D1808054

UNDERSTANDING HEALTH COMMUNICATION TECHNOLOGIES

Pamela Whitten

David Cook

Editors

Foreword by Jonathan D. Linkous

JOSSEY-BASS
A Wiley Imprint
www.josseybass.com

Published by Jossey-Bass
A Wiley Imprint
989 Market Street, San Francisco, CA 94103-1741   www.josseybass.com

Jossey-Bass books and products are available through most bookstores. To contact Jossey-Bass directly call our Customer Care Department within the U.S. at 800-956-7739, outside the U.S. at 317-572-399386 or fax 317-572-4002.

Jossey-Bass also publishes its books in a variety of electronic formats. Some content that appears in print may not be available in electronic books.

Library of Congress Cataloging-in-Publication Data

Understanding health communication technologies / Pamela Whitten and David Cook, editors.—1st ed.
    p.; cm.
    Includes bibliographical references and indexes.
    ISBN 0-7879-7105-7 (alk. paper)
        1. Telecommunication in medicine—Case studies. [DNLM: 1. Telemedicine—United States.
    2. Organizational Case Studies—United States. W 83 AA1 U55 2004] I. Whitten, Pamela. II. Cook,
    David, 1970-
    R119.9.U53 2004
    610'.28—dc22   2004006416

Printed in the United States of America
FIRST EDITION
HB Printing   10 9 8 7 6 5 4 3 2 1

CONTENTS

Figures, Tables, and Exhibits   x

Preface   xiii

Foreword   xxi

    Jonathan D. Linkous

The Editors   xxiii

The Contributors   xxv

PART ONE: IMPLEMENTATION   1

1 Problems with Implementation: The Story
of a Home Telecare Trial   3

    Frances S. Mair, Derek Hibbert, Carl R. May, Robert Angus, Tracy Finch,
Angela Boland, Jane O'Connor, Alan Haycox, Chris Roberts, Simon Capewell

2 Challenges in Launching a Malaysian Teleconsulting Network   11

    Richard Wootton, Mohamad Suhaimi Mohamad Tahir

3 Social Aspects of Implementing a Medical Information System: Cure or Symptom?   19

Ronald E. Rice

4 Telemedicine at Shriners Hospitals for Children: One Size Does Not Fit All   30

Mark L. Niederpruem, Robert Gerding, Mary E. Kautto, Peter Armstrong, Jana L. C. Lindsey, Katherine Y. Vigil, Cary Burcham, Michael Moushui, Shannon M. Lehman, Donald Lighter

PART TWO: MANAGEMENT AND OPERATIONS   37

5 Home Telehealth: Overcoming Buy-In Issues   39

Bonnie Perry Britton, Rhonda Chetney

6 A Model for Persuading Decision Makers and Finding New Partners   46

Glen Effertz, Steven Beffort, Alistair Preston, Frank D. Pullara, Dale C. Alverson

7 Leadership Issues Facing an E-Start-Up Management Team   59

James Patterson, Gary M. Shulman

8 A Health Care Information System in Greece: Key Factors, Self-Organization, and Take-Home Lessons   69

Angelina Kouroubali, Don E. Detmer, Manolis Tsiknakis, Stelios Orphanoudakis

9 The Anatomy of Failure? Teledermatology in an English City   80

Carl R. May, Maggie Mort, Tracy Finch, Frances S. Mair

PART THREE: COMMUNICATION   89

10 Research as Dialogue: Health Communication and Behavior Change in Patients' Natural Habitat   91

Linda M. Harris, Rita Kobb, Patricia Ryan, Adam Darkins, Gary L. Kreps

11 Diagnosing the Communication Infrastructure in Order to Reach Target Audiences: A Study of Hispanic Communities in Los Angeles   101

Pauline Hope Cheong, Holley A. Wilkin, Sandra Ball-Rokeach

12 The Role of Telehospice in End-of-Life Care   111

Collette M. Clemens, Beverly Davenport Sypher, Gary C. Doolittle

13 Doctor and Patient Interactions During Telemedicine:
    Clashes of Perceptions and Reality   118

Jeanine W. Turner, James D. Robinson, Adil Alaoui, James F. Winchester,
Alan Neustadtl, Walid Gabriel Tohme, Betty A. Levine, Jeff Collmann,
Seong K. Mun

PART FOUR: OUTCOMES   127

14 Teletherapy for Childhood Depression: Where Is the Evidence?   129

Eve-Lynn Nelson

15 Serving Children with Disabilities in Rural Iowa   138

Dennis C. Harper

16 Crisis Telehealth as a Cost Management Strategy   145

Susan L. Dimmick, Samuel G. Burgiss, Nikki Cook

17 Using Point-of-Care to Reduce Medication Errors   151

Chris L. Tucker, Russell Carlson

18 The United Kingdom Virtual Outreach Project   160

Paul Wallace

19 The Financial Side of a Tele-Oncology Practice   171

Gary C. Doolittle, Ashley Spaulding, Ryan Spaulding

PART FIVE: EDUCATION   179

20 The Role of the Internet in Prostate Cancer Survivors'
    Illness Narratives   181

Michael Irvin Arrington

21 Successful Web Site Construction and Management:
    Harnessing the Skill and Enthusiasm of Volunteers   187

Marlene M. Maheu, Joseph P. McMenamin

22 Multimedia Education for Gestational Diabetes Patients   193

Deborah C. Glik, Sally F. Shaw, Gloria M. Chinea, Amy Myerson

23 New Paradigms for Continuing Education: Training Providers How to Use Technology   203

Thomas S. Nesbitt, Thu P. Tran, Jana Katz

24 Telehealth in Cyberspace: Virtual Reality for Distance Learning in Health Education and Training   212

Dale C. Alverson, Stanley M. Saiki Jr., Thomas P. Caudell

25 The SEEDS Project: From Health Care Information System to Innovative Educational Strategy   225

Judith J. Warren, Katherine A. Fletcher, Helen R. Connors, Anita Ground, Charlotte Weaver

PART SIX: UNIQUE APPLICATIONS   233

26 Bringing Care Home to the Rural Elderly: Clinician and Patient Satisfaction with Telehealth Communication   235

Carma L. Bylund, Bonnie Wakefield, Jane E. Morse, Annette M. Ray

27 Systemwide Rollout of Doctor-Patient Secure Web Messaging: The University of California, Davis, Virtual Care Experience   244

Eric M. Liederman, Eric M. Zimmerman, Marcos A. Athanasoulis, Margaret A. C. Young

28 Low-Vision Reaching Out Through Telemedicine: The Process of Implementing One Ophthalmic Subspecialty   251

Jade S. Schiffman, Gina G. Wong, Rosa A. Tang

29 Internet-Based Specialty Consultations: A Study of Adoption Challenges   261

Paul Heinzelmann, Joseph Kvedar

30 Telerehabilitation: A Harvest of Multidisciplinary Services   268

Cynthia Scheideman-Miller

PART SEVEN: TECHNOLOGY 275

31 Sustainable Security: Building Virus and Vulnerability
Management into an Organization's Culture 277

C. Scott Blanchette, David T. Noll

32 Designing Technology: A Case of Vendor and Provider
Partnership 284

Audrey Kinsella, Kim Lee, Brenda Ecken

33 Behind the Applications: Making Technology Transparent 289

Sally R. Davis, Pamela Whitten

PART EIGHT: POLICY 297

34 Policy and the Origins of the Arizona Statewide
Telemedicine Program 299

Ronald S. Weinstein, Gail Barker, Sandy Beinar, Michael Holcomb,
Elizabeth A. Krupinski, Ana Maria Lopez, Alison Hughes, Richard A. McNeely

35 The Long and Winding Road to Medicare Reimbursement 310

Joseph A. Tracy, Karen E. Edison

36 Addressing Barriers to Access for Uninsured in Western New York
State: WNYhelpnet.org 319

Thomas Hugh Feeley, Denise M. Rizzo, Jeannine M. Osborne

37 Using Computer Technologies to Provide Relevant Cancer
Information to Vulnerable Populations: The NCI Digital Divide
Pilot Projects 328

Gary L. Kreps, David H. Gustafson, Peter Salovey, Rosemarie Slevin Perocchia,
Wayne Wilbright, Mary Anne Bright, Cathy Muha, Carol C. Diamond

38 Bridging the Digital Divide: Lessons from the Health
InterNetwork India 337

Joan Dzenowagis, Andrew Pleasant, Shyama Kuruvilla

Name Index 347

Subject Index 351

FIGURES, TABLES, AND EXHIBITS

Figures

2.1   Installed Teleconsulting Terminals   13

4.1   Shriners Hospitals Telemedicine Program Host and Remote Sites, April 2003   33

6.1   New Mexico Department of Corrections Facilities   48

6.2   Explaining Telehealth in the Business Case   50

6.3   Prison Population Growth, Historical and Projected, 1975–2002   51

8.1   Health Care Facilities and the HYGEIAnet Network Infrastructure   70

10.1   An Interpersonal Symptom Management System: A Working Model   97

11.1   Metamorphosis Research Design   103

11.2   Top Ten Ways That Hispanics Get Information on Health and Medical Care   106

15.1   Teleconsults for Children with Disabilities   141

17.1   Reported Error Rate as a Percentage of Total Doses Dispensed   157

18.1   Case Example of Telemedicine Clinical Consultation   164

18.2   Responses to Overall Patient Satisfaction by Randomized Group   168

19.1   Using Telemedicine Technology to Provide Care to a Rural Patient   172

22.1   Original and New Characters for the Gestational Diabetes Multimedia CD-ROM   199

22.2   New Main Menu and Chapter Interfaces for the Gestational Diabetes
       Multimedia CD-ROM   200
23.1   Participant Feedback on the Telemedicine Learning Center
       Curriculum   209
24.1   The Virtual Patient with a Blood Pressure Cuff, Neck Brace,
       and Head Bandage   215
24.2   Schematic Depiction of the Patient Simulator Input and Output
       System   216
24.3   The Studio, Screen, and Student User Using the Touch Screen   217
24.4   Students Working as a Team in the Virtual Reality Environment Despite
       Physical Separation over Distance   218
26.1   Patient Receiving Telehealth Services   236
28.1   System for Tele-Ophthalmology   253
28.2   Patient Electronic Episode   259
34.1   Arizona Telemedicine Network   305
36.1   The Western New York State Region   321

Tables

2.1   Equipment Installed at the Teleconsulting Sites   13
2.2   Teleconsulting Activity in Various Store-and-Forward Networks   15
4.1   Shriners Hospitals Locations and Services   31
6.1   Distance and Travel Time in New Mexico   51
6.2   IP Intranet One-Time and Recurring Costs   52
6.3   Videoconferencing One-Time and Recurring Costs   53
6.4   Transportation Costs by Location   54
6.5   Percentage of Trips Saved, by Year   54
6.6   Breakeven Analysis   56
19.1   Hays Practice Costs   173
19.2   Horton Practice Costs   174
33.1   Examples of Upper Peninsula Telehealth Network Adaptations   294
36.1   WNYhelpnet.ORG User Statistics, December 2002–May 2003   323
36.2   WNYhelpnet.ORG Category Use by User Status   324
38.1   Estimated Internet Access, 2002   339
38.2   Indian Government Health Service Facilities   340
38.3   Key Comparisons Between Karnataka and Orissa, India   341

Exhibits

13.1   Topics Raised During Doctor-Patient Interactions   121
18.1   Trial Hypotheses   162
21.1   Most Popular Article Departments in SelfhelpMagazine   190
28.1   Protocol for Video and Audio Clip for Low-Vision
       Remote Examination   256

PREFACE

In his influential work *Understanding Media: The Extensions of Man* (1964), Marshall McLuhan stated "that any technology gradually creates a totally new human environment" (p. viii). Indeed, the advent of new and innovative health communication technologies promises to revolutionize the landscape of health care delivery. For example, telemedicine technologies may use interactive video and clinical peripheral devices to enable a physician or health care provider to visit a patient at a distant location in real time. Telehealth technologies broaden the telemedicine connotation beyond simply medical purposes to include nursing and educational applications. The more recent metaphor of e-health appears to expand these ideas further to include Web-based solutions and a paradigm shift from health care provider-driven approaches to more patient-centered delivery models. Computerized patient records or electronic medical records are one example of this trend, especially when technologies enable patients to access their health information on the Web and become more empowered in their own care.

There is no denying that health communication technologies will play a critical role in facilitating health care delivery in the next decade and beyond. However, although these trends have been quite effective at penetrating the mainstream media, they have been considerably less effective at moving into mainstream medicine. We, along with many other researchers, theorists, and practitioners, believe it is only a matter of time before this change occurs. Still, understanding why this revolution has not caught on sooner, or become more widespread, is a critical

question we all must ask. This book seeks to answer this question by bringing together world-renowned experts to share their successes and failures through their
experiences. We hope that the lessons industry pioneers have learned can be shared
with students in the classroom, researchers seeking to expand our knowledge within
this realm, and perhaps most important, health care providers and administrators
developing their own applications to enhance the quality of care they provide.

Employing a Case Study Approach

One of the best ways to understand how and why a certain innovation or intervention developed the way it did is by using a case study approach. This approach
provides "a touchstone of reality" (Haytin, 1988, p. 41) for the reader in making
"visible the qualitative features of organizational life" (Sypher, 1990, p. 3). In other
words, case studies enable us to address contemporary problems and challenges
within one context that have transferable relevance to other settings. Students reading this book can use the experiences of others to shape their own ideas on how to
develop innovations in health care. Academicians may use the efforts described
to develop research and theories into the adoption and development of tomorrow's
health delivery systems. New practitioners and even other industry pioneers can
compare their own experiences with the initiatives outlined here to fine-tune or
reengineer efforts of their own. And, finally physicians, nurses, and other health
professionals may be encouraged to implement health communication into their
own practices after learning from the experiences of their peers.

Outline of the Book

The book is organized into eight parts representing common themes across thirty-
eight cases from diverse disciplines, industries, and nationalities to include: implementation, management, communication, outcomes, education, unique applications,
technology, and policy. Each case is complemented with a set of open-ended discussion questions at its conclusion.

Implementation

Devising a plan to adopt a certain technology and implement it into routine daily
practice is a common starting point for the majority of cases in this text. Part One
groups cases that focus on the implementation process itself as the critical lesson
of their overall experience. In Chapter One, Mair and her colleagues describe the

problems encountered in implementing a home telecare clinical trial in the United Kingdom. They describe the professional and organizational dynamics that serve as barriers to the implementation of their teletrial service. In Chapter Two, Wootton and Tahir describe the trials and tribulations of implementing a national telehealth network in Malaysia. They explain why the $5.5 million effort was withdrawn from service after two years while the government opted to replan the implementation effort. Rice's case in Chapter Three tells the story of how a medical records information system was implemented into one health care organization. Part One concludes with Chapter Four by Niederpruem and colleagues, who detail the multitude of challenges in implementing a telemedicine network in the Shriners health system, an organization with twenty-two hospitals in three countries and sixteen U.S. states.

Management and Operations

Traditionally the notion of management or operations refers to the activities involved in four general functions: planning, organizing resources, leading, or coordinating (McNamara, 2003). The cases in Part Two provide a sampling of key operational issues related to the delivery of services using communication technologies. The case by Britton and Chetney in Chapter Five argues that organizations will not maximize the use of new technologies without formal strategic efforts to secure buy-in from key providers. Effertz and colleagues provide concrete suggestions in Chapter Six for the creation of a business plan, illustrated in their case about the deployment of telehealth in the New Mexico Correctional Department. In Chapter Seven, Patterson and Shulman address the issue of leadership in their presentation of a start-up company. In Chapter Eight, Kouroubali, Detmer, Tsiknakis, and Orphanoudakis address the challenge of managing change as illustrated from a project to create a health information infrastructure on the island of Crete in Greece. Finally, in Chapter Nine, May, Mort, Finch, and Mair provide an intriguing case of a teledermatology project that was relaunched in response to local market competition.

Communication

The contributors in Part Three share a common focus on understanding the effect technology has on routine communication practices or the role communication plays in socially constructing the way participants come to understand the initiative in which they participated. Harris and her colleagues from the National Cancer Institute and the Veteran Affairs department describe in Chapter Ten a theoretical framework they are using in a telehealth home application for chronic patient populations. Their research-as-dialogue model blends patient-provider interactions with evidence-based medicine and quality-of-care concerns. In Chapter Eleven, Cheong, Wilkin, and Ball-Rokeach describe the Metamorphosis project, an effort to work with families and communities within the Hispanic neighborhoods of Los Angeles to better understand how health communication may have a positive impact on their health problems. The next case, by Clemens, Sypher, and Doolittle in Chapter Twelve, looks at using health communication technologies in the hospice setting. In Chapter Thirteen, the final case in Part Three, Turner and her colleagues look specifically at doctor-patient interactions during telemedicine consultations.

Outcomes

In recent years, the Centers for Medicare and Medicaid Services has stressed the importance of outcomes as indexes of quality of care. Conducting research regarding some form of outcome is challenging and often difficult to measure. In addition, there are a wide variety of relevant outcomes to consider, ranging from costs to impacts on health status. Part Four provides cases that offer a sampling of outcome results from a diverse array of projects. In Chapter Fourteen, Nelson highlights a patient within a project designed to deliver teletherapy for childhood depression. Next, in Chapter Fifteen, Harper presents a case on telemedicine for children with disabilities in rural Iowa to provide an overview of patient and provider satisfaction, economic indicators, and changes in the parental role in this team-to-team model. Dimmick, Burgiss, and Cook provide an enlightening case in Chapter Sixteen on the use of crisis telehealth as a cost-saving strategy in Tennessee. Tucker and Carlson demonstrate in Chapter Seventeen the reduction in medication errors that occured when a Veterans Administration hospital implements point-of-care medication administration technology. Wallace offers a case in Chapter Eighteen of a virtual outreach model of care employed in the United Kingdom that resulted in unanticipated outcomes of higher costs and follow-up referrals. Finally, in Chapter Nineteen, Doolittle, Spaulding, and Spaulding detail the financial considerations of a tele-oncology practice in Kansas.

Education

With rapidly changing advances in the medical field, it is becoming increasingly difficult for health care providers and patients to stay abreast of the latest relevant treatment information. In current health care practice, an information and knowledge gap exists among the medical research community, the specialized practice community, the general practice community, and the lay patient. One possible solution to facilitate access to information, support services, and education is through distance instructional media such as interactive video or the Internet. The cases presented in Part Five highlight a range of innovative technological applications to provide information and education. In recognition that not everyone fully embraces the Internet when they have been diagnosed with a disease, Arrington provides three composite narratives in Chapter Twenty that illustrate the range of Internet use among prostate cancer survivors. In Chapter Twenty-One, Maheu and McMenamin describe SelfhelpMagazine, one of the first privately developed mental health Web sites designed to translate scientific information into plain English for a worldwide readership. Glik, Shaw, Chinea, and Myerson present in Chapter Twenty-Two a case on the development of an interactive multimedia program available in a bilingual format (Spanish and English) created to help pregnant women with gestational diabetes mellitus manage their diabetes. In Chapter Twenty-Three, Nesbitt, Tran, and Katz provide an interesting twist to the notion of education in their analysis of a training program developed specifically to teach providers how to employ telehealth technologies. In Chapter Twenty-Four, Alverson, Saiki, and Caudell present a virtual reality initiative, Project TOUCH (Telehealth Outreach for Unified Community Health), a joint initiative between the Universities of New Mexico and Hawaii with simulations and education processes embedded in virtual reality environments, artificial intelligence, and experiential active learning. The final chapter in Part Five, by Warren, Fletcher, Connors, Ground, and Weaver, provides an overview of a unique project at the University of Kansas School of Nursing that integrated a clinical information system into the nursing school's curriculum.

Unique Applications

Part Six highlights initiatives with a unique clinical focus, a novel context for delivery, or some combination of both. In Chapter Twenty-Six, Bylund, Wakefield, Morse, and Ray describe four separate programs using telehealth technologies in a home for elderly rural Iowans within the Veterans Affairs health system. Liederman, Zimmerman, Athanasoulis, and Young at the University of California, Davis, examine in Chapter Twenty-Seven the successful pilot implantation of a Web-based patient messaging service. In Chapter Twenty-Eight, Schiffman, Wong, and Tang describe the approach and rationale for providing tele-ophthalmic services for rural and elderly patients in Texas. Heinzelmann and Kvedar in Chapter Twenty-Nine analyze adoption issues relating to Internet-based specialty consultations. Chapter Thirty, by Scheideman-Miller, describes the nuances of developing a telerehabilitation service in schools in Oklahoma.

Technology

Technology is at the heart of every case in this book. The chapters in Part Seven, however, provide an inward focus on key issues related to technology. In Chapter Thirty-One, Blanchette and Noll address one of the most important issues facing technology deployment today: security. Kinsella, Lee, and Ecken provide an example in Chapter Thirty-Two of a provider organization that has partnered with an equipment vendor to tailor equipment for a Pennsylvania-based home telehealth project. Finally, Davis and Whitten provide an overview in Chapter Thirty-Three of a Michigan-based telemedicine project's endeavor to create a transparent technology solution.

Policy

Emergence of the Internet and diffusion of high-bandwidth telecommunications technologies are just beginning to enable innovative applications to address burgeoning needs for greater access to health care services at lower cost. In order to maximize the effective use of technology to deliver health services around the world, it is vital that key health providers, regulators, and policy experts work together. Part Eight presents an important set of cases that illustrate formal efforts regarding policy in the immediate and long term. Weinstein and colleagues document in Chapter Thirty-Four the policy efforts employed to create a cutting-edge statewide telehealth program in Arizona. In Chapter Thirty-Five, Tracy and Edison jump to the national level, examining the efforts that led to the federal reimbursement for telehealth. This part also provides cases that demonstrate initiatives that may ultimately have an impact on state, national, and international policy through efforts to eliminate digital divides. Feeley, Rizzo, and Osborne detail in Chapter Thirty-Six the efforts in New York State to design a Web site to warehouse, organize, and simplify existing services for the uninsured. Kreps and colleagues outline in Chapter Thirty-Seven four National Cancer Institute–funded Digital Divide Pilot projects that tested new strategies for narrowing the digital divide regarding cancer information for vulnerable populations in the United States. In the final chapter, Dzenowagis, Pleasant, and Kuruvilla present an important World Health Organization–funded endeavor to use information technology to support public health services in India.

In Summary

We are deeply grateful to have such a wide array of programs and initiatives with world-renowned experts willing to share their experiences within this book. We thank all of them for their commitment and effort to make this endeavor a worthwhile experience for all of us. We also thank Jossey-Bass for having faith in our proposal and believing in the idea that a large readership is interested in health communication technologies and can learn through the experiences of industry pioneers. We hope that readers will learn as much from these case studies as we did from participating in the creation of the book.

References

Haytin, D. L. *The Validity of the Case Study.* New York: Peter Lang, 1988.

McLuhan, M. *Understanding Media: The Extensions of Man.* Cambridge, Mass.: MIT Press, 1964.

McNamara, C. "Introduction to Management." 2003. [http://www.mapnp.org/library/mng_thry/mng_thry.htm].

Sypher, B. D. *Case Studies in Organizational Communication.* New York: Guilford Press, 1990.

FOREWORD

Meeting challenges in providing health care in this still-new century requires a fundamental change to the face of health care delivery. Certainly, some of these challenges have already revealed themselves. Rural and medically underserved residents struggle to attain access to adequate health services. Growing concerns to address medical errors and improve the quality of care are equally paramount. And the cost of providing services, achieving adequate reimbursement, and providing affordable pharmaceuticals continue to plague policymakers. Attempting to address these challenges, let alone solving them completely, can be an overwhelming proposition. Consider further the vast disparities across the globe in providing the most basic health care, and the obstacles that lay ahead may seem overwhelming.

Despite these challenges, there is hope. The editors and authors of this book collectively illustrate the promise of health communication technologies in bridging gaps in access and narrowing the quality chasm to revolutionize the future of health care delivery. In fact, as the case studies reveal, the future is already here in many instances. This book provides a unique opportunity to learn from the firsthand experiences of experts from around the world. With its focus on the lessons learned from both successful and failed initiatives, this book provides a refreshing opportunity to learn from the accomplishments and mistakes of others. And with its multidisciplinary approach through eight unique parts, the book promises to appeal to a broad audience.

The use of case studies is an important strategy to solve the misleading separation of theory and practice. An interesting array of cases can put a reader in touch with a world of technology in health that would take years to experience fully. Pamela Whitten and David Cook have included a set of cases in this book that reach beyond standard examples of technology-based interventions. Although these cases provide an important sampling of projects that employ communication technologies to deliver health services, more important are the unique complexities within the health system that are revealed.

The significance of the contribution made by the editors of this book can not be overstated. Anyone interested in the role that technology can play in improving the health care delivery challenges of the twenty-first century should read this book. Indeed, the cases within provide a road map for students, academic researchers, and practitioners in the field. I believe this collection of cases will add significantly to our collective insight regarding communication technologies and health.

> *Jonathan D. Linkous*
> Executive Director
> American Telemedicine Association

THE EDITORS

Pamela Whitten, Ph.D., is an associate professor in the Department of Telecommunications at Michigan State University. She is also a Senior Research Fellow for Michigan State's Institute of Healthcare Studies. In her current position, Whitten is responsible for conducting technology- and health-related research, as well as teaching graduate and undergraduate telecommunications courses. Whitten's research focuses on the use of technology in health care with a specific interest in telehealth and its impact on the delivery of health care services and education. She is currently launching projects to create wireless networks in four Michigan nursing home facilities that employ Tablet PCs to provide telemedicine services to the bedside and to create and evaluate a diabetes Web site for low-literate adults. Her other active research projects range from telepsychiatry to telehospice and telehome care for patients with chronic obstructive pulmonary disease and congestive heart failure. Prior to joining the faculty at Michigan State in 1998, Whitten ran the telemedicine program for the state of Kansas through the University of Kansas Medical Center. She received her Ph.D. in organizational communication from the University of Kansas, M.A. in communication from the University of Kentucky, and B.S. in management from Tulane University.

David Cook, Ph.D., has been involved with the implementation and research of health communication technologies for the past seven years, initially as the director of the Center for TeleMedicine and TeleHealth and more recently as the director of Health and Technology Outreach at the Kansas University Medical Center (KUMC) in Kansas City, Kansas. His current charge is to align the health and technology outreach efforts of the state's lone academic medical center in developing and extending the institution's mission to serve the health care needs of the state. Cook's body of work includes projects to implement technologies in health facilities, home health care, and K–12 schools. His most recent project involves using interactive video and Web resources to train health care providers in the area of bioterrorism. His research articles and presentations have targeted health care access, technology adoption, patient-provider perceptions, and implementation and delivery of health communication technologies. Cook received his B.A. in political science and speech communication from Iowa State University and his M.A. and Ph.D. in organizational communication from the University of Kansas.

THE CONTRIBUTORS

Adil Alaoui, M.S., is affiliated with the Imaging Science and Information Systems Center in the Department of Radiology at Georgetown University Medical Center, Washington D.C.

Dale C. Alverson, M.D., is the director of the Center for Telehealth and a professor of pediatrics and OB/GYN at the University of New Mexico Health Sciences Center, Albuquerque, New Mexico.

Robert Angus, M.D., is a faculty member at the University Hospital Aintree National Health Service Trust, Liverpool, United Kingdom.

Marcos A. Athanasoulis, M.P.H., Dr.P.H., is the chief technology officer at Evalu-Metrix LLC located in Massachusetts.

Peter Armstrong, M.D., F.R.C.S.C., F.A.C.S., is director of Medical Affairs at the Shriners Hospitals for Children, International Shrine Headquarters, Tampa, Florida.

Michael Irvin Arrington, Ph.D., is an assistant professor in the Department of Communication Studies at the University of Kentucky, Lexington, Kentucky.

Sandra Ball-Rokeach, Ph.D., is a professor and director of the Metamorphosis Project in the Annenberg School of Communication at the University of Southern California, Los Angeles, California.

Gail Barker, M.B.A., Ph.D., is affiliated with the College of Medicine at the University of Arizona, Tucson, Arizona.

Steven Beffort is affiliated with the Robert O. Anderson School and Graduate School of Management at the University of New Mexico, Albuquerque, New Mexico.

Sandy Beinar, is affiliated with the College of Medicine at the University of Arizona, Tucson, Arizona.

C. Scott Blanchette is affiliated with the Stanford University Medical Center, Palo Alto, California.

Angela Boland is affiliated with the Mersey Primary Care R&D Consortium in the Department of Primary Care at the University of Liverpool, Liverpool, England.

Mary Anne Bright is affiliated with the Cancer Information Service Program in the Office of Communications at the National Cancer Institute, Bethesda, Maryland.

Bonnie Perry Britton, M.S.N., R.N.C., is director of Clinical Development for American Telecare, Greenville, North Carolina.

Cary Burcham, R.N., M.B.A., C.N.A.A., B.C., is affiliated with the Shriners Hospital for Children, Tampa, Florida.

Samuel G. Burgiss, Ph.D., is a faculty member at the University of Tennessee Graduate School of Medicine and director of the University of Tennessee Telehealth Network, Knoxville, Tennessee.

Carma L. Bylund, Ph.D., is the director of AGGME Outcome Project for New York Presbyterian Hospital, affiliated with the Center for Education Research and Evaluation, Columbia University Medical Center in New York City, New York.

Simon Capewell, Ph.D., is a faculty member of the Department of Public Health at the University of Liverpool, Liverpool, United Kingdom.

Russell Carlson, R.N., BSN, is affiliated with the National Bar Code Medication Administration Joint Program Office in the Veterans Health Administration Office of Information, Topeka, Kansas.

Thomas P. Caudell, Ph.D., is a faculty member in the Department of Electrical and Computer Engineering and the director of Visualization Laboratory at the Center for High Performance Computing, at the University of New Mexico, Albuquerque, New Mexico.

Pauline Hope Cheong is an assistant professor in the School of Informatics, State University of New York, Buffalo, and is affiliated with the Metamorphosis Project in the Annenberg School of Communication at the University of Southern California, Los Angeles, California.

Rhonda Chetney, R.N., M.S., is affiliated with Sentara Home Care Services, Chesapeake, Virginia.

Gloria M. Chinea, M.P.H., is affiliated with the Health Ministries and Healthy Beginnings initiative at the St. John's Regional Medical Center and St. John's Pleasant Valley Hospital, Oxnard, California.

Collette M. Clemens, M.A., is affiliated with Lands' End, Dodgeville, Wisconsin.

Jeff Collmann, Ph.D., is a faculty member in the Imaging Science and Information Systems Center in the Department of Radiology at Georgetown University Medical Center, Washington, D.C.

Helen R. Connors, Ph.D., R.N., F.A.A.N., is a faculty member at the University of Kansas School of Nursing, Kansas City, Kansas.

Nikki Cook, M.S.U., graduated with a master of science degree from the University of Tennessee College of Social Work in December 2003.

Adam Darkins, M.D., F.R.C.S., M.P.H., is affiliated with the Department of Veterans Affairs, Veterans Health Administration, and Telemedicine Strategic Healthcare, Washington, D.C.

Sally R. Davis, M.A., is affiliated with the Telehealth and Management Development department at the Marquette General Health System, Marquette, Michigan.

Don E. Detmer, M.D., M.A., is professor emeritus and professor of medical education at the University of Virginia in Charlottesville, Virginia. At the time of the research he was the Dennis Gillings Professor of Health Management and the director of Cambridge University Health at the Judge Institute of Management, University of Cambridge, U.K.

Carol C. Diamond, M.D., M.P.H., is affiliated with the Information Technologies for Better Health initiative at the Markle Foundation, New York, New York.

Susan L. Dimmick, Ph.D., is a faculty member at the University of Tennessee Graduate School of Medicine in the Department of Radiology, and is manager of research and evaluation for the UT Telehealth Network.

Gary C. Doolittle, M.D., is a faculty member of the Division of Hematology and Oncology at the University of Kansas Medical Center, Kansas City, Kansas.

Joan Dzenowagis, Ph.D., is project manager of the Health InterNetwork initiative at the World Health Organization, Geneva, Switzerland.

Karen E. Edison, M.D., is chair of the Department of Dermatology and medical director of the Missouri Telehealth Network at the University of Missouri, Columbia, Missouri.

Brenda Ecken, M.Ed., B.S.N., R.N., is affiliated with ViTel Net, Reston, Virginia.

Glen Effertz, M.B.A., is affiliated with the Center for Telehealth in the Health Sciences Center at the University of New Mexico, Albuquerque, New Mexico.

Thomas Hugh Feeley, Ph.D., is a faculty member in the School of Informatics and the Department of Communication at the University at Buffalo, State University of New York, Amherst, New York.

Tracy Finch, Ph.D., is a faculty member at the University of Newcastle upon Tyne and the Centre for Health Services Research, United Kingdom.

Katherine A. Fletcher, Ph.D., R.N., is an associate clinical professor at the University of Kansas School of Nursing, Kansas City, Kansas.

Robert Gerding is affiliated with the Shriners Hospitals for Children, International Shrine Headquarters, Tampa, Florida.

Deborah C. Glik, SC.D., is a faculty member in the UCLA School of Public Health, Los Angeles, California.

Anita Ground, B.S.N., M.B.A., R.N., is affiliated with the Cerner Corporation, Kansas City, Kansas.

David H. Gustafson, Ph.D., is a professor of industrial engineering at the University of Wisconsin, Madison, Wisconsin.

Linda M. Harris, Ph.D., is affiliated with the Health Communication and Informatics Research Branch of the National Cancer Institute, Bethesda, Maryland.

Dennis C. Harper, Ph.D., is faculty member in the Carver College of Medicine at the University of Iowa, Iowa City, Iowa.

Alan Haycox, M.D., is affiliated with the Prescribing Research Group in the Department of Pharmacology, University of Liverpool, Liverpool, United Kingdom.

Paul Heinzelmann, M.D., is affiliated with Partners Telemedicine at Harvard Medical School, Boston, Massachusetts.

Derek Hibbert is affiliated with the Mersey Primary Care R&D Consortium in the Department of Primary Care at the University of Liverpool, Liverpool, United Kingdom.

Michael Holcomb, B.S., is affiliated with the Arizona Telemedicine Program at the University of Arizona's College of Medicine, Tucson, Arizona.

Alison Hughes, M.P.A., is affiliated with the Arizona Telemedicine Program, Tucson, Arizona.

Jana Katz is a member of the Center for Health and Technology at the University of California Davis Health System, Sacramento, California.

Mary E. Kautto, R.N., M.A., is affiliated with Shriners Hospitals for Children, Minneapolis, Minnesota.

Audrey Kinsella, M.A., M.S., is research director for information for Tomorrow Home Telehealth Planning Services, Kensington, Maryland.

Rita Kobb, R.N., is affiliated with the Department of Veterans Affairs, Bay Pines, Florida.

Angelina Kouroubali, Ph.D., is an affiliated research scientist at the Center of Medical Informatics and Health Telematics Applications at the Institute of Computer Science, Foundation for Research & Technology-Hellas, Crete, Greece. At the time of the research she was a Ph.D. candidate at the Judge Institute of Management, University of Cambridge, U.K.

Gary L. Kreps, Ph.D., is the Mandell Professor of Health Communication at George Mason University, Fairfax, Virginia.

Elizabeth A. Krupinski, Ph.D., is a faculty member in the Department of Radiology and affiliated with the Arizona Telemedicine Program at the University of Arizona, Tucson, Arizona.

Shyama Kuruvilla is affiliated with the Health InterNetwork initiative at the World Health Organization, Geneva, Switzerland.

Joseph Kvedar, M.D., is affiliated with Partners Telemedicine and is vice chairman of the Department of Dermatology at Harvard Medical School, Boston, Massachusetts.

Kim Lee, M.S.N., R.N., B.C., is affiliated with the Home Nursing Agency, Altoona, Pennsylvania.

Shannon M. Lehman, R.N., B.S.N., is affiliated with Shriners Hospitals for Children, Erie, Pennsylvania.

Betty A. Levine, M.S., is a faculty member in the Imaging Science and Information Systems Center in the Department of Radiology at Georgetown University Medical Center, Washington, D.C.

Eric M. Liederman, M.D., M.P.H., is a faculty member in Clinical Information Systems at the University of California Davis Health Systems, Sacramento, California.

Donald Lighter, is affiliated with the Shriners Hospitals for Children, International Shrine Headquarters, Tampa, Florida.

Jana L. C. Lindsey, R.N.C., is affiliated with the Shriners Hospitals for Children, Honolulu, Hawaii.

Jonathon D. Linkous, is the president of the American Telemedicine Association, Washington, D.C.

Ana Maria Lopez, M.D., M.P.H., is affiliated with the Arizona Telemedicine Program at the University of Arizona, Tucson, Arizona.

Marlene M. Maheu, Ph.D., is a consultant based in San Diego, California.

Frances S. Mair, M.D., is a faculty member in the Department of Primary Care at the University of Liverpool, Liverpool, United Kingdom.

Carl R. May, Ph.D., is affiliated with the Center for Health Services Research in the School of Population and Health Sciences at the University of Newcastle upon Tyne, Newcastle upon Tyne, United Kingdom.

Joseph P. McMenamin, M.D., J.D., is affiliated with McGuireWoods LLP, Richmond, Virginia.

Richard A. McNeely, M.A., is affiliated with the Arizona Telemedicine Program at the University of Arizona's College of Medicine, Tucson, Arizona.

Jane E. Morse, R.N., is affiliated with the Veterans Affairs Medical Center, Iowa City, Iowa.

Maggie Mort, Ph.D., is a faculty member at the Institute for Health Research at Lancaster University, Lancaster, United Kingdom.

Michael Moushui is affiliated with the Shriners Hospitals for Children, Tampa, Florida.

Cathy Muha is affiliated with the National Cancer Institute, Gaithersburg, Maryland.

Seong K. Mun, Ph.D., is director of the Imaging Science and Information Systems Center in the Department of Radiology at the Georgetown University Medical Center, Washington, D.C.

Amy Myerson, M.A., is affiliated with the UCLA School of Public Health and the UCLA Health and Media Research Group in the School of Public Health, Los Angeles, California.

Eve-Lynn Nelson, Ph.D., is affiliated with the Center for Telemedicine and Department of Pediatrics at the Kansas University Medical Center, Kansas City, Kansas.

Thomas S. Nesbitt, M.D., is director of the Center for Health and Technology in the University of California Davis Health System, Sacramento, California.

Alan Neustadtl, Ph.D., is a faculty member in the Department of Sociology, University of Maryland at College Park.

Mark L. Niederpruem, F.A.C.H.E, is affiliated with the Shriners Hospital for Children, Springfield, Massachusetts.

David T. Noll, is affiliated with Stanford University Medical Center, Palo Alto, California.

Jane O'Connor, is affiliated with the South Sefton Primary Care Trust, Waterloo, Liverpool, England.

Stelios Orphanoudakis, Ph.D., is the director of the Foundation for Research & Technology-Hellas, and Professor of Computer Science at the University of Crete, Greece.

Jeannine M. Osborne, C.S.W., M.S., is affiliated with the University at Buffalo Department of Family Medicine, Buffalo, New York.

James Patterson, Ph.D. is a faculty member in the Communication Department at Miami University, Oxford, Ohio.

Andrew Pleasant is affiliated with the Health InterNetwork initiative at the World Health Organization, Geneva, Switzerland, and a visiting lecturer at Brown University, Providence, Rhode Island.

Rosemarie Slevin Perocchia, R.N., M.Ed., is affiliated with the Cancer Information Service of New York at the Memorial Sloan-Kettering Cancer Center, New York.

Alistair Preston, Ph.D., is a faculty member in the Anderson School of Management at the University of New Mexico, Albuquerque, New Mexico.

Frank D. Pullara, M.D., is affiliated with the health services initiative at the New Mexico Corrections Department, Santa Fe, New Mexico.

Annette M. Ray, R.N., B.S.N., is affiliated with the Veterans Affairs Medical Center, Iowa City, Iowa.

Ronald E. Rice, Ph.D., is the Arthur N. Rupe Chair in Communication in the Department of Communication at the University of California, Santa Barbara, Santa Barbara, California.

Denise M. Rizzo, M.S., is affiliated with the University of Buffalo Family Medicine Research Institute and is the finance director for Health for All of Western New York, Hamburg, New York.

Chris Roberts, is a faculty member in the School of Epidemiology and Health Sciences at the University of Manchester, Manchester, United Kingdom.

James D. Robinson, Ph.D., is a faculty member in the Department of Communication at the University of Dayton, Dayton, Ohio.

Patricia Ryan is affiliated with the Department of Veterans Affairs, Bay Pines, Florida.

Stanley M. Saiki Jr., M.D., is a faculty member in the Department of Medicine at the University of Hawaii, and is the director of the Pacific Telehealth and Technology Hui, Tripler Army Medical Center/VA, Honolulu, Hawaii.

Peter Salovey, is the Chris Argyris Professor of Psychology in the Department of Psychology at Yale University, New Haven, Connecticut.

Cynthia Scheideman-Miller, M.H.A., is affiliated with INTEGRIS Health, Oklahoma City, Oklahoma.

Jade S. Schiffman, M.D., is a clinical associate professor, University Eye Institute, University of Houston, Houston, Texas.

Sally F. Shaw, Ph.D., is a staff member at the Glendale Adventist Hospital, Glendale, California.

Gary M. Shulman, Ph.D., is the chair of the Communication Department at Miami University, Oxford, Ohio.

Ashley Spaulding is affiliated with the University of Kansas Medical Center, Kansas City, Kansas.

Ryan Spaulding, Ph.D., is the director of the Center for Telemedicine and Telehealth at the University of Kansas Medical Center, Kansas City, Kansas.

Beverly Davenport Sypher, Ph.D., is a professor of Communication and Associate Provost for Special Initiatives, Purdue University, West Lafayette, Indiana.

Mohamad Suhaimi Mohamad Tahir resides in Selangor Darul Ehsan, Malaysia and is affiliated with the MSC Technology Centre Sdn Bhd.

Rosa A. Tang, M.D., M.P.H., is a faculty member of the Department of Ophthalmology at the University of Texas Medical Branch, Galveston, Texas.

Walid Gabriel Tohme, Ph.D., is a faculty member in the Imaging Science and Information Systems Center in the Department of Radiology at the Georgetown University Medical Center, Washington, D.C.

Thu P. Tran is affiliated with the Center for Health and Technology in the University of California Davis Health System, Sacramento, California.

Joseph A. Tracy is the executive director of the Missouri Telehealth Network at the University of Missouri Health Care, Columbia, Missouri.

Manolis Tsiknakis is researcher and coordinator of the Center of Medical Informatics and Health Telematics Applications at the Institute of Computer Science, Foundation for Research & Technology-Hellas, Crete, Greece.

Chris L. Tucker is affiliated with the National Bar Code Medication Administration Joint Program Office in the Veterans Health Administration Office of Information, Topeka, Kansas.

Jeanine W. Turner, Ph.D., is a faculty member in the McDonough School of Business at Georgetown University, Washington, D.C.

Katherine Y. Vigil, R.N., is affiliated with the Shriners Hospitals for Children, Salt Lake City, Utah.

Bonnie Wakefield, Ph.D., R.N., is an investigator in the Center for Research in the Implementation of Innovative Strategies in Practice (CRIISP) at the Veterans Affairs Medical Center, Iowa City, Iowa.

Paul Wallace, M.D., is a faculty member in the Department of Primary Care and Population Sciences at the Royal Free and University College Medical School, London, United Kingdom.

Judith J. Warren, Ph.D., R.N., B.C., F.A.A.N., is a faculty member of the University of Kansas School of Nursing, Kansas City, Kansas.

Charlotte Weaver, Ph.D., R.N., is affiliated with the Cerner Corporation, Kansas City, Missouri.

Ronald S. Weinstein, M.D., is director of the Arizona Telemedicine Program at the University of Arizona's College of Medicine, Tucson, Arizona.

Wayne Wilbright, M.D., M.S., is affiliated with the Medical Informatics and Telemedicine Program at Louisiana State University's Health Sciences Center, New Orleans, Louisiana.

Holley A. Wilkin is affiliated with the metamorphosis project in the Annenberg School of Communication at the University of Southern California, Los Angeles, California.

James F. Winchester, M.D., is medical director of Renal Tech International, New York, New York.

Richard Wootton is director of research of the Centre for Online Health at the University of Queensland, Brisbane, Australia.

Gina G. Wong, O.D., is an adjunct assistant professor at the University of Houston College of Optometry, Houston, Texas and is affiliated with the Department of Veteran Affairs Northern California Healthcare System, Sacramento Medical Center, Mather, California.

Margaret A. C. Young, M.S., is affiliated with the Relay Health Corporation, San Francisco, California.

Eric M. Zimmerman, M.P.H., M.B.A., is affiliated with the Relay Health Corporation, San Rafael, California.

PART ONE

IMPLEMENTATION

Courage is being scared to death—but saddling up anyway.

JOHN WAYNE

CHAPTER ONE

PROBLEMS WITH IMPLEMENTATION

The Story of a Home Telecare Trial

Frances S. Mair, Derek Hibbert, Carl R. May, Robert Angus, Tracy Finch, Angela Boland, Jane O'Connor, Alan Haycox, Chris Roberts, Simon Capewell

Telecare is a rapidly growing field of clinical activity and technical development. New technologies have caught the attention of clinicians and policymakers worldwide because they offer the potential to solve structural problems around inequalities of service provision and distribution. This is particularly true in the United Kingdom (National Health Service Executive 1998), the location of the trial described here. However, we know that globally, despite an abundance of pilot and demonstration work, telecare has not yet penetrated routine health care practice in any systematic way. There is a tendency for grant-funded health telecare projects to discontinue when the grant funding ceases rather than become services that are integrated into routine practice.

This trial investigates the use of a nurse-led home telecare service to address the problem of high hospital admission rates of patients with chronic obstructive pulmonary disease (COPD). It is particularly novel in that it involves the provision of home telecare services to individuals suffering from an acute exacerbation of a chronic illness. This is quite distinct from the way home telecare services have

We acknowledge funding for the project from the following sources: NHS Modernisation Fund, Mersey Primary Care Research and Development Consortium, and Astra Zeneca. T.F.'s contribution to this chapter was funded from the Department of Health Research Initiative in Information and Communication Technology (ICT/032).

traditionally been employed: to maintain patients with relatively stable chronic health conditions at home through the use of routine monitoring of important health parameters.

This type of intervention, a nurse-led home telecare service, was thought particularly suitable for COPD for several reasons. COPD is a condition of the lungs characterized by largely irreversible airflow obstruction and results in considerable disability in the later stages. COPD is the second most common noncommunicable disease. It affects 600 million people worldwide and causes about 30 million deaths per year (Murray and Lopez, 1997). In the United Kingdom, it affects over 1.5 million people and accounts for approximately 12 percent of acute medical admissions, costing the health service over £500 million per year (National Health Service Executive, 1996). COPD is a condition of middle and later life and represents a major component of the primary care workload. It generates over twice the number of consultations arising from asthma and four times the consultations with angina (McCormick, Fleming, and Charlton, 1995). There are both clinical and economic reasons that make exploration of new methods of service delivery for this patient population particularly valuable.

The telecare equipment used in this study consists of an analogue video telephone and peripheral devices that provide distant measurement of physiological parameters: pulse, blood pressure, temperature, and pulse oximetry. The key objective of this study is to describe the professional and organizational dynamics that may serve as barriers to the implementation of the telehealth service.

A Description of the Trial Interventions

A team of specialist nurses based within a hospital emergency department intercepts patients being admitted for exacerbations of COPD. The team provides a thorough, standardized clinical assessment of the patient (history taking, physical examination, and basic investigations) supported by the respiratory medical team to determine if, with additional medication and nursing support, care at home is possible. If the exacerbation is judged to be mild to moderate and home care is considered feasible, the patient is randomized to one of the trial arms: home telecare or face-to-face nurse home visits. Patients randomized to either arm of the study receive a medication package, including antibiotics, steroids, and nebulized bronchodilators, and social care support, if required, until the patient is stable. Those randomized to home telecare receive most of their intensive nursing support by means of telecommunications technology; nursing support in the other trial arm is with face-to-face nurse home visits. Typically, both types of nursing support packages are continued for fourteen days, when patients are discharged unless there are clinical concerns.

The Process of Implementation

Running in tandem with the randomized controlled trial was a qualitative evaluation that examined the process of introduction and implementation of the home telecare technology into the health care setting described. The observation period extended over thirteen months. Data for this ethnography were drawn from various sources, the main one being the researchers' field notes: a diary that records details of day-to-day activity on the trial and included accounts of meetings between those involved in the trial and the work undertaken to move the project along. We also kept records of e-mail correspondence and project meetings and undertook semistructured interviews with professionals involved at the introductory phase of the trial to gain their perspectives. All of these resources were then coded using software for qualitative data analysis and analyzed in accordance with ethnographic principles, especially the techniques of constant comparison (May, 1998).

The Struggle to Make the Telecare System Fully Operational

The nursing team participating in the trial served two large and extremely busy teaching hospitals located approximately six miles apart. The home telecare service was initiated at only one of these hospitals in an effort to make monitoring of the project easier. In addition, budgetary restrictions limited the number of telecare units available for the service. It was therefore thought sensible to focus the service on a single hospital catchment area. Furthermore, this project received grant support from the National Health Service (NHS) Modernization fund, a U.K. Department of Health fund that aimed to support a range of innovative methods of health care delivery. The project team submitted an application for £200,000 in funding from this source but received only £80,000. These funds had to be used for both equipment purchase and project evaluation. The project was therefore operating on an extremely tight budget.

When the equipment arrived, one-to-one training regarding the service and use of the equipment was given to each of the nurses who were to be involved in providing the home telecare service. However, it soon became clear that there were a number of obstacles to routine use of the telecare service in practice: concerns about risk management, professional resistance and patient resistance, workload pressures, and technical problems.

Risk Management

There were concerns about issues relating to risk and the telecare service. The nurses involved in the study were concerned that the system would increase the risk to patients. The home telecare service was not generally seen by the nurses in terms of a progressive extension of their professional practice. Instead, it was usually more critically received as something that took them a step away from a holistic model of nursing care (May, 1992; Davies, 1995).

Shortly after these observations, it became apparent that the number of patients being successfully recruited was far fewer than expected. Further exploration revealed that where patients raised concerns or expressed a lack of confidence, the nurses were assuming their refusal rather than explaining the trial further to encourage participation. In part, this related to the nurses' own uncertainties about the equipment, including their relative inexperience in terms of setup and operation. At this point, the project was in the process of being piloted, which amplified professional uncertainties as nurses adapted to the new system and its associated practices. What was important here was that professional assessments of risk attributed to the system were perceived and acted on in ways that affected the possibilities for its implementation. The strategies that actors employed to manage risk and uncertainty, in the context of implementing telecare systems, were of major importance. It became increasingly clear that there were numerous possible reasons for recruitment difficulties that extended well beyond ideas of risk.

Professional Resistance

As the service was introduced, it quickly became apparent that team members had many reservations about the utility and acceptability of the telecare equipment for both themselves and the patients. A commonly expressed view was that the home telecare service was likely to be of only limited value to them. Unfortunately, initial problematic experiences with the telecare equipment seemed to reinforce this view. The problems nurses encountered sometimes related to the well-recognized limitations of the technology.

For example, the nurses noted adverse effects on communication resulting from the fact that when using the videophone, there was a delay in relaying speech. Some nurses thought that this had a negative affect on their usual consultation style, as the following remark from the field notes illustrates: "Nurse 11 felt the delay on the line was a problem—she said it felt like she was talking 'over' the patient."

Patient Resistance

Users of this service were usually frail, older individuals with a number of co-morbidities. At the time of invitation to the service, they were also experiencing acute breathlessness associated with the exacerbation of COPD. The nurses noted that it was difficult to persuade these individuals to try home telecare.

Patient resistance reinforced professional resistance as the ensuing recruitment difficulties meant that all the nurses did not get the opportunity to experience the telecare equipment in action and as a consequence did not feel able to recommend the idea of the service to patients. Low use also affected professional confidence relating to use of the equipment.

Workload Pressures

Another difficulty in getting the service running at an acceptable level was the existing workload pressures that the nursing team experienced. Due to circumstances beyond our control, the service was introduced during a particularly busy time of the year for the nursing team, and so external pressures on the team to deliver the traditional face-to-face home care service were increased. Setting up the telecare equipment in patients' homes, while having long-term potential time-saving benefits (in terms of reduced home visits to patients), proved to be time-consuming in the short term. For instance, the nurses' initial lack of familiarity with equipment setup and the need to complete the trial documentation meant that two nurses, rather than the usual one, went out to the patient's home for the initial visit.

A third nurse was also needed at the hospital base station to test the connection and make sure the system was working effectively. Thus, three nurses were involved in initial setup for each patient. This was clearly excessively labor intensive and problematic for the nursing team, especially when considering the competing demands on their time.

Technical Problems

The equipment used in the trial initially proved unreliable. There were problems with poor audio and visual quality and poor connectivity. Equipment that had worked well when demonstrated under ideal conditions proved less effective when placed in the real-life setting of patients' homes, where the quality of telephone lines could be in doubt and lighting and general conditions could be suboptimal. This lack of reliability and dependability of the equipment during the initial phases generated another major barrier to the early success of the project and served to reinforce the existing negative perceptions of nurses who were being asked to provide the telecare service.

Addressing the Problems

The success of this project was seen to depend largely on the extent to which the nurses were able to integrate their clinical roles with the demands of the evaluation. At this site, much of the work (both clinical and evaluative) was delegated to the nursing team, who were thus placed in a position of dual responsibility: responsible not only for the success of the home telecare system as a clinical service but also to have a major role in measuring and evaluating its success. Maintaining the commitment and cooperation of the clinical actors was seen to be of primary importance. Regular team meetings were therefore arranged in an effort to provide ongoing motivation and support.

With regard to risk management, this issue was discussed at length with individual members of the nursing team. The trial protocol had been designed with safety as a paramount feature. Therefore, nurses had the ability to default to a face-to-face home nursing visit if at any time they felt uneasy about the clinical safety of a home telecare visit. In practice, the nurses were sometimes more persistent in trying to make the telecare contacts work than might be expected from this. However, in an effort to allay the nurses' concerns, it was emphasized on a number of occasions that their clinical judgment should take precedence over home telecare considerations.

The workload pressures could not be easily resolved. However, positive steps were taken to try to alleviate problems posed by initial equipment setup. After discussions with the equipment vendor, it was agreed that the vendor would act as a point of contact to help with initial equipment setup.

The technical problems encountered also added to risk management fears and adversely affected the providers' perceptions of the service. Resolving these difficulties was seen as crucial to the success of the service. Subsequently, all the initial videophone units were replaced with upgraded versions. The audio and visual quality of the videophone consultations consequently was much improved.

The nurses were given additional training to help the patients become more confident and willing to participate. As a result, we expanded the trial to include a second hospital served by the same nursing team in order to increase the number of patients eligible for the trial. The eligibility criteria for the study were also broadened beyond intercepting patients suffering from an acute exacerbation of COPD in the emergency room. Now, individuals who have been too ill for home telecare and are therefore admitted to hospital with an acute exacerbation of

COPD but who are subsequently deemed eligible for early hospital discharge with home care support are being invited to participate.

Professional resistance remains to some degree but has lessened with time. This is due to a combination of factors: increasing familiarity with the equipment, growing experience of providing the service in a new manner, and increased reliability of the equipment. We continue to monitor this issue in our study design.

Current Status of the Project

The home telecare project described in this chapter is ongoing. Recruitment now takes place in two hospital sites. The eligibility criteria for the service have been broadened, and the volume of patients using the service is increasing. Additional funding has been secured from two sources: a Department of Health Primary Care Research Consortium and a pharmaceutical company. The feedback from the nursing team has become more positive, with fewer day-to-day problems and concerns being raised with the researchers.

Discussion Questions

1. Professional resistance to home telecare services can be a factor in inhibiting the integration of such services into routine health care practice. How should you approach assessing the levels of such resistance in advance of introducing this service? What do you think can be done to try to overcome this potential difficulty?

2. Enrolling participants in home telecare projects is frequently problematic. Provide an example of a project where difficulties with recruitment were identified as an important issue. Describe the types of difficulties that were encountered and how these were addressed.

3. What do you think are the best ways to identify barriers to recruitment to home telecare services?

4. Where use of telecare services is low, especially initially, maintaining confidence in setup and use of equipment can be difficult. Identify some ways to minimize this problem.

References

Davies, C. *Gender and the Professional Predicament in Nursing.* Bristol, Pa.: Open University Press, 1995.

May, C. "Individual Care? Power and Subjectivity in Therapeutic Relationships." *Sociology*, 1992, *26*, 589–602.

May, C. "The Preparation and Analysis of Qualitative Data." In B. Roe and C. Webb (eds.), *Research and Development in Clinical Nursing Practice*. London: Whurr, 1998.

McCormick, A., Fleming, D., and Charlton, J. *Morbidity Statistics from General Practice: Fourth National Study 1991–2*. London: Office of Population Censuses and Surveys, 1995.

Murray, C.J.L., and Lopez, A. D. "Global Mortality, Disability, and the Contribution of Risk Factors: Global Burden of Disease Study." *Lancet*, 1997, *347*, 1436–42.

National Health Service Executive. *Burdens of Disease: A Discussion Document*. Leeds, U.K.: Department of Health, 1996.

National Health Service. *Information for Health: An Information Strategy for the Modern NHS 1998–2001*. London: Health Service Executive, 1998.

CHAPTER TWO

CHALLENGES IN LAUNCHING A MALAYSIAN TELECONSULTING NETWORK

Richard Wootton, Mohamad Suhaimi Mohamad Tahir

This case study describes a national teleconsulting network that was installed in Malaysia in 2001 and two years later was withdrawn from service while the government replanned it. The teleconsultation application represented one of four pilot projects within an overall national telehealth program in Malaysia. The program was conceived in 1997 as a strategic initiative to transform the nation's health care system toward integrated and seamless delivery of health care and improved health outcomes (Yusof, Neoh, bin Hashim, and Ibrahim, 2002; Yadav and Lin, 2001; Ariff and Teng, 2002; Suleiman, 2001; Abidi and Yusoff, 1999). Fundamental to this strategy was the underlying shift from the traditional focus on curative services and medicine to wellness, people, services, and the use of technology. The teleconsultation project had these stated aims (Suleiman, 2001):

- Enhancing the capabilities of primary care centers
- Extending the reach of specialized health care

This chapter reflects the personal opinions of the authors and not necessarily the views of their employing organizations.

- Optimizing the use of specialists, who are available only at large general hospitals
- Reducing patient transfers

The teleconsultation project was advertised in an international Request for Proposal (RFP) in 1999. Seven companies participated in the RFP process. The government, through the Ministry of Health, awarded the contract to a U.S.-based company through a local agent, who carried out the customization and implementation. The contract was valued at $5.5 million and covered work over two and a half years, starting in April 2000. The technical component of the work was to supply, install, and operate a national teleconsultation network. The service component was network operation in Malaysia and the provision of access to medical experts from other parts of the world, who were already part of the U.S.-based company's existing network.

The teleconsulting network operated via store-and-forward transmission. Network terminals were located in "hub" and "spoke" hospitals; cases requiring a specialist's opinion were sent from a referring hospital to a specialist located at a hub, or level 1, hospital. The referring hospitals were subdivided into larger district hospitals (level 2) and smaller hospitals or health centers (level 3). At each site, a teleconsultation coordinator was designated and then trained to prepare cases for transmission using the system. The coordinator prepared the required information, such as X-ray and laboratory results, in digital format. The information could also include scanned paper documents, voice annotations, and electrocardiogram scans. After preparing the case, the coordinator alerted the specialist at the receiving site, transmitted the information, and awaited the response from the teleconsulting system.

Data

During the contract period from March 28, 2001, to October 11, 2002, equipment was installed at forty-one sites across Malaysia (Table 2.1 and Figure 2.1): four level 1 hospitals and thirty-seven referring sites.

At the end of the contract period, the company provided teleconsulting activity data. Most of the data were verified in a subsequent review by the consultants appointed by the government. There were 1,104 teleconsultation cases from March 28, 2001, to October 11, 2002, for a consultation rate of approximately 700 cases per year. The average rate was therefore 2 cases per day for the network of forty-one sites. The majority of cases involved teleradiology.

FIGURE 2.1. INSTALLED TELECONSULTING TERMINALS.

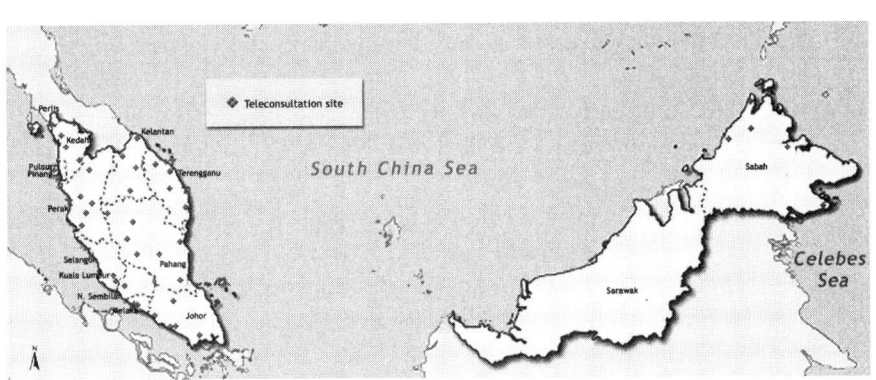

TABLE 2.1. EQUIPMENT INSTALLED
AT THE TELECONSULTING SITES.

Level	Number of Sites	Location	Equipment at Each Site
1	4	Major hospitals in the capital and large towns	Three teleconsulting terminals for data capture, sending and receiving, and diagnosis
2	21	District hospitals	Two teleconsulting terminals for data capture and sending and receiving, respectively
3	16	Health centers and hospitals (the health centers were located a few kilometers from district hospitals)	Two teleconsulting terminals for data capture and sending and receiving, respectively

Problems and Issues

There were five main problems identified from this experience:

- Teleconsulting activity was perceived to be low.
- The equipment was installed mainly in hospitals and therefore had no role in enhancing primary care.
- There was no evidence that patient transfers had been reduced. Indeed, there were no mechanisms to collect such data.
- There was a high turnover of teleconsultation coordinators.
- Network readiness and reliability were poor.

Activity

The teleconsulting use rate was perceived (by the government) to be low. Perhaps the government's expectations were unrealistic. To examine this, it is instructive to compare the level of teleconsulting activity in the Malaysian network with reported activities from similar teleconsulting networks elsewhere in the world. Reported teleconsulting activity rates in other store-and-forward networks have ranged from 100 to 1,300 cases a year, with network sizes ranging from 3 to 220 sites (see Table 2.2).

Thus, the activity on the network under discussion (700 cases per year) falls within the range of those listed. This is also the case for activity per site (17 cases per year per site), which falls within the range of those listed (5 to 370 cases per year per site). Regardless of whether the network operation was strictly cost-effective, its characteristics do not appear to be markedly different from those of other store-and-forward networks in the world.

Equipment

Four of the sixteen level 3 health centers had X-ray equipment. However, the health centers with X-ray facilities were not provided with a digitizer to facilitate X-ray transmission. None of the sixteen level 3 health centers had the specialist drugs required to treat patients, which resulted in patients' being referred physically to the nearest hospital rather than electronically using the teleconsulting network.

Mismatched Referral Patterns

Some of the network configurations did not match actual referral patterns. The review of the pilot discovered that this had a lot to do with the nonalignment of administrative policy and procedures. The teleconsultation coordinators could use

TABLE 2.2. TELECONSULTING ACTIVITY IN VARIOUS STORE-AND-FORWARD NETWORKS.

Operator	Number of Sites	Activity (Cases per Year)	Activity (Cases per Year per Network Site)
Blue Cross (United States)	20	100	5
Swinfen Charitable Trust (United Kingdom)	12	100	8
Arizona (United States)	9	400	44
People's Liberation Army (China)	220	1000	5
WorldCare (United States)	3	1,100	370
U.S. Army (United States)	10	1,300	130
Malaysia case study	41	700	17

the system to liaise directly with specialists at a level 1 site, but they could take full advantage of this facility only if that hospital was also the next referral hospital in the conventional (paper-based) referral process. Otherwise, the system was used mostly for general communication with the specialist at the level 1 hospital. In these cases, the teleconsultation coordinator would usually revert to the conventional process of referring to the intermediate district hospital (where the coordinators' superiors were located, that is, the normal line of reporting). It was then the responsibility of the district-level doctors and administrators to follow through. The teleconsultation coordinators felt that the use of the system bypassed their superiors, and they were reluctant to do this very often.

Also, when prescriptions did come back relating to telehealth cases, the patients often had to be transferred to the bigger hospitals because of the lack of facilities and medicines at the health centers.

Coordinators

There was a high staff turnover among those designated as teleconsultation coordinators. After three years of training coordinators, only 5 percent of the participants remained from the initial group. It appeared that hospital administrators had not considered the role of the teleconsultation coordinator when making transfers of personnel. To ensure that teleconsulting services are conducted smoothly, there is also a need to ensure that teleconsultation coordinators are selected from medical assistants or health assistants who are technically inclined.

Network Readiness and Reliability

Network readiness and reliability was a frequently reported problem. In smaller towns, bandwidth was usually limited to 19.6 or 28.8 Kbps, which was often not fast enough for satisfactory transmission of digital images. More critical was the reliability of the network, which was well below 98 percent for major towns and lower than 95 percent for the smaller towns and health centers. This is one of the principal reasons that the government halted the pilot project.

Implications and Lessons Learned

The implementation of the pilot project incurred an expenditure of several million dollars and resulted in teleconsultations for about a thousand patients. The cost per case was of the order of thousands of dollars—perhaps ten or a hundred times the cost of obtaining a second opinion by conventional means, particularly in the case of radiology reports. Although cost-effectiveness was not considered in the pilot project, activity levels were perceived to have been low, and the project was therefore replanned by the Ministry of Health and relevant stakeholders.

The fundamental problem was the attempt to establish a relatively large telehealth network in an environment where the clinicians who were supposed to use it could not see any obvious benefits. A forty-one-site teleconsulting network is a relatively ambitious project; the average network size of mature telemedicine networks in the United States is seventeen sites (Dahlin, Watcher, Engle, and Henderson, 2001). Furthermore, there were concerns that in using the system, referrers would be bypassing their district-level administrators, which would not be sanctioned. In other words, the policy and procedures between the referring sites and the receiving sites should have been aligned beforehand to take account of the new process enabled by teleconsulting.

Although the overall teleconsultation project began with clear objectives, the actual implementation lost sight of some of these. There were technical problems with the network, and the training did not comprehensively address the needs of the teleconsultation coordinators.

Promotion and the management of change were not adequate. The company was required to carry this out as part of the contract, but the government viewed this portion of their services as unsatisfactory. In fairness, though, the government did not allocate sufficient resources and senior management support for this change initiative. Although the company was responsible for providing awareness and training programs, the government project team did not fully address the policy and procedures required in the light of the changes in process.

Current Status of the Project

The original project was completed on schedule and without any significant delay. However, at the time of writing, the teleconsulting system has been shut down while the Ministry of Health replaces the private network with a network of more suitable bandwidth. The government also took over the network operating center on completion of the contract.

With regard to integration with other systems, such as the existing patient registration systems and the lifetime health record (other applications under the national telehealth program), only a proof of concept has been carried out. Full integration is stalled because of problems with other subsystems and applications, the lack of readiness of the necessary infrastructure, and policy mismatch. The government is also considering other teleconsulting providers for the next phase of the overall telehealth project.

The local agent has secured the rights and the source code for the software used for the teleconsulting service. The company has submitted a proposal to the government for a two-year maintenance service for the system.

As a result of the review of the pilot project, the government and its policy-makers are rethinking the approach to teleconsulting and the need to align it with the overall telehealth program, as well as other modernization initiatives in the public health sector. It must be stressed that the project was a pilot specifically to test the efficacy of the teleconsulting approach.

With the wisdom of hindsight, a much smaller pilot project—perhaps two or three sites—should have been conducted before anything more ambitious was attempted. Generally, it is a mistake to plan for a "big bang" implementation in any health-related information technology work. It is far better to grow incrementally from a pilot project. As has been pointed out before, "Telemedicine projects implemented prematurely and without a feasibility study can quickly begin drifting in a sea of dashed expectations" (Stumpf, Zalunardo, and Chen, 2002, p. 45). One might also observe that projects adrift in a sea of dashed expectations are sometimes lost without trace.

Discussion Questions

1. What is the best method of predicting whether a proposed telehealth solution makes sense?
2. How do you obtain independent telehealth advice from people who have practical experience in the area and are not interested parties?

3. What is the right index of success? Is it activity? Is it proof that consultations by telehealth are quicker or cheaper than by the conventional alternative?
4. What are the principles of successful change management?

References

Abidi, S. S., and Yusoff, Z. "Telemedicine in the Malaysian Multimedia Super Corridor: Towards Personalized Lifetime Health Plans." *Studies in Health Technology and Informatics,* 1999, *68,* 283–288.

Ariff, K. M., and Teng, C. L. "Rural Health Care in Malaysia." *Australian Journal of Rural Health,* 2002, *10,* 99–103.

Dahlin, M. P., Watcher, G., Engle, W. M., and Henderson, J. *2001 Report on U.S. Telemedicine Activity.* Portland, Ore.: Association of Telehealth Service Providers, 2001.

Stumpf, S. H., Zalunardo, R. R., and Chen, R. J. "Barriers to Telemedicine Implementation." *Healthcare Informatics,* Apr. 2002, 45–49. [http://www.healthcare-informatics.com/issues/2002/04_02/stumpf.htm].

Suleiman, A. B. "The Untapped Potential of Telehealth." *International Journal of Medical Informatics,* 2001, *61,* 103–112.

Yadav, H., and Lin, W. Y. "Teleprimary Care in Malaysia: A Tool for Teleconsultation and Distance Learning in Health Care." *Asia-Pacific Journal of Public Health,* 2001, *13,* S58–61.

Yusof, K., Neoh K. H., bin Hashim, M. A., and Ibrahim I. "Role of Teleconsultation in Moving the Healthcare System Forward." *Asia-Pacific Journal of Public Health,* 2002, *14,* 29–34.

CHAPTER THREE

SOCIAL ASPECTS OF IMPLEMENTING A MEDICAL INFORMATION SYSTEM

Cure or Symptom?

Ronald E. Rice

To help provide better care for patients, improve communication between departments, store information, control costs, and regulate the provision of health care, health care organizations implement medical information systems using a wide variety of technologies (Eder, 2000; Kissinger and Borchardt, 1996; Packer, 1985; Rice and Katz, 2001; Rognehaugh, 1999; Street, Gold, and Manning, 1997). In this way, we can think of medical information systems as "cures" for certain organizational problems or illnesses.

General positive impacts include improved timeliness of health care, improved format of reports to physicians and administrators, increased access to multisource databases to improve the quality of the health care process, and the introduction of management controls to contain health care costs (Lincoln and Korpman, 1980). However, as with all other organizational technologies, they may also lead to increased workloads, shifted work roles, loss of autonomy, fragmented and rationalized jobs, and conflict about evaluation of information (Braverman, 1974; Hirschheim, 1985; Johnson and Rice, 1987; Kling, 1980; Markus, 1984). Many hospital information systems indeed encounter dissatisfaction, interference, resistance, or failure due to factors such as poor system design, improper fit with organizational and social features, negative attitudes and social relationships within the hospital, medical norms about technology and patient care, and national health policies (Brenner and Logan, 1980; Dowling, 1980; Lindberg, 1979; Smith and Kaluzny, 1986). In these ways, we might also think of medical information systems as "symptoms" of deeper organizational problems or illnesses—that is, that why and how such systems are implemented may primarily reflect or uncover current conditions and assumptions rather than serve to solve some of those same conditions and assumptions.

This confusion between "cure" and "symptom" is partially due to the fact that social and organizational factors tend to be overlooked in information system design and implementation, but they often play the primary role in influencing the success or failure of these hospital information systems. This case reports quantitative and qualitative insights into the two-year process of implementing an integrated medical records information system in one health care organization. In the end, it is not clear whether the system was primarily a cure for the organization's information ailments or primarily a symptom of deeper organizational problems.

The System, People, and Sources

The setting is the student health service of a large urban university. The service employs between 100 and 125 full- and part-time employees, as well as numerous student workers, and treats upward of 600 student patients per day.

The system implemented in this setting was an integrated medical records information system running off a dedicated minicomputer with networked dedicated terminals and printers. The vendor and system planners designed the computerized system to approximate the paper-and-pencil systems previously used in various departments, with the most immediate and pressing problem being patient scheduling. Note this fundamental assumption: the underlying processes, work flows, and job designs were not in question and thus not redesigned; rather, the system was designed to cure current problems in information gathering, distribution, billing, and analysis. By the end of the study period, many system functions were operating:

- Scheduling appointments for patients and physicians
- Creating a common database for student demographic and eligibility information
- Generating encounter forms (which patients received when they checked in at the front desk and then took with them to each department, and which were used to note all treatment and billing information for later entry into the system)
- Entering codes for diagnoses, tests, and services performed
- Reconciling written encounter forms with data entered in the computer
- Generating reports

As students showed up for their appointments or were admitted for on-the-spot treatment, they were given an encounter form generated by the system, which they carried with them throughout their visit to the clinic and handed to the cashier before they left. This form was used to consolidate information about test requests and clinic activities and was used as the basis for entering data into the system and eventual corroboration with departmental entries for billing and analysis. The vendor's complete system could provide a wide range of integrated applications. Long-term goals and applications included functions for communicating orders for tests, reporting of lab results, analyzing patient outcomes for medical research, and identifying trends to plan for seasonal resources. However, as of the end of this study it was primarily an information collection, management, tracking, and reporting system.

The Study

The general study approach used questionnaires, moderately structured interviews, observations, and archival data collected at three time periods: several months before the new information system was implemented (T1), several months after implementation had begun (T2), and approximately one year after the second survey (T3). Researchers also observed individuals using both the previous pencil-and-paper system and the computer system in the course of their daily work. Of the 111 employees at the health service at T1 (some were seasonal or part time, so the figure of 111 overstates the number of relevant respondents), 88 were still employed at T3; 74 of these 88 employees (84 percent) completed both T1 and T3 questionnaires. The end of the T3 questionnaire asked for some open-ended comments on what the employees thought were good and bad aspects of the system and the implementation process. We also interviewed eleven people: the cashier supervisor, the appointments secretary, a lab tester, a nurse administrator, a scheduling assistant, a nurse in women's health care, the supervisor of scheduling (also a triage nurse), a nurse with wide administrative responsibilities, and two assistant administrative analysts in finance and personnel.

Problems and Issues

The following sections summarize the employees' perceptions of and experiences with organizational aspects of the new system.

Positive Aspects of the System

The survey gathered seventy-four comments on positive aspects of the system, grouped into eight categories (we provide the percentage of comments comprising each category and example comments):

- Diversity of benefits (23 percent: "improve data collection, retrieval, dissemination capabilities and potentially improve quality of care")
- Information retrieval (22 percent: "easier-to-retrieve information about patients and whatever lab work has been ordered")
- Analysis and reporting (18 percent: "using one encounter sheet from which invaluable information can be input, thus potentially producing reports such as types of patients and diagnoses")
- Not enough use of system to be able to comment (12 percent)
- Decreased paperwork (11 percent: "automatic checklist lab ordering has lowered waiting time")
- Improved scheduling (7 percent: "can see if a patient has other appointments scheduled in student health")
- New or enjoyable job (4 percent)
- Better and more services (4 percent: "the system keeps advancing clinics, patients, employees")

The personal interviews also emphasized the significance of the system for information storage and retrieval. One person said that she "is now retrieving information instead of files." Formerly, if they wanted file information, they had to fill out and sign a form requesting a student's file, have someone pick up the slip, and bring the chart back. There was always a sense that much time was spent filling in forms. They used to have to flip through separate pages per doctor and per day to find an appointment. One particular benefit will be that they can get otherwise missing information on a patient—directly from the information entered as part of the student's registration database.

Negative Aspects of the System

The employees provided nearly as many comments on negative aspects of the system:

- Slow response time and questionable system reliability (30 percent: when the system goes down, there is no verification of who has been seen)
- Increased workload and use of paper (19 percent: "cancellations of appointments do not correspond with the computer and the appointment cards—this doubles the work")

- Problems with procedures and patient flow (19 percent: "takes too long and double-booking occurs frequently")
- Problems with documentation and training (14 percent: "not everyone knows how to use it and I think everyone should know at least the basics")
- Reports and formats (7 percent: "reports are still not available easily, which was one of the main reasons for purchasing the system")
- Insufficient communication with experts and consultants (4 percent)
- Not sufficient system use to have an opinion (4 percent)
- Ergonomics, insufficient involvement/participation, and other (1 percent each)

The personal interviews also raised negative aspects of the system, such as the lack of fit of the system to the actual jobs—for example, "In one of the clinics, appointments start at 8:15 and happen every half-hour. But the system starts on the hour, at 9 A.M., and allows appointments every hour. They can't change it manually. So the appointment folk know this, and have learned to skip around the fixed times."

Attitudes Toward the System

Attitudes toward a computer system are a central focus of information system implementation research (Ives, Olson, and Baroudi, 1983; Lucas, 1981; Schultz and Slevin, 1975) and may vary widely across professions and departments, as new roles and relations may be introduced (Aydin, 1989; Counte, Kjerulff, Salloway, and Campbell, 1987; Fischer, Stratmann, Lundsgaarde, and Steele, 1987).

The employees did have generally positive attitudes toward the computer system ("the system will be, or is, worth the time and effort required to use it," a 7-point scale) at both T1 and T3. The mean attitude for all employees, however, decreased significantly from 6.02 (agree) at T1 to 5.27 (between slightly agree and agree) at T3 ($p < .01$). Medical personnel reported a lower assessment and a statistically significant decrease from T1 to T3 (5.86 to 4.84—closer to slightly agree than to neutral, $p < .01$). The initial decision to emphasize administrative (scheduling, billing, medical records) over medical applications (diagnosis, trend analysis) resulted in the negative physician attitudes at T3, although administrators were attempting to convince physicians that the system would eventually benefit them as well. Members of the nonmedical occupations also reported a slight, but not statistically significant, decline from 6.19 to 5.77, but were more positive at both time periods.

A summary regression analysis showed that positive attitudes at T3 were moderately explained by support from one's work unit for learning how to use the system, organizational policies that support learning about and experimenting with the system, and lower levels of system use. Reasons for the diversity of attitudes seem due to age (less willing to change), prior computer experience, more professional experience, fear of making a mistake, and some technophobia. A final general theme was the importance of both presenting, and having, reasonable expectations: "People look for it to be perfect, but it's not."

Implementation and Training

The implementation process was characterized by ongoing informal communication, sandwiched into a busy work schedule that tried to encourage the use and development of new system-based procedures. Individuals often selected their own contacts to discuss the computer system, and individuals in medical records and in finance and personnel assumed the role of computer liaison or "guru" for workers in a number of departments.

Survey respondents provided nearly fifty comments about the implementation process, grouped into six categories:

- Need more frequent updating, training, professional instruction, and a user manual (20 percent)
- Insufficient implementation experience or system use to have an opinion (20 percent)
- Involvement and communication (17 percent: "More people who are working with the system, and people affected by it, i.e., the clinicians, should have been involved in choosing a system")
- Debugging and timing of implementation stages (17 percent: "I would have agreed to pay for the system after it was tested and had proved to be doing what it should have done from the beginning")
- Vendors or equipment (15 percent: "Would have looked at more providers, systems and options")
- Documentation and procedures (11 percent: "The program for the generation of requisition slips is poorly designed. It has too many steps and commands and I feel it could be greatly improved upon!")

Overall, the interviewees had mixed feelings about the ease of learning the system and felt that experimentation with the system was important to learning but was not supported by the organization—for example, "The problem comes from those who really want to know how the system works and the meaning of alternatives on the menu. Some terms are too complicated or misleading." Another staff member said that she learned by making mistakes and solving them, as she "fiddles around with it during extra time. Now that the system's up, however, there's not so much time to do this."

Departmental Interactions

Integrated hospital information systems that create common databases require health care departments to cooperate, increasing interactions among departments, such as between nurses administering drugs and a pharmacy's billing practices and subsequent revenues (Aydin, 1989; Aydin and Rice, 1991, 1992). These interdependencies necessitate standardized forms, terminology, and policies and procedures agreed on by the departments involved. In turn, common access to standard resources may reduce dependence on other departments for access to information, possibly reducing conflict. Computers can trigger social dynamics that may either modify or maintain the structure of the organization (Barley, 1986; Stryker, 1981).

Overall, employees perceived a very slight increase in information exchange with all other health service departments ($M = 4.53$ where 4.00 is "no change" and the range is 1 to 7). Nonmedical personnel perceived greater increases than did medical personnel. Members of the medical records department perceived greater increases in information exchange with all other departments than did employees in any of the other departments ($p < .01$), while medical records, the lab, primary care, and finance and personnel were the departments mentioned by members of other departments as being most involved in increases in information exchange. Communication-based forms of involvement in implementation (communicating with systems personnel and trainers, communicating about new ways to use the system, and receiving support from supervisors for doing so) were the most important factors in predicting increases in interdepartmental information exchange.

Job Design

There was little or no job redesign accompanying the system implementation. One interviewee felt that "the results are very unfair; the job descriptions do not reflect the changed responsibilities in people's jobs." These were discussed in the light of the new system, but no changes followed. In fact staff "absorbed the implementation" in their "spare time." As a result, many personnel had no spare time or energy left. Thus, paradoxically, the system created a need for more help and staff. But the administrative analysts insisted that in the long run, the essential benefit would be better service to the students.

Thus, without any intentional policy or strategy, some system characteristics forced changes in job designs and organizational interactions.

Complex Consequences

One of several paradoxes associated with the system was the summer analysis project started up by the service's director. During the summer, students had to pay for their services unless they obtained special insurance, but even then, the routines were different than they were during the regular year. Before the system, there was no insight as to the effect of all these students and different pricing policies. This was important because most of the health care service's supplemental income came during the summer, and the same problems arose every summer, but the service had no information on the reality of the situation. The director had one of the assistant administration analysts manually log all cash receipt forms to identify the scale of this problem. She saw it as a one-time special project, which ended up lasting the entire following year because it took so much clerical time to enter all the data, which she analyzed using a spreadsheet program. With the new system and its ability to capture service, demographic, and billing information, staff could now do the same kinds of analysis they did for the summer analysis all year long. The consequence was that what was seen before as a special project, one of several that researched unique problems, now took up nearly all the student work hours, as well as some of the analyst's time, so the finance office had no additional resources to do the special projects, including learning more about the system and analyzing what kinds of reports could be done.

Implications

Not surprisingly, this medical information system was designed to overcome limitations of paper-based work and had a wide variety of positive and negative outcomes. Perhaps more surprising, a new, complex medical information system may really be more of a symptom than a cure. It can provide an occasion to reveal or engage many underlying processes and problems in the organization, ranging from technical policies, and implementation and job design decisions, to social norms across departments and professions. The assistant administration analyst noted that the system "brings to light all these operational problems," such as a disorganized or tangled procedure. It makes obvious the need for policies and procedures. Why does the system do this if the policies and procedures and staff were not needed before the system? The respondents thought about this question and basically decided that before the system, things were a mess but had not been perceived as such. Rather, they felt that the main problem or organizational illness was the dependence on paper-based work processes. They thought that the growing awareness of the need for policies and procedures, and the need to run an efficient and effective organization, was a change associated with the new administrators. As the service grew, it began to need organization. This need for improved organization was part of the rationale for the system (for example, to obtain demographic data, have more accurate information). Once the system was in place, it "forces you to articulate things"—not only to have accurate data input but to understand how jobs and processes are related. Before, there were always several ways to do a procedure because each person or supervisor could solve it differently. With the new system, it was necessary to know and use the proper way to do the procedure.

The primary implication from this and other studies is that the social aspects of system implementations are by far the most critical aspects—both as influences on and outcomes from organizational change associated with the system. In this sense, while medical information systems may be seen by some as a "cure" for organizational problems, they may also be "symptoms" of underlying organizational assumptions, managerial policies, and social roles.

Discussion Questions

1. What are some of the central communication problems and issues associated with the implementation of this information system?

2. What are two implementation procedures or policies you would have changed if you had been in charge? Why? How would things have been different with these changes?

3. What are some components and functions of a health care institution that are necessary to provide good patient care but are not visible or obvious to the patient?

4. Identify and debate trade-offs between two technical system characteristics or features and two social system characteristics or features.

5. List and describe two examples each of what you would consider to be successful and unsuccessful aspects of the information system in this case.

6. From the results provided in one of the seven organizational aspects, identify and analyze how problems or issues associated with the implementation of the medical information system were actually symptoms of underlying organizational problems or illnesses.

7. Based on one of the associated journal articles (Aydin and Rice, 1991; 1992;

Rice and Anderson, 1993; Rice and Aydin, 1991), discuss one of the examples or results from this case in more detail.

References

Aydin, C. E. "Occupational Adaptation to Computerized Medical Information Systems." *Journal of Health and Social Behavior*, 1989, *30*, 163–179.

Aydin, C. E., and Rice, R. E. "Social Worlds, Individual Differences, and Implementation: Predicting Attitudes Toward a Medical Information System." *Information and Management*, 1991, *20*, 119–136.

Aydin, C. E., and Rice, R. E. "Bringing Social Worlds Together: Computers as Catalysts for New Interactions in Health Organizations." *Journal of Health and Social Behavior*, 1992, *33*(2), 168–185.

Barley, S. R. "Technology as an Occasion for Structuring: Evidence from Observations of CT Scanners and the Social Order of Radiology Departments." *Administrative Science Quarterly*, 1986, *31*, 78–108.

Braverman, H. *Labor and Monopoly Capital: The Degradation of Work in the Twentieth Century.* New York: Monthly Review Press, 1974.

Brenner, D. J., and Logan, R. A. "Some Considerations in the Diffusion of Medical Technologies: Medical Information Systems." In D. Nimmo (ed.), *Communication Yearbook,* Vol. 4. Thousand Oaks, Calif.: Sage, 1980.

Counte, M. A., Kjerulff, K. A., Salloway, J. C., and Campbell, B. C. "Implementing Computerization in Hospitals: A Case Study of the Behavioral and Attitudinal Impacts of a Medical Information System." In J. G. Anderson and S. J. Jay (eds.), *Use and Impact of Computers in Clinical Medicine.* New York: Springer-Verlag, 1987.

Dowling, A. F. Jr. "Do Hospital Staff Interfere with Computer System Implementation?" *Health Care Management Review*, 1980, *5*, 23–32.

Eder, L. B. (ed.), *Managing Healthcare Information Systems with Web-Enabled Technologies.* Hershey, Pa.: Idea Group Publishing, 2000.

Fischer, P. J., Stratmann, W. C., Lundsgaarde, H. P., and Steele, D. J. "User Reaction to PROMIS: Issues Related to Acceptability of Medical Innovations." In J. G. Anderson and S. J. Jay (eds.), *Use and Impact of Computers in Clinical Medicine.* New York: Springer-Verlag, 1987.

Hirschheim, R. A. "Assessing Participative Systems Design: Some Conclusions from an Exploratory Study." *Information and Management*, 1983, *6*, 317–327.

Hirschheim, R. A. *Office Automation: A Social and Organizational Perspective.* New York: Wiley, 1985.

Ives, B., Olson, M. H., and Baroudi, J. J. "The Measurement of User Information Satisfaction." *Communications of the ACM*, 1983, *26*, 785–793.

Johnson, B., and Rice, R. E. *Managing Organizational Innovation: The Evolution from Word Processing to Office Information Systems.* New York: Columbia University Press, 1987.

Kissinger, K., and Borchardt, S. *Information Technology for Integrated Health Systems.* New York: Wiley, 1996.

Kling, R. "Social Analyses of Computing: Theoretical Perspectives in Recent Empirical Research." *Computing Surveys*, 1980, *12*, 61–110.

Lincoln, T. L., and Korpman, R. A. "Computers, Health Care, and Medical Information Science." *Science*, 1980, *210*, 257–263.

Lindberg, D.A.B. *The Growth of Medical Information Systems in the United States*. San Francisco: New Lexington Press, 1979.

Lucas, H. Jr. *Implementation: The Key to Successful Information Systems*. New York: Columbia University Press, 1981.

Markus, M. L. *Systems in Organizations: Bugs and Features*. Boston: Pitman, 1984.

Packer, C. L. "Historical Changes in Hospital Computer Use." *Hospitals*, Jan. 16, 1985.

Rice, R. E., and Anderson, J. G. "Social Networks and Healthcare Information Systems: A Structural Approach to Evaluation." In J. Anderson, C. Aydin, and S. J. Jay (eds.), *Evaluating Health Care Information Systems: Approaches and Applications*. Thousand Oaks, Calif.: Sage, 1993.

Rice, R. E., and Aydin, C. "Attitudes Towards New Organizational Technology: Network Proximity as a Mechanism for Social Information Processing." *Administrative Science Quarterly*, 1991, *36*, 219–244.

Rice, R. E., and Katz, J. E. (eds.). *The Internet and Health Communication: Expectations and Experiences*. Thousand Oaks, Calif.: Sage, 2001.

Rognehaugh, R. *The Health Information Technology Dictionary*. Gaithersburg, Md.: Aspen, 1999.

Schultz, R. L., and Slevin, D. P. "Implementation and Organizational Validity: An Empirical Investigation." In R. L. Schultz and D. P. Slevin (eds.), *Implementing Operations Research/Management Science*. New York: American Elsevier, 1975.

Smith, D. B., and Kaluzny, A. D. *The White Labyrinth*. Ann Arbor, Mich.: Health Administration Press, 1986.

Street, R. L. Jr., Gold, W., and Manning, T. (eds.). *Health Promotion and Interactive Technology: Theoretical Applications and Future Directions*. Mahwah, N.J.: Erlbaum, 1997.

Stryker, S. "Symbolic Interactionism: Themes and Variations." In M. Rosenberg and R. H. Turner (eds.), *Social Psychology, Sociological Perspectives*. New York: Basic Books, 1981.

CHAPTER FOUR

TELEMEDICINE AT SHRINERS HOSPITALS FOR CHILDREN

One Size Does Not Fit All

Mark L. Niederpruem, Robert Gerding, Mary E. Kautto, Peter Armstrong, Jana L. C. Lindsey, Katherine Y. Vigil, Cary Burcham, Michael Moushui, Shannon M. Lehman, Donald Lighter

An organization with twenty-two hospitals in three countries and sixteen states in five time zones offering three product lines poses specific challenges of introducing telemedicine technologies. In 1998, Shriners Hospitals for Children (SHC) embarked on harnessing the technologies to serve children within its care using telemedicine. This was undertaken to serve difficult-to-reach populations in geographical areas distant to the host hospital and to reduce the time and dollars related to travel for the patient and families and for the physicians and clinicians. The need to establish a process to achieve this integration was envisioned early on and resulted in the Telemedicine Governance Council. This organizational body has afforded the planning, coordination, and implementation of this ongoing project.

Reviewing the process that has taken place to date will highlight the challenges and strategies used by SHC to achieve its objectives. An examination of the stages within this development process will identify the variables that need to be considered when implementing a system in an organization that is geographically diverse.

At this time, SHC is involved in three distinct services. The hospitals were originally founded to be orthopedic hospitals to serve the population with polio in the 1920s; hence, pediatric orthopedics is the largest service component of the system. Children from birth to eighteen years of age who have orthopedic or related problems are seen at nineteen of the twenty-two hospitals. Second, in the

1960s, SHC expanded its mission to include pediatric burn patients. Currently, four facilities provide services for burn injuries and related plastic reconstructive surgeries. Third, SHC provides services for spinal cord–injured patients at three of the facilities. These services provide comprehensive medical and rehabilitation services for this injury. A list of hospitals and the services provided is in Table 4.1.

The subtitle of this chapter, "One size does not fit all" refers to the differences experienced in applying telemedicine to SHC. The differences primarily are in the geographical location and the makeup of that hospital's market. Some hospitals are located in large metropolitan areas and others in small to medium-sized metropolitan areas. Each metropolitan area has its own service delivery model that has evolved over the course of time, including the presence of nonprofit, religious-based, and for-profit health care service delivery models. Because of SHC's presence for the better part of eighty years, SHC's role has been well integrated into the fabric of the community. The way health care is delivered in one section of the country can be quite different from that delivered in another section of the country.

TABLE 4.1. SHRINERS HOSPITALS LOCATIONS AND SERVICES.

Hospital	Location	Orthopedics	Burns	Spinal Cord Injury
Boston Hospital	Boston		X	
Canadian Hospital	Montreal, Canada	X		
Chicago Hospital	Chicago	X		X
Cincinnati Hospital	Cincinnati, Ohio		X	
Erie Hospital	Erie, Penn.	X		
Galveston Hospital	Galveston, Tex.		X	
Greenville Hospital	Greenville, S.C.	X		
Honolulu Hospital	Honolulu	X		
Houston Hospital	Houston	X		
Intermountain Hospital	Salt Lake City, Utah	X		
Lexington Hospital	Lexington, Ky.	X		
Los Angeles Hospital	Los Angeles	X		
Mexico City Hospital	Mexico City	X		
Northern California Hospital	Sacramento, Calif.	X	X	X
Philadelphia Hospital	Philadelphia	X		X
Portland Hospital	Portland, Ore.	X		
St. Louis Hospital	St. Louis, Mo.	X		
Shreveport Hospital	Shreveport, La.	X		
Spokane Hospital	Spokane, Wash.	X		
Springfield Hospital	Springfield, Mass.	X		
Tampa Hospital	Tampa, Fla.	X		
Twin Cities Hospital	Minneapolis, Minn.	X		

Although there are several differences in SHC hospitals, there are also unifying themes that illustrate the similarities of the hospitals working to integrate telemedicine to their daily practices. Such similarities as smaller facilities (under sixty beds) provide a more controlled environment to introduce new ideas. A corporate body that promotes a new intervention is seen as a similarity and unifying force as to the introduction and adaptation of a new technology. Also when surveyed, the eleven hospitals engaged at this time had similar themes for putting resources into this new technology: reaching unserved or underserved areas and improving patient and family satisfaction with decreased travel time and missed school and work.

Why Telemedicine, and Why Now?

SHC has eleven of the twenty-two facilities at various stages of implementing telemedicine. The facility with the most experience represents over five years of operational experience, and the facility with the least experience is currently being brought on-line. Figure 4.1 highlights the program sites.

Typical reasons for implementation run true with the SHC case study as well, such as saving time, money, and transportation costs. However, within these broad areas, there are issues that SHC sites were addressing specific to their locale. The first of note is increasing accessibility for patients requiring specialized care. Improving efficiency of both time and dollars is another main reason this project has been undertaken. Forgoing the inconvenience of having to take the day off from work and a day off from school, traveling a good distance, incurring travel costs and incidental costs, and then returning home proves to be a burden on the family. In addition, the specialist must move to the patient. Finally, two of the eleven hospitals indicated, as part of their proposals, that they would use equipment related to telemedicine for professional education. This would seem to be a commonsense approach to having guest lecturers come or to attend didactic sessions in a more convenient manner. However, to date, only one hospital has taken advantage of this technology. The reasons for not having developed this aspect more are unclear. But as time constraints continue to become a factor in everyone's lives, telecommuting and tele-educational sessions appear to be a partial answer.

Putting the Pieces Together

The implementation of telemedicine at SHC has been accomplished in a number of different ways. Nevertheless, some common themes do emerge from the broader picture, regardless of the length that the program has been running.

FIGURE 4.1. SHRINERS HOSPITALS TELEMEDICINE PROGRAM HOST AND REMOTE SITES, APRIL 2003.

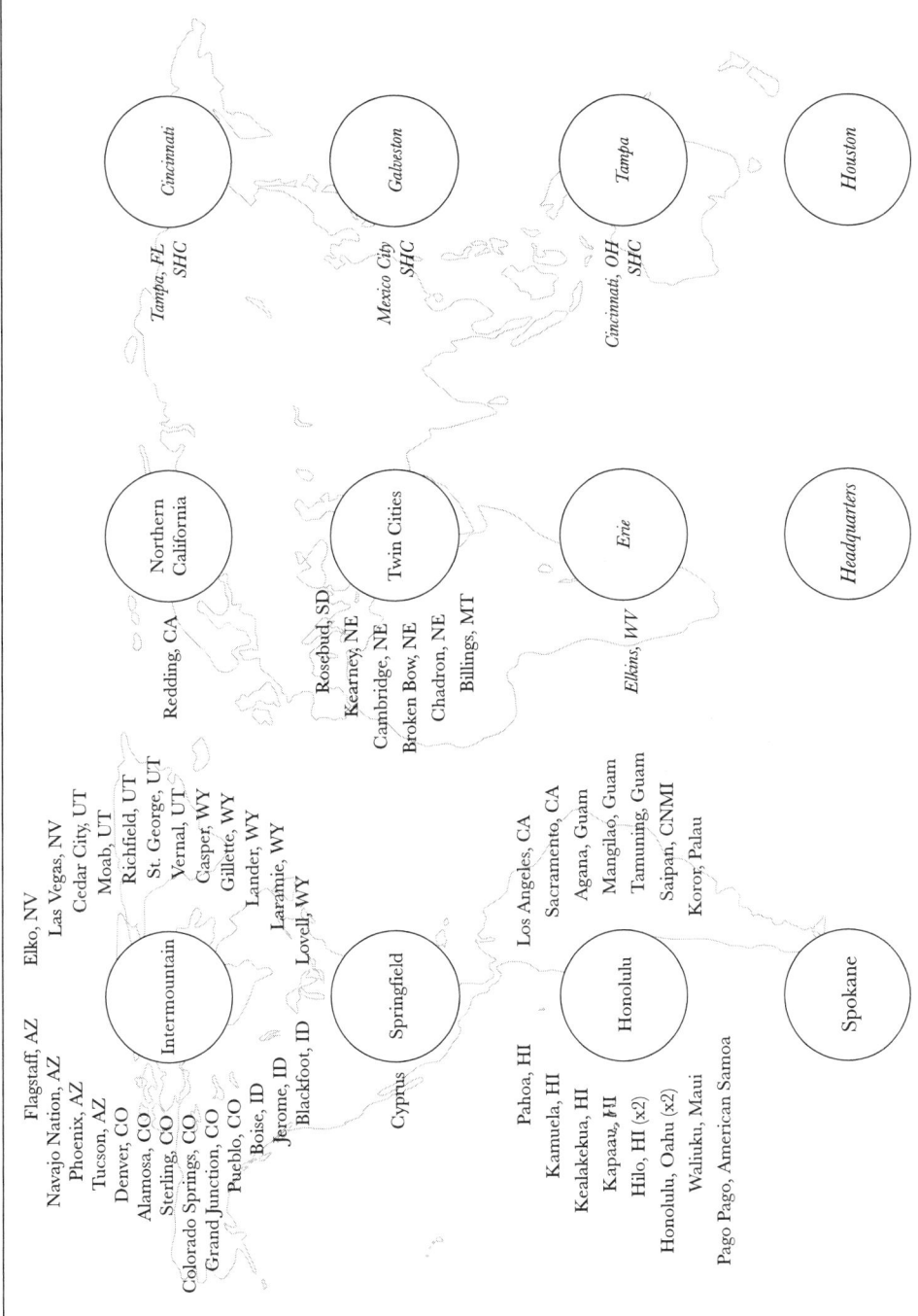

First and foremost, a project must have vision: the vision of harnessing a technology for improved patient care. The vision does not need to come from the highest point in the organization, although corporate support is an essential component. Vision may come from the champions within an organization who see the potential of adding another tool to deliver care at the time it is needed, where it is needed, and by the appropriate person. Champions ensure buy-in from the appropriate groups necessary to succeed. Included among these are physicians as well as other clinical and nonclinical staff who will help facilitate or create roadblocks to its implementation.

Integration is a second strategy to consider to help facilitate the implementation of telemedicine. Although the key component is the physician-patient relationship, the supporting cast of characters is long and essential for care to be rendered effectively, efficiently, and safely. Integration needs to be incorporated into the fabric of the organization so that it is accepted and so that individuals do not have to go out of their way to accommodate another demand on their time.

A third benefit to implementation suggests the need to use a phased approach, as one facility noted. Hoping to receive equipment, connect it, and then schedule a dozen patients to be seen the first hour is unrealistic. As with most other activities, competencies grow with experience. One must not set expectations too high, thereby setting the program up for early failure. One program recognized this early, noting that telemedicine has an important application for all components of clinical services, including the three service areas of SHC organization. However, initial energy focuses on follow-up with burn reconstruction patients only. This concentration will help to minimize the effects of misstarts while providing an opportunity to gain a practical understanding, including technical issues of the telemedicine program.

Due to the multisite nature of SHC, a fourth strategy is to establish technological standards early in the process. The Telemedicine Governance Council did this, with the aid of an external consultant who was well versed in the technology aspect of telemedicine and videoconferencing. The challenge in setting technical and equipment standards is not only choosing a solution; it is staying abreast of the technology wave. Therefore, one must pick a point when establishing a standard and go from that point forward. Fortunately, the baseline technical standards have been set by the regulatory and trade groups of the communications arena, and this has served all of telemedicine well so as not to have competing technologies creating unnecessary inefficiencies and redundancies in the system. Establishing standards for equipment and transmission purposes was achieved following a routine review of vendors.

Lessons Learned

One of the predominant lessons learned has been the importance of having a trained, competent person at the remote site to present the patient. Due to the wide degree of variability of the remote sites, the issues in achieving this were broad.

A second lesson relates to the importance of the organization's commitment in supporting the initiative. For example, clinical and administrative champions are necessary to bring about a successful implementation. This includes dedicating the amount of time and resources necessary to assist introducing this technology into any organization.

Another common lesson relates to the feasibility and appropriateness of the technology. The technology's ease of use, limitations, and reliability all illustrate potential strengths and shortcomings in implementing a service. In the short period that telemedicine at SHC has been operational, the technology has advanced rapidly; it has become easier to use, more reliable, and less costly.

Consistent with other studies, there is a high degree of patient satisfaction with the use of telemedicine. There was a 99 percent comfort level identified by the most active program within SHC for 2002, which has been consistent since the beginning of the program. Anecdotally, we would concur that the patients and families are ready for this technology. The limitations appear to be on the provider's side, freeing up time, identifying champions, and making it a routine part of the hospital operations.

Another anecdotal observation is that the acceptance level may be positive in part because wait times are less for a telemedicine encounter. Since telemedicine is scheduled at specific times due to communication costs, providers are on time, and so the satisfaction level may be increased.

One program expressed an increased awareness by those at the host site of the cost associated with travel for patients or families. This may describe in part the satisfaction noted with patients and their families because they are receiving services in a more cost-effective manner.

The lessons learned are not much different from other programs launched in recent years; however, the detail noted and anecdotal observations will help future programs address these issues early on. We believe that telemedicine will become another tool in continuing efforts to reach patients who need specialized services. Just as traditional consults have developed over telephones and now e-mail, the day is not too far away when telemedicine will be a recognized standard of care for accessing specialized services.

Discussion Questions

1. Shriners Hospitals for Children has undertaken a broad implementation planned for telemedicine. How is this experience different from or similar to experiences that your own program has had or other programs of which you are knowledgeable?
2. If you were a provider in an underserved area, how would the approach described in this case study enhance or hinder your accessing specialized care?
3. What components are missing from the Shriner Hospitals for Children implementation described in this case study?
4. If you were seeking to implement a telemedicine program in a large geographical area, what would be the top three areas you would consider?
5. In looking at outcomes for programs such as described in this case study, what variables might you review to determine the effectiveness? The efficiency? The return on investment?

PART TWO

MANAGEMENT AND OPERATIONS

In the business world, the rearview mirror is always clearer than the windshield.

WARREN BUFFETT

CHAPTER FIVE

HOME TELEHEALTH

Overcoming Buy-In Issues

Bonnie Perry Britton, Rhonda Chetney

No other aspect of technology-delivered health services has received the attention and enthusiasm attributed to providing care directly into patients' homes. Home telehealth began with home health agency nurses conducting "live" audiovideo visits from the agency to a patient at home. Patients were primarily home bound with chronic illnesses, such as heart failure, chronic obstructive pulmonary disease, or diabetes. The patient and nurse could see and hear each other. The nurse conducted physical assessments; collected objective and subjective data such as blood pressure, heart rate, pulse oximetry, and weights; and listened to heart and lung sounds.

Early pioneers have demonstrated high patient and provider satisfaction. In addition, programs have documented home health agency cost savings, hospital and payer cost savings, and increased nurse productivity (Britton, Engelke, Still, and Walden, 1999; Britton, Engelke, Rains, and Mahmud, 2000; Chetney, 2003; Chetney and Sauls, 2003; Jerant, Rahman, and Nesbitt, 2001; Johnston, Wheeler, Deuser, and Sousa, 2000; Lewis, 2001; Roupe and Young, 2003; Shea and others, 2002; Slater and Chetney, 2003; Starren and others, 2002; Wilver, 2001). As a result, home telehealth is expanding rapidly in multiple directions.

Since early 2000, providers have been expanding from mostly home health nurses providing patient encounters to all members of the multidisciplinary team.

Dietitians conduct nutritional counseling, education, and dietary regimen compliance monitoring. Speech therapists conduct speech therapy visits, and physical therapists evaluate stroke and head injury patients. In addition, the locations of both the patient and the provider are changing. Telehealth professionals are located in home health agencies, hospital and outpatient disease management programs, and outpatient clinics, to name a few. And patients are now located not only in their homes but also in assisted living facilities, group housing, schools, and clinics. Home telehealth includes a wide range of services, from telemonitoring (transmission of digitized clinical data) to synchronous visits between providers and patients. One of the main issues facing any home telehealth integration is provider buy-in. Creating and sustaining buy-in is critical for the success of any program.

Many factors affect nurse buy-in. These factors vary across implementation sites and providers, so it is essential to develop a multifaceted plan to build and sustain buy-in. This case study highlights a Sentara Home Care Services disease management program that incorporates strategies for nurse buy-in during development and implementation of a disease management program for heart failure, the Cardiac Connection.

Home Telehealth at Sentara

In 2000, Sentara began incorporating interactive home telehealth into its existing heart failure disease management programs. Cardiac Connection was established with the goal of decreasing hospital readmissions and emergency room visits for patients with heart failure. Improving the well-being of these patients was paramount to the success of the program.

Patients are identified and screened at the time of referral to determine the New York Heart Association classification for their disease. Consent is obtained from the patient for participation in the program. Once patients meet the criteria for inclusion, they are enrolled in the program.

Sentara's nurses use Aviva 1010 XR equipment (American TeleCare) that combines live audio and video with a telephonic stethoscope and other medical peripherals (blood pressure meter, electronic scale, pulse oximeter, finger stick blood sugar) to conduct patient encounters. The nurse and patient can see and talk to each other while the nurse gathers objective and subjective information for a clinical assessment of the patient's status. A central workstation, located in the home health office, enables the nurse to assess the patient's current status and, when needed, intervene rapidly, preventing an exacerbation of the heart failure. In addition to storing documentation (weight gain, blood pressure, and vital signs), the nurse can graph the patient information to fax to the physician.

Patients are taught correct placement for the blood pressure cuff and stethoscope and machine and camera operation. A nurse in the agency office uses a central workstation to initiate a practice encounter while the in-home nurse is present. Making the first encounter while the nurse is in the home helps determine additional learning needs. This concurrent encounter also increases in-home nurse confidence in the accuracy of the technology. Teamwork develops as the nurses work together to ensure that the patient is using the unit safely and effectively. As of fall 2003, nurses had provided more than two thousand home telehealth encounters to patients enrolled in Sentara's telehealth programs.

Strategies to Secure Nurse Buy-In

In order to ensure nurse acceptance and utilization of this program, a management strategy with nine steps was developed to maximize nurse buy-in.

Step One: Select a Telehealth Leader

The first critical step is to select a home telehealth champion. This person is usually responsible for promoting and overseeing the implementation phase, obtaining nurse buy-in, developing clear objectives for deployment of the equipment, and measuring outcomes, which can then be used to demonstrate the benefits of the program. This person is also usually responsible for marketing the program to physicians and payers. The champion needs to be the main communicator to the staff.

Step Two: Involve Visiting Nursing Staff from the Beginning

The next critical step is to include field staff in the process of selecting home telehealth equipment that meets the needs of the patient populations. Including the nurses at the beginning helps the agency choose a product that is user friendly in the field and encourages the staff to have a stake in the success of the product they select. Sentara included a select group of field nurses in the selection process to test and try various products. It selected nurses to be trained as "train the trainers" on the home telehealth equipment. Nurses were chosen who had lengthy experience with the point-of-care documentation product and were comfortable using a laptop computer.

Choosing a nurse who was familiar with technology and not fearful of it contributed to the ease of learning the product. Most nurses were chosen because they were enthusiastic about trying something different and were open to change. Many of these nurses had recently completed a Windows class that helped with learning the central workstation. Staff attended demonstrations by vendors regarding the technology and the options available for the patient and the staff. Several small pilots were completed that included the visiting nursing staff in testing the technology. Staff nurses then had input into the selection of the specific product. The staff at Sentara chose to partner with American TeleCare for its telehealth vendor.

Step Three: Pique Interest

The designated home telehealth champion should conduct informal presentations to all nursing staff. The purpose of the presentations is to inform the staff of how other agencies have successfully used home telehealth, allay staff anxieties regarding new technology, pique interest, and answer questions. The presentations covered current research and outcome studies, real-time examples, and the rationale for implementing interactive home telehealth. The field nurses who participated in the selection process were also involved in telling their experiences during the pilot phase.

Step Four: Select a Model of Care

Sentara chose a case management model of care where nurses selected their patients, installed home telehealth equipment in the home, and conducted in-home visits co-mingled with telehealth patient encounters. Both types of visits were provided by the same nurse. This model of care delivery was different from most other telehealth programs that use a nurse at the central station to conduct home telehealth patient encounters and a different nurse in the home to conduct in-home visits. Although the Sentara model may not be as cost-efficient as the traditional model, it was successful because the nurses did not feel as if they were being replaced by the telehealth nurse. This model also minimized intimidation of having another nurse "follow up on them" and encouraged nurses to use the telehealth technology for their patients. Patients benefited from the continuity provided from seeing the same nurse in their home as well as through the video monitor.

One of the first patients followed under this model was a retired female with heart failure who was dealing with her own health and numerous family social problems. Her husband was an alcoholic and would not assist in her care. Her daughter was experiencing personal problems and kept moving in and out of the home at various times. Whenever this happened, the patient's stress level would increase, and she generally had difficulty controlling her disease. Home telehealth was a lifeline for this patient. The patient was receiving routine in-home visits, co-mingled with home telehealth encounters from the same nurse, with whom she had developed a close relationship. With home telehealth, the nurse was able to teach the patient to identify triggers that would exacerbate her condition. When the patient began to feel a change in her condition, she would call the nurse, who would then initiate a home telehealth encounter to assess the patient's condition. Effective stress and medication management during these difficult times prevented numerous emergency room visits and admissions for this patient. The clinical effectiveness of the technology helped the nurse realize that being able to see the patient without delay helped her intervene quickly and effectively and was more efficient than driving to the patient's home to provide the care.

Step Five: Define Process and Policy

Sentara developed written guidelines to assist the nursing staff in identifying appropriate patients for the program. Nurses can seek advice from the telehealth champion regarding patient selection guidelines for referral to the telehealth program. Keeping these guidelines simple helped with buy-in from the nursing staff. Developing or enforcing overly stringent criteria for inclusion can deter referrals to the program. Keeping it simple and broad encourages staff to consider more patients appropriate for telehealth.

Step Six: Train Staff

Nurses received training as home telehealth "train the trainers." Two days of hands-on training was provided by the vendor, American TeleCare. Staff nurses and clinical managers were trained on equipment software and hardware, patient installation, and education. The nurses were validated for competence in using the central station and installing the patient station and patient education. Nurses who were interviewed said that the training was adequate and additional practice with the equipment reduced their anxiety.

Step Seven: Make Documentation Easy

Sentara incorporated a telehealth service option into the point-of-care documentation system. Sentara documents telehealth encounters on the same visit note that staff use for in-home visits. The agency views a telehealth encounter as a skilled visit and believes the documentation should be the same. Incorporating the option to differentiate the actual visit contact as a telehealth encounter allows the agency to compile statistical and cost data related specifically to telehealth. The field staff also benefit from knowing that the telehealth encounter will be factored into their productivity.

Step Eight: Address Productivity Issues

Staff are given extra productivity credit for the initial equipment installation and patient education. Normally, a revisit is equal to one productivity hour. Telehealth equipment installation and patient education are awarded a productivity equivalent of 1.5, and the actual telehealth encounter receives 0.5 productivity credit. Initially, the visits or encounters were not given extra productivity credit, an issue that created a hesitance among the staff to recommend their patients to the telehealth program. Sentara surveyed staff and found that most nurses would refer more patients if they received additional credit for the initial equipment installation and patient education visit. Once the revised productivity policy was instituted, staff referrals increased; nurses enjoyed using the equipment and enjoyed decreased travel time, creating more buy-in to the program.

Step Nine: Provide Ongoing Buy-In Activities

The home telehealth champion attended staff meetings to review staff nurses' role in home telehealth, provide updates regarding progress, and share patient success stories. Cost savings and improved patient outcomes are shared with the staff to demonstrate the benefits from the program. A newsletter publishes stories regarding the program. The staff is rewarded for referrals to the program with movie tickets and other employee recognition programs. New staff nurses receive home telehealth training during orientation so they understand that home telehealth is an integral part of Sentara's care delivery. Staff photos are used in marketing brochures, television clips, and other public relation activities. The field staff have also been used to market the program directly to physicians. Periodic surveys of the staff are conducted to gain insight into improvements to the program. Staff recommendations about new technology or ideas are taken seriously and implemented when appropriate.

Discussion Questions

1. How does interactive home telehealth change your thoughts on remote patient care delivery?
2. Why is the management of provider buy-in an important strategic aspect of any project employing new technologies for health delivery?
3. Are there different issues that must be considered for development of provider buy-in versus sustainability of provider buy-in? If so, what are they?
4. What would occur if an organization does not formally address provider buy-in?

5. On a scale of 1 to 10, with 10 being the highest, how would you rate the importance of provider buy-in to the success of a telehealth project?

References

Britton, B., Engelke, M., Rains, D., and Mahmud, K. "Measuring Costs and Quality of TeleHomecare." *Home Health Care Management and Practice,* 2000, *14,* 27–32.

Britton, B., Engelke, M., Still, A., and Walden, C. "Innovative Approaches to Patient Care Management Using TeleHomecare." *Home Health Care Consultant,* 1999, *13,* pp. 11–12, 14–16.

Chetney, R. "The Cardiac Connection Program." *Home Healthcare Nurse,* 2003, *21*(10), 680–686.

Chetney, R., and Sauls, E. "A Picture Speaks Louder Than Words . . . But a Digital Camcorder Tells the Whole Story." *Homehealth Care Nurse,* 2003, *21*(10), 645–646.

Cryer, L., and Wilmsen, P. "Telehealth: An Integrated Clinical and Information System Solution." *Supplement to the Remington Report,* July–Aug. 2002, pp. 11–13.

Jerant, A., Rahman, A., and Nesbitt, T. "Reducing the Cost of Frequent Hospital Admissions for Congestive Heart Failure: Randomized Trial of a Home Telecare Intervention." *Medical Care,* 2001, *39*(11), 1234–1245.

Johnston, B., Wheeler, L., Deuser, J., and Sousa, K. H. "Outcomes of the Kaiser Permanente Tele-Home Health Research Project." *Archives Family Medicine,* 2000, *9*(1), 40–45.

Lewis, P. "VHA Home Telemedicine Study Results in a Savings of $23 Million." *Remington Report,* Sept.–Oct. 2001, pp. 10–12.

Roupe, M., and Young, S. "Interactive Home Telehealth: A Complementary Addition to Disease Management Programs." *Remington Report,* July–Aug. 2003, pp. 14–16.

Shea, S., and others. "Columbia University's Informatics for Diabetes Education and Telemedicine (IDEATel) Project." *Journal of the American Medical Informatics Association,* 2002, *9*(1), 49–62.

Slater, S., and Chetney, R. " Using Telehealth Technology to Manage Wound Care and Asthma Patients at Sentara Home Care Services." *Home Health Care Management and Practice Journal,* 2003, *15*(2), 166–167.

Starren, J., and others. "Columbia University's Informatics for Diabetes Education and Telemedicine (IDEATel) Project." *Journal of the American Medical Informatics Association,* 2002, *9,* 25–26.

Wilver, D. "A PPS Success Story. Telehomecare: How an Agency Benefits Financially, Clinically, and with the Community." *Remington Report,* July–Aug. 2001, pp. 26–28.

CHAPTER SIX

A MODEL FOR PERSUADING DECISION MAKERS AND FINDING NEW PARTNERS

Glen Effertz, Steven Beffort, Alistair Preston,
Frank D. Pullara, Dale C. Alverson

An inmate sits isolated in prison trying to turn his life around, preparing for a new lease on life and release back into society. Unfortunately, he is hepatitis C virus (HCV) positive, as are nearly one-third of his fellow inmates. Without treatment, he faces the risk of death from end-stage cirrhosis, liver failure, or liver cancer. With treatment, he could be completely cured, with a 50 percent cure rate even with the most resistant strains of the virus. But treatment is not an option. Treatment, even if available, would be complicated and require a highly trained specialty team usually available only at high-level medical centers, inaccessible to most prisoners. In fact, a newly implemented telehealth system is bringing that specialty team to him and his primary care providers. He now has a new lease on life.

This tale began when the new medical director of the New Mexico Corrections Department (NMCD) appeared at the Center for Telehealth at the University of New Mexico (UNM). He asked why NMCD was not using telehealth within its health system because it just made sense. Nevertheless, this was a time that state corrections was under a severe budget crunch and could not consider any new expense like implementing a telehealth network. The NMCD medical director needed a business plan, which the Center for Telehealth agreed to develop in partnership with our business school, the Anderson Schools of Management, at UNM. That document proved to be the critical step that led to implementation of a full telehealth system connecting all state prisons in New

Mexico with links to outside networks at UNM, the Department of Health, and other providers as far away as Illinois. Now the system is being used to provide mental health services to inmates at significant cost savings. For the first time, prison inmates in New Mexico are being treated for HCV through a telehealth-enabled program providing case-based co-management between specialists and primary care providers. This is an enormous public health breakthrough.

The New Mexico State Department of Corrections consists of nine facilities throughout the state (Figure 6.1). Inpatient care is provided at the Los Lunas facility. Subspecialty and tertiary care is concentrated (outside the corrections system) in the Albuquerque area. Distance between facilities can be greater than five hundred miles. Local access to specialty health care in many of the locations is slight or nonexistent. The cost of transportation for inmates is extremely high, often involving overtime pay for security officers. Security problems and public safety are also major concerns: any trip out of the corrections facility involves a risk of escape attempts. Bringing providers to the institution poses its own set of problems: many providers are unwilling to make long trips and expect to be reimbursed for their travel time at their regular hourly rate. This case study presents the rationale and detail for the business plan that ultimately resulted in a telehealth program for New Mexico's prison system.

Considering a Business Case

On the surface, this seems like an open-and-shut case. There is a need for medical services, the services can be provided through telehealth, there are probable cost savings, and the project could have positive effects outside the system. We have an in-house champion. Do we need any further work? The answer is, emphatically, yes.

Turisco (2000) stated that health care organizations have not traditionally used any type of formal planning for information technology investments. She points out that this has often resulted in unsuccessful projects and poor return on value. Neumann, Blouin, and Byrne (1999) emphasized that all technology proposals should be formally reviewed through a "growth-efficiency capital filter" (p. 14)—essentially a business case. Austin (1999) concluded that "a feasibility analysis is a necessary but not sufficient condition for the success of a business project" (p. 42).

Turisco (2000) explained that the business case includes "people, process, and technology changes" (p. 12). Jennett, Gao, Hebert, and Hailey (2003) identified six potential policy levels at which benefits can be expected: encounter level, program level, organizational level, regional level, provincial level, and national

FIGURE 6.1. NEW MEXICO DEPARTMENT
OF CORRECTIONS FACILITIES.

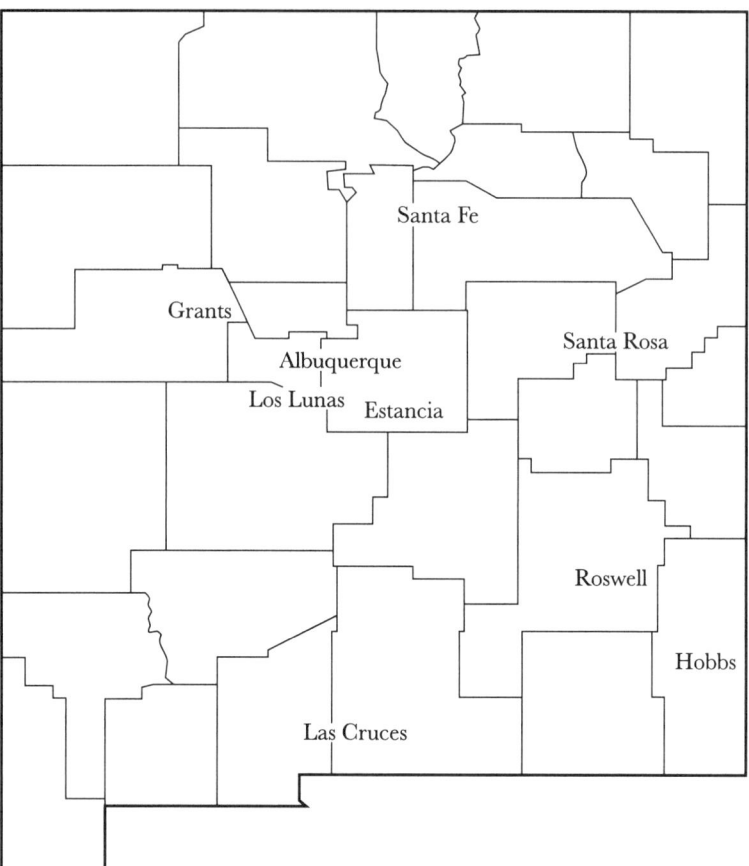

level. Both researchers point out that policy implications may differ radically at each different level. Fortunately, we can limit our business case to two or three relevant levels. In this situation, we are concerned with benefits at the encounter and organizational levels.

Pellissier and others (2001) emphasized that knowing the intended audience for the business case is extremely important. Their point of view is that the business case "concisely answers what the reader needs to know, rather than a landfill of collected information" (p. 6). Knowing the audience will also guide the technological and financial sophistication of the presentation, and the level of detail.

A number of researchers (Neumann, Blouin, and Byrne, 1999; Pellissier and others, 2001; Schmidt, 1997; Turisco, 2000) have discussed the use of cost and revenue (or cost savings) data in business cases. Much of the literature is geared more toward for-profit enterprises, and thus there is a good deal of discussion about the relative merits of return on investment, internal rate of return, payback period, and other financial approaches for evaluating projects. The important point is that the analysis must include a detailed table showing net cash flow. An analysis that takes into account the time value of money is useful but not essential. These researchers also mention the importance of intangible benefits. Turisco (2000) emphasizes that a dollar value for the benefits should be ascertained whenever possible. Neumann and others (1999) point out that it may sometimes be useful to think about the qualitative benefits that a project may bring.

The Business Case for the New Mexico Corrections Department

Of course, the best way to demonstrate what a business case should look like is to show an actual one. What follows is an annotated version of the business case that we prepared for the New Mexico Corrections Department.

What Is Telehealth?

The business case is usually presented to an audience that is, at best, only marginally familiar with the concept of telehealth. It is therefore essential to introduce and define the concept early in the case. In our case relating to the NMCD, much of our intended audience were not familiar with the concept. Figure 6.2 provides the initial explanation.

Why Telehealth?

We next lay out some quantitative (but nonfinancial) arguments for why telehealth would be effective in the New Mexico corrections system. The first factor has to do with the growth, both historical and projected, in the prison population, which will translate into a growing need for health care services (Figure 6.3).

The next factors examined had to do with the local health care providers. First, the number of providers per 100,000 population in New Mexico is lower than the national average (194 versus 226). Second, New Mexico is a geographically large state (the fifth largest) with a large percentage of health care providers

FIGURE 6.2. EXPLAINING TELEHEALTH IN THE BUSINESS CASE.

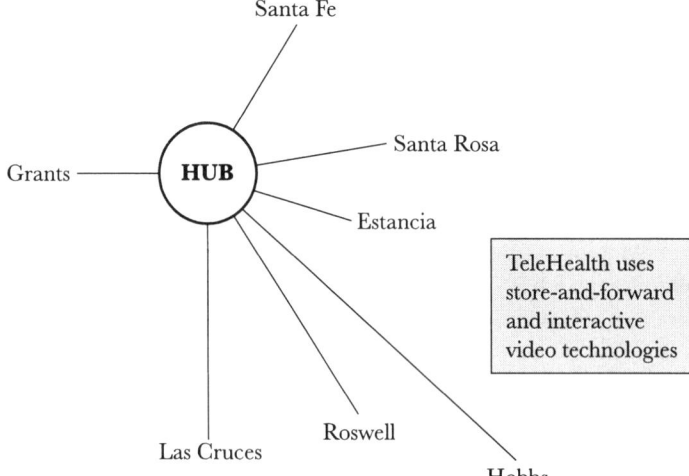

located in one small area. The last of the initial arguments involves the geographical spread of the state. With the concentration of health care providers in the Albuquerque area, driving time from Albuquerque becomes a significant barrier to the provision of services (Table 6.1).

Telehealth Costs and Savings

The next section in the business plan was the core of the business case: the financial justification for the project. Before laying out any justification, though, we needed to be more specific as to what exactly was involved in the project. We proposed that the department install a videoconferencing system that would be available in all nine of its facilities. We soon determined that the current telecommunications infrastructure would not be sufficient to support this system. There were several issues that brought about this conclusion:

- Existing network bandwidth was used to capacity.
- Committed information rates varied at each facility.
- Latency was not proven to meet minimum requirements.

FIGURE 6.3. PRISON POPULATION GROWTH, HISTORICAL AND PROJECTED, 1975–2002.

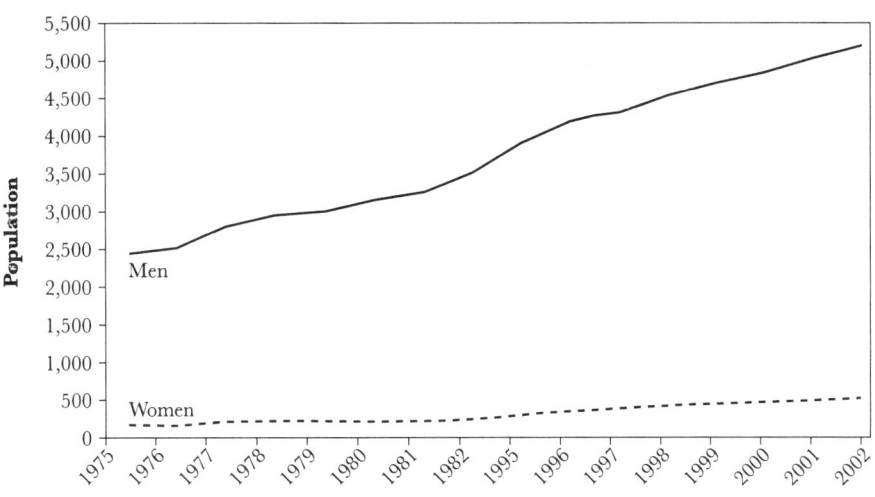

Note: The figures are for the end of the fiscal year. Those for 1975 to 2000 are actual; those for 2001 and 2002 are projected.

TABLE 6.1. DISTANCE AND TRAVEL TIME IN NEW MEXICO.

Location	Miles	Travel Time (hours)
Santa Fe	118	2
Los Lunas	48	1
Estancia	120	2
Grants (Men)	156	3
Grants (Women)	156	3
Santa Rosa	228	4
Hobbs	630	10
Las Cruces	446	7
Roswell	398	6

We proposed an upgrade to meet the following minimum requirements:

- Simulate an intranet with a virtual private network, switch virtual circuit, or a private virtual network.
- Guarantee a committed information rate of 384 Kbps with bursting up to 512 Kbps to support a single quality connection of interactive video.
- Guarantee latency under 250 milliseconds round trip.
- Guarantee quality of service from the provider and network managers.

Costs. The business case must account for both one-time and recurring costs. The initial cost of infrastructure improvements, including the Internet protocol (IP) intranet, would be $61,800, with an operating cost for these improvements of $51,100 per year (Table 6.2). There would also be costs for the videoconferencing equipment in each of the sites (Table 6.3).

Savings. This is the heart of the matter. With all of the associated benefits, both internal and external, will the system pay for itself? There are, of course, instances where the system does not have to pay for itself. If the benefits are spread across a number of constituencies, some outside agency may be willing to take on at least a partial subsidy for the system. For the NMCD, we knew that subsidy was extremely unlikely and that we would have to find cost savings.

TABLE 6.2. IP INTRANET ONE-TIME AND RECURRING COSTS.

	Cost	Cost per Site	Number of Sites	Total
One-time equipment costs				
Internet protocol intranet	Routers	$2,300	9	$20,700
	Installation	700	9	6,300
Primary rate interface	Connection			
switched network	equipment	4,300	1	4,300
(Los Lunas)	Gateway	30,000	1	30,000
	Installation	500	1	500
Total one-time equipment costs				$61,800
Annual recurring costs				
Internet protocol intranet	Telecom charges	$4,200	9	$37,800
Primary rate interface				
switched network	Telecom charges	6,300	1	6,300
	Maintenance	5,500	1	5,500
	Long distance	1,500	1	1,500
Total recurring costs				$51,100

As is often the case for telehealth projects, we immediately looked to transportation costs. The corrections system is spread out over a large geographical area, with health care providers concentrated in Albuquerque. It turned out that the department had been tracking their transportation activity and that data were available for the previous year's medical travel from each facility to Albuquerque. The department was also able to supply some data regarding transport costs:

- Transport cost per mile: $0.51
- Average officer salary with benefits: $18.13
- Average officers per transport: 1.5

In addition, on average, 75 percent of the officers transporting inmates were being paid overtime. We assumed an average consult time with the health care professional of three hours. From this, we were able to estimate the annual cost of transporting prisoners for medical reasons (Table 6.4).

Because of training considerations and the lack of availability of specialty and subspecialty practitioners, the project would have to be phased in. Also, there would always be the need for some transports, for instance, for medical emergencies or hands-on therapy. We were able to find evidence suggesting that transports could be reduced by 60 to 70 percent in mature systems. Based on these factors, we assumed a system that would be phased in with increasing transportation savings as additional specialties were brought in (Table 6.5).

TABLE 6.3. VIDEOCONFERENCING ONE-TIME AND RECURRING COSTS.

	Cost	Cost per Site	Number of Sites	Total
One-time equipment costs				
	Videoconferencing unit	$10,500	9	$94,500
	Monitor	600	9	5,400
	Cart	800	9	7,200
	T1 channel service unit	600	9	5,400
	Hub extenders	1,200	9	10,800
	Installation	2,000	9	18,000
Total one-time equipment costs				$141,300
Annual recurring costs	Maintenance	$1,290	9	$11,610
Total recurring costs				$11,610

TABLE 6.4. TRANSPORTATION COSTS BY LOCATION.

	Transport Cost per Trip	Custody Cost per Trip	Total Cost per Trip	Trips per Year	Annual Cost
Santa Fe	$60	$187	$247	317	$78,256
Los Lunas	24	150	174	437	76,138
Estancia	41	150	191	90	17,141
Grants (men)	80	224	304	161	48,800
Grants (women)	80	224	304	224	67,955
Santa Rosa	116	262	378	218	82,258
Hobbs	321	524	845	443	373,988
Las Cruces	227	374	601	293	175,983
Roswell	203	374	577	121	69,692
Total					$990,211

TABLE 6.5. PERCENTAGE OF TRIPS SAVED, BY YEAR.

	Year 1, 20 Percent	Year 2, 40 Percent	Year 3, 60 Percent	Year 4, 70 Percent	Year 5, 70 Percent
Santa Fe	$15,651	$31,302	$46,953	$54,779	$54,779
Los Lunas	15,228	30,455	45,683	53,296	53,296
Estancia	3,428	6,856	10,285	11,999	11,999
Grants (men)	9,760	19,520	29,280	34,160	34,160
Grants (women)	13,591	27,182	40,773	47,569	47,569
Santa Rosa	16,452	32,903	49,355	57,580	57,580
Hobbs	74,798	149,595	224,393	261,792	261,792
Las Cruces	35,197	70,393	105,590	123,188	123,188
Roswell	13,938	27,877	41,815	48,785	48,785
Total savings	$198,043	$396,083	$594,127	$693,148	$693,148

Cost Analysis. How do the costs and demonstrated possible savings go together? Table 6.6 shows the usual configuration for a project, with high up-front costs offset by savings in future years.

In this case, the savings are far greater than the cost outlays. Any analysis should, however, take into account the time value of money. A simple calculation will show that the payback period for this project is 1.2 years. If we were working in the private sector, we would want some comparison with other investment opportunities. Calculation for this project would show a net present value of $1,764,753 with a 4 percent discount rate.

Externalities

Since this is a project that the government was paying for, it was important to point out the benefits that do not serve the Department of Corrections directly but will be of utility to other state agencies and to the general public.

First, a corrections network could be an important step toward the formation of a statewide telehealth alliance. There are several dimensions to this possible alliance. A telehealth alliance could bring together providers of health services to alleviate some of the capacity constraints caused by the shortage of physicians in the state and even out the disparities in medical services between rural and metropolitan New Mexico.

The lack of affordable broadband could be compensated for by connecting existing and proposed telehealth networks to create a network of networks that will provide broader access and increased connectivity. An alliance of medical, technical, and management expertise would also enable the service providers to operate in a well-managed technological and administrative environment, leading to a sustainable telehealth system in New Mexico.

In a larger sense, the project could be of enormous economic value to a rural state like New Mexico. The development of communications infrastructure could provide access and bandwidth to the communities where the correctional facilities are located. A successful project would establish proof of concept to demonstrate the validity of a remote delivery system. Health services and education are both critical issues in rural economic development, and both can be delivered over the infrastructure developed to deliver either.

Problems, Lessons, and Implications

Most of the problems faced in implementing the system were anticipated. Connectivity with the telecommunication providers was identified early on as a potential bottleneck, and it has proven to be so. Scheduling issues were also

TABLE 6.6. BREAKEVEN ANALYSIS.

	Year 0	Year 1	Year 2	Year 3	Year 4	Year 5
Cash inflow						
Transportation savings		$198,043	$396,083	$594,127	$693,148	$693,148
Total cash inflow		$198,043	$396,083	$594,127	$693,148	$693,148
Cash outflow						
Telecom one-time costs						
Routers	$20,700					
Installation	$6,300					
Connection	$4,300					
Gateway	$30,000					
Installation	$500					
Telecom recurring costs						
Internet protocol						
telecom charges per year		$37,800	$37,800	$37,800	$37,800	$37,800
Primary rate interface						
telecom charges per year		$6,300	$6,300	$6,300	$6,300	$6,300
Maintenance per year		$5,500	$5,500	$5,500	$5,500	$5,500
Long distance		$1,500	$1,500	$1,500	$1,500	$1,500
Video one-time costs						
Videoconferencing unit	$94,500					
Monitors	$5,400					
Roll-about carts	$7,200					
T1 channel service units	$5,400					
Hub extenders	$10,800					
Installation	$18,000					
Video recurring costs						
Maintenance per year		$11,610	$11,610	$11,610	$11,610	$11,610
Total cash outflow	$203,100	$62,710	$62,710	$62,710	$62,710	$62,710
Net cash flows	($203,100)	$135,333	$333,373	$531,417	$630,438	$630,438

Payback period: 1.2 years
Net present value
@ 4 percent: $1,764,753

anticipated: having the inmates available and ready as soon as the consultant comes on-line is a major problem.

At times, the primary providers within the correctional system have seen some of the telehealth initiatives as an additional burden to their clinical responsibilities and not integrating well into their clinical schedules. Ongoing discussions with providers and the medical contractor are necessary to address these issues, improve the clinical operations, and enlist their support. Critical to success is the facilitation of open communications between the corrections medical director, Frank Pullara, and the medical director of the medical services contractor, who employs the providers, contracts for services, and manages the health plan, including making decisions regarding provision of care to individual inmates and need for transfer out of their facility for those services.

Getting reports back from external consultants is a problem that predates telemedicine. The system being used will allow the consultant to type in a report during or immediately after the appointment and send it electronically.

A prospective business case can serve not only as a persuasive document but also as a source of performance measures against which success can be determined. Those measures provide the data to see if expectations were truly met and the program was potentially sustainable. Although this case has not yet reached the stage at which its value can be assessed, the project will live or die based on whether the cost savings projected in the business case are realized and the users and decision makers perceive real values achieved.

DISCUSSION QUESTIONS

1. Why are business plans important to developing a telehealth program?
2. What items are crucial for a good business plan?
3. Once a program is implemented, what is the ongoing role of the business plan?
4. What are the issues related to sustainability of telehealth?
5. What are the unique challenges of implementing telehealth with corrections?
6. What lessons learned can be translated into the noncorrectional environment?

REFERENCES

Austin, C. "The Coming of the Information Age to Healthcare." *Frontiers of Health Care Management,* 1999, *15*(3), 40–42.

Jennett, P. A., Gao, M., Hebert, M. A., and Hailey, D. "Cost-Benefit Evaluation of Telehealth: Implementation Implications for Regions and Communities." Sept. 2003. [http://itch.uvic.ca/itch2000/jennett/jennett.htm].

Neumann, C., Blouin, A., and Byrne, E. "Achieving Success: Assessing the Role of and Building a Business Case for Technology in Healthcare." *Frontiers of Health Services Management*, 1999, *15*(3), 3–28.

Pellissier, S., and others. *General Methodology for Business Case Analysis.* Fredrick, Md.: U.S. Army Medical Research and Materiel Command, May 2001.

Schmidt, M. *What's a Business Case? And Other Frequently Asked Questions.* Boston: Solution Matrix, 1997.

Turisco, F. "How to Justify the Investment: Principles for Effective IT Management." *Health Management Technology*, Mar. 2000, pp. 12–13.

CHAPTER SEVEN

LEADERSHIP ISSUES FACING AN E-START-UP MANAGEMENT TEAM

James Patterson, Gary M. Shulman

Health is one of the most common on-line search topics, with 36 million adults searching for health-related information in 2002 (Fox and Fallows, 2003). Recent studies, however, indicate that over 50 percent of the health information found on the Internet is misleading, inaccurate, or outdated (Berland and others, 2001). To address this growing problem, Jack Abbott, a prominent physician, and Drew Peterman, a youthful communications consultant conceived of the idea to create an Internet search engine that would filter health information found on the Web and provide users with information tailored to their specific needs. Abbott was convinced that the concept for a smart health search engine would be an easy sell to investors given the recent boom in Internet investments.

This case study identifies challenges facing a start-up management team during the organization's inception and through its early transitional stages of development. Transformational leadership issues that emerge from the analysis include trust, vision, empowerment, decision-making style, and organizational culture. (The names of the organizations, products, and organizational members used in this case analysis have been changed.)

Background

At the time Jaxsurf was conceived, Abbott owned LEDREX, a small health technology company that sold high-end medical equipment to physician practices.

Peterman worked as Abbott's director of technology, and both frequently expressed their frustration with LEDREX's restricted vertical market and lagging sales. While brainstorming ways to expand into the exploding Internet health space, the idea for the Jaxsurf search engine was conceived. Abbott and Peterman agreed to move forward with a consumer-based search engine, and Abbott agreed to provide the seed money to get the idea off the ground.

Peterman and Abbott knew that to develop the search engine technology, they would need an incredibly talented team. Both knew many suitable candidates who, in the light of the excitement of the Internet boom, were ready to take a risk on such a venture. They first hired Chris Bloom, a technology wiz and friend of Peterman. Bloom came in as a founder to serve as the chief technological officer of the new organization. They next hired Taylor Lee, a young but well-respected investment banker. Abbott was concerned about Lee's limited experience, and the team agreed to hire Lee as a director of finance rather than as a chief financial officer even though the duties would be commensurate with the title. Finally, the team hired Pat Hummel to serve as director of sales and marketing. Abbott would be the CEO, and Peterman would serve as the organization's director of Internet development.

With the core management team in place, Jaxsurf was ready to move forward.

Choosing Between an Entrepreneurial and a Bureaucratic Model

Over the first few months, the management team thrived in an environment of uncertainty and challenge. Despite scarce resources and dwindling funds, they focused their attention on making quick decisions and boot-strapping processes to conserve resources. Peterman, Bloom, and Hummel worked on developing a blueprint for the search technology. Abbott leveraged his medical expertise to begin development of the filtering and rating system, while Lee worked on generating budgets and strategies for securing outside funding. Team members readily accepted responsibility for tasks and seemed to take pride in the organization they were in the process of creating. Team members valued autonomy and did not hesitate to make decisions based on "their gut." Block (1991) characterizes such actions as a positive political dynamic common to entrepreneurs. When organizational members strive for excellence, act with courage, and value autonomy, the political dynamic at play is a healthy one and often works against the bureaucratic mentality common to most organizations (Block, 1991).

The excitement the management team felt was heightened by the whirlwind buzz of the Internet boom. For the entire team, however, one thing was clear: if Jaxsurf had any chance of survival in the consumer health Internet space, the organization would have to grow fast and would need substantial funding.

Jaxsurf succeeded in generating moderate interest among potential investors, but none of them wanted to be the first in. It became clear to the management team that they needed to land a lead investor willing to commit significant capital to the venture. The CEO pitched Jaxsurf to a close relative known for investing in early-stage businesses. Surprisingly, the investor quickly committed $1 million to the organization, and most of the other potential investors followed suit.

With more than $1 million in the bank, the management team faced a new reality: accountability—not to each other but to a handful of external constituents investing in them. This new reality had a profound effect on how the management team would choose to behave.

In the first meeting after funding was secured, Abbott announced he wanted to delegate the development of the rating system to Pat and hire additional employees to work on testing and rating health sites. He felt his efforts were best served managing the organization now that Jaxsurf had funding. At first, Peterman and Bloom, the other founders, did not object; in fact, they had serious doubts about the quality of the rating system Abbott was developing. Hummel, they felt, was an extremely accomplished executive and would have little trouble adjusting to the new role. But Abbott's decision to turn over the rating system to Hummel worried them. Did Abbott feel, as they did, that he was failing at producing a sufficient rating system? If so, what function would Abbott fill now that his key responsibility had been delegated to someone else?

For Peterman and Bloom, the answer was forthcoming. Abbott began to focus his efforts on managing the rest of the team, delegating tasks and questioning key processes. His primary concern was not the expertise of the management team but the management team's ability to execute in the largely unexplored Internet space. He felt the organization needed to outsource key functions and hire additional personnel with specialized expertise. Abbott had family money behind the venture and wanted to take more control over organizational operations, act more cautiously, and rely more heavily on outside expertise.

While the rest of the management team wondered if Abbott's new-found doubts about the team's performance were somehow related to his own failure to produce an adequate rating system, they were not totally against the idea of outsourcing. The organization had, as far as they were concerned, gone public, and they were reluctant to take on more responsibility that might eventually hold them accountable. The addition of external investors, coupled with the CEO's overt concerns about the team's ability to execute, made the fear of failure a real possibility. As one team member explained, "In the beginning, making decisions was easy. There was no money, and we had very few resources. We did not hesitate because there were no other alternatives to consider."

In the end, many of the key organizational functions were outsourced at considerable expense. Accounting and payroll were outsourced to a local accounting firm. The Web interface, usability testing, and marketing also were turned over to outside companies. In addition, the company hired five raters, a ratings manager, and four engineers.

With the new employees and additional partners, the management team focused their attention on managing people and systems and outsourcing key functions to external partners viewed as more experienced. The team moved forward with caution, adopting a wait-and-see approach to decision making. It seemed that the very funding designed to fuel entrepreneurialship depleted it. As one founder put it, "Jaxsurf became just another bureaucracy."

(Micro)Managing a Talented Team

Over the next few months, Abbott began to distance himself from the rest of the management team. He focused his attention on developing detailed organizational charts, devising procedures for tracking progress, and holding organizational members accountable for execution deadlines. Despite the addition of four outside partners and ten new employees, the management team, with the exception of Abbott, remained highly cohesive. One team member would later comment, "It was one of the best team experiences I have ever had. I have never worked with a better group of competent, incredibly talented people in the thirty years I have been in private industry."

While the management team had always acknowledged Abbott as the CEO of the organization, he had seemed more like a colleague than a superior. They acknowledged the need to structure the organization for external investors, but they felt it was understood that the core team would continue to function as colleagues, with little or no hierarchy. Now, with the addition of outside investors, Abbott seemed to focus his attention on managing them, and his apparent new initiative to surveillance and second-guess the key functions of the organization was not well received by the remaining team members. To the rest of the team, the well-structured organization portrayed in private placement memos and corporate documents was now being thrust on them, threatening the collaborative and autonomous environment they needed to thrive.

Two critical decisions that Abbott made only further isolated him from the rest of the management team. First, with the addition of new personnel, Abbott sought to formalize the organization of the company. He issued an organizational chart that clearly placed him above the other founders and management team members. He called the chart an "organization of accountability," and it was clear that all of the remaining team members were now accountable to him. When he presented the chart at a regular company meeting, Peterman, frustrated and impulsive, quickly shouted, "And who are you accountable to?" Abbott responded, "Myself," to which Bloom quickly and calmly added, "and the investors." A fact Abbott knew too well. Several of the investors were becoming nervous given recent developments in the Internet market. The Internet, as a fertile ground for business, was imploding. The Internet buzz was wearing off, and a good idea and hefty investments were not enough to make it in the highly competitive Internet space.

At that same meeting, Abbott announced he had developed an e-mail tracking system to keep tabs on who was doing what: he wanted all members of the management team to document how they spent their time in daily reports to him. Both of these initiatives were not well received by the rest of the team for three reasons. First, the remaining team members strongly believed that Abbott had missed more deadlines and failed to execute more initiatives than any other team member. Second, Abbott was the only one in need of daily reports since he had taken himself out of the loop by turning over the rating system to Hummel. Finally, it seemed that Abbott had somehow redefined their relationship from cocollaborators to one of superior-subordinate.

Many of the team members began to voice concerns with Abbott's style of leadership. They felt he was spending time developing procedures and regulations to monitor and control them rather than leveraging his charisma to inspire and motivate them. They were already self-motivated and felt they thrived best in a flexible environment where they had the freedom to make decisions and manage themselves. In this regard, the rules and procedures Abbott was implementing were impeding their progress, not enabling it.

Studies indicate that many technologically advanced firms need to alter their hierarchical management systems (Cohen and Bradford, 1989) as a result of eroding power structures and less information control brought about by emerging technologies (Humphreys, 2001). Bass (1985) first expressed the need for a new type of leader for such organizations; transformational leaders focus on the "general awareness and acceptance of the purposes and missions of the organization" (p. 43) by drawing on deeply held value systems. They create clear visions of the future, use their inspiration to influence others, stimulate creativity, and lead with honesty and integrity (Conger, 1999). Studies have clearly linked these transformational qualities to follower effort, performance, and satisfaction with the leader, particularly in technology organizations (Whittington and Goodwin, 2001). In contrast, transactional leaders focus their efforts on establishing reward systems to motivate employees. Transactional leaders often employ rewards and punishments so that subordinates will follow rules and regulations (Humphreys, 2001).

Most of the team members interviewed noted they initially found Abbott to be "likable" and "charismatic." However, they also noted that these qualities often were overshadowed by Abbott's efforts to structure the organization and enforce rules. As one team member noted, "I came onboard excited about the organization. Abbott was so passionate about the potential success of the business. Then he began to dictate how things should be done. He should have stayed focused on what he does best—inspiring people."

Removing a Key Team Member

In the following months, the relationship between Abbott and the rest of the team deteriorated even more. To Abbott, Lee seemed the most defiant with respect to the rules and procedures he was trying to implement. As a result, Abbott announced his decision to the rest of the team to fire Lee. He told them that Lee had constantly missed deadlines and was not expending the effort necessary to bring in additional investors. In addition, Lee was not providing the daily progress updates he had requested in the previous company meeting. Bloom quickly responded, "Abbott, we are all behind on deadlines—it's not just Lee. Lee can't approach investors until the product is complete and the marketing materials are finished." Hummel felt the team was working extremely well together and resented Abbott's efforts to disrupt the team three months short of launching the core product. Nevertheless, Abbott moved forward with the firing process, spending considerable time meeting with the organization's attorney and documenting what he felt were Lee's incompetencies.

Bloom, Hummel, and Peterman could not understand why Abbott would move to fire Lee when the team was working so well together and so close to completing the Jaxsurf search engine. Abbott, for his part, did not understand why members of his team, particularly Bloom and Peterman as cofounders, were not supporting his decision to fire Lee. In the end, Peterman and Hummel threatened to walk out if Abbott fired Lee. While their bold and impulsive action demonstrated the team's collective loyalty to one another, it also left Abbott with a solid defeat. Trust in him, it seemed, was all but gone. In addition, the team was directly challenging him with threats.

Bedfellows, Adversaries, Allies, and Opponents

It was clear to Abbott that the other team members did not share his vision for how the organization should operate. The success of his vision, however, depended directly on the expertise and experience of the management team. The Lee incident proved to him that to remove one team member would likely mean that others would leave on their own accord. At the same time, replacing the entire management team was not an option. Peterman and Bloom were founders who held considerable shares of stock in the company. While Abbott might be able to negotiate settlement agreements for their departure, the organization had little incentive to offer new employees at their level. In addition, the company's cash reserves were running out, and it was still months away from having a viable product necessary to enter the sales cycle. Abbott sensed that the trust level among the other organizational members was incredibly low but continued to argue with them about even the simplest of issues.

In his book *The Empowered Manager,* Block (1991) expresses the need for leaders to build support for their vision. In the political environment of organizing, those we need to influence can be identified on the basis of two dimensions: trust and agreement. Allies and opponents have high levels of trust for leaders but differ significantly in their level of agreement with decisions made by the leadership (Block, 1991). Bedfellows and adversaries equally distrust the leadership of the organization but with one key difference: bedfellows generally agree with decisions made by the leadership, while adversaries do not.

Abbott knew he had no allies among the other team members but felt he might be able to force agreement among the management team by documenting opinions voiced and decisions made by the other team members. The process, however, backfired. Organizational members resented the fact that Abbott felt compelled to "catch them" contradicting themselves, and his action only further depleted trust and agreement with his decisions.

When his attempt to force agreement failed, Abbott may have felt an alternative way to build allies was to hire them. Mark Fine, a close personal friend, had recently left his family business amid rumors of bankruptcy. Abbott's relationship with Fine was strong, and he felt his years of experience running a company would be invaluable to Jaxsurf. Abbott approached the management team and made his case for hiring Fine to help keep the product development on schedule. Hummel quickly spoke up: "Do you really think someone who bankrupted his own business is what we need?" Bloom added, "Abbott, we just don't have the money." After much discussion, the rest of the management team left for the weekend convinced they had succeeded in demonstrating to Abbott that hiring Fine would not be a good decision for the company.

After the weekend, Scott, Peterman, Hummel, and Lee arrived to find Fine sitting at a desk in the corner of the office. It appeared to them that Abbott had moved forward with hiring Fine despite their objections. For Lee and Peterman, this reinforced their belief that Abbott was not acting in the best interest of the company. Several months later, they negotiated settlement agreements with the organization and left. Hummel, feeling the organization would never succeed under its current leadership, left shortly after.

Addressing Problems of Trust, Operations, and Leadership

The management team at Jaxsurf did implement several measures to address the problems of trust, operations, and leadership. Sensing trust was incredibly low among the three founders, they held a retreat over a weekend at a mountain resort. The idea was for the three of them to get away from the pressures and confines of the office and family and work through the various issues causing problems among them. Over the weekend, they discussed the culture of the organization, differences in management and conflict styles, the vision of the organization, and their future plans for the organization. Each founder would later describe the retreat as a success in helping them sort out the many issues facing the management team. Translating the ideas that came out of the weekend, however, proved to be difficult, if not impossible. The increasing pressure to get the core product to market with limited resources and dwindling funds left little time for them to focus on the organization's management problems. As one founder noted, "It became business as usual."

To deal with the issues of outsourcing key organizational functions and fears of bureaucracy reigning at Jaxsurf, the team decided to appoint a board of advisers to help with all the major functions of the organization. Eight noted leaders in the fields of health, business, and technology were appointed to the board. The team, concerned about the need to bring in additional funds, opted to appoint high-profile advisers to the board, many of whom did not live in the same geographical region as the organization. The advisers were an impressive assemblage of abilities and expertise, but the management team found it difficult to engage them on any substantive level. The advisers' busy schedules and geographical restrictions made it difficult for them to provide any useful service to the organization.

Finally, the founders agreed to appoint Bloom as chief operating officer of the organization. Bloom would follow the other team members' progress with the various projects under development and report directly to Abbott. That way, the team would have very limited contact with Abbott while Abbott remained in the loop. Most of the management team felt this new shift in the chain of command was a positive step for the organization. As one member noted, "When Bloom took over as COO, we started to build momentum. While it may seem as if it created additional bureaucracy for the organization, it actually eliminated more than it created. We should have done that sooner."

Lessons Learned

Start-up companies have the strategic challenges of first designing or creating a high-performance organization and then sustaining viability during later stages of developmental change. Changes can be internal (for example, more new employees, technological breakthroughs, new work processes) or external (for example, market conditions, competition, economic, political, supply chain relationships). The following issues are relevant to Jaxsurf and highlight the importance of adopting a transformational leadership style in these types of organizations.

From the beginning, organizational members must receive an orientation to answer the question, "Why am I here?" This applies to the founding members of the organization and those who join later. An effective orientation period or program communicates a sense of purpose and instills a team or organizational identity for members. Organizational members who cannot answer this question are more likely to feel disoriented, uncertain, and even fearful.

The second issue focuses on building trusting relationships among organizational members by implicitly posing the question, "Who are you?" When answered ideally, it results in mutual respect, authentic behavior, caring, openness, and reliability. If time or circumstances do not allow for building trust or contribute to mistrust, members will often behave cautiously and project a facade that hides their true feelings and attitudes. Lack of trust or mistrust can contribute to a negative political climate in the organization.

Goal clarification clearly communicates to members explicit assumptions regarding work, integrates goals, and promotes a shared vision. By providing answers to the question, "What are we doing here?" members are more likely to avoid feelings of apathy, cynicism, skepticism, and inappropriate internal competition.

Effectively answering the question, "How will we do what we do?" builds member commitment to the organization. The issues of role definition, resource allocation, and decision making are resolved. If these issues are left unresolved, members are more likely to exhibit dependence on, or resistance to, leadership. A typical leadership reaction to the unresolved situation is to micromanage details and job functions of others.

Finally, the process implementation issue is resolved by explicitly addressing, "Who does what, when, and where?" Disciplined execution of strategy comes from member understanding, acceptance, and alignment with clearly stated processes. When implementation processes are not explicitly communicated, the consequences are often confusion, conflict, missed deadlines, and nonalignment. Start-ups must be sensitive to revisiting this issue frequently, as processes may require changes as the organization moves from the creating to the sustaining stages of development.

We can learn from the Jaxsurf case the important lesson that open communication is central to addressing each of the above issues, which all have implications for individual and organizational performance. It is a leadership responsibility to focus regularly on establishing a dialogue about these issues among organizational members. These issues must be revisited frequently as the start-up organization makes the transition from a new enterprise to one that is built to last.

Discussion Questions

1. What actions contributed to the level of trust at Jaxsurf? What might have been done to increase mutual trust?
2. What did each team member do to contribute to the leadership situation at Jaxsurf? What should Abbott have continued doing? Started doing? Stopped doing?
3. To what extent were voices heard at Jaxsurf? What could be done to enhance participative decision making at Jaxsurf? How might participation have improved a decision that was made at Jaxsurf?
4. How were qualities of Jaxsurf culture manifested? How did the culture at Jaxsurf change? How might more positive cultural qualities been created at Jaxsurf?
5. What factors or events contributed to the level of role definition at Jaxsurf? What might have been done to increase role clarity or reduce role ambiguity at Jaxsurf?
6. What are Jaxsurf's key strategic advantages? Which of these strategic advantages had the greatest potential to contribute to a strong culture at Jaxsurf? How might Jaxsurf better leverage its strategic advantages?
7. To what extent was there a shared vision at Jaxsurf? How did the vision affect the work of key organizational members? How might have alignment with a shared vision among Jaxsurf members been enhanced?

References

Bass, B. *Leadership and Performance Beyond Expectations.* New York: Free Press, 1985.

Berland, G., and others. "Health Information on the Internet: Accessibility, Quality, and Readability in English and Spanish." *Journal of the American Medical Association*, 2001, *285*(20), 2612–2621.

Block, P. *The Empowered Manager.* San Francisco: Jossey-Bass, 1991.

Cohen, A., and Bradford, D. *Influence Without Authority.* New York: Wiley, 1989.

Conger, J. "Charismatic and Transformational Leadership in Organizations: An Insider's Perspective on These Developing Streams of Research." *Leadership Quarterly*, 1999, *99*(10) 145–170.

Fox, S., and Fallows, D. *Health Searches and Email Have Become More Commonplace, But There Is Room for Improvement in Searches and Overall Internet Access.* Washington, D.C.: Pew Internet and American Life Project, 2003.

Humphreys, J. "Transformational and Transactional Leader Behavior." *Journal of Management Review*, 2001, *1*(3), 149–159.

Whittington, J., and Goodwin, V. "Transformational Leadership, Goal Difficulty, and Task Design: Independent and Interactive Effects on Employee Outcomes." In *Academy of Management Proceedings.* Briarcliff Manor, N.Y.: Academy of Management, 2001.

CHAPTER EIGHT

A HEALTH CARE INFORMATION SYSTEM IN GREECE

Key Factors, Self-Organization, and Take-Home Lessons

Angelina Kouroubali, Don E. Detmer, Manolis Tsiknakis, Stelios Orphanoudakis

The Greek Ministry of Health has initiated reforms toward decentralizing health care services and developing integrated health care information systems (HCIS) at a regional level. However, a large number of these plans have yet to be implemented. Currently, health care institutions follow their own agendas, allocate budgets for information development independent of government plans, and base their local initiatives on the personal motivation of medical and technical personnel. HYGEIAnet is one of these initiatives developed by the Foundation for Research and Technology-Hellas (FORTH), one of the leading research institutions in Greece. The Institute of Computer Science at FORTH undertook the development of the regional infrastructure to provide high-quality HCIS and computer training to public institutions throughout the island of Crete. HYGEIAnet differs from other local initiatives throughout Greece in that it spans all levels of health care across a region. Implementations took place between 1998 and 2002 across Crete, aiming at securing regular use of the technology in health care facilities beyond the end of the project. The regional network infrastructure between primary care facilities and hospitals is presented in Figure 8.1.

HCIS in primary care health centers was among the first to be implemented. The complete information system included an electronic health record (EHR), a laboratory information system, a radiology information system, and telemedicine services. The primary care regional network was designed to support patient data management, monitoring of health indicators, assessment of population

FIGURE 8.1. HEALTH CARE FACILITIES AND THE HYGEIANET NETWORK INFRASTRUCTURE.

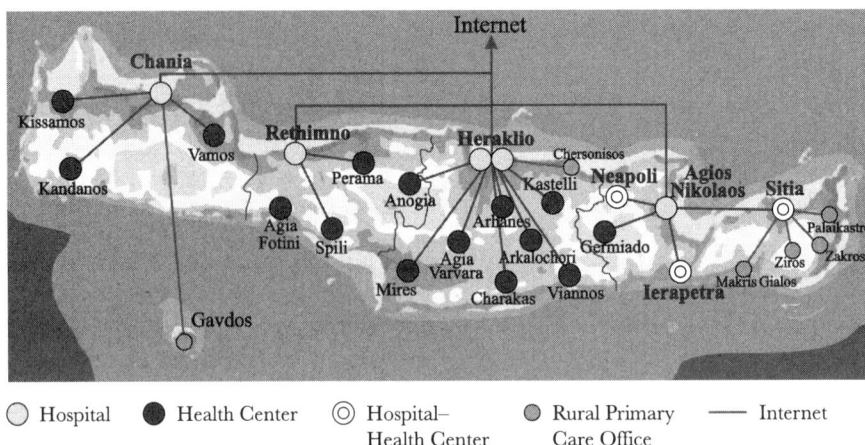

○ Hospital   ● Health Center   ◎ Hospital–   ● Rural Primary   —— Internet
                                        Health Center   Care Office

health needs, teleconsultations, and automation of health care processes. When the project was initiated in 1998, there were no computer facilities or network infrastructure in health centers. To understand the context in which implementation and change took place, it is important to illustrate the state of primary care in Crete at the time of the research.

Primary care in Greece is an undervalued and underrepresented medical specialty. Generally health centers are very loosely organized. They are often understaffed, collaborations among health care providers in the clinics are limited, and written job descriptions are lacking. Typically, even paper-based patient records are not used in health centers. The absence of health records and the limited communication among professionals means that the fundamental principle of continuity of care is largely ignored. Exceptions are found in health centers where employees with sensitivity, personal interest, and effort have incorporated health records, teamwork, and community outreach into their routines.

To raise the standards of primary care delivery and the esteem of general medicine as a specialty, the section for Social and Family Medicine of the University of Crete Medical School initiated educational and research activities. It established a network of health centers to promote patient information recording and health assessment by medical students and primary care providers. This effort gave visibility to best practices in primary care, defined as evidence of teamwork, maintenance of paper- or computer-based records, and community outreach. When providers engage in these activities, more people come into contact with one another, issues are discussed, ideas are exchanged, and information is given greater value. Information about best practices often created a challenge for others to change.

The need for continuity of care and information exchange has introduced an imperative call for successful implementations of HCIS (World Health Organization, 2002). HYGEIAnet is a particularly useful case to study change because the implementation was essentially organic. There was no central body to require change against a tight time schedule or to plan an explicit implementation strategy. Hence, the factors that emerged from studying change springing from within can contribute to an understanding of change initiatives in similar settings elsewhere.

Knowledge and Practice Today

Evidence now confirms that HCIS that are successfully developed and implemented can improve health care efficiency and effectiveness (World Health Organization, 2002). However, their implementation is frequently resisted and results in failures (Anderson, 1997; Kaplan, 1997). The challenge of identifying techniques to ease the incorporation of information technology into health care organizations remains important (Sittig, 1994; Aarts and Peel, 1999).

Change initiatives have focused on the elaborate identification and control of individual, structural, technology, process, and environmental variables to ensure the success of change initiatives. However, despite the importance of a variety of factors in influencing implementation success and managing change, controlling, anticipating, and predicting factors does not avoid the occurrence of unpredictable events (Goldstein, 1994). Furthermore, experience has shown that change is often a natural and productive feature of even small organizations. This view of change is especially relevant to health care organizations where the autonomy of doctors and the unique case of each patient require flexible and adaptable responses.

The understanding of change as an ongoing process is facilitated when shifting from the traditional view of organizations as machines to seeing organizations as complex adaptive systems. Complexity theory advocates that resistance to change is not an inherent characteristic of organizations, but a temporary state of equilibrium (for a detailed analysis of complexity theory concepts, see Dooley, 1997; Plsek and Greenhalgh, 2001). In practice, change occurs as emergent and ongoing while the complex adaptive system self-organizes. Self-organization is a self-generated and self-guided process of transformation that does not need to be externally driven or hierarchically controlled (Goldstein, 1994). Information is said to be the nutrient of self-organization (Wheatley and Kellner-Rogers, 1996). Information flow enriches the organization, offering opportunities for growth and change. An increase in information flow through education, contact with professionals, cultural trends, and the media often precedes transformation.

Complexity theory helped us understand how change occurred in primary care clinics in Crete. The nonmandated, organic character of implementation and the loose regulation of primary care clinics offered an environment where change was equivalent to self-organization. The research focused on eight primary care clinics throughout the island to identify factors that influenced implementation and transformation toward best practices within clinics. An interpretive methodology was used, and data were collected over two years as events took place. A longitudinal design is particularly relevant in studies of innovation, since the researcher can explore the processes of learning, adaptation, and progressive change that occur within information systems in research settings (Pettigrew, 1990). Data collection was done mainly through observation and face-to-face interviews with senior management, designers and system administrators, and clinic personnel.

Key Factors

The HCIS was well received in all eight health centers, although individual use varied from no activity to daily use. The main users of the HCIS were health care providers and laboratory technicians. Some nonmedical personnel used the system for administrative tasks. Avid users generally felt that the HCIS introduced efficiency and effectiveness to their work. However, there were people who felt unable to use the HCIS or uninterested in using it due to limited training, lack of time, or motivation. Innovative use of HCIS was usually coupled with already established best practice activities such as teamwork, health care research, patient data recording, and community activities.

The decision to get involved with the technology rested solely with individual employees, who took the initiative to introduce a voluntary change in their everyday work practices. Technology, education, leadership, organizational structures, and the environment were five key factors that contributed to the variation of implementation experience and the degree of change in the clinics. These factors are not unique to primary care clinics in Crete; they are frequently identified in other implementation initiatives around the world (see Lorenzi and others, 1997; Larsen, 2001). However, each factor operates uniquely in different contexts, enriching our understanding of change and implementation.

Technology

The introduction of the HCIS in health centers increased the information flow available to the clinics and initiated self-organization. The technology, a novelty for health center staff, provided opportunities to improve daily practices. In three health centers, the general practitioner used the EHR to enter data during consultation. Two midwives created a personal database for their patients to identify population needs. Often ambulance drivers and support staff used the system for leisure activities, such as browsing the Internet or playing games. Occasionally, practical aspects of installation and maintenance hindered self-organization, leading to the conclusion that equipment must work very reliably if it is to be used at all.

Education

Educational activities occurred at two levels. FORTH offered basic computer training to health care employees throughout Crete. This was important since in Greece, basic computer skills are largely absent in the majority of the population. The second level of education occurred through the section of social and family medicine that offered primary care education and research activities oriented to general practitioners. Information about primary care best practices was circulated, creating small clusters of health care providers interested in improving their daily work. The degree of participation of health center employees in training and primary care activities reflected the extent of technology use and related change.

Employees reported that the educational activities increased the information flow in health centers and made them aware of opportunities that previously they had overlooked. Training in basic computer skills was useful to employees even if they did not intend to use the computer for health care activities. However, when training occurred before the installation of equipment or was too brief to meet actual needs, otherwise willing employees were not able to use the technology, a situation that could clearly be solved. In addition to formal training, the arrival of the Internet and increased computer use generally helped stimulate clinic employees to acquire new skills even if they were not directly interested in HCIS.

Leadership

Typically, health center employees blamed the shortcomings of the public health care system on inadequate organization of primary care services; in fairness, staffing shortages in some circumstances clearly had an impact on the organization. Despite these complaints, innovative activities occurred in the health centers. The paradox of providing services in a seemingly disorganized environment is attributed partly to the culture of *philotimo*, which was best expressed through appropriate leadership. *Philotimo* literally means "friend of honor," describing the feeling of self-esteem and sense of duty that governs day-to-day behavior. It was the most commonly heard word among health center employees when they wanted to explain why things worked in the clinic.

Leadership that relies on *philotimo* implies trusting that employees will show sufficient interest and responsibility to perform their work. Several employees consider the culture of *philotimo* a negative aspect of the Greek public sector because it introduces a high element of uncertainty. However, trusting the capacity of individuals for creative change to improve their work and facilitate their life was essential for successful change initiatives across sites. Other cultures might refer to this as focusing on worker morale and team spirit or pride in working for a competent organization. Appealing to the employee's sense of *philotimo* created an atmosphere of collaboration and learning that focused on improving the efficiency and effectiveness of patient care. Such health centers succeeded in incorporating best practices throughout the organization.

Organizational Structures

The presence or absence or even relative strength of health center structures such as department integration, regulations, incentives, and staffing are important in determining the degree of change that occurs. Health centers faced several shortcomings, such as loose or scant regulations, lack of formalization of activities, and limited resources that acted against the optimal functioning of the clinic. Nevertheless, strong leadership helped mitigate some of these shortcomings.

Staffing was one of the most influential structural factors for the implementation effort. The introduction of HCIS relied on interested health care providers. Employees with sufficient interest for the HCIS were among the first to receive equipment and training, and these employees in turn influenced other health care providers to use the technology. Health care providers with training on primary care best practices were familiar with the importance of the HCIS and promoted its use. In some cases, there were no personnel to use the equipment, or the small number of employees had too large a workload to allow them to spend time learning the technology. For example, one clinic had a single pediatrician to cover the needs of a rather large geographical area. She complained that having thirty patients waiting did not allow her time to learn how to use the EHR. Certain specialties, such as home health visitors and laboratory personnel, are underrepresented in health centers, hindering community outreach activities and the function of the laboratory.

Environment

The relationship between the clinic and its environment was the final factor that influenced implementation and change. Among other things, the environment included the patient population served by the health center and external pressures, such as those from the Ministry of Health. Both patients and the Ministry of Health had the capacity to influence technology-based change. Clinics that involved patients more actively in their care and provided improved services such as community outreach and complete patient records increased the expectations of the community and set standards that were then followed independent of staff turnover. The formal requirements of the Ministry of Health, such as monthly reports of health data, challenged employees to use computers to facilitate reporting processes.

Implications for Policy and Practice

In health centers, organizational change occurred when operations incorporated elements of primary care best practices. A key to these changes may be the greater availability of information considered useful by the practice. Some health centers had already started changing their daily activities to incorporate best practices prior to the implementation of HCIS. The HCIS was welcomed to assist the ongoing change and certainly enhanced the timeliness and availability of information. There were, however, health centers that initiated change solely on the installation of the HCIS. In these centers, the technology triggered organizational change because it provided opportunities that challenged health care providers in keeping detailed patient records or ordering tests on-line.

In addition, the introduction and use of the technology contributed to the transformation of relationships among some employees. Collaboration was the exception rather than the norm in health centers. However, the introduction of the technology established collaboration within the domains of research, education, and daily activities. Contrary to the popular belief that presents physicians as notoriously resistant to change, the experience of HYGEIAnet revealed otherwise. The majority of physicians and other health care providers were ready to learn, collaborate, and transform their daily work under the appropriate conditions: adequate capacity in terms of technology, education, and staffing and conditions that provided freedom, fostered responsibility, generated connections, and cultivated relationships around desired information. This is a decidedly optimistic message and one that is too often ignored or denied.

The Ministry of Health in Greece has recognized the importance of primary care and information systems in the organization of the health care sector. However, policy does not explicitly address the development of both the primary care sector and information systems in parallel. Government policy is particularly important in recognizing, encouraging, and developing initiatives that are already taking place rather than ignoring or denigrating developments on the front line. In addition, to sustain regionwide efforts, it is important to account for ongoing maintenance and financial support, currently lacking in Crete.

Management of HCIS implementation requires attention to multiple success factors that have been identified from research and experience. However, implementation lessons are not readily transferable to multiple contexts. It is essential to consider the meaning of success factors and recommendations to any particular implementation effort. Instead of developing exact implementation plans to cultivate the necessary conditions for generating change from within, implementation methods might be more productively focused on loose control, encouragement of innovation, and direction setting around a few easily understood and sensible goals. These methods appear to produce faster results than the traditional plan-and-control mentality. Indeed, precise planning may take too long, be inappropriate, not be followed, or be openly resisted.

Technology Recommendations

HCIS need to be available and functional at the place and time of decision making. The need to examine the way technology is used in particular contexts is essential to understanding and anticipating technology outcomes. A detailed examination looking for those things that employees are most attracted to in an information system may provide a way to tap into user aspirations. Direct experience suggests that simply getting reliable e-mail communications up and running can be transformational.

HCIS should ultimately benefit patients. Consumer demands for information and participation in managing chronic illnesses will most likely shape the nature of clinical management and the respective roles of providers and patients in ways that cannot be fully anticipated at this time (Coye and Detmer, 1998). Providers will need the support of appropriate knowledge sources and communication technologies to stay up to date with the vast amount of information that is gradually becoming available to all audiences through the Internet.

Education Recommendations

One of the major components involved in innovation and change is education. To improve primary care services and facilitate the incorporation of primary care information systems, education in both primary care and information systems is important. The research identified the following components of education as important in implementing HCIS in primary care: the incorporation of primary care and information systems education in medical school, continuing education for health care providers, and computer training based on the specific needs of individual employees. High priority should be placed on demonstrating the usefulness of the technology and the way it supports individual services and work performance. Finally, health care personnel in leading positions, such as directors of health centers, need to attend management and leadership training to be able to contribute to the better management of their organizations.

Leadership Recommendations

The natural tendency of agents to change can be greatly influenced through leadership. The complex adaptive systems approach to leadership introduces the notion of coordination and facilitation rather than direct control and planning. Leadership should offer employees the opportunity to be creative while supporting an environment that is sufficiently flexible to allow the organization to observe its performance and learn how to grow at the personal and collective levels.

Conclusion

The rapid increase in the incidence of chronic illness, commensurate with the aging of many populations across the globe, requires a reorganization of health care systems based on personal relations and the exchange of relevant information. Health care information systems are "a prerequisite for coordinated, integrated, and evidence-informed health care" (World Health Organization, 2002, p. 37). Organizing primary care services, improving communication throughout the health sector, and implementing information systems require considerable change. The nature of the medical profession has an inherent component of uncertainty and transformation (Heeks and others, 1999). According to its philosophical foundations set in ancient Greece, it is a profession in flux, where continuous education and improvement is occurring (Pellegrino, 2001). Hence, if health care providers view their profession as a vocation, the assumption of reluctance to change is a paradox. The current competitive environment in health care calls for approaching change not as a problem to resolve but as an opportunity to improve health care delivery and customer care. The need for continuous transformation applies especially to primary care, the specialty with the largest range of variation in health conditions.

Managing change as a process of self-organization requires noticing, encouraging, and amplifying new ways of doing things. Eventually novel processes may be incorporated into the way the work group or organization operates. In managing a complex organization, emphasis should be placed on individuals and their relationships. Individual enthusiasm, commitment, and personal ability contribute to the emergent behavior of complex adaptive systems. To influence change, leaders need to create systems "that disseminate rich information about better practices, allowing others to adapt those practices in ways that are most meaningful to them" (Plsek and Wilson, 2001, p. 748).

Discussion Questions

1. If you were to move into a new region and were charged with implementing a computer-based health information network for primary care clinics, what would be your top priorities?
2. If your charge was to create a network to link primary and secondary care providers, what would be your top priorities?
3. How would you assess your progress?
4. How would you offer leadership to this effort?
5. What would be the essential components of your HCIS, and what priority would you give to its functional components? Why?
6. What would you include in a health information technology educational program for (a) entry-level health professionals, (b) practicing health professionals, and (c) information technology support personnel?

References

Aarts, J., and Peel, V. "Using a Descriptive Model of Change When Implementing Large Scale Clinical Information Systems to Identify Priorities for Further Research." *International Journal of Medical Informatics*, 1999, *56*, 43–50.

Anderson, J. G. "Clearing the Way for Physicians' Use of Clinical Information Systems." *Communications of the ACM*, 1997, *40*(8), 83–90.

Coye, M. J., and Detmer, D. E. "Quality at a Crossroads." *Milbank Quarterly*, 1998, *76*(4), 759–769.

Dooley, K. "A Complex Adaptive Systems Model of Organization Change." *Nonlinear Dynamics, Psychology, and Life Sciences*, 1997, *1*(1), 69–97.

Goldstein, J. *The Unshackled Organization: Facing the Challenge of Unpredictability Through Spontaneous Reorganization*. Portland, Ore.: Productivity Press,, 1994.

Heeks, R., Mundy, D., and Salazar, A.. *Why Health Care Information Systems Succeed or Fail.* Manchester, U.K.: Institute for Development Policy and Management, 1999.

Kaplan, B. "Organizational Evaluation of Medical Information Resources." In C. Friedman and J. Wyatt (eds.), *Evaluation Methods in Medical Informatics*. New York: Springer-Verlag, 1997.

Larsen, K.R.T. "Antecedents of Implementation Success: A Comprehensive Framework." Paper presented at the Hawaii International Conference on System Sciences, Hawaii, 2001.

Lorenzi, N. M., and others. "Antecedents of the People and Organizational Aspects of Medical Informatics: Review of the Literature." *Journal of the American Medical Informatics Association*,, 1997, *4*(2), 79–93.

Pellegrino, E. *Physician Philosopher: The Philosophical Foundation of Medicine.* Charlottesville, Va.: Carden Jennings Publishing, 2001.

Pettigrew, A. M. "Longitudinal Field Research on Change: Theory and Practice." *Organization Science*, 1990, *1*(3), 267–292.

Plsek, P. E., and Greenhalgh, T. "Complexity Science: The Challenge of Complexity in Health Care." *British Medical Journal*, 2001, *323*, 625–628.

Plsek, P. E., and Wilson, T. "Complexity Science: Complexity, Leadership, and Management in Healthcare Organisations." *British Medical Journal*, 2001, *323*, 746–749.

Sittig, D. F. "Grand Challenges in Medical Informatics." *Journal of the American Medical Informatics Association*, 1994, *1*(5), 412–413.

Wheatley, M. J., and Kellner-Rogers, M. (1996). "Self-organization." *Strategy and Leadership*, July–Aug. 1996, pp. 18–24.

World Health Organization. *Innovative Care for Chronic Conditions: Building Blocks for Action.* Paris: World Health Organization, 2002.

CHAPTER NINE

THE ANATOMY OF FAILURE?

Teledermatology in an English City

Carl R. May, Maggie Mort, Tracy Finch, Frances S. Mair

One of the striking features of the general field of telecare is the disparity be-tween the large numbers of reports of successful local initiatives and ser-vice developments, and the failure of these systems to become widely diffused and routinely embedded in the organizational delivery of health care. This is espe-cially evident in the United Kingdom, where despite high-level policy support and much enthusiasm for telecare (National Health Service Executive, 1998), it has largely failed to be taken up as a means of health care delivery at a local level.

Britain is a small country (nowhere is more than ninety miles from the sea) with a large population (around 60 million). Arguments in favor of telecare are therefore somewhat different from countries where uneven geographical distri-bution of specialist health care is the problem. Instead, policymakers have focused on the efficiency gains derived from using new technologies to modernize services by increasing throughput and distributing care from areas of high demand to other centers (May, Mort, Mair, and Williams, 2001), while emphasizing to pa-tients the benefits of reducing traveling and waiting times.

We gratefully acknowledge the time and candor willingly given to us by participants in this study, who must necessarily remain anonymous. We acknowledge with thanks contributions to our work made by our collaborators: Linda Gask and Nikki Shaw. Research for this chapter was funded by the U.K. Economic and Social Research Council (grant L218 25 2067), to which we also extend our thanks.

Since the mid-1990s, we have followed the introduction, development, evaluation, and implementation of ten telecare services through consecutive studies that used qualitative and observational sociological techniques. In total, these studies have involved more than three hundred separate episodes of data collection and analysis (these are described in detail in May and others, 2003). In this chapter, we examine one of these services, which offered a teledermatology outreach clinic in an English city. A condition placed on our research by local research ethics committees was that individuals, organizations, and their location would remain anonymous in our published reports, and we gladly honor that condition in this chapter.

We provide an analysis of what seems at first sight to be the failure of a teledermatology service. But on closer examination, this analysis tells the story of the way that a group of clinicians successfully used the service to solve both a structural and a political problem.

Teledermatology in an English City

Teledermatology began in the city at the beginning of 1995, and since then it has gone through four phases. The first of these was an experimental service that used real-time videoconferencing to connect hospital-based dermatologists with doctors and patients at family practitioners' offices. This service involved a small group of academic clinicians interested primarily in research about continuing medical education. They saw triadic consultations between a dermatologist, family practitioner, and patient as a means of improving the quality and consistency of dermatological practice in primary care. The rationale for the study was similar to that underlying a recently published large, randomized controlled trial of triadic consultations in primary care in the United Kingdom (Wallace and others, 2002). However, in the course of our study, we found that clinicians quickly began to question its value. One clinician told us that the patient, family practitioner, and dermatologist "all had to be there at the same time, and it took time to load the software, . . . so although it was good for educational purposes and probably good for complex cases where you are wanting to have a case conference, it probably would not be realistic to take that forward as a normal form of dermatological services."

Image quality was poor, and so it was difficult to discriminate between trivial and serious lesions, especially on darker skin tones. Moreover, matching the availability of the three participants also proved difficult. For the chief of the dermatology department, this organizational problem was a crucial obstacle to the effective delivery of the service. In fact, the image quality available from the videoconferencing system was sometimes so poor that dermatologists had to rely on the family practitioner acting as their proxy and describing the rash or lesion to them.

Technical and organizational problems overwhelmed this service, which was not regarded as a success and concluded in late 1996.

Building Evidence for Practice

Since triadic videoconferencing had failed to produce the anticipated benefits, the family practitioners' enthusiasm for teledermatology rapidly waned. The dermatologists remained interested, but argued that if they were to use teledermatology as a diagnostic tool without the presence of a proxy (the family doctor), they needed both better image quality and robust evidence of clinical effectiveness and safety. One of the dermatologists saw this as a crucial political move to provide strong evidence about the utility of telecare in health services: "If you look at every other aspect of patient management, whether it be—particularly if you look at introducing new surgical techniques or new drugs—they have to go through very rigorous evidence-based overviews before they are introduced into the health service. . . . But now we have got something that really is the same as a way of managing patients. It's being introduced—or they are trying to introduce—it without any recognised controlled trials."

The most senior dermatologist was able to find research and development funding for a randomized, controlled clinical trial of a store-and-forward telecare system versus conventional face-to-face encounters, where high-quality digital images of skin lesions (suspected tumors) were stored and forwarded from one hospital outpatient clinic to another, and where histological examination was the gold standard test of concordance. Three hundred sixteen patients were entered into the trial. The results were promising.

The clinical trial, of course, was undertaken in highly controlled conditions, quite unlike those experienced in everyday practice. But the evidence that it produced was, according to the model of biomedical research that informed it, of very high quality. By the end of 1998, the dermatologists were reassured that teledermatology could be clinically effective and was safe, and they went on to publish their results in highly regarded clinical journals.

By then, enthusiasm for continuing to work in the field was beginning to wane: the dermatologists' conventional service was under pressure, and the waiting time for nonurgent appointments had reached thirty-five weeks by the beginning of 1999. Both the dermatologists and the family doctors whose patients were referred to their clinic saw this as completely unacceptable, and teledermatology became regarded as "a distraction from our core business," according to the service manager. Additional funding was made available to provide extra clinics, but this brought another problem into the foreground. A national shortage of consultant dermatologists meant that more hospital-based clinics could not be provided because additional dermatologists could not be found to run them. The department therefore began to plan an outreach service, employing specialist nurses to provide community-based triage clinics that would, the chief of dermatology said, "sort the wheat from the chaff."

A Shift from Clinical Experiment to Experimental Clinic

Circumstances changed suddenly at the beginning of 1998, when a for-profit tele-dermatology provider began to offer a rapid diagnostic service to family doctors in another part of the city. The dermatologists recognized, again in the words of the chief of dermatology, that "there was lots of threat" from this service: the for-profit service would destabilize the market for his department's services (the department was effectively a monopoly supplier), and hence its income stream, and he was concerned that the rapid diagnosis that the for-profit service offered was not backed up by peer-reviewed evidence of clinical safety and effectiveness.

What followed from this was the rapid conversion of plans for the nurse-outreach clinic into plans for a nurse-run teledermatology clinic for family doctors in the department's area. An outreach nurse would tour primary care facilities, taking digital photographs of patients' skin lesions and other problems and recording basic patient data, and these would then be sent by e-mail to the dermatologists' hospital department. They would be reviewed by doctors, who would make a diagnostic decision and management plan, which could then be sent on to the patient's family doctor. Sinister symptoms, or uncertain problems, could be sent directly to the hospital department for face-to-face consults.

From the start, dermatologists were uncertain, and sometimes very skeptical, about the capacity of this new way of working to deliver the kind of clinical data that they felt they needed to work with. One of them told us:

> When we examine a patient normally, there's more to it than simply looking at the rash or the individual lesion. So often palpation and texture play a large part in it. That's one issue. The second issue, which is perhaps more important, is that, even if one can make an accurate diagnosis, often that isn't all that the consultation needs to do. A lot of the information which you get from a patient relates to other issues than the actual clinical diagnosis—the impact that a skin problem might be having on them, for example. So we might have two people who've got what is visually an identical-looking rash. One of them might be completely not bothered, but the other person might be devastated. And those sorts of more subtle clues about patient's anxiety and the impact the problem is having on them, I suspect, will be a lot more difficult to get with teledermatology.

Hardware and organizational systems that had been proved in the earlier clinical trial were brought back into service, and the department's dermatologists began to pilot-test them on a much wider population. At the same time, negotiations with family practitioners to roll out a teledermatology service formed around two important points. First, dermatologists were able to stress that the service was evidence based and that there was a scientific justification for it by emphasizing their peer-reviewed papers in clinical journals. Second, they were able to enroll family doctors into a novel system of practice that promised to resolve the existing structural problem of long waiting times, and so secure funding for modernizing their service. In doing this, they were able to capture the terrain of innovation claimed by the for-profit provider, while claiming their own conventional knowledge base and the continuity of service that stemmed from it. The political problem for the department was solved: a contract was signed, the market for the departments' service stabilized, and the dermatologists began to work to set the new service in train.

Teledermatology in Practice

In fact, it was several months before the teledermatology service was able to roll out anything approaching clinical practice. In tests, the imaging system that had been previously directed at well-defined skin lesions on a largely white population proved inadequate to deal with the much wider range of dermatological disease experienced in the inner-city areas from which new patients were drawn, areas that included substantial Afro-Caribbean and South Asian minority populations. Diffuse lesions and rashes were hard to detect on different skin tones, just as they had been in videoconferenced triadic consultations several years before. The original hardware was therefore abandoned. New hardware was obtained—coincidentally from the same company whose equipment was used by the for-profit competitor. It took time to bring this into service in a way that seemed to work.

Elsewhere (Mort, May, and Williams, 2003), we have observed that one of the key problems for the dermatology department was managing the move from a clinical experiment (the randomized, controlled trial) to an experimental clinic (the rolled-out service). At the center of this problem was the changed knowledge that the dermatologists needed to use to judge diagnostic effectiveness. In the trial, the adjudicating criterion was convergence: How closely did telediagnosis accord to conventional face-to-face diagnosis? There was a concrete means of assessing this by using laboratory tests as a gold standard. But the strictly controlled mechanisms of the clinical trial could not be applied in real practice, they were too time-consuming for everyday clinical work, and they focused on too specific a diagnostic category: skin tumors. This meant that the dermatologists had to move to another kind of criterion: their confidence that they had enough accurate clinical data to make a reliable diagnosis and management decision.

Attempts to achieve this were organized not around the digital image itself but around the accompanying clinical information that the outreach nurse collected alongside it. The nurse would use an on-line protocol for recording this information in a structured way. In practice, this structured data collection was quickly found to be insufficient, and a free text box, originally intended for marginal notes, assumed considerable importance as nurses began to use this to provide information of central importance to the diagnostic and management process. Another dermatologist explained the importance of this:

> Because we've also asked them [the nurses] for more subtle things like "patient worried sick, needs to be seen" because some of that's soft feel that you get. . . . Obviously the nurses aren't so used to seeing patients and having responsibility for the assessment of patients, so that's been quite a difficult learning curve for them to take on that responsibility, and we don't have them making diagnosis; they have a nurse opinion. We've actually modified the form to have the nurse opinion in there. . . . I think the most valuable thing is "unknown" or "I don't know" because that's the honest answer if you don't know what it is or "it looks like eczema". The free text is very useful for all sorts of things, the bits you can't get from a photograph, like "the widespread rash is now cleared but now they've got something completely different from the referral letter and it's whatever . . . ."

In this situation, the question of the intermediary became significant. The design of the service laid emphasis on the hardware, but we can argue that the real intermediary rapidly became the outreach nurse (just as the family practitioner had taken on a proxy role in the earlier videoconferencing study). The dermatologists became dependent on the nurses in a way that they had not anticipated or intended. This happened because the dermatologists never gained sufficient confidence in the images that were transmitted to them to make consistent diagnostic decisions, and they found themselves increasingly reliant on the nurses' opinions as a parallel interpretation of the image. This lack of confidence had an important consequence: it meant that dermatologists found themselves recalling about 60 percent of their patients for a conventional face-to-face consult at the hospital. So while the structural waiting list problem was solved (in fact, the waiting list plummeted to virtually zero in six months), because patients had been "seen" by the dermatology department, the dermatologists' own workload was significantly increased because they had to "see" these patients again. Moreover, the loss of subtle knowledge about the patient—about the material presentation of skin problems and their psychosocial impact—left the dermatologists feeling not only uncertain about their diagnostic decisions and management strategies but also feeling deskilled. Once the waiting list had been cleared, there was little enthusiasm to continue the service, and it was discontinued.

Implications

Champions of telecare celebrate success, but it is equally important to understand failure. Nevertheless, defining success or failure is itself sometimes a problem. In the latter context, the story of this teledermatology service can be understood in several ways. It tells us that:

- It is difficult to translate a system configured through highly structured clinical research protocols into the messy business of everyday clinical practice.
- The introduction of a telecare health service reconfigures relationships between different kinds of clinicians—in this case, between doctors and nurses.
- Technological innovation is difficult to manage and generates additional labor and complexity for different groups.

One interpretation of these different elements of the story that we have told might be that the hardware used, and the clinical abilities of the dermatologists themselves, were the problem. We might argue that they had underestimated the complexity of the new system that they were bringing into service. But the hardware was very similar to that used by the successful and high-volume for-profit service provider. That company used (and still does) a nearly identical model of service delivery: nurse-led outreach clinics, transmitting digital images of skin lesions and rashes to a distributed network of consultant dermatologists. The dermatology department's system emulated that of the for-profit provider but seemed unsuccessful in use; it failed to normalize and become routinely embedded in practice.

However, an alternative interpretation of this story suggests an entirely different outcome—one in which the apparently failed system was actually highly successful:

- It achieved its explicit objective. In six months, nearly two hundred patients were seen, and the thirty-five-week waiting time that was in place when the service was rolled out was reduced to two weeks. Teledermatology solved a structural problem in the organization of health care.
- The market for the dermatology department's service was contractually stabilized. This locked out competition from the for-profit provider. Teledermatology solved a political problem in the organization of health care.

In parallel, the dermatology department was therefore able to produce an account of the "failure" of teledermatology, while at the same time achieving material "success" that stabilized and supported its own clinical service. The teledermatology service was a short-term intervention. It was a tool to deal with a structural and political problem but could also be effectively used to resist further development. They had tried it, giving it their best shot, and it did not work. In a relatively small community of practice located in a local health care system under pressure, that was a powerful story for them to tell. As far as we know, neither the dermatology department nor the family practitioners that it serves have experimented further with teledermatology in the two years since the service concluded.

Discussion Questions

1. Can you think of a telecare service where the definition of success or failure is equally ambiguous? What conflicts and difficulties are in play? How are they being worked out?
2. What kinds of evaluation methods are most effective in drawing out lessons from politically and structurally contentious telecare interventions?
3. Organizational and technical complexity are major problems in health care systems on a large scale. Can telecare be effectively integrated into complex patterns of service delivery? What is needed to achieve this? How can it best be organized?

References

May, C., Mort, M., Mair, F. S., and Williams, T. "Factors Affecting the Adoption of Tele-healthcare Technologies in the United Kingdom: The Policy Context and the Problem of Evidence." *Health Informatics Journal*, 2001, *7*, 131–134.

May, C., and others. "Health Technology Assessment in Its Local Contexts: Studies of Tele-healthcare." *Social Science and Medicine*, 2003, *57*, 697–710.

Mort, M., May, C. R., and Williams, T. "Remote Doctors and Absent Patients: Acting at a Distance in Telemedicine." *Science Technology and Human Values*, 2003, *28*, 274–295.

National Health Service Executive. *Information for Health: An Information Strategy for the Modern NHS, 1998–2001*. London: National Health Service Executive, 1998.

Wallace, P., and others. "Joint Teleconsultations (Virtual Outreach) Versus Standard Outpatient Appointments for Patients Referred by their General Practitioner for a Specialist Opinion: A Randomised Trial." *Lancet*, 2002, *359*, 1961–1968.

PART THREE

COMMUNICATION

Extremists think "communication" means agreeing with them.

LEO ROSTEN

CHAPTER TEN

RESEARCH AS DIALOGUE

Health Communication and Behavior Change in Patients' Natural Habitat

Linda M. Harris, Rita Kobb, Patricia Ryan, Adam Darkins, Gary L. Kreps

Knowing is the process of communicative interaction.

RALPH D. STACEY (2001)

When we straddle dams across great rushing rivers, we harness the powerful forces at work to generate energy. This case study describes how theoretically architected patient-provider interactions can harness the naturally occurring currents of human dialogue to generate evidence-based health care. This focus on the dialogue is to bring attention to the powerful forces at work within human interaction to monitor and adapt to threatening conditions. At the heart of the case study is the dialogue that transpires between a cancer patient and his care provider.

Special thanks go to Neeraj Arora, health systems analyst, Division of Cancer Control and Population Studies, National Cancer Institute, for his keen insights into systems theory and patient-provider communication. Also, our gratitude goes to Neale Chumbler for allowing us to borrow heavily from early drafts of prepublished work and for his continued research leadership. Chumbler is research health scientist at the Veterans Administration, Health Services Research and Development/ Rehabilitation Research and Development Rehabilitation Outcomes Research Center at the North Florida/South Georgia Veterans Health System and an assistant professor in the Department of Health Services Administration at the University of Florida.

Research as Dialogue Case Study

This case study focuses on a particular point in time for cancer patients and their informal caregivers: the weeks immediately following diagnosis, during which they undergo chemotherapy. These weeks are both a hopeful and a difficult period—hopeful because a growing number of cancers can often be reduced to manageable chronic conditions, but difficult because the treatment itself can cause threatening side effects. The stakes are very high for the patient, the informal caregiver, and the health care provider organization. The patient is at risk of dying if treatment is not forthcoming and of horrible pain and other debilitating conditions as well, and of being removed from home if his symptoms are not managed successfully. The informal caregiver is at risk of becoming overwhelmed with the burden of care. And, the provider organization is at risk of paying for the dramatically increasing costs of institutional care if symptoms are not managed successfully at home.

Coordinating Symptom Management Through Daily Dialogue

Al Logan is an eighty-year-old veteran who was awarded a purple heart in combat during World War II. He has lived with his wife, Pat, near Lake City, Florida, since his retirement in 1990. In summer 2003, Logan is diagnosed with colon cancer. Upon the advice of his oncologist, he chooses to begin chemotherapy treatments. Al opts to participate in a home cancer care pilot study sponsored by the Veterans Health Administration (VHA) and the National Cancer Institute. Although he travels to the outpatient clinic in Lake City for treatments, his life is otherwise not interrupted by unnecessary travel. In fact, before the treatments begin, he and Pat are visited by a VHA health care professional. Together, they establish a baseline of his symptoms and a symptom management plan. Rita Ryan, the care coordinator assigned to Al, also brings them a personal, in-home communication and monitoring appliance and demonstrates how to engage in daily dialogues with her through this appliance.

Ongoing coordinated communication between Al and Rita is at the heart of this innovative health care process. Al and Pat are treated as equal partners in care. They are responsible for monitoring and reporting Al's health status, for performing many self-care activities, and for adjusting these activities based on feedback they receive. They are supported by a twenty-four-hour communication link to Rita.

As a cancer patient undergoing chemotherapy, Al is at risk for experiencing fatigue, pain, nausea, and depression. In addition, functional ability will be a key to Al's health status during his six weeks of treatment. To facilitate monitoring regarding these symptoms as well as functional ability, we selected questions for their daily dialogues that have been tested for their reliability and validity.

Through dialogue, the Logans and their care coordinator establish an individual baseline for Al's health status and quality of life, collect self-report data, and make behavioral adjustments to health status changes on a daily basis. Outcomes data generated during patient-provider conversations are automatically linked to the patient's computerized patient record, capable of capturing, aggregating, and reporting on individual trend data in near real time. Each patient's record is also part of a larger patient database in which normative trends can be calculated and reported. The enterprise system is relatively mechanistic; it is designed to simply store and share data. Because it is networked and automatically linked to the VHA enterprise-wide outcomes knowledge base, it is part of an enterprise-wide learning system, informed by the data generated from the population of patients and care coordinators who are monitoring, assessing, and adjusting to patients' symptoms each day.

Thinking Inside the Box

Although the care coordinator is an infrequent visitor in the veteran's home after their initial visit, they communicate daily. The personal communication and monitoring appliance is used to integrate outcomes questions and answers into this ongoing flow of patient-provider communication. The text-messaging appliance is a small box. It is a Web-based store-and-forward application that connects through a secured network to the care coordinator through the Internet from the patient's home by a toll-free number, requiring no technological know-how. Within this electronic box, each individual's action is feedback for the other's inquiry and adaptation. In addition, the interpersonal dynamic feeds outcomes data into the larger enterprise system that collects and stores baseline patient data against which individual trend data, as well as normative data, can be fed back to inform adjustments that need to be made to sustain satisfactory health status.

First Day of Dialogue: Before First Chemotherapy Treatment

Al turns on the communication and monitoring appliance and is greeted with questions taken from pretested scales, each related to one of the most common symptoms he is likely to face (fatigue, nausea, depression, pain) and one question related to his functional activity level—for example, "Within the past 24 hours do you feel more tired than usual?" (At less frequent intervals, questions related to quality of life are asked by phone.)

Al's yes or no answers and his pain score indicate that he is experiencing his usual level of energy, has no symptoms of nausea, feels typically upbeat, has no pain, and is functioning at his usual activity level. Al's initial baseline responses are automatically recorded in the VHA patient database and his computerized personal record, which is transparent to his multidisciplinary health care provider team. Al participates in this routine dialogue each day. For the first week, through his first chemotherapy treatment, Al's responses reveal no change in his symptom-free health status. However, two days after his first treatment, the dialogue takes a different course.

Day 10: Monitoring and Reporting

Two nights after his first chemotherapy treatment, Al begins to feel nauseated. The following morning, he responds to each of the questions the same as before, except for the question measuring his nausea symptom level. This time he answers yes to whether he had felt like or had thrown up in the previous twenty-four hours.

When Al's report appears on Rita's computer screen that day, Al's positive feedback appears as a red flag that a change in Al's symptoms has occurred, triggering a phone call according to the care coordinator protocol. In their phone conversation, Al explains that his medicine has made him nauseous, and he has lost his appetite. Rita assures him that this is common for two days after chemotherapy; however, she reviews his treatment options based on the cancer care guidelines adopted by the VHA. Assessing the need for further support, Rita says that she will have a dietitian call them to review menu options while he is undergoing chemotherapy.

Al and Pat have a conversation with the dietitian, and Pat tries smaller servings of more appropriate foods. They read nausea management literature Rita mails to them after retrieving it from the National Cancer Institute's Cancer Information Service Web site. Over the next several days, Al and Pat work out a diet plan that keeps him at a level of nausea they find tolerable.

Al continues to monitor his symptoms and functional activity level during his daily dialogues with Rita. His answers suggest he is managing to sustain a health status level he finds satisfactory and that his quality of life is satisfactory to him. On day 24, Al records another change.

Day 24: A Change in Health Status

Al's fatigue level has begun to concern his wife. She encourages him to provide a different answer to this daily fatigue question, knowing this will trigger a personal response from Rita. So on day 24, after the third treatment, Al answers yes to the question about whether he is more tired than before. His yes triggers a red flag for Rita and prompts another phone call.

Managing During the Chemotherapy

During the ten weeks of chemotherapy, Al experiences significant nausea and fatigue. He and Pat manage the nausea to their satisfaction with self-care, supported by dietary guidance. His fatigue is discovered to be a result of anemia, which his oncologist diagnosed and treated. Despite these health problems, Al continues to report a satisfactory quality of life and remains very satisfied with his care. Al's baseline and the data gathered as part of his daily dialogues are now part of his computerized personal record and are also part of the larger cancer care population knowledge base at the VHA.

The interactions between Al and his health care provider are similar to many other doctor-patient conversations, with an important exception: their daily dialogue is generating the evidence they need to manage Al's symptoms. Their dialogue serves as an engine propelling them toward greater and greater efficiencies in symptom management through coordinated monitoring, adaptation, and caregiving. This dynamic is a hybrid, made up of the science of evidence-based medicine (with empirically structured dialogues that make up the monitoring and reporting part of the process) and the art of interpersonal communication (with open-ended dialogues) where human creativity, spontaneity, and fidelity play their role.

Research as Dialogue Model

Despite the natural capacity for humans to perform conjoint monitoring, adaptations, and care giving, these actions have gained little attention as health communication acts in practice or research. Within the medical system today, these are services or interventions "delivered to" a patient or sometimes something a patient does for himself or herself (self care). Slight attention has been focused on coordinated care, much less coordinated care as an act of communication. Instead, patient-provider communication is more typically focused on functions such as relationship establishment, information exchange, and shared decision making (Arora, 2003). In fact, one does not find acts such as reciprocity, coordination, monitoring, or adapting among the "essential sets of communication tasks," according to the Kalamazoo consensus statement regarding communication in medical encounters (Makoul, 2001).

This case study demonstrates that human dialogue is the patient's natural habitat and that within it, powerful forces are at play propelling and constraining how we adapt to threats to the health of the patient. This habitat is far from static; it is the fluid social context in which we generate, confirm, and act on our knowledge about our experiences and ourselves.

This dynamic, we believe, is at the heart of what evidence-based health care sets out to accomplish: a continuous feedback loop between evidence of what works and health-improving actions. Theoretically, architected patient-provider dialogues hold within them the primary elements of outcomes research and health improvement: an ongoing context of reciprocal expectations that each participant will be responsive to the other (usually referred to as adherence in other research models but referred to here as feedback); mutual monitoring, inquiries, observations, and adaptations to deviations from the norm (usually referred to as interventions in other research models but is self-care in our model); and the recording of changes in health status, in the form of longitudinal aggregated data.

Our research-as-dialogue model is informed by those who view human systems as complex and adaptive (Kreps, 1990; Weick, 1969; Plsek, 2001) and human interaction as the generator of meaning and knowledge (Vygotsky, 1962; Bruner,

1968; Stacey, 2001, 2003). Stacey, following complexity sciences, describes knowledge as "not so much a database of individually discovered facts, but more of an interpersonally powered self-organizing process" (2001, p. 96).

Plsek (2001) describes how self-regulating change occurs naturally during the interactions of complex, adaptive systems. He further makes a useful distinction between mechanistic systems and adaptive systems, holding that while engineers or architects might design mechanistic systems where the interactions do not vary, the design of an adaptive system is more like that of the work of a farmer: "The farmer simply creates the conditions under which a good crop is possible" (p. 315). In our model, we created these conditions by structuring a significant part of their dialogue according to scientifically validated questions, asked by a credible and trusted professional, who expected and received the feedback needed to anticipate and adjust to problem symptoms.

Feedback is the engine that propels interpersonal interaction and the conjoint generation of meaning and knowledge. The causal mechanism of feedback in the interpersonal system may be best described by Gouldner (1960), who identified the "norm of reciprocity," a universal force of self-fulfilling expectations that others will respond in kind. Capella and other contemporary communication theorists have noted that "mutual adaptation is the defining characteristic" of this reciprocal give and take, from the first interpersonal interactions between infants and their mothers to public debate (Capella, 1991, p. 104; see also Stacey, 2003). Paradoxically, this mutual expectation for reciprocity carries with it universal normative forces strong enough to compel humans to keep responding to each other, even under the duress of being involved in unwanted, repetitive, even abusive conversations (Cronen, 1979). This suggests that just as there is the potential for generative dialogue between patient and provider, there is potential for degenerative dialogue as well. Since the consequences for either have a far-reaching impact on the health status of the patient, our model draws attention to the need to provide patients and providers the tools to monitor and adjust their interactions accordingly.

When these views come together, they form a model for conducting outcomes research within provider-patient dialogue. We expect, based on this way of thinking, that providers and patients, when given the opportunity, can perform in complex and adaptive ways, that their interactions can contain highly personalized and effective acts of care giving, and that the knowledge they generate together can be flexible and fluid enough to anticipate and counter frequent and serious health threats.

Following this approach, our research-as-dialogue model guides the design of coordinated symptom management dialogues for patients and providers to monitor, assess, and adjust to evidence of changes in health status, within the context of their ongoing relationship. After an initial set of empirically validated questions setting the dialogue process in motion, the specific words and messages are left up to the participants to craft. The naturally occurring mutual obligations to reciprocate propel these conversations toward the achievement of their outcome goals.

Figure 10.1 represents the interpersonal symptom management system, functioning within a larger health care enterprise system that has been developed in a way that harnesses their natural capacity to coordinate the management of Al's symptoms. There are multiple hierarchical contexts of systemic interaction in this model—the enterprise level and the interpersonal level—each informing the other concerning evidence of what is working, what is not, and under what circumstances.

Taken together, successful management of these symptoms and functional physical activity level can determine whether a cancer patient undergoing chemotherapy can avoid institutional care. In addition, patients and providers can keep a daily account of the quality of health care, the quality of life, and the satisfaction level of the patient.

FIGURE 10.1. AN INTERPERSONAL SYMPTOM MANAGEMENT SYSTEM: A WORKING MODEL.

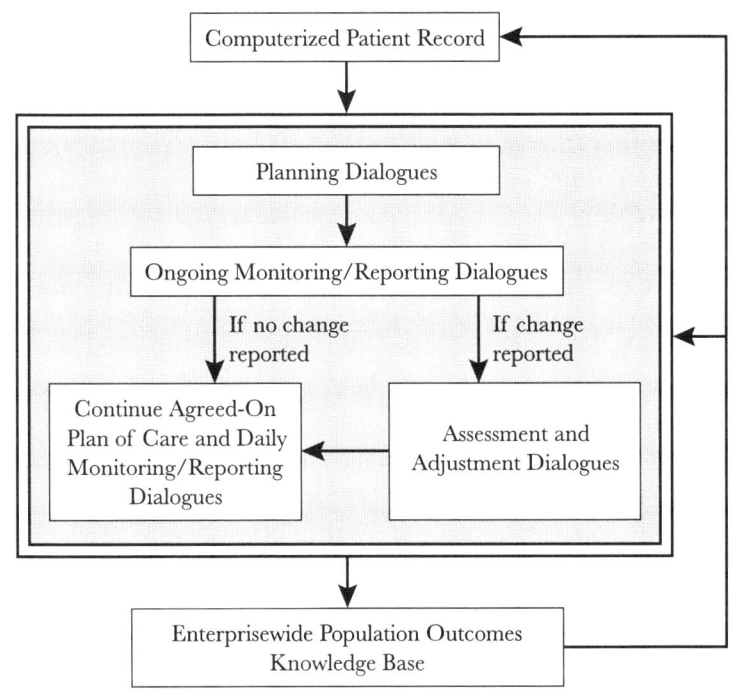

Outcomes and Current Status

Preliminary evaluations of the initial home telehealth pilot project compared home telehealth care with usual VHA care for patients with a variety of chronic conditions. Data suggest that the desired cost-reduction outcomes are being achieved. Overall, comparisons of the intervened group findings to the comparison group found that the intervened group showed considerably greater improvements on all measures (Meyer, Kobb, and Ryan, 2002).

At this writing, the cancer care project is just getting under way in Florida. Therefore, we do not yet know if the home telehealth model will achieve the same level of cost savings and quality for cancer care as it has for other chronic conditions. However, regardless of the outcomes themselves, we see great promise in the patient-provider system as a generator of actionable outcomes data because it is designed to adapt quickly and reliably to unacceptable outcomes. We believe the nature of this dyadic system has potential, in the aggregate, to become the locus of self-monitoring, self-regulating health care throughout the VHA system.

Conclusion

In 2001, the Institute of Medicine and the Committee on the Quality of Health Care in American published a vision of the twenty-first-century health care system: "providing care that is evidence-based, patient-centered, and systems-oriented" (Institute of Medicine, 2001, p. 20). Achieving this vision for an entire national health care system seems to be a daunting challenge, and it is not evident that health communication plays a major role. Health communication has been viewed primarily as an enhancement to the health care process, not as a dynamic dyadic system. However, when we focus on the interpersonal system as a complex, adaptive engine of care, redesigning the health care system seems much more manageable. From this vantage point, we see that within the patient-provider dyad, there are naturally occurring interpersonal forces at work, such as the norm of reciprocity and the ability to monitor and adapt to each other, propelling them to coordinate their health care activities.

We believe that if patient-provider conversations are structured to capitalize on the natural human capacity to reciprocate, monitor, and adapt and are supported with an enterprise-wide electronic communication system, we can realize the Institute of Medicine vision, one dyad at a time. And if, as others have noted, the health care system is "like politics—not an institution, but a set of collective behaviors that are formed and influenced through communication processes"

(Finnegan and Viswanath, 1990, p. 14), then our task as health communication researchers is to design patient-provider dialogues that are isomorphic with the natural flow of human interaction and allow them to flourish throughout the health care enterprise. This case study suggests we would benefit in this effort from a model of health communication that takes into account the remarkable synergy that can take place within dialogue.

Discussion Questions

1. Traditionally, research and interventions have been conducted separately. What are the implications for each of integrating these two activities?
2. How might this model be applied to clinical trials?
3. How should privacy and confidentiality issues be resolved in this approach to research and care delivery?
4. How does this model of research compare to classic controlled, randomized trials?
5. What are some hypotheses that would flow from this theoretical model?

References

Arora, N. K. "Interacting with Cancer Patients: The Significance of Physicians' Communication Behavior." *Social Science and Medicine,* 2003, *57,* 791–806.

Bruner, J. *Acts of Meaning.* Cambridge, Mass. Harvard University Press, 1968.

Capella, J. N. "Mutual Adaptation and Relativity of Measurement." In M. Montgomery and S. Duck (eds.), *Studying Interpersonal Interaction.* New York: Guilford Press, 1991.

Cronen, V. E. "A Theory of Rules Structure and Episode Types, and a Study of Perceived Enmeshment in Unwanted Repetitive Patterns." In D. Nimno (ed.), *Communication Yearbook III.* New Brunswick, N.J.: Transaction Books, 1979.

Finnegan, J. R., and Viswanath, K. "Health and Communication: Medical and Public Health Influences on the Research Agenda." In J. Bryant (ed.), *Communication and Health: Systems and Applications.* Mahwah, N.J.: Erlbaum, 1990.

Gouldner, A. W. "The Norm of Reciprocity: A Preliminary Statement." *American Sociological Review,* 1960, *25,* 161–178.

Institute of Medicine. *Crossing the Quality Chasm: A New Health System for the Twenty-First Century.* Washington, D.C.: National Academy of Sciences, 2001.

Kreps, G. "The Social Systems Theory of Organization." In G. Kreps, *Organizational Communication.* New York: Longman, 1990.

Makoul, G. "Essential Elements of Communication in Medical Encounters: The Kalamazoo Consensus Statement." *Academic Medicine,* 2001, *76,* 390–393.

Meyer, M. A., Kobb, R., and Ryan, P. "Virtually Healthy: Chronic Disease Management in the Home." *Disease Management,* 2002, *5*(2), 87–94.

Plsek, P. " Redesigning Health Care with Insights from the Science of Complex Adaptive
    Systems." In Institute of Medicine, *Crossing the Quality Chasm: A New Health System for the
    Twenty-First Century.* Washington, D.C.: National Academy Press, 2001.
Stacey, R. D. *Complex Responsive Processes in Organizations: Learning and Knowledge Creation.* New
    York: Routledge, 2001.
Stacey, R. D. *Complexity and Group Processes: A Radically Social Understanding of Individuals.* New
    York: Brunner-Routledge, 2003.
Vygotsky, L. *Thought and Language.* Cambridge, Mass.: MIT Press, 1962.
Weick, K. *The Social Psychology of Organizing.* Reading, Mass.: Addison-Wesley, 1969.

CHAPTER ELEVEN

DIAGNOSING THE COMMUNICATION INFRASTRUCTURE IN ORDER TO REACH TARGET AUDIENCES

A Study of Hispanic Communities in Los Angeles

Pauline Hope Cheong, Holley A. Wilkin, Sandra Ball-Rokeach

Maria is a first-generation Mexican immigrant who is married with three children, ages two, four, and five. She and her family rent a house and share it with her husband's extended family. Maria's mother-in-law takes care of all five children in the household while the parents work. Maria and her husband work long hours between multiple jobs in order to pay bills and send money back to their family and to home-town projects in Mexico. Although both parents work hard, they cannot afford health insurance for the whole family. The state of California has several subsidized programs that could assist them, but Maria is afraid that if she signs up her two younger American-born children, she might expose the older undocumented child and create inequity in treatment for her children. When Maria has questions about health or child care issues, she tends to talk to other parents or get information from the Spanish-language television stations.

Maria is a composite character we have created based on our interactions with residents in four Los Angeles Hispanic communities over a two-year period. Her story is based on our observations during our field visits to the areas, the interviews we conducted with community leaders and newspapers, and our telephone survey and focus group interviews with residents. One of our most important findings for health communicators and practitioners that emerge from our research with residents like Maria is that new health communication technologies are not currently as effective as other media tools (Cheong, 2004).

Since 1998, the Metamorphosis project (Figure 11.1) has engaged in a thorough examination to uncover the nature and well-being of families and their communities in various diverse multiethnic neighborhoods in Los Angeles (http:// www.metamorph.org). All the neighborhoods are located within ten miles of the Los Angeles civic center and contain residents representative of 90 percent of the Los Angeles population, thereby reflecting a good picture of this urban area's montage of ethnicities and social backgrounds (Matei and others, 2001). The Metamorphosis project is part of an ongoing research of the Community and Technology program in the Annenberg School for Communication, University of Southern California. In 2002, we formed a research partnership with First 5 LA (formerly known as Proposition 10), the county's Commission for Healthy Families and Children. The commission is a citizen initiative approved by California voters in the November 1998 election. The proposition created the Children and Families First Program to "promote, support, and optimize [the] early childhood development" of children from the prenatal stage until their fifth birthday. The program also assists families and others who care for young children. Ultimately, the program seeks to "optimize the development and well-being of all children, from the prenatal stage until their fifth birthday by increasing resources, ensuring access to services, and improving the abilities of families, communities and providers of services"(http://www.first5.org). With this partnership, we have expanded the community research focus of the project to include the concerns of family health and child care and to develop a strategy of community change.

Hispanic communities, which have been growing steadily in Los Angeles County, are relatively lacking in terms of health and child care resources. Hispanics have the highest birthrates in Los Angeles County and are the largest and fastest-growing ethnic group (Los Angeles County Department of Health, 2000). Hispanics in Los Angeles County have the highest rates of child poverty and the lowest percentage of children with health insurance (Los Angeles County Children's Planning Council, 2002; United Way, 2000). Hispanic children and youth also have the second highest rates of hospitalization (Los Angeles County Department of Health, 2000). According to self-reports, Hispanic adults form the largest population of Los Angeles adults in poor health (Los Angeles County Department of Health, 2000). These statistics compel health interventions and an urgent need for health practitioners to reach this population and understand their media connections. This challenge requires the use of research methods that afford access to first- and second-generation immigrants with no or limited English-language skills; they constitute 30.3 percent of the Los Angeles County Hispanic populations (U.S. Bureau of the Census, 2000). This case study describes how the communication infrastructure theoretical approach can be applied to the understanding and application

FIGURE 11.1. METAMORPHOSIS RESEARCH DESIGN.

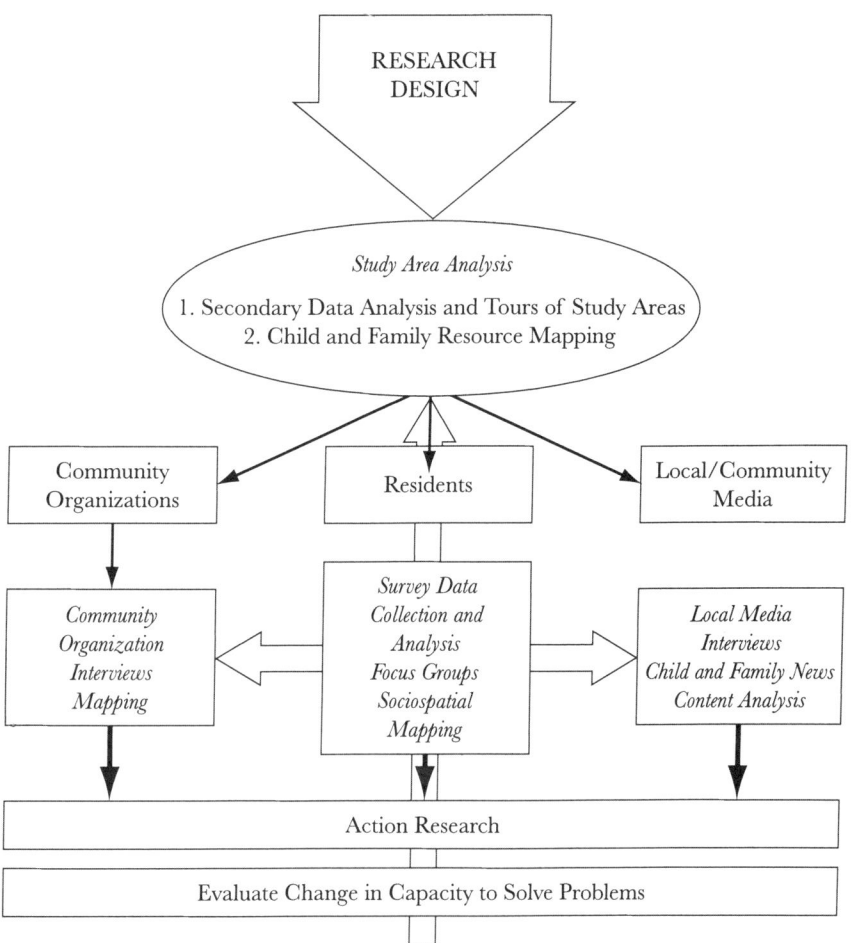

of a range of communication technologies for the purposes of reaching underserved communities.

The Communication Infrastructure Approach to Understanding Media Connections

The communication infrastructure approach involves a diagnosis of communities by examining two components: the storytelling network and the communication action context (Ball-Rokeach, Kim, and Matei, 2001). The storytelling network comprises the integrated links between the residents, community organizations, and local media that enable storytelling about the community as well as health issues. For example, in a strong storytelling network, neighbors talk to each over the backyard fence about the neighborhood. They talk about upcoming events, new threats or new opportunities, where to go for health services, and the like. Community organizations with service, cultural, sports, or other missions also encourage their clients or members to talk with others about neighborhood issues, for example, health care, child care, safety, and the schools. In addition, local media, from the church or temple newsletter to a free bulletin to a commercial newspaper or radio station, provoke neighborhood storytelling by covering the activities of community organizations and community institutions.

The second component of the communication infrastructure, the communication action context, is the environment in which families, organizations, and media operate. It comprises all the important factors in a community that influence whether storytelling about critical health issues occurs. Such factors may include availability of child and health care services in the areas, street safety, and the condition of local grocery stores and products. This context can enable storytellers and neighborhood storytelling when, for example, there are safe streets that allow people to congregate in public spaces or to join in the activities of community organizations. Unsafe streets limit or constrain the storytelling process.

A key conclusion from prior investigations in eight diverse communities of Los Angeles is that when the trinity of storytellers—residents, community organizations, and local media—encourages one another to talk about the resources and problems of the local community, residents develop a sense of belonging that leads them to unite with others to tackle shared problems (Ball-Rokeach, Kim, and Matei, 2001; Kim, 2003).

In this way, the Metamorphosis project takes an ecological approach to understanding peoples' health problem solving behavior as a function of their communication and resource environments as well as group and individual characteristics (Cheong, Wilkin, and Ball-Rokeach, 2003).

Some of the salient questions pertaining to reaching families and meeting their health concerns include: What are the various ways in which residents obtain health information in their everyday lives? What is the nature and quality of residents' media connections to a range of older and newer media, as well as mainstream and local ethnically targeted media? Recent studies show the importance of local ethnically targeted media for new immigrant populations (Chan, 2002; Project for Excellence in Journalism, 2004). We are also interested in uncovering residents' connections to these crucial, but often overlooked, local ethnically targeted media, available in the preferred language of newer immigrant populations. The Metamorphosis project has unusual databases that identify not only the different media technologies that are available to residents in our study areas, but also which media the residents connect with in their everyday lives.

The following section highlights some of our research findings about media connections for health from Hispanic residents in our study areas. These results are based on telephone survey and focus groups held between December 2002 and March 2003. For the purposes of this case study and to illustrate our research collaboration with the First 5 Los Angeles Commission for Healthy Families and Children, we are concentrating on the findings from the 327 families who have children five years old and younger. We also recruited people from this sample to participate in focus groups. In February 2003, we held five focus groups, which were conducted in Spanish with the goal of uncovering more in-depth information about community, family, and child issues. Participants told their stories about general issues of concern in their communities and about their children and families.

Results

The majority of respondents (84 percent) chose to respond to the telephone survey interview in Spanish; the rest of the population (16 percent) completed the survey in English. This linguistic preference has implications for the choice of communication technologies employed, as well as the design and promotion of health interventions among new immigrant populations.

From the survey responses, we ranked the top ten ways that respondents get information on medical and health care. As illustrated in Figure 11.2, television and interpersonal communication overwhelmingly rank the highest. Other media channels, such as radio and the Internet, are used by less than 10 percent of our respondents. We observe a similar pattern when it comes to getting information about raising children. Interpersonal communication, television, books, and magazines are among the more popular sources of information as compared to both newspapers and the Internet, which are less than 5 percent of respondents use.

FIGURE 11.2. TOP TEN WAYS THAT HISPANICS GET INFORMATION ON HEALTH AND MEDICAL CARE.

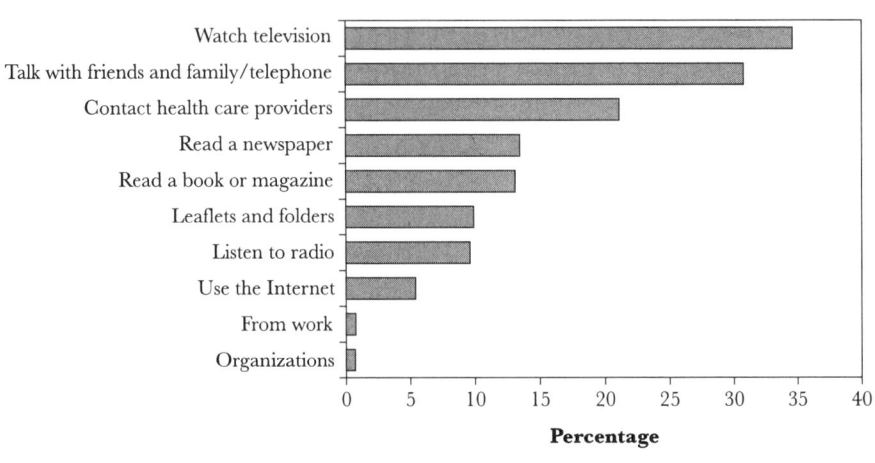

Note: N = 327.

A further investigation into the specific media channels that our target population connects to reveals that the majority of respondents who connect to television, newspapers, and the radio for health and child care information go to ethnically targeted media. For example, of the 34 percent who connect to television for health care information, 67 percent of them connect to Spanish-language television. Of the 14 percent who go to the newspaper to discover health information, 50 percent choose to read Spanish-language newspapers. Thus, we observe a stronger connection with Spanish-language community media than with the mainstream and English-language media. This reflects the large percentage of first- and second-generation immigrants (88.3 percent) who are most comfortable communicating in their native language and probably also go to these channels because they are more culturally and ethnically relevant to them. Participants from the five focus groups also said that they referred to local and ethnically targeted media for information pertaining to their health care; for example, residents in the city of South Gate mentioned that they usually tune into Spanish radio and watch Spanish television.

Further exploration into Internet connection patterns revealed that less than one-third of our respondents connect to the Internet at home, at work, or at any other location. This figure is dramatically smaller than the numbers found for other ethnic groups in our previous study areas. Still, even for Latinos, these numbers are quite low. For example, in our 2001 survey, 68 percent of the Latinos in the City of Glendale reported connecting to the Internet at home, work, or another location. This information shows that findings about Latinos from one area cannot be generalized to other areas even within a city such as Los Angeles.

Nevertheless, we were interested in discovering whether even these small numbers of Internet connectors connected to the Internet for health information. Of those who do connect, half of the respondents have sought health information online. This provides some hope that as more people in the community start to connect on-line, we might expect this medium to become a means of providing health information to the group. However, at this point, there are not enough people connecting to the Internet to justify its use as a main channel to reach this population. Furthermore, no participant in the focus groups mentioned or talked about the Internet as a source for information for health and child care issues in their community. Most of our respondents, like Maria, prefer media targeted to their ethnic group. These are the key health storytelling media that promote health storytelling among residents.

Implications and Lessons Learned

The Metamorphosis project's orientation to health communication is community based and grounded in an ecological and contextualized approach to the analysis and application of communication technologies to health promotion and problem-solving behaviors. Our approach deals with how health communicators and practitioners might use knowledge of the key health storytellers to tailor health campaigns.

We believe that a solution to reaching new immigrants lies in our multilevel approach, where we uncover the key players in the target group's communication infrastructure. Our goal was to uncover the new immigrants' media connections in order to determine how best to reach them. From our case study analyses of distinct Hispanic communities, we have examined and investigated peoples' complex media profiles, including their connections to newer as well as older media and particularly local ethnically targeted media. Our research has illustrated the importance of empirically understanding the range of media technologies that residents use in their everyday lives in order to discern the best ways to reach a particularly hard-to-reach but burgeoning audience, the new Hispanic immigrants.

The stories of Maria's family and others in these four Los Angeles County communities illustrate the importance of health communication program and campaign designers to identify the media connection patterns of the specific community they are trying to reach. In the case of Maria and her family, new communication technologies are not the most effective way to reach them. Ethnically targeted local media are a more effective means.

It is important to note that with all the optimism behind new technologies in health communication, there are still certain populations, like the newer Hispanic immigrant groups, that are not connecting to the Internet. This highlights the importance of pinpointing the specific media channels used by the target populations, including a thorough investigation of ethnic and local media. It also involves identifying the key players in the storytelling network, such as the community organizations involved in direct storytelling about the neighborhood and their health concerns. In order to best reach target audiences, health practitioners need to understand the importance of the different media within the greater communication infrastructure.

Future Research Plans

We are beginning to interview the community organizations and the producers of local media identified in the survey. In order to measure the quality of child, family, and health stories told in the local media, we plan to do a news content analysis. We are also in the process of designing action research to increase the likelihood that community organizations and local media not only tell more health and family stories tailored to the concerns and conditions of local residents, but also that they get to know one another better, and thereby strengthen the neighborhood storytelling network.

Three years after initiating action research in the form of intervention workshops, we plan to evaluate community change. We aim to find out if the storytelling network becomes stronger or more integrated as revealed by greater volume of neighborhood storytelling (for example, about child and health issues) and, equally important, by more storytelling synergy where community organizations and local media stimulate each other and provoke ongoing conversations among residents. With a strong and synergistic storytelling network, messages that effectively get through to one storyteller (such as a resident or a local newspaper) are much more likely to get amplified or spread through the network, greatly increasing their reach and their impact.

In the future, we plan to continue to work with First 5 Los Angeles and other similar agencies to assist them in reaching their target populations most effectively. We hope to expand community studies to other communities and other ethnic populations within Los Angeles. Our intervention challenge is to create links between storytellers where there are none as revealed in our research or to strengthen existing links. For health interventions, the challenge is to become part of the community's storytelling network by knowing which communication channels are used, getting to know the producers of these media, and knowing which organizations in an area are important in the everyday lives of residents and deploying these organizations in intervention efforts. If we succeed, we have reason to believe that relatively long-lasting effects might be obtained because residents like Maria and her family members may come and go, but with the more stable presence of local media and community organizations, the storytelling network may endure.

Discussion Questions

1. How does the communication infrastructure approach to health intervention change your thinking about employing communication technologies for the dissemination of health care information?
2. If you were designing a media campaign for underserved communities, what kinds of media would you identify as critical to these populations? What factors would you consider as you make these decisions?
3. What are the advantages and disadvantages of using a combination of older and newer media, as well as mainstream and local ethnically targeted media, for reaching new immigrant communities?
4. If you were conducting health communications research, what questions might you ask to uncover the nature of residents' connections to a variety of media in their everyday lives?
5. What considerations should you have when designing an Internet-based health campaign? What unique problems may you face when designing a campaign for new immigrant groups?

References

Ball-Rokeach, S. J., Kim, Y-C., and Matei, S. "Storytelling Neighborhood: Paths to Belonging in Diverse Urban Environments." *Communication Research,* 2001, *28*(4), 392–428.

Chan, V. "Study: Ethnic Media Fills Increasingly Important Role." *Quill,* 2002, *90,* 34–35.

Cheong, P. H. "Media Relations, Threat and Health Problem Solving Behaviors: Extension and Application of Communication Infrastructure Theory and Research." Unpublished doctoral dissertation, University of Southern California, 2004.

Cheong, P. H., Wilkin, H. A., and Ball-Rokeach, S. J. "Tapping into Virtual Resources: Newer and Older Media in Health Promotion." Paper presented at the Virtual Learning in Health Communication Conference, Annenberg School of Communication, University of Southern California, Los Angeles, Apr. 11, 2003.

Kim, Y.-C. "Storytelling Community: Communication Infrastructure and Civic Engagement in Urban Spaces." Unpublished doctoral dissertation, University of Southern California, 2003.

Los Angeles County Children's Planning Council. *Children's Scorecard.* Los Angeles: Los Angeles County Children's Planning Council, 2002.

Los Angeles County Department of Health. *The Health of Angelenos: A Comprehensive Report on the Health of the Residents of Los Angeles County.* Los Angeles: Los Angeles County Department of Health, 2000.

Matei, S., and others. Metamorphosis: A Field Research Methodology for Studying Communication Technology and Community." *Electronic Journal of Communication,* 2001, *11*(2). [http://www.cios.org/getfile/matei_V11n201].

Project for Excellence in Journalism. *The State of the News Media.* Washington, D.C.: Project for Excellence in Journalism, 2004.

U.S. Bureau of the Census. *English Language Proficiency of Spanish Speaking Population. Los Angeles County, California.* Washington, D.C.: U.S. Government Printing Office, 2000. [http://www.census.gov/main/www/cen2000.html].

United Way, Los Angeles. *American Dream Makers, Latino Profiles Study Report.* Los Angeles: United Way, Los Angeles, 2000. [http://www.unitedwayla.org/pfdfiles/ADM.pdf].

CHAPTER TWELVE

THE ROLE OF TELEHOSPICE
IN END-OF-LIFE CARE

Collette M. Clemens, Beverly Davenport Sypher,
Gary C. Doolittle

Each year, more than 885,000 people use the services of one of the thirty-two hundred hospice programs in the United States (National Hospice and Palliative Care Organization, 2002). While this might seem like a fairly large rate, it represents a relatively small portion of those eligible. Although hospice is recognized as a critical part of end-of-life care and nine out of ten Americans agree that dying at home is the ideal, over half of the terminally ill die in a hospital setting. Access, financial constraints, personal preferences, lack of physician referrals, late diagnoses, and the primary caregiver requirement all appear to constrain hospice care.

One proposed solution that has the potential to reduce some of the barriers to hospice care is telemedicine, "a form of telecommunications that delivers health care remotely" (Davis, 1995). It has the potential to overcome the geographical isolation obstacle to timely and quality medical care (Telemedicine Research Center, 1997). "The more contact patients have with health care services, even telemedically, the less likely they are to run to the hospital" ("The Final Hurry," 1997, p. 342), and a reduction in hospital visits means a reduction in health care costs. In 2002, health care workers made 458 million visits to over 6.2 million people at a cost exceeding $33 billion, or approximately $70 to $80 per visit (National Hospice and Palliative Care Organization, 2002).

The Case of Kendallwood's Telehospice Program

To explore the possibilities of telemedicine in the hospice setting, the University of Kansas Medical Center (KUMC) in Kansas City, Kansas, in cooperation with Kendallwood Hospice, also in Kansas City, launched an in-home collaborative project during 1998 to serve hospice patients in both Kansas and Missouri. Telehospice, as it was called, both visually and aurally connects hospice patients and their caregivers with care providers at different locations. This connection (through a camera, television, and telephone) allows patients and caregivers to interact with health care professionals across a new medium and create a new communication context for delivering health care.

The case study presented here was conducted at the beginning of the Kendallwood Telehospice program and points out that Telehospice became much more than the technology itself, even though the technical features made it possible. Through in-depth, focused interviews, hospice patients and caregivers provided firsthand accounts of their experiences with a new use of health communication technology in an acutely sensitive situation. Our focus was not to assess whether end-of-life care was enhanced through this medium; rather, the goal was to understand what sense the caregivers and patients made of Telehospice.

The Participants

Participants were selected from the patient base at Kendallwood Hospice. Archival data provided general demographic information, travel time, and directions to patients' houses. The location of their homes was an important consideration due to the limited range of the connections between the hospice base station and the patients' homes (Doolittle and Allen, 1997). Some participants lived as far as two hours from the Kendallwood Hospice Centers.

In all, seventeen individuals participated in interviews: four patients, six caregivers of patients who are now deceased, and seven individuals who were caregivers at the time of the interviews. Although the number of participants for this study was not large, their experiences demonstrate what can be learned from a small, intensely studied group in a very distinctive setting.

What We Learned

At the onset of each interview, patients talked about their experiences with hospice care. When patients and caregivers talked about hospice, there was an enormous outpouring of positive sentiment. In many respects, Telehospice was constructed as the people who had become a critical part of their life during this incredibly emotional time. The hospice workers were described by the caregivers as "helpful, wonderful, fantastic, good people, excellent, religious, spiritual, and people who simply just care."

In effect, the medium became the person on the other end, but this happened only after a brief overview of the technical aspects of the units. The respondents began by talking about *its* buttons, tools, technical know-how, sounds, and so forth. They also talked about trying to get *it* to work, how *it* was something new so it was a "privilege to have one to use." Others described *it* as cutting edge or "practically out of this world; it was just kind of awesome, I'd say," and a great many people talked about Telehospice as a combination of a television and a telephone.

Not unexpectedly, the descriptions of Telehospice began with technical details, but the neutral messages about cables and wires were overpowered rather quickly by the possibilities and pitfalls of this technology. It was in these second-level descriptions that the technology transformed into a person. In effect, it was personified, it acted, and it was constrained. "It" helped, "it" comforted, "it" provided security, but "it" also acted differently in different situations.

Telehospice was seen as help (answers and assistance in their care-giving efforts), as security (reassurance that emergencies could be addressed quickly with the help of health professionals), as useful (capable of doing something they might be unable or ill equipped to do on their own), as comfort (a relief, consolation, or support), as access (a means to get care much quicker or in rural areas, to get any hospice care at all). Finally, Telehospice was considered easy to use and nonthreatening. As the medium took on human-like qualities, the picture grew in complexity.

Descriptions about help varied. Some described specific instances, and others provided the general examples of help. One caregiver said, "The nurse can look at her body and kinda decide what's hurting her and what she needs." Another said, "You just feel like the nurse is there with you helping you with the patient at the time. And she can see what's going on better than you can tell someone what's going on."

Another woman who cared for her ill mother talked about the security Telehospice presented: "I always felt better when I got off the system. Because when I got off the system, I know someone in a short while, someone is going to be coming through that door. That was one of the reasons why I felt so much better. But had they not, I'm sure they would have relieved my fears by assessing the situation and explaining it to me to the extent to where I would not have been upset. I would have been okay."

Such examples illustrate situation-specific advantages, both tangible and emotional, for placing the units in the homes of hospice patients. Each of the caregivers' stories suggests that the communication made possible because of the technology was not just part of Telehospice; it was, in fact, hospice care. Mediated communication, in this sense, constituted a secure community of caring.

Part of that caring was captured in expressions of Telehospice as comfort or to relieve worry, provide consolation, relieve pain, or simply provide some tangible form of support. One woman stated, "It's knowing that there's someone somewhere who cares, and when I don't know what to do, they do. It's a source, it's a consolation, and it's peace of mind."

Telehospice also made palliative care possible for some who had no other end-of-life options. Kansas has a fairly dispersed population, and several of the hospice patients and caregivers visited as part of this project were an hour or two from the base office or from nurses' homes. This distance made it difficult for health care professionals to get to them quickly, and even more difficult for them to get to health professionals. Not surprisingly, another recurring theme in the participants' talk was the issue of access. A widowed woman, who had lost her husband just four days prior to the interview and lived several miles outside an urban area on an unmarked dirt road, shared this: "There is times that our roads get pretty bad and drifted and we never know what they're gonna do. And they said they could see him, they could do a lot with how he was looking." They could not have, and probably would not have, she said, gotten any help had they not had Telehospice.

Access is also linked to ease of use. Caregivers seemed almost surprised at how easy the technology was to use. They repeatedly said it was just a matter of pushing a few buttons, getting everything going, and then the connection was up and running. This may account for their early conversational switch to other aspects of the technology.

Conversely, hospice patients and their caregivers described what most felt was one of the biggest disadvantages of Telehospice: the shortcomings of the technology itself and limited sound and picture quality. One family had a hard time making a connection. They had the equipment but never could connect with a picture of the nurse. After loading updated software, they were able to make the unit work, but the caregiver had already formed negative opinions about the technology, and at the time of the interview, she had yet to use the equipment. A few others had problems with the small buttons on the units. There were also problems reported with the overall picture quality. Most complained of a jumpy picture.

While Telehospice possibilities were mostly thought to be constrained by technological difficulties, about a third of those interviewed worried that it depersonalized their hospice care, was an intrusion in their home, and substituted for face-to-face interactions. Consequently, the usefulness of it was questioned, but only three families felt Telehospice had little to no use, and their comments constituted only 9 percent of the total. This small percentage suggests even those who felt Telehospice was useless did not talk about it in much detail, and such scattered perceptions were overshadowed by the stronger, more elaborate, and vivid descriptions of possibilities.

Even so, some people conveyed a dislike for the system, and others said they would rather see the nurse in person, even though they felt positive overall about Telehospice. "I like that," one patient said pointing to the unit, "but I still like to see the nurse. See the nurse only comes out once a week and I know it takes a load off her, but sometimes I'd like to see her more often." As a caregiver pointed out, "It was neat, but it's just not like having Alma [a nurse] here to pat my hand and kiss me goodbye."

An even smaller percentage of the families felt the units were more than unessential: they saw them as disruptive. One respondent said, "It cluttered the house as far as I was concerned. Well, it sat on the kitchen table. Anyway when he got really bad sick, he wouldn't be able to go to the table anyway. And we didn't have a place in our bedroom to put it, to hook it up."

To summarize the interview results, participants initially described Telehospice in very neutral, concrete terms (its buttons, cables, and wires), but such understandings quickly developed into the more personal, advantageous, constitutive terms. More than half (55 percent) of the total messages focused on the positive aspects of Telehospice. Another 8 percent focused on the rather neutral technical aspects, and about a third of the messages focused on pitfalls. Clearly, there were more advantages for this technology than disadvantages, and the greatest strengths focused on how it transcended the technology itself and made possible a community of care that might not otherwise exist for those at the end of their life and those who were taking care of them.

Conclusions and Implications

Ultimately, Telehospice provided patients and caregivers with help when a care team member could not be physically present in their homes. The participants constructed a sense of security that someone was visually there twenty-four hours a day, seven days a week if necessary. "It"—the product, the process, and the interpretation of both—provided access to care and a resultant sense of comfort and ease.

Perhaps the most interesting and illuminating development was the apparent shift in respondents' descriptions. The "them" (nurses, volunteers, and other helpers) who provided help, comfort, and security became an "it" (Telehospice), which took on those same roles. While this type of technology was not developed to substitute for hands-on in-home care, it has been socially constructed as a way to extend the hospice philosophy by augmenting traditional care as well as creating a new kind of care that broadens the meaning of "giving more life to each day."

In essence, Telehospice is a communication context for hospice health care professionals, hospice patients, and their caregivers. For most of the users, this technology and the sense made of it influenced how death was experienced and care was managed. Participants saw this technology as helpful, comforting, and secure. In effect, it took on a life and gave more life, reasons enough to explore further the possibilities of Telehospice. This case study demonstrates how in-home communication technology can reinvent the possibilities of hospice care.

As the world of health care changes to an increased emphasis on relationships between providers, insurers, and patients, technology can play an increasing role in developing relationship-centered health care communities. Of course, programs like Telehospice are hardly a panacea for health care improvements and access. There are very real concerns about the depersonalized feelings some participants expressed in this study. At the same time, this study highlights how telemedicine can provide access to health care for those who have few, if any other, options, especially in terms of end-of-life care.

The findings also suggest new areas of research and new technological capabilities that have not been considered. Specifically, this case study points to the emotionally and physically challenging job of the caregiver and helps us understand how the requirements of this role may constrain hospice participation. A neglected aspect of Telehospice, and perhaps of hospice care in general, is the social support needed for caregivers to sustain their roles. The technology that supported this project could have been exploited more fully to connect caregivers with one another. The technology could connect them with one another in the same way that it connected them and the patients with health care professionals. The capability, know-how, and perhaps motivation are there. The possibility for another level of health care is made possible by creating virtual support groups for caregivers.

This study deepened our understanding of how mediated communication created health care possibilities in end-of-life situations. The findings provide knowledge that is unique to the specific events in each of these people's lives, but it has prescriptive power for others in similar situations. It presents what Chen and Pearce (1995) call "local knowledge" and "practical wisdom." It also presents what Ostwald (1962, p. 312) calls "wisdom in action, and hence a moral intelligence." It reminds us that we have an ethical responsibility as researchers to be sensitive, respectful, understanding, and careful in our judgments and recommendations. Ultimately, we must remember that hospice, the care beyond the cure, is a telemedically unique and acutely sensitive context.

Discussion Questions

1. If you were a hospice patient, how do you think you would feel about using this technology as part of your care? Would your feelings change if you were a caregiver? Why or why not?
2. What uses of telemedicine can you think of in addition to those introduced in this case study?
3. What are some limitations of this study? What are the limitations of studying hospice care in general? What are the limitations of case studies in investigations such as this one?
4. What are the strengths of this study? What potential is there in any study of hospice? What are the advantages of the case study method for studying hospice?
5. What kind of ethical responsibilities confront a hospice researcher?
6. What other research do you think needs to be done in the area of Telehospice? More specifically, what questions about Telehospice would you like to have answers to? What methods would you use to generate data to answer these questions?

References

Chen, V., and Pearce, W. B. "Even If a Thing of Beauty, Can a Case Study Be a Joy Forever? A Social Constructionist Approach to Theory and Research." In W. Hurwitz (ed.), *Social Approaches to Communication*. New York: Guilford Press, 1995.

Davis, J. "Telemedicine Begins to Make Its Case." *Fortune*, Nov. 27, 1995. [http://www.fortune.com/fortune/articles/0,15114,375601,00.html.I].

Doolittle, G. C., and Allen, A. "Practicing Oncology via Telemedicine." *Journal of Telemedicine and Telecare*, 1997, *3*, 63–70.

National Hospice and Palliative Care Organization. *NHPCO 2002 National Data Set*. Alexandria, Va.: National Hospice and Palliative Care Organization, 2002. [http://www.nhpco.org/files/members/2002NationalDataSet.pdf].

Ostwald, M. (trans). *Nicomachean Ethics*. Indianapolis: Bobbs-Merrill, 1962.

Telemedicine Research Center. "Telemedicine Information Exchange." Jan. 29, 1997. [http://tie.telemed.org/scripts/getpage.pl?page=whatis].

CHAPTER THIRTEEN

DOCTOR AND PATIENT INTERACTIONS DURING TELEMEDICINE

Clashes of Perceptions and Reality

Jeanine W. Turner, James D. Robinson, Adil Alaoui,
James F. Winchester, Alan Neustadtl, Walid Gabriel Tohme,
Betty A. Levine, Jeff Collmann, Seong K. Mun

The doctor walks into his office and turns on a video monitor. Immediately, he views the dialysis unit located fifteen miles away, and a nurse greets him. She pushes the monitor to the bed of the first patient, and the doctor begins to talk to the patient about his condition. After a brief consultation, the nurse asks both the patient and the doctor if they are finished and then wheels the monitor to the next dialysis chair.

This scenario describes the type of telemedicine discussed in this case study. We focus on the changing dynamics involved in moving a communication encounter from a face-to-face environment to a virtual environment and discuss what that might mean to the participants involved. The mediated environment changes the context for interaction, and in changing the context it transforms many of the assumptions about clinical encounters.

This project was funded in whole with federal funds from the National Library of Medicine under contract N01-LM-6–3544.

Project Phoenix

This case study is part of a larger study called Project Phoenix, a telemedicine program funded by the National Library of Medicine that used a personal computer–based telemedicine system to manage end-stage renal disease (ESRD) patients on hemodialysis at Georgetown University Medical Center. The doctor in the case study is a nephrologist at Georgetown University Medical Center. Prior to this telemedicine project, the doctor made rounds at the medical center and at a dialysis unit called Union Plaza about fifteen miles away. The unpredictability of Washington, D.C., traffic could turn a fifteen-minute trip across town into a two-hour ordeal. The doctor completed his rounds twice a week.

Once the telemedicine system was set up, he continued to see the patients in person at Georgetown (thirty-five patients) twice a week. He saw his patients at Union Plaza (forty-three patients) once in person and once over the telemedicine system. Although an ideal study would have had no in-person interactions at Union Plaza, to comply with District of Columbia regulations, he visited each patient once in person for a traditional visit and once over telemedicine. (For a full description of this study and its analysis, see Turner and others, 2003.)

Perceptions of Telemedicine

Many times during the research of telemedicine, the focus of attention is on the technology and its ability to replicate traditional clinical encounters. This study focuses on the difference between the two settings. Specifically, it examines communication. As communication involves multiple individuals with multiple perspectives, understanding what each individual brings to the telemedicine encounter is important. With telemedicine, using some type of communication technology, health care occurs within a virtual environment created by the verbal and nonverbal communication cues made available. This added complication makes the study of communication in this environment all the more interesting. The focus of this study was to gain insight into the changing nature of the virtual environment and its impact on the communication taking place.

Traditional provider-patient communication involves two main tasks: information exchange and relationship development (Cegala and others, 1996). One study of patient satisfaction with videoconferencing-based teleconsultations found that patients were satisfied with telemedicine on both dimensions but more satisfied with the informational dimension than the relational dimension (Mekhjian and others, 1999). This study examined the conditions under which telemedicine might be deemed appropriate from both a health care practitioner and a patient perspective.

The Study

First, we engaged in participant observation in person and using telemedicine to study the communicative interactions that took place between the doctor and the patient. We observed the patients as they interacted with the doctor for six months. During this time, we noted the topics of conversation that were introduced. We were not trying to distinguish between the two settings at this time but rather seeking to develop a list of topics discussed. With this list of topics, we then developed a coding scheme for analyzing the sessions themselves. We also used these observation sessions to develop an interview guide for exploring patient and health care practitioner perceptions of telemedicine interactions.

We conducted interviews with twelve of the patients at the telemedicine site along with one nurse and one physician. The patient interviews took place at the end of their dialysis session and averaged forty-five minutes to an hour in length. Two researchers were present: one conducted the interview, and the other took extensive notes. At the end of each session, these notes were typed and compiled. The researchers discussed the interview and added to the notes where necessary. Direct quotations from patients were noted in order to record the patients' actual words whenever possible. Finally, we coded conversations between the doctor and patient by indicating on a coding sheet each time a specific topic was introduced into the conversation (Exhibit 13.1).

Between May 1998 and March 1999, we coded 147 patient encounters. Fifty-one were face-to-face encounters at the telemedicine-enhanced site, forty-seven were telemedicine encounters at the telemedicine-enhanced site, and forty-nine were face-to-face encounters at the control site. All patient encounters were coded using the same physician. Three coders were trained in use of the coding scheme, and they maintained an inter-coder agreement of .95 indicating close to complete agreement on the coded items (Holsti, 1969). If the topic came up during the interaction, the topic received a 1; if not, it was coded 0. A section was added so that the coder could insert anything that occurred during the interaction that was not included in the coding scheme.

Interview Results

Separate interviews were conducted with patients and practitioners to gain insight into these perceptions from key groups.

EXHIBIT 13.1. TOPICS RAISED DURING DOCTOR-PATIENT INTERACTIONS.

Topics Raised
- Social or nonclinical topics
- Routine checks
- Medication refills*
- Access problems*
- Change in dialysis*
- Referrals to other specialists*
- Medication changes*
- Medication orders*
- Travel-related concerns
- Labs and reports
- Patient complaints
- Family discussions
- Confidential discussions
- Patient education

Special Situations
- Need for physical checks (by the nurse or physician)
- Physician interruptions
- Times when the patient refused to interact
- Technical problems

*Topics that the interview patients suggested were equivocal situations requiring a face-to-face interaction.

Patient Perspectives

A patient who is seeking medical care is experiencing some uncertainty. This uncertainty can range from little to great, depending on the patient's familiarity with the condition and provider. For example, a patient who discovers a lump in her breast may experience high uncertainty about her condition because she does not know what the lump means, but feels comfortable with her physician because she has been seeing that doctor for many years. Another patient with a chronic illness who has moved to a new area of the country may experience low uncertainty about the condition but high uncertainty about a new physician. Telemedicine is introducing an additional uncertainty: a new context for receiving care. Patients are familiar with seeing a physician in a face-to-face environment in a doctor's office, and telemedicine transforms that environment.

Within this study, patients were familiar with the physician and were experiencing a chronic illness. We asked them under what conditions they would like to experience a telemedicine consultation. The patients' responses can be categorized within different stages of uncertainty: low, moderate, and extreme. During low periods of uncertainty, patients suggested that telemedicine provided a wonderful tool. Increased access to the physician allowed patients to receive a routine check of their symptoms to make sure that things were okay. Said one patient, "If there are no problems . . . H_2O okay, blood pressure okay . . . you should be fine. . . . then telemedicine works great." Another patient said, "Telemedicine is great for people who only need to see their doctor once a month." During periods of extreme uncertainty, for example, a crisis situation, patients also felt telemedicine was a great alternative. For example, if a patient had a precipitous drop in blood pressure while connected to the dialysis machine at the clinic and the doctor was not there, telemedicine offered a great opportunity. The physician could quickly be available to the patient; without telemedicine, this access would not be possible.

However, patients noted that during periods of moderate uncertainty—for example, a medication needed to be changed or the patient had a problem with a graft or access site—then the patients felt face-to-face consultation would be a better option. Some patients even suggested that they might save information from a telemedicine visit to a face-to-face visit to make sure that it was communicated correctly. For example, one patient suggested that medication changes required an in-person visit: "It's [telemedicine] pretty good but when the doctor changes your prescription. I wait until the doctor comes in person; then I get the prescription myself and take it to the pharmacy." Another patient noted, "Yesterday they couldn't stick me right. I would have liked to have Dr. W here to look at my abscess and talk to the nurse about it."

The interviews with the patients indicated that their acceptance of telemedicine as an alternative to traditional care varied depending on their condition. During periods of low uncertainty (essentially maintenance of their illness) or high uncertainty (when they were happy with any access to the doctor), they felt telemedicine was effective. However, during periods of moderate uncertainty, the patients preferred face-to-face consultation. These differing perceptions suggest that the "presence" offered by telemedicine is different from the presence offered in a traditional face-to-face encounter. A comment from a patient that underlines this point suggested that it was easier to lie over telemedicine. He said, "After a holiday weekend when I have not kept to my diet the way I am supposed to, it is much easier to lie about what I ate over telemedicine than to look at Dr. W in the eye. When he is here, I feel more guilty about it than when he is in his office."

Health Care Practitioner Perspectives

The nurses and physician we talked to had interesting perspectives to share about telemedicine. None of them could pinpoint a time during the three-year implementation of the telemedicine system that they needed a face-to-face encounter rather than telemedicine to resolve a particular issue. Returning to the uncertainty paradigm, it makes sense that the health care practitioners would face a different degree of uncertainty than the patients did. Since the health care practitioners were familiar with treating dialysis patients, there were few situations that would create a moderate or even high degree of uncertainty about treatment options. As a result, it may be that telemedicine was appropriate from the health care practitioners' perspectives because they, like the patients, enjoyed telemedicine as an alternative under periods of low uncertainty. The key distinction between the two groups is that patients often had different perceptions of uncertainty than the health care practitioners did.

The nurses commented that they liked the control over the clinical encounter that telemedicine gave them. During telemedicine encounters, the nurse decided when the encounter was over. She (all the nurses at the unit were female) decided when to move the monitor to the next bed. During face-to-face interactions, the nurse followed the doctor's lead as he moved from patient to patient.

The physician noted that telemedicine was effective from a clinical practice perspective but added that it became monotonous after a while. He tended to get bored sitting in one location viewing patient after patient. He also perceived that the telemedicine interactions took longer when in fact there were no significant differences in the time it took to perform a telemedicine consultation versus a traditional consultation.

Analysis of Communication Behaviors

The interviews with the patients suggested that they approached telemedicine encounters differently than they approached a traditional clinical encounter. To determine whether their actual behavior matched these perceptions, we coded their conversation topics during telemedicine encounters and compared them to their traditional face-to-face encounters, as well as a control group. We found no significant difference in the number of topics introduced in telemedicine interactions versus those in the face-to-face or control sessions. Therefore, although patients suggested that they might save information to discuss during face-to-face settings, the coded behaviors do not suggest that.

While patients perceived differences between traditional and telemedicine settings, the health care practitioners were quick to note that they treated the two conditions the same. However, we found that the physician was interrupted during face-to-face encounters, whereas we did not find any evidence of interruptions during telemedicine interactions. Specifically, while treating a patient at the dialysis clinic, the physician was sometimes called away to answer a question or respond to a telephone call. The fact that the two conditions (telemedicine versus traditional) were treated differently by others may be a reflection of the newness of the technology and an initial reluctance to interrupt a technology session. As the newness wears off, interruptions may be more likely.

Finally, the fact that the physician felt bored during telemedicine points to the very different presence offered by the two conditions. During a face-to-face clinical encounter, he is in charge, moving much like a celebrity from one fan to the next. He holds court and is the center of attention in the room with nurses following behind him. Telemedicine provides a very different situation. The nurse is now in charge and is in control of the cues that the physician hears and sees. During a face-to-face visit, the physician can hurry the encounter along through his nonverbal behavior. During a telemedicine encounter, the nurse determines when all of the questions have been resolved.

Major Findings from the Study

This study of telemedicine suggests several interesting findings:

- Perceptions do not always match actual behavior.
- Patients' perceptions of uncertainty during a clinical encounter do not necessarily match those of their health care provider.
- The uncertainty created by the illness or concern may influence a patient's acceptance of telemedicine.
- Communication environments created through telemedicine vary from that of a traditional encounter.

Implications for Telemedicine Development and Diffusion

What kind of implications do these findings have for telemedicine deployment? First, this study underlines the important perspective of the consumer patient. It does not matter how many research findings report no significant difference between telemedicine and traditional interactions: a patient who perceives them differently may approach them differently. Therefore, a patient with an opportunity for telemedicine or a face-to-face encounter may make this decision based on comfort level with her or his condition. Telemedicine's effectiveness from the health care practitioner's perspective must also be balanced with the patient's perceived sense of its effectiveness.

Similarly, although the patient reported acting differently depending on whether he or she received telemedicine or a face-to-face encounter, the results suggest the patient did not. Therefore, the critical decision in attracting a patient to a telemedicine setting is during the preperception stage when making decisions about whether to try it. From a health care practitioner perspective, this study illustrates how telemedicine changes the context of the clinical encounter in many communicative ways. The nurse is given an elevated role in the encounter, and the physician loses some autonomy because he or she must rely on the eyes and ears of the nurse. Finally, although quantitative differences in topics introduced were not detected, qualitative differences in the actual conversations may vary between conditions. For example, the patient who feels more comfortable lying during telemedicine interactions provides an interesting insight into the changes in the cues present within telemedicine encounters.

Telemedicine creates an interesting communicative environment for understanding health care delivery. This case study opens up many issues to consider when assessing the viability of telemedicine for the delivery of care.

Discussion Questions

1. If people perceive they will communicate differently during telemedicine than they actually do, what are the implications of this when marketing telemedicine services?
2. We noted that the changing communication dynamic changed the role relationships and power between the doctor and the nurse. Do you see these changes being stabilized, or will the system find a way to revert back to the traditional power relationships?
3. How can patients' perceptions regarding telemedicine interactions influence implementation of these systems?
4. How can what we learned about health care practitioner perceptions influence future implementation of telemedicine systems?
5. Under what conditions would you be comfortable with a videoconferencing-based telemedicine interaction? Why?

References

Cegala, D., and others. "Components of Patients' and Doctors' Perceptions of Communication Competence During a Primary Care Interview." *Health Communication*, 1996, *8*, 1–27.

Holsti, O. R. *Content Analysis for the Social Sciences and Humanities.* Reading, Mass.: Addison-Wesley, 1969.

Mekhjian, H., and others. "Patient Satisfaction with Telemedicine in a Prison Environment." *Journal of Telemedicine and Telecare*, 1999, *5*, 55–61.

Turner, J. W., and others. "Understanding the Contribution of Context to the Communication Environment of telemedicine Interactions." *Health Care Management Review,* 2003, *28*(2), 7–18.

PART FOUR

OUTCOMES

If we knew what it was we were doing, it would not be called research, would it?
ALBERT EINSTEIN

CHAPTER FOURTEEN

TELETHERAPY FOR CHILDHOOD DEPRESSION

Where Is the Evidence?

Eve-Lynn Nelson

Sam was not only the best rebounder on his basketball team, but he was the class math whiz and his scouting group's star. But my first interaction with Sam was following an intentional overdose. Over the past few months, Sam's friends no longer called because he yelled at them over nothing. His grades slipped, and he wanted to sleep all the time. He just didn't care anymore. What had changed in Sam's life?

Just like Sam, one in forty children and one in twelve adolescents experience depression. The symptoms affect every aspect of a child's life, interfering with academic, social, and family functioning. Children with depression experience the same symptoms as do adults with depression. They have problems with mood, particularly irritability; problems with concentrating; problems with behavior, including agitation or lethargy; and problems with physiological regulation, including changes in appetite, sleep, and energy (American Psychiatric Association, 1994).

Psychologists at Kansas University Medical Center (KUMC) see children with depression in their offices every day. But for every child seen, approximately two children go without services (Wu and others, 2001). Despite the high morbidity associated with childhood depression—suicide is the third leading cause of child and adolescent death—many barriers to care get in the way of treatment. Many patients live hours from KUMC and have no child psychiatrists or psychologists in their counties. Telemedicine provides specialty mental health care at a distance. For example, children like Sam are often seen in Kansas's rural telemedicine outreach clinics (Ermer, 1999) and in the TeleKidcare setting (Cain and others, 2001).

Tele–Mental Health

Effective treatments for childhood depression exist, including psychotherapy and medication options (Barnard, 2003). One of the most effective options is cognitive behavioral therapy (CBT), which involves challenging negative cognitions and increasing adaptive behaviors. Telemedicine offers one way to match effective treatments with children with depression. Clinical telemedicine has been used in almost every imaginable clinical setting and specialty (Krupinski and others, 2002). Tele–mental health services began over forty years ago (Baer, Elford, and Cukor, 1997) and have been described across diagnoses, including posttraumatic stress disorder (Deitsch, Frueh, and Santos, 2000), gender identity issues (Ghosh, McLaren, and Watson, 1997), depression (Cerda, Hilty, Hales, and Nesbitt, 1999), anxiety (Manchanda and McLaren, 1998), agoraphobia (Cowain, 2001), and eating disorders (Bakke, Mitchell, Wonderlich, and Erickson, 2001). Case studies with children suggest effective treatment over interactive televideo (ITV) for oppositional defiant disorder (Rendon, 1999), family conflict (Paul, 1999), and externalizing behaviors (Miller and others, 2002). Across twenty-nine tele–mental health studies, Miller (2003) found positive results in terms of satisfaction and doctor-patient communication.

Tele-mental health generates strong opinions ranging from, "It's obviously the same as face-to-face care" to "It's obviously a second-rate system." Such opinion has real impact on the ability to provide telehealth services, as clinicians face reimbursement difficulties, licensing challenges, and privacy concerns. Mental health providers in Kansas found such mixed reactions. Families receiving psychotherapy over interactive televideo have been overwhelmingly satisfied with services (Ermer, 1999). They praise the system for allowing them to get help without having to travel miles or wait months to see a professional. But other professionals and potential telehealth sites are more skeptical about tele–mental health services. Numerous "what-ifs" are raised, including worries that an adequate therapeutic relationship cannot be established over the technology and that the clinician will miss important diagnostic and treatment indicators.

The best way to answer these divergent opinions is to complete research. But such data are difficult to collect because randomized controlled trials are expensive and time-consuming, require systematic data management, and are logistically challenging when working with clinics across a wide geographical area. For example, Hersh and others (2001) found only 25 articles out of the 4,628 reviewed articles that met their criteria: head-to-head comparison between traditional and ITV care.

This case study focuses on the story of conducting a randomized controlled trial in the telehealth setting. The goal is to describe different problems and solutions in research. Sam will guide us as he moves from study participant to study completer.

Challenge 1: Design and Redesign

The design was a work in progress over the eight-month course of planning. From a pure science perspective, the first design was the best possible model to address the research question and rule out alternative causes. The subsequent designs were the best possible designs balancing the ideal scientific model with ethical concerns and recruitment practicalities.

Design 1

The original design called for children with depression to be randomly assigned to three different conditions: cognitive-behavioral therapy over ITV, cognitive–behavioral therapy face-to-face, or a wait list control of educational materials and standard care. The standard of care was referral to the community mental health center and other local providers. This three-group design is the most powerful way to answer how the treatment delivery system affects outcome. The design tests whether change can be attributed to the intervention rather than just getting better over time.

Design 2

The first design revision was in response to Internal Review Board (IRB) concerns. The researchers completed three IRB reviews through KUMC, Kansas University, and the school system targeted for recruitment. The IRB did not accept the community standard of care as an ethically acceptable control condition, even though the families would have been eligible for the treatment at KUMC following the eight-week wait list time. This set the bar higher for the tele–mental health intervention. It had to be shown equivalent to or more advantageous than the best possible clinic-based care rather than to the community standard received by most children.

The new design was a simplified two-group design. Children with depression were randomized to either therapy over ITV or therapy face-to-face. This allowed the researchers to address the central treatment delivery question: How does face-to-face intervention compare with the same intervention over interactive televideo? The IRB also raised concerns about long-term treatment. In response, all participants received psychotherapy and referral as needed at no charge for one year.

Design 3

Initially, the researchers planned to use the school-based TeleKidcare systems. Begun in 1998, TeleKidcare is the country's first school-based telemedicine program. KUMC partnered with the Kansas City, Kansas, school system to increase access to health care for urban students. TeleKidcare uses PC-based interactive televideo to link the school nurse's office to the KUMC health care provider. In planning the telehealth depression study, the TeleKidcare school nurses were very enthusiastic about the project. They gave compelling examples of children in their schools who struggled with depression and faced numerous stressors, from losing family members to violence to repeatedly failing classes. But due to time and recruitment considerations, the final technology selection was two ITV units based on-site at KUMC. Because of this implementation change, the research question was one of treatment efficacy: whether therapy over ITV leads to improvements comparable to therapy face-to-face.

Challenge 2: Getting and Keeping Participants

Recruitment and retention were two of the greatest challenges in implementing the research protocol. Challenges related to the stringent inclusion criteria and the multiple sessions required for therapy completion.

Recruitment

Recruitment was done in urban, suburban, and parochial school districts. Many strategies were used to get the word out about the project. Some were broad tactics: advertising in the local parents' newspaper, sending out over fifteen hundred letters to school personnel, meeting personally with over a hundred school representatives, and attending school events to pass out brochures. Not surprisingly, the most effective strategy was personal contacts. One example was meeting with local school nurses through providing free continuing-education lectures about childhood depression. The researcher also had to answer misinformation that was circulated about the program, such as the rumor that the study was funded by the pharmaceutical industry to promote a particular medication.

Enrollment and Dropout

The project received 112 general inquiries from schools, health professionals, and parents about possible referral to the program. From this, 66 evaluations were completed, resulting in 51 children qualifying for the study. Three-quarters of children qualifying for the study enrolled. Enrollment and dropout were consistent over the sixteen-month enrollment period and did not vary across groups. As in many other studies, recruitment started painfully slowly and gained momentum right as recruitment was ending, largely based on increasing referral from the same sources and other families who had participated in the study.

Thirty-eight families enrolled, and twenty-eight families completed the study. The reasons for dropout included "too busy for the appointment," "feels the child is doing better and no longer needs intervention," "poor parent/guardian health," "moving," and "entering the juvenile justice system." Each child recruited had a unique story and presenting symptoms that cannot be fully captured by the research results. As a case study, I describe how one participant, Sam, completed each component of study and challenges around implementation.

Challenge 3: Getting Started

At the time of the study, Sam, a Caucasian male, was eleven years old. He attended a suburban school and lived with his mother in a single-parent household. Like the majority of children in the study, he presented not only with mood concerns but also with attention-deficit hyperactivity symptoms. He had a family history of both mood and anxiety disorders. He had been moody in the past, but was irritable more days than not and had made a suicide attempt. He wanted to stay in the house all the time and no longer had any appetite. In addition, he was experiencing many stressors, including no friends due to his irritability and bossiness, a drop in grades due to difficulty concentrating, and frequent arguments with his mother over anything and everything.

Answering Questions

Before enrollment in the study, Sam and his mother completed a standardized interview and questionnaires to evaluate Sam for Major Depressive Disorder, as formally defined by the *Diagnostic and Statistical Manual of Mental Disorders* (DSM-IV; American Psychiatric Association, 1994). Two outside raters had to agree the child met the strict depression criteria before he could be enrolled in the research protocol. It is important to have therapy options for children who do not meet the full depression criteria. But research protocol requires a clear definition of the targeted population.

Next Steps

Because he met the depression criteria, Sam was eligible for participation in the study, and like 75 percent of those eligible, his family chose to enroll. The next step was completing the consent and assent process. Through the IRB process, the consent form grew to a ten-page document that parents frequently found difficult to understand. In trying to describe every possible detail and risk associated with the project, the final consent was often more confusing than enlightening to many parents. Sam also had to complete two assents based on the differing requirements of KUMC and Kansas University IRBs. After agreeing to participate, Sam was randomized to a treatment group: by coin toss, Sam was part of the ITV condition.

Working Together

The next step was following the CBT protocol with Sam and his mother. By family and therapist report, all treatment elements were feasibly implemented in the ITV and face-to-face groups. Because Sam was in the ITV condition, care was taken to make sure materials were available on both the tele-therapist and patient side. For example, when completing the Feelings and Thoughts worksheet, there was a copy for the therapist and for Sam in his ITV room.

Like most other school-aged children, Sam was curious about the technology. In addition, he was impulsive and prone to touch things without thinking, such as pretending to be a rock star using the system microphone. Part of this is positive and reflects comfort using the technology and talking over the system. But the researchers attempted to "child-proof" the telemedicine room, such as removing as many technological distractors as possible, as well as setting ground rules with the participants about appropriate use of the equipment, such as, "Do not touch the keyboard." Similar limit setting was done in the face-to-face setting.

In the first session, the therapist explained to Sam that the technology was "special phone lines so we can see and hear each other at the same time." Reassurances were given that unlike regular television, the session could be seen only by Sam and the therapist. It was also important to set clear expectations about therapy because the therapist has less control over the participants. For example, Sam's mother was instructed ahead of time to wait in the waiting room during the child portion of the session rather than waiting out of view of the camera or right outside the ITV-room door. There was only one equipment difficulty across Sam's eight sessions, and this required rebooting the systems.

Posttest

At the end of the study, Sam and his mother completed the same interview as the beginning of the study. They also completed the self-report measures concerning behavior and satisfaction.

Following treatment, Sam no longer met the DSM-IV criteria for childhood depression, just as 82 percent of the other children treated in the study. Importantly, the ITV and face-to-face groups did not differ significantly in the number of children who, like Sam, no longer were depressed at the end of the study.

Discussion

Sam is a telehealth success story of one. Over the course of the eight sessions, his depression remitted, and he made gains in psychological, social, family, and academic functioning. Sam was presented as an example participant. "Sam" could have been the most popular girl struggling with her father's death or the least popular second grader benefiting from basic social skills. The randomized controlled trial allows the researcher to look at the group of participants as a whole and provides valuable information about how effective the telehealth intervention was across diverse children.

Sam's case example is compelling, but only the efficacy design can address the mixed opinions about telehealth presented in the introduction. Randomized controlled trials answer the question, "Where's the evidence?" Comparing the ITV group and the traditional group leads to the persuasive response that teletherapy is as effective as the same treatment presented face-to-face for this group of children with depression.

Future Applications and Conclusion

The next telehealth step is implementing a similar telemedicine treatment protocol within the community. This meets telehealth's goal to take the best possible treatments and provide access to individuals who would otherwise be unable to receive care. There are many exciting possibilities for catching the children with depression who currently go without treatment. Telehealth could be used to link therapists miles away with children in rural settings or could be used to link therapists with settings common to the child, such as the school or the pediatrician's office. Collaboration between child psychologists and child psychiatrists using ITV is another area for clinical investigation.

But many research questions must be addressed as this research moves from the controlled KUMC environment to the community setting. A "one-size-fits-all" approach will not work when implementing telehealth protocols such as this in each community. Factors to consider include the urban or rural setting, the telemedicine room setup, the presenter, the format, the session characteristics, the outcome measures, the patient population, and the treatment package. Efficacy trials must also contend with adapting to the ever-changing technology and develop protocols across delivery systems. Multisite trials with comparable measures will be the best way to address how each component affects treatment outcome and acceptability.

Future research will address questions about diagnostic accuracy over ITV, as well as long-term follow-up using the technology. Researchers may investigate not only whether depression recurs but also whether the telehealth treatment may delay recurrence, may decrease the intensity and duration of future episodes, and may increase the recovery time given treatment booster sessions.

We now have research evidence that this tele–mental health intervention works. But the researchers must put back on their clinician and advocate hats to make use of the information. The data alone will not change minds or bring services to children. Clinical researchers must use the full range of communication strategies to educate the public about options and to persuade funders, including granting agencies and insurance providers, about the value of these telehealth services.

Discussion Questions

1. Detail the advantages and disadvantages of relying on individual case studies and satisfaction studies in telehealth versus randomized controlled trials.
2. Outline ethical dilemmas in the design, implementation, and interpretation of telehealth efficacy trials.
3. What are the potential challenges to conducting a diagnostic accuracy trial for childhood depression evaluated over ITV?
4. What communication strategies could one use to get the word out about the results of telehealth efficacy trials such as this?
5. Describe how you could apply the lessons from the case study in setting up a randomized controlled trial in a different telehealth specialty.

References

American Psychiatric Association. *Diagnostic and Statistical Manual of Mental Disorders.* (4th ed). Washington, D.C.: American Psychiatric Association, 1994.

Baer, L., Elford, R., and Cukor, P. "Telepsychiatry at Forty: What Have We Learned?" *Harvard Review of Psychiatry*, 1997, *5*, 7–17.

Bakke, B., Mitchell, J., Wonderlich, S., and Erickson, R. "Administering Cognitive-Behavioral Therapy for Bulimia Nervosa via Telemedicine in Rural Settings." *International Journal of Eating Disorders*, 2001, *30*(4), 454–457.

Barnard, M. U. *Helping Your Depressed Child.* Oakland, Calif.: New Harbinger, 2003.

Cain, S., and others. "Telepsychiatry Services in an Urban School District for 2000–2001." Poster session at the meeting of the American Academy of Child and Adolescent Psychiatry, Honolulu, 2001.

Cerda, G. M., Hilty, D. M., Hales, R. E., and Nesbitt, T. S. "Use of Telemedicine with Ethnic Groups." *Psychiatric Services*, 1999, *50*(10), 1364.

Cowain, T. "Cognitive-Behavioral Therapy via Videoconferencing to a Rural Area." *Australian and New Zealand Journal of Psychiatry*, 2001, *35*(1), 62–64.

Deitsch, S. E., Frueh, B. C., and Santos, A. B. "Telepsychiatry for Post-Traumatic Stress Disorder." *Journal of Telemedicine and Telecare*, 2000, *6*(3), 184–186.

Ermer, D. "Experience with a Rural Telepsychiatry Clinic for Children and Adolescents." *Psychiatric Services*, 1999, *50*(2), 260–261.

Ghosh, G. J., McLaren, P. M., and Watson, J. P. "Evaluating the Alliance in Videolink Psychotherapy." *Journal of Telemedicine and Telecare*, 1997, *3*, 33–35.

Hersh, W. R., and others. "Clinical Outcomes Resulting from Telemedicine Interventions: A Systematic Review." *BMC Medical Information and Decision Making*, 2001, *1*(1), 5.

Krupinski, E., and others. "Clinical Applications in Telemedicine/Telehealth." *Telemedicine Journal*, 2002, *8*(1), 13–48.

Manchanda, M., and McLaren, P. "Cognitive Behaviour Therapy via Interactive Video." *Journal of Telemedicine and Telecare*, 1998, *4*(Suppl. 1), 53–55.

Miller, E. A. "Telepsychiatry and Doctor-Patient Communication—An Analysis of the Empirical Literature." In R. Wootton, P. Yellowlees, and P. McLaren (eds.), *Telepsychiatry and e-Mental Health.* London: Royal Society of Medicine Press, 2003.

Miller, T. W., and others. "Telemedicine: A Child Psychiatry Case Report." *Telemedicine Journal*, 2002, *8*(1), 139–141.

Paul, N. "Telepsychiatry, the Satellite System and Family Consultation." *Journal of Telemedicine and Telecare*, 1999, *3*(Suppl. 1), 52–53.

Rendon, M. "Telepsychiatric Treatment of a Schoolchild." *Journal of Telemedicine and Telecare*, 1999, *4*(3), 179–182.

Wu, P., and others. "Depressive and Disruptive Disorders and Mental Health Service Utilization in Children and Adolescents." *Psychiatric Services*, 2001, *52*, 189–195.

CHAPTER FIFTEEN

SERVING CHILDREN WITH DISABILITIES IN RURAL IOWA

Dennis C. Harper

Why can't we have these services in our town? I can't afford to leave work for so long, but I can't afford not to get them for my child.

PARENT OF A SPECIAL NEEDS CHILD

Children and youth with special needs present a complex array of health care requirements that remain throughout their life span. The health care needs referred to in this chapter include chronic health disabilities (diabetes, epilepsy, cystic fibrosis), developmental and behavioral disorders (cerebral palsy, spina bifida, attention deficit hyperactivity disorder, mental retardation, autism), and traumatic injuries (traumatic brain injury, spinal cord injuries).

Families usually have to travel substantial distances to obtain services from an interdisciplinary team of pediatric experts. Usually this team needs to relate and consult with local professionals to facilitate treatment recommendations. Traditional service models include the client and family visiting multiple individuals in different clinics or teams of professionals in clinics and the communication of information in the standard written report, whenever it arrives. Much time, energy, often great distances, costs, and long waits for appointments and late communications characterize these traditional evaluation and treatment service systems (Glueckauf, 2002).

One parent consumer noted, "We are still going through the same thing as parents did 30 years ago . . . there is all this new technology . . . if we had telemed-

This project has been funded with federal funds from the National Library of Medicine under contract N01-LM-6–3548.

icine none of this would happen" (Wheeler, 1998, p. 16). It is not surprising that telehealth would be considered for providing multispecialty health care services for children and youth with special needs. As early as the 1990s, professionals in rural New York (Wheeler, 1998) and rural Georgia (Karp and others, 2000) began offering multidisciplinary services to children with special health care needs at remote locations from hospital settings. Remote health care is the future for much of rural America (Antezana, 1997).

Iowa is a rural state with an estimated seventy thousand children who have a variety of developmental disabilities, and parents and professionals often travel long distances to Iowa's tertiary center, the Center for Disabilities and Development (CDD), for evaluation and treatment of children who exhibit complex health care concerns. The CDD is a specialized hospital, part of the University of Iowa Hospitals and Clinics, providing treatment and evaluation for people with chronic health care concerns and disabilities. A telemedicine consultation service for children and youth with health and developmental disorders, using a specialized interdisciplinary team, has been developed and is ongoing. This clinical service is unique in that teams of professionals at both sites, with parents with children present, complete the evaluations. The emphasis of this consultation service is on team-to-team health and behavioral consultation on children and youth in Iowa's school settings. This team-to-team consultation permits comprehensive parent and professional dialogue, professionally guided evaluation procedures, and real-time discussion of evaluation results and treatment recommendations.

Real-time communication is achieved by using the Iowa Communication Network, digital service level three (DS3), which is a 45 Mbps fiber-optic cable network linking ninety-nine counties to eight hundred sites throughout Iowa, located in hospitals, schools, and selected public buildings. This National Library of Medicine–funded project used three studio sites in southwestern rural Iowa, approximately one hundred miles from University Hospitals with a population base of seventy-five thousand families. The three sites (two in educational settings, one in a small regional hospital) all had studios with push-to-talk microphones, Sony large screen monitors, and ceiling-mounted cameras or Sony handheld cameras. Evaluation of these consultation services focused on parents and professional consumers located in rural Iowa. The study answered two overall questions: What services can be effectively provided using telemedicine? and Will rural patients, families, and providers be satisfied with telemedicine consultations?

Telemedicine Encounters

Patients and families of the CDD telemedicine consultations were scheduled cooperatively by the hospital-based scheduling center and a local (distant site) predesignated coordinator. This local coordinator remains a key aspect of such community-based services. When the child and the family arrived at the telemedicine site, the coordinator or team leader of the distant site was responsible for reviewing procedures for the telemedicine conference and dealing with information related to confidentiality, parental consent, and specific session record keeping. The team leader acted as both the case manager and the facilitator for the telemedicine encounter.

A series of protocols for patient presentation and consultation was established prior to the encounters for each clinical area. A general consultation protocol (GCP) was collaboratively developed covering in detail etiquette of telemedicine encounters. This was the guiding template for the evaluation sessions. The GCP was the basis for training new local providers prior to specific consultations. It outlined logistics for sessions, designated leadership and specific responsibilities of participants, processing of confidential releases and reports, summaries of clinical consultation, and follow-up arrangements. Four subspecialty protocols were developed collaboratively between the local (CDD) team and the distant site team in rural Iowa. These protocols focused on children with severe behavior disorders, children with swallowing disorders (dysphagia), children needing assistive technology services, and children and youth with unmet health needs, primarily traumatic brain injury. Figure 15.1 depicts the process of telemedicine consultation.

Evaluation Results

The following section outlines several lessons learned and research outcomes from the experiences of using telemedicine to provide services to rural children in Iowa with disabilities.

Satisfaction

A comprehensive patient and professional satisfaction survey was developed cooperatively and administered by the Iowa Institute for Social Sciences, an independent social science consulting firm at the University of Iowa. This survey consisted of a fifty-five-item phone-based survey for each parent and professional area and reviewed multiple areas of satisfaction with the telemedicine encounter. For professionals, questions focused on the quality of the information using the telemedicine venue in comparison to the traditional face-to-face on-site evaluations and consultations. Multiple response scales were used (Likert and specific categories) in the survey. Treatment groups consisted of parents or other caregivers

FIGURE 15.1. TELECONSULTS FOR CHILDREN WITH DISABILITIES.

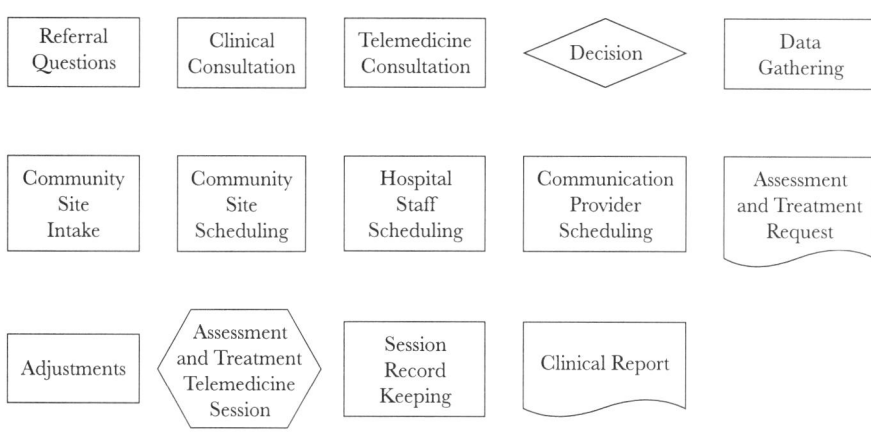

and professionals who participated in the telemedicine encounters, and control groups consisted of parents or other caregivers and professionals who had no experience with telemedicine encounters but prior experience with the CDD treatment system. Parent or other caregivers and controls were matched on socioeconomic status and general problem referral, professionals having prior referral history with the CDD, and having had received traditional clinical and evaluation services (Harper, 2001a).

One hundred subjects (patients and families) were enrolled, and 73 families agreed to participate in the final interviews, for a participation rate of 73 percent. Complete data were available on 55 patient families. The control groups (family control) consisted of 64 families, 50 of which completed these interviews, for a participation rate of 78 percent. Providers (research-treatment) consisted of 192 individuals; 135 participated for a 71 percent participation rate. Of the 45 provider-controls contacted, 36 agreed to an interview, for a participation rate of 80 percent. All analyses were completed by contrasting matching groups (treatment versus control) using two statistical tests: Fisher's Exact Test and the Wilcoxon rank sum test. Significance levels were set at .05 in all instances. Statistical comparisons of treatment versus controls on all demographics were nonsignificant, thereby ensuring the comparability of the research contrasts.

Parent-Caregiver Evaluation of Telemedicine

Parents as consumers report a very high degree of satisfaction (98 percent satisfied to very satisfied) with virtually all aspects of services provided by the care teams. These positive evaluations include the quality of care provided, time with health care providers, reported positive attitudes of health care providers, and increased positive regard of telemedicine. Parents reported that they are as satisfied with telemedicine consultations as they are with face-to-face care.

Provider and Professional Evaluation of Telemedicine

Providers (physicians, nurses, social workers, educational and psychological specialists, and teachers) reported that telemedicine consultation provided access to high-quality care (88 percent), was viewed as a time saver (96 percent), and provided better care (81 percent). Providers who were in favor of using consultation had more ongoing contact with telemedicine, reported that families were very positive toward consultations, and reported that more communication was permitted by telemedicine consultation. Finally, providers reported that telemedicine consultation was as good as face-to-face direct consultations for the majority of clinical work involved. As noted by a local pediatrician, "I was skeptical at first about this technology; however, my patients are now requesting this, and it does save time in coordinating the complex cases." These providers report telemedicine as more favorable and see it as a process providing access to higher-quality care, are positive toward receiving positive and regular feedback from patients, and tend to have higher participation rates in telemedicine consultations while viewing this type of consultation as productive in their use of their own professional time (Harper, 2001b). These telemedicine consultations were also seen as enhancing the skill of local professionals.

Economic Analysis

Telemedicine is a major cost saver to local families and local professionals. The average saving to the local district (professionals and parents) was $971 per telemedicine session. This figure includes costs of on-site team consultation and travel by the team to the local community. Average cost for parents for out-of-pocket savings was $125 per session. Reimbursement from private insurance carriers is beginning to support these services. The future success of such consultations is related to broader acceptance of these telemedicine services by parents, professionals, and the insurance industry.

Major Highlights

Data from our analyses pointed to a range of important outcomes and benefits, including:

- Parents become care managers during participation in telemedicine.
- Recommendations for treatment are presented and discussed in real time, promoting efficiency, coordination, direct practical applicability for the patient, and more immediate implementation.
- Follow-up can occur more frequently and in a more timely manner for families and patients.
- Increased professional collaboration and rapport is possible and a major benefit.
- Major savings occurs for families in out-of-pocket costs by staying in the community.
- Parents and consumers report very high satisfaction with all aspects of telemedicine services.
- Local professionals and service providers report high satisfaction of telemedicine services.
- Professionals (local providers) report high satisfaction with easy access to tertiary medical consultation.
- The CDD is committed to the use of ongoing refinement and dispersion of telemedicine on a statewide basis.
- University-based clinicians have acknowledged the building of new partnerships and a network to ongoing telemedicine consultations; the global professional community is getting smaller.

Future Challenges for Telemedicine in Iowa and the Nation

Telemedicine is much more than video-interactive consultation and needs to be integrated into an informational structure in the health care domain. Our telemedicine program is considering interaction within a complex array of services for patients and providers to include Internet access to Web-based systems for health care information, referral making, and access to all health care systems. This would be cross-integrated to the medical record systems, as well as direct contact with all tertiary professionals in the state (Bashshur, Sanders, and Shannon, 1997).

We must now explore interactive information systems for patient care beyond the Iowa Communication Network. Although the fiber-optic network is outstanding in promoting a number of real-time contacts to over eight hundred sites throughout Iowa, we now need to explore connections through the Internet directly to patient homes and into professionals' offices.

Scheduling of telemedicine consultation by a large number of agencies and individuals is one of the major challenges within the health care system of the University of Iowa Hospitals and Clinics and other health care programs. It may be advantageous to explore intranets to coordinate specific and confidential information for particular groups of patients with designated professionals. Finally, telemedicine researchers need to consider designing protocols to evaluate the efficacy of treatments delivered over telemedicine venues. Randomized and controlled clinical studies are likely to have the best likelihood of providing specific information about the efficacy of this technology. Telemedicine needs to become a regular and accessible tool for all health and allied health providers as part of our training in health education.

Discussion Questions

1. Is it important to study patients' and providers' attitudes toward technology-based services? Why or why not?
2. Is there any potential relationship between economic outcomes and satisfaction with telehealth?
3. Does this case require further outcomes research, or should it simply provide ongoing services now?
4. What is the relationship between the process for providing telehealth in this case and patient and provider perceptions?

References

Antezana, F. "Telehealth and Telemedicine Will Henceforth Be Part of the Strategy for Health for All." 1997. [http://www.who.ch//].

Bashshur, R. L., Sanders, J. H., and Shannon, G. *Telemedicine: Theory and Practice.* Springfield, Ill.: Charles C. Thomas, 1997.

Glueckauf, R. L. "Telehealth and Chronic Disabilities: New Frontier for Research and Development." *Rehabilitation Psychology,* 2002, *47*(1), 3–7.

Harper, D. C. *Telemedicine Services for Children with Disabilities in Rural Iowa: From Research to Practice.* Bethesda, Md.: National Library of Medicine, National Institutes of Health, 2001a. CD-ROM.

Harper, D. C. "Team Based Telemedicine for Children with Disabilities in Rural Iowa." *Telemedicine Journal and e-Health,* 2001b, *7*(2), 123.

Karp, W. B., and others. "Use of Telemedicine for Children with Special Health Care Needs." *Pediatrics,* 2000, *105*(4), 843–847.

Wheeler, T. "Telemedicine and Special Needs Children." *Telemedicine Today,* 1998, *6*(4), 16–20.

CHAPTER SIXTEEN

CRISIS TELEHEALTH AS A COST MANAGEMENT STRATEGY

Susan L. Dimmick, Samuel G. Burgiss, Nikki Cook

This case study focuses on cost management as a central strategy in a state-mandated program where overcoming distance obstacles and reducing response time were crucial to the effective management of psychiatric emergencies. Tennesseans living in the Appalachian region of the state have historically been underserved for mental health needs. Of the fifty counties that comprise the eastern third of the state, thirty-five (70 percent) are designated as mental health professional shortage areas (http://bphc.hrsa.gov/databases/newhpsa/newhpsa.cfm). With so many unmet needs for access to mental health expertise, an already critical shortage has exacerbated the problem of dealing with patients who present with a psychiatric crisis. These patients usually present in a hospital's emergency room, where medical staff feel inadequate to the task of dealing with this type of crisis.

In Tennessee, a mobile crisis team (MCT) is responsible for assessing individuals to determine whether immediate hospitalization is warranted. This is part of a state-mandated process for any individual who requires emergency voluntary psychiatric hospitalization and is completed in conjunction with an emer-

Funding for this program and research was provided in part by a grant from the Office for the Advancement of Telehealth, Health Resources and Services Administration, U.S. Department of Health and Human Services.

gency room physician. This consultation leads to a decision regarding the best disposition for each individual, based on clinical needs. In rural areas of Tennessee, and particularly in the mountainous terrain of Appalachia, an MCT often is on the road for several hours to reach a patient in crisis. In the meantime, hospital emergency staff or law enforcement personnel (and sometimes both) must stay with the patient, resulting in lost productivity and costly expenditures of time.

Managing Costs, Distance, and Response Time

To increase response time and to reduce travel costs, the University of Tennessee Telehealth Network (UTTN) partnered with Ridgeview Psychiatric Hospital's MCT and a rural emergency room in Scott County, Tennessee, to pilot a program that used video-mediated psychiatric assessments to determine whether hospitalization is necessary for patients presenting in crisis.

Prior to telehealth, individuals in crisis were generally taken to the emergency room at Scott County Hospital in Oneida. The emergency room staff called Ridgeview's MCT in Oak Ridge, and the mobile crisis staff then traveled to Oneida to do assessments. The trip to Oneida usually takes an hour and a half, but this can develop into a two- to three-hour trip one way depending on road conditions.

Ridgeview's MCT developed a telemedicine protocol for voluntary and involuntary patients that provides the guidelines for telemedicine communication between MCT and Scott County Hospital. The MCT philosophy is to "provide psychiatric evaluation to any individual meeting emergency criteria for psychiatric hospitalization and/or emergency outpatient treatment" (Ridgeview Psychiatric Hospital and Center, 2001).

When a patient presents in psychiatric crisis in the Scott County Emergency Department, emergency department staff call the MCT office with a referral. A registered nurse or physician provides MCT with clinical and demographic information, and they mutually agree on a time frame for a telehealth encounter. Meanwhile, the patient and Scott County emergency department staff together review and discuss confidentiality issues prior to the encounter. This dialogue should result in a verbal agreement for telehealth assessment and faxing of a signed written release of a consent form to MCT.

If the patient is considered safe and cooperative and can remain alone during the telehealth assessment, emergency department staff wait outside the telehealth encounter room until the assessment is complete. After assessment, the patient is escorted to the hospital's social work office. Scott County clinical personnel then consult with the MCT professional using the telehealth system to review the case for a final disposition. Hospital staff and MCT provide the results of a final disposition to the patient.

When the final disposition is voluntary, MCT completes its assessment notes and faxes them to emergency department personnel. Scott County staff obtain precertification for outpatient services or voluntary admissions. When the final disposition is involuntary, Scott County staff and MCT staff work on the appropriate paperwork, with MCT obtaining precertification. The patient must have constant supervision until this process is completed and the patient is escorted to an in-patient unit.

Data Collection Methods

Data were collected through a triangulation approach. Consultation data, including patient demographics, response time, consultation time, and case disposition, were collected by Ridgeview Psychiatric Hospital and Center's MCT and faxed to UTTN. Follow-up case disposition for hospitalizations was collected through a secondary analysis of Ridgeview records. UTTN analyzed differences in response time, psychiatric diagnosis, and hospitalizations both before and after the intervention with crisis telehealth. Personnel at both Scott County Hospital and Ridgeview conducted a financial analysis of the impact of the crisis telehealth program on the handling of emergency psychiatric cases (University of Tennessee Graduate School of Medicine, 2000).

Crisis Telehealth Program Results

Scott County Hospital reported to UTTN, "Telemedicine has made a big impact on our delivery of services. It has significantly decreased the amount of time each client spends in the emergency room, from 3 to 5 hours down to 45 minutes." This time period reflects the total amount of time spent in the emergency department, as opposed to response time for access to a crisis professional, which declined from ninety-nine minutes on average to eighteen minutes. Scott County Hospital also reported, "In the first three months of using the telemedicine system, we have noted a savings of approximately $130 per patient."

Ridgeview concurred: "The impact that has taken place is absolutely beyond anyone's expectations. MCT staff can respond to requests for intervention within five minutes. The benefits to all parties involved have been exceptional, especially from the point of view of timely interventions and easy access to services." Ridgeview reported a savings of $120 per patient.

Ridgeview conducted two separate financial projections for maintenance of the current crisis telehealth program (scenario 1) and for expansion to an adjacent county (Campbell County) in scenario 2. In both projections, the first three years cover the three-year Office for the Advancement of Telehealth (OAT) grant period, which funded the original crisis telehealth demonstration, and the last two years are postgrant years.

Scenario 1: Maintaining Services in Scott County

The telecommunication costs include the monthly charge for maintaining the lines needed for the service to Scott County. This by far represents the largest portion of the cost throughout the five-year period. Beginning in year 2, salary and benefits represent the clinical staff cost of expanding services to include physician consultations and therapy. Equipment maintenance costs are budgeted in years 2 through 5 to cover any cost of maintaining the current equipment.

In years 1, 2, and 3, the project relies on OAT funding and other community funding identified by the University of Tennessee Telehealth Network to cover most of the program cost during those years. Medical revenues are generated by providing doctor consultations and therapy services to Scott County using the current telemedicine network. In years 3 and 4, services are expanded, thus increasing the amount of medical revenues to help cover the loss of OAT funding.

Although in years 4 and 5, the program shows a small gross shortfall ($5,503 in each year), if considering the additional cost savings, the program generates a net surplus in each of those years. The cost savings represents the travel cost and salary and benefit cost that would have been incurred if the clinicians were required to travel to Scott County. These savings are clearly a substantial benefit of the program.

Scenario 2: Maintaining Services in Scott County and Expanding Services to Campbell County

All costs, funding sources, and cost saving described in scenario 1 are also included in this financial projection. In addition, costs, funding sources, and cost savings associated with expanding services to Campbell County in year 3 are included.

Beginning in year 3, telecommunication costs are increased to include the cost of maintaining the necessary lines needed for providing services to Campbell County. Again, this represents the majority of the costs associated with providing services to Campbell County. Salary and benefits are increased from scenario 1 by $525 in year 3 and by $4,350 in years 4 and 5, representing the cost of clinical staff providing the services in Campbell County.

Medical revenues are increased by $900 in year 3 and by $7,800 in years 4 and 5, representing the revenue generated by providing physician consultations and therapy services in Campbell County.

As in scenario 1, this financial projection also shows a small gross shortfall (approximately $9,000) in years 3, 4, and 5. However, when considering the cost savings generated by the program, the bottom-line net surplus for the program is $98,174 at the end of the five-year period. Again, these cost savings represent the travel cost and salary and benefit cost that would have been incurred if the clinicians were required to travel to the Campbell County location. These savings also represent a substantial financial benefit of the program.

Crisis Telehealth: Lessons Learned

Although there were definitive cost savings and response time reductions, the state office of mental health wanted evidence that there were no significant differences in diagnoses or hospitalizations between seeing a patient in crisis face-to-face versus seeing a patient in the crisis telehealth program. A comparison of diagnoses made in the six months preceding crisis telehealth intervention and the first six months of crisis telehealth implementation found no statistically significant difference between a diagnosis made in the face-to-face mode versus the telehealth communication mode. There was a small but statistically significant difference in hospitalizations, with four more hospitalizations occurring during the first six months of crisis telehealth intervention period. Based on this evidence, the state granted a waiver for the crisis telehealth program to continue providing video-mediated crisis assessment.

Sheila Musharbash, team leader for Ridgeview's MCT, noted, "There continues to be resistance in the emergency department when personnel deal with psychiatric clients. Many emergency personnel want to deal only with cardiac patients and other typical types of emergency patients. Our solution is to continue to provide education and to be diplomatically assertive. We remain firm that the provision of crisis telehealth fills a need for the patient and results in cost efficiencies for providers."

Discussion Questions

1. Why is it important to analyze cost outcomes for a technology-based intervention?
2. This case focuses on cost outcomes, but also discusses health outcomes in the lessons learned. Why did the authors include these data as well?
3. Analyze the approach and subsequent results employed in this case to document cost savings.
4. How would this project have ended up in the long term if no cost analyses were conducted? Would it still be operational?

References

Ridgeview Psychiatric Hospital and Center. "MCT.112, Policy and Procedure, Telemedicine
Protocol." July 24, 2001. [http://bphc.hrsa.gov/databases/newhpsa/newhpsa.cfm].

University of Tennessee Graduate School of Medicine. "Scott County Telemedicine Project,
Telemedicine Strategic/Financial Plan, Phase II." Knoxville: University of Tennessee
Graduate School of Medicine, 2000.

CHAPTER SEVENTEEN

USING POINT-OF-CARE TO REDUCE MEDICATION ERRORS

Chris L. Tucker, Russell Carlson

According to the 1999 report from the Institute of Medicine, as many as ninety-eight thousand Americans die each year due to medical mistakes made by physicians, pharmacists, and other health care professionals. Of these deaths, many are due to medication errors (Weiss, 1999). Efforts to develop wireless, real-time bar code medication administration software that would have an interface with existing Veterans Information Systems and Technology Architecture (VistA) began in 1992 with the visionary insight of G. Sue Kinnick, a registered nurse. She had observed an employee at the Seattle Tacoma International Airport using a handheld device to scan a bar code in her rental car. She believed the VA could use the same technology to track medications given to veterans and shared the idea with the administration at the Topeka Veterans Affairs Medical Center (VAMC), planting the seed for what would become the VA's Bar Code Medication Administration (BCMA) program. The Colmery-O'Neil VAMC developed and implemented a prototype medication administration system.

The VA's under secretary for health approved the development of the project in August 1998 as the VA's automated medication administration system. During August 1999, the BCMA project came to fruition when the VA successfully implemented the software in its 173 medical centers nationwide. It was not surprising that this new software received a mix of reactions from hospital staff experienced with the more traditional manual method of administering medications to patients. Yet it still managed to demonstrate quickly how it could dramatically reduce medication errors.

Project Design and Description

The overall medication management process is a complex series of interrelated subsystems that involve numerous hand-offs and the coordination of numerous disciplines. Most medication administration errors are the result of multiple system failures that are due to faulty system design (Leape and others, 1995).

Manual systems create adverse drug events in a number of ways:

- Incomplete order handoffs between the various hospital disciplines involved in the process
- Order misinterpretation
- Incomplete or improper transcription
- Communication breakdowns
- Faulty drug identity checking
- Rule violations
- Faulty dose checking
- Drug stocking and delivery problems
- Slips and memory lapses
- Lack of standardization of terms and procedures

The primary requirements of the computerized system were to ensure the patient receives the correct medication, in the correct dose, and at the correct time and to visually alert staff when the proper parameters were not met. Nurses scan bar codes on patient wristbands as well as bar codes on each medication administered. The system validates the accuracy of the administration, visually alerting the user if any of the "five rights" (right patient, right drug, right dose, right time, and right route) are not met, and documents the administration.

The BCMA system required the software to be developed and supported by a nationwide team of practitioners and technical experts. The system also had to integrate with the existing VA hospital pharmacy and nursing software programs. Other system requirements included limiting variation that required staff to learn several different procedures, using protocols, and reducing reliance on memory, making it difficult to make an error by forcing functions. Minimizing user-entered keystrokes and maximizing automated sign-ins and security checks also played a key role in the software design. The software reduces reliance on short-term memory by providing real-time access to medication order information at the patient's bedside and a system of reports to remind clinical staff when medications need to be administered or have been overlooked or when the effectiveness of doses administered should be assessed. It also alerts staff to potential allergies, adverse reactions, special instructions concerning a medication order, and order changes that require action.

The process of identifying software requirements resulted in the development of a system that records One-Time, On-Call, Stat, and Now orders in addition to the regularly scheduled and as needed (pro re nata; PRN) medications. The system is flexible enough to allow the nurse to record refused medications, document the refusal reason, request missing doses electronically from the pharmacy, and record early or late medications approved for administration by a physician outside the regular administration window.

The software offers a comprehensive package of management and accountability tools, including the following:

- Automated Due list, generated by the nurse, which lists immediately prior to each administration time the medications to be administered.
- PRN effectiveness list that alerts the nurse to record the effectiveness of PRN after they have been given.
- Paperless medication administration history, which electronically records the nurse's initials and the exact time the medication was scanned as given in a conventional medication administration record (MAR) format.
- Patient medication log that is used by all clinical staff and can be accessed throughout the medical center to review patient medication needs. With this report, clinicians can review the number of doses or times a drug has been recorded as given for a user-specified date range.
- Missing dose requests that automatically print on a designated printer in the pharmacy, alerting pharmacy personnel when a dose should be reissued. The missing dose software also captures the nurse ID, the drug requested, the time requested, and the reason the dose was missing. These functions are carried out at the time the nurse is administering medication, thereby reducing the reliance on memory, minimizing user-required keystrokes, and minimizing workflow disruption.

Hardware considerations involved the use of a wireless local area network to create a system that automatically communicates to the existing mainframe computer system, VistA, in real time. It was important that no data downloading was required. The system needed to automatically reference several different service component software systems to create a real-time device, automatically communicating critical information back to the nurse while passing medications. End users wanted an easy-to-use, lightweight, and portable device to provide a point-of-care data entry and retrieval system.

Since nurses administering medications move from patient to patient and ward to ward, the automated system required mobility. To achieve this real-time mobility, the software requires a continuous Ethernet connection to the VA hospital information system database. Nurses use laptop computers and handheld bar code scanners. In areas of the hospital that do not require clinician mobility, wired networking can be used. BCMA places real-time information in the hands of the clinical staff and thereby decreases the possibility of medication errors.

The virtual due list (VDL), which replaces the manual system's paper MAR, allows the nurse to view medications that are due to be administered for a selectable administration window and offers additional safety checks not possible with manual systems. If a nurse attempts to administer a medication outside the scheduled administration window, the system provides appropriate safety alerts. These safety alerts must be reviewed using the nurse's clinical judgments prior to continuing with the medication administration. The VDL displays current administration status such as given, held, or refused. This administration status has reduced the occurrence of medication being omitted that should have been administered. Because the computer displays only active orders, the potential for administering a discontinued or expired order is eliminated.

Collaboration

Changes in technology often demand changes in procedures and policies as well as standardization of terms and processes. Historically, pharmacy and nursing have not worked cohesively to address issues related to drug delivery and administration. This lack of communication has led to an incomplete understanding of the medication management process and created barriers to patient safety. An important step in implementing BCMA was the development of a multidisciplinary team to address these issues and foster understanding of the entire process. This team creates an environment for change that benefits patient care, reduces handoffs, and improves communication and efficiency. Order interpretation and procedural guidelines created through this multidisciplinary approach ensure that nursing, pharmacy, and providers interpret and carry out the medication order in a consistent and uniform manner. This approach makes certain the physician understands when the order will be carried out regardless of the ward where a patient is assigned. In addition, the multidisciplinary concept ensures the pharmacy drug delivery process is aligned with nursing expectations.

Procedural and process standardization provides many benefits for both improved patient outcome and enhanced pharmacy-nursing communication. The electronic transcription process ensures that both pharmacy and nursing use the same electronic document for dispensing and administering medications. The electronic transcription process also requires pharmacy and nursing verification of the same electronic order. Because nursing and pharmacy share the transcription process, any discrepancies in transcription are frequently identified during the verification process and corrected before a transcription error causes patient harm.

Development of an automated missing dose process makes certain that electronic requests for missing doses are processed and delivered to the nurse within defined time limits by reducing unnecessary handoffs in the request process. Each electronic request creates an entry in a missing-dose file. Reports are available within BCMA to allow managers to track and trend both the volume of missing doses submitted for a specific drug and the location where the missing dose originated.

The pharmacy is responsible for ensuring that all medications distributed within the facility contain readable bar codes. Adherence to bar code labeling requirements reduces both nursing and pharmacy frustration with implementation of an electronic scanning system. Electronic labeling procedures eliminate the need for handwritten labels that may not be legible. The bar code labeling software contains fields for patient name, ward location, instructions, filled by, checked by, drug name, and dosage ordered.

Computerization allows multiple users to access medication administration information at the same time without competing for or attempting to locate a paper record. Interruptions for the nurse administering medications and the potential for medications to be omitted during the administration process are reduced. Computerization also helps prevent administering medications outside the medication administration window, because the information is presented to the medication nurse even if another individual is accessing the patient's medication administration information.

Outcomes

Implementing an electronic system is a complex endeavor, which involves the training and integration of several hospital disciplines and the establishment of policies and procedures that consider the needs of the users as well as the needs of the system.

Some BCMA users, as well as the professional unions, were concerned that the enhanced tracking and reporting tools created might contribute to an increase in punitive actions when medication errors did occur. However, management did assure staff that inaccurate medication administration was considered the end result of a chain of events possibly set in motion by poorly designed processes and not the result of one individual's action. Reporting of inaccurate medication administration must be in a positive, nonpunitive review process that includes the trending of root cause and end result. The intent of BCMA software is to provide the nurse with an additional check-and-balance system that augments, but does not replace, clinical judgment.

Implementation and training for staff and support personnel included the appropriate use of the software, as well as hardware support and troubleshooting, and exposure to processes and procedural changes required to convert to a completely electronic record. Hands-on training is essential to ensure that end users develop a comfort level when converting from a paper system to an electronic process. Allowing nurses to use the system in their particular setting in a non-threatening environment and at their own pace has proven beneficial.

Training must include not only the use of the software module but also the appropriate use of a bar code scanner to ensure its safe operation. Within the VA, each facility was asked to send appropriate representatives from nursing and pharmacy to one of several national training sessions. These sessions provided users with the tools and knowledge required to deploy the software at their facilities. In addition, national support networks are used to provide ongoing assistance and information sharing between facilities and provide access to national support specialists.

In some locations, nursing staff were unfamiliar or uncomfortable with using computers. To help ensure that staff had basic MS Windows-based skills, the VA training office purchased, and provided to all facilities, disk-based training for Word 97, Excel 97, PowerPoint 97, and MS Windows NT 4.0 Introduction. VA intranet sites are available to all users. These Web sites are devoted to national training materials, software updates, development notes, and field best practices.

Communication is of paramount importance to the successful implementation of any new software. Each facility was encouraged to establish a multidisciplinary focus group and a mail group to communicate system-related concerns, such as hardware failures, software problems, procedural requirements, and ongoing support for the project.

At the Colmery-O'Neil VAMC, of the almost 1.9 million patient doses dispensed in 1993 (the last full year of data using a completely manual system) and of the 409 reported medication errors, the reported error rate was 0.0217 percent, or 21.7 incident reports for each 100,000 units. The error rate for 2001 was 0.0030 percent or 3.0 incidents per 100,000 units, with 460,795 units dispensed and 22 reported errors. This is an 86.2 percent improvement in the reported error rate for fiscal year 2001 over that of 1993 (Figure 17.1).

Figure 17.1 compares the types of reported medication errors between 1993 and 2001. In each category of error, fewer errors occurred while the electronic system was in use, as is demonstrated by the following:

FIGURE 17.1. REPORTED ERROR RATE
AS A PERCENTAGE OF TOTAL DOSES DISPENSED.

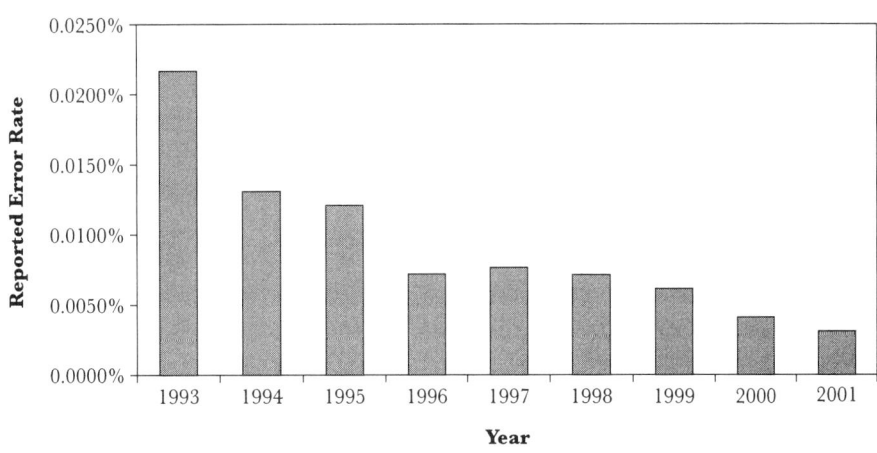

- 75.47 percent improvement in errors caused by the wrong medication being administered to a patient
- 61.97 percent improvement in errors caused by the incorrect doses being administered
- 93.48 percent improvement in wrong patient errors
- 87.41 percent improvement in wrong time errors
- 70.34 percent improvement in errors caused when medications scheduled for administration were not given

The Colmery-O'Neil VAMC has also reduced the number of missing doses by 68 percent through the analysis of missing dose data by identifying drug storage and delivery problems, unit-dose drug cart filling inconsistencies, and drug packaging concerns. Reducing the number of missing doses has reduced workflow interruption and improved dispensing accuracy.

The success of BCMA is due to the collegiality of patient care providers (nurses, pharmacists, doctors), technical support (information management, biotechnical engineers), and administration. Veterans are beneficiaries of this innovative computerized medicine administration system that improves patient's safety.

Preliminary evaluations of this project's outcomes support the original premise that a computerized medication administration process will reduce medication errors, improve medication administration process and procedures, and enhance documentation of medication administration data.

Implications and the Future

BCMA has proven effective in reducing medication administration errors. Now that we have addressed the primary concern of patient safety and medication errors, we need to focus more on the actual end users: the nurses. Continued incorporation of human factors engineering principles as well as improving the ergonomics of the software and hardware being used at our facilities will improve overall acceptance and user satisfaction. We must continue to identify the physical, biomechanical, postural, and physiological consequences of interacting with the software and the associated hardware. Addressing these issues will lead to better overall compliance with the system's intended use and improve retention of nurses.

Future goals of the BCMA project are to improve its interaction with other clinical software packages such as Vital Signs, Laboratory, Dietary, and our computerized patient record system in an effort to streamline efficiency, and provide needed clinical data to support sound clinical decisions regarding patient care. Further integrating the interfaces with other clinical software will provide a seamless transition to the end user, improve user satisfaction, and promote efficiency. Development is also underway to provide the same inpatient safety features of BCMA to patients who receive medication treatments in outpatient clinic settings.

Discussion Questions

1. What role can new technologies play in reducing human errors?
2. What kinds of organizational issues had to be addressed in order for this project to be deployed?
3. Do the outcomes data provide compelling evidence for the need for this technology?
4. What other types of outcomes studies would benefit this project?
5. Explain the statement from the case, "Implementing an electronic system is a complex endeavor."

References

Leape, L. L., and others. "Systems Analysis of Adverse Drug Events." *Journal of the American Medical Association*, 1995, *274*, 35–43.

Weiss, R. "Thousands of Deaths Linked to Medical Errors." *Washington Post*, Nov. 30, 1999, p. A1.

CHAPTER EIGHTEEN

THE UNITED KINGDOM VIRTUAL OUTREACH PROJECT

Paul Wallace

The Virtual Outreach project was established in order to determine whether there were advantages to using real-time videoconferencing as an alternative to outpatient (ambulatory clinic) referral. Based on the outreach clinic model, where specialists perform outpatient clinics in general practice (GP) surgeries (similar to primary care clinic settings in the United States), the prime motivation for undertaking the project was the frustration of both patients and clinicians at the poor levels of communication.

There are often major difficulties in sharing understanding between the patient, the GP, and the consultant. The GP may not adequately describe in the referral letter her or his understanding of the patient's problem and the reason for the referral. The specialist may not understand the patient's problem from the written communication, and the patient may not be able to clarify this to the specialist. As a result, there is often confusion about the reason for referral, unnecessary duplication of tests and other investigations, and poor understanding by the patient of the views of the examining specialist. Patients are frequently seen repeatedly in outpatient clinics, because of the specialist's inability to discharge them back to the GP's care.

Theoretical Underpinnings and Data Gathering

Real-time joint medical consultations were shown in the Netherlands to result in major reductions in unnecessary investigations and treatments and to reduce substantially the need for hospital outpatient follow-up. A series of studies were carried out on joint consultations between GPs and a variety of different specialists (Vierhout and others, 1995; Vlek, 2000). In the Maastricht studies series, the joint consultations were organized as monthly meeting between a group of four or five GPs with one specialist. Each GP could bring in one or two patients who were reassessed. Overall, the acceptance of the joint consultations was high. As a result of a learning effect and a higher level of skills, the joint consultations were shown to reduce the number of patients referred to specialist care. In addition, joint consultations seemed to have an important impact on communication problems between GPs and consultants, as the difference between the GP's reason for referral and that perceived by the specialist clearly diminished.

The problem with the Netherlands model of joint consultation was that it required the GP, patient, and consultant all to be physically present in the same place at the same time. The joint teleconsultation appeared to offer a solution for this important problem by allowing the patient and the GP to stay in the general practice, with the consultant "beamed in" using an integrated switched digital network (ISDN) link and PC-based software.

A key aim of the virtual outreach project was to ensure that the joint teleconsultations were subjected to rigorous clinical and economic evaluation, and accordingly a fully scaled randomized, controlled trial, and a comprehensive economic evaluation were planned. The key hypotheses to be tested in the trial are shown in Exhibit 18.1.

The Project

The project was established in two locations, one in central London and the other in semirural Shropshire and mid-Wales. Some sixty GPs and ten specialists in each of the settings agreed to participate. With the aid of substantial research funds obtained primarily from the Research and Development National Health Service Health Technologies Assessment initiative, videoconferencing equipment and ISDN lines were installed. The specialties represented in the project were endocrinology, gastroenterology, orthopedics, rheumatology, ears-nose-throat (ENT) surgery, neurology, respiratory medicine, and urology.

Training Sessions

We undertook a series of training sessions for both the GPs and the hospital specialists prior to their involvement in the trial. Participants in the urban and the rural arms of the trial were invited to a programmed training event with opportunities

EXHIBIT 18.1. TRIAL HYPOTHESES.

Main trial: To test the hypotheses that virtual outreach would:
☐ Reduce offers of hospital follow-up appointments
☐ Reduce numbers of medical interventions and investigations
☐ Reduce numbers of contacts with the health care system
☐ Have a positive impact on patient satisfaction and enablement
☐ Lead to improvements in patient health status

Economic evaluation: To test the hypotheses that virtual outreach would:
☐ Incur no increased costs to the National Health Service
☐ Reduce the costs incurred by patients attending outpatient appointments
☐ Reduce the time taken off work

to learn from the investigators about the background and proposed conduct of the trial, to get hands-on experience with the equipment to see how it worked, and to have some opportunity to undertake role-play and discuss with GP and specialist colleagues how best to undertake the joint teleconsultations. In addition, the research nurses in both arms of the trial undertook outreach visits to the practices to show the general practitioners and their associated staff how the equipment worked. They left a demonstration video for use by the practice staff.

Establishing the Service

Each of the consultants indicated their availability for teleconsultations. Generally it was not possible for them to have protected time for the teleconsultations, and appointments were thus usually shoehorned into routine schedules at the beginning or end of a normal outpatient (ambulatory) clinic. Participating GPs' preferred times were at the beginning or end of a surgery or in the period in the middle of the day between surgeries. Again, there was usually no protected time available for these appointments. In each location, a project office was established to handle incoming referrals and coordinate the allocation of joint consultation appointments times. This entailed complex cross-checking of specialist availability against GP availability and then confirming the proposed appointment with the patient. Appointment letters were sent to all three parties. All referrals were communicated as for normal outpatients by a GP referral letter, and following the teleconsultation, the specialist wrote a letter to the GP, summarizing the content of the consultation and the recommendations for future management of the patient.

The Joint Teleconsultation

For the patients, this was an entirely novel way to undergo their consultation with the specialist. Not only did they find themselves in their GP's practice, a place familiar to most of them, but they also had their family doctor with them during the session. Moreover, the hospital specialist, far from dominating the situation as often occurs in the standard outpatient consultation, was present only through the videolink. As one patient put it, the consultant was effectively a "doc-in-the-box."

In most cases, the GP began the consultation by introducing the patient to the specialist. The specialist would then have the opportunity to speak with the patient and the GP in order to obtain further information relevant to the patient's presenting problem. Certain aspects of examination could be undertaken during the consultation. For example, it was possible to obtain a direct view through the camera of a possible thyroid enlargement (goiter) or to obtain an examination "by proxy," where the GP would examine the patient on behalf of the specialist, such as an orthopedic examination of the knee. Once the specialist had completed this set of tasks and had formulated an appropriate management plan, this was communicated directly to both the patient and the GP. There was the opportunity for each to clarify areas of uncertainty with the specialist. The GP was able to act as the patient's advocate, prompting clarification from the specialist or asking for more detailed information about aspects of the proposed management plan. An illustrative case follows:

Joe is an eight year old child with recurrent ear infections. At the age of five, he had had surgical insertion of grommets, but although the grommets were extruded successfully eighteen months later, he has been left with a perforation of his right tympanic membrane and continues to get middle ear infections quite frequently. At his last consultation with his mother, Mrs. S, his GP, Dr. B, decides to refer back to his ENT surgeon, Mr. Q, to assess whether Joe would benefit from further surgery. The referral takes place during the trial, and Mrs. S is approached about her willingness for Joe to be included. She gives her consent, and a few days later hears that Joe's appointment is to be scheduled as a joint teleconsultation at Dr. B's surgery.

When Joe and his mother arrive for the appointment, they are taken into a special room in the practice where Dr. B joins them. Dr. B greets them and shows them the equipment, a PC with a small video camera mounted on top, explaining how it is supposed to work. At that moment, the phone rings, and Mr. Q's face appears on the TV screen. He greets Dr. B, who returns the greeting and introduces Joe and his mother. During the joint consultation. Mr. Q asks Dr. B to give him further details of Joe's problems, checking that the information in the hospital record corresponds to Dr. B's understanding of the situation. Every now and again, Dr. B turns to Joe and Mrs. S for clarification or confirmation. Having reviewed the history, Mr. Q turns to Joe and his mother, asking them to tell him how things have been since the last operation. Mrs. S tells him of the recurrent episodes of ear infection that Dr. B has had to manage, sometimes with antibiotics, and Joe confirms how painful and unpleasant they have been. Mr. Q then asks Dr. B for some further details relating to tests and treatments he has prescribed for Joe and then asks Dr. B to examine Joe's ears (Figure 18.1). Dr. B examines Joe's ears with an auroscope, describing his findings to Mr. Q as he does so. Mr. Q listens, prompting at intervals for specific pieces of information about the appearance and the size of the perforation of the right tympanic membrane.

At the end of the consultation, Mr. Q suggests that Joe should come to his clinic for a further appointment to enable him to examine the ear directly in order to decide whether he would benefit from surgery. He arranges a date for this appointment and checks with Mrs. S as to whether this would be convenient. Mr. Q has not been able to make the definitive decision based only on Dr. B's findings, but with prompting from Dr. B, Joe and Mrs. S are able to ask Mr. Q about the likelihood of surgery and the particulars of admission, should this prove necessary. They check possible dates, and Mr. Q offers to arrange admission (if he decides that this is indicated) so that it would coincide with Joe's half-term holiday. The joint teleconsultation concludes with a brief discussion between Dr. B and Mr. Q about the general indications for further surgery following grommet insertion and the likely prognosis. This is followed by an exchange of greetings among all parties and Dr. B then shuts down the video-

FIGURE 18.1. CASE EXAMPLE OF TELEMEDICINE CLINICAL CONSULTATION.

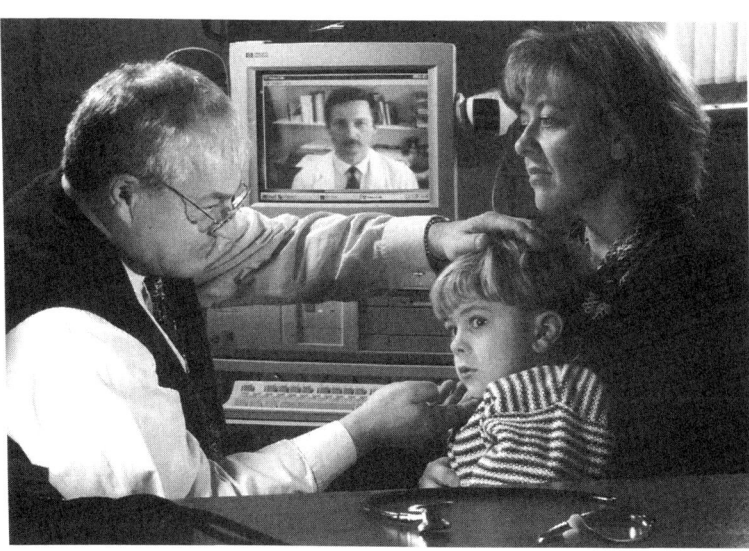

conferencing program. He spends the next ten minutes reviewing the discussion and the decisions made with Joe and his mother. From the time Mrs. S and Joe entered the special consulting room to the time they left, twenty-five minutes have elapsed.

The Trial and the Constraints It Imposed

The project was established as a randomized, controlled trial in order to enable rigorous evaluation of the effectiveness and costs in the London and Welsh settings of virtual outreach relative to routine outpatient consultations. In addition, a qualitative study was carried out, involving interviews, videorecordings, and direct observation. As a result, the participants in the trial were subject to a rather large number of constraints. The general practitioners had no control over which of their patients were included in the trial or (naturally) which intervention their individual patients ended up receiving. This meant that they found themselves involved in virtual outreach on some occasions when they did not feel that their presence was likely to be beneficial to themselves or the patient. The specialists taking part had to work under rather difficult circumstances. There was no dedicated teleconferencing suite in either of the hospitals, and they had to undertake teleconsultations in addition to their usual outpatient load. The technical aspects of the virtual outreach service were inevitably significantly constrained by cost considerations. As a result, we used ISDN2 lines, which gave picture and sound of only moderate quality and reliability. The GPs had no access to peripherals such as fiber-optic instruments for ear examinations, which could have made a substantial difference to outcome, for example, in the case of ENT referrals.

Although we spent considerable time with a small number of participants in the feasibility and pilot stages, there was limited time to develop the intervention for the majority of the main trial participants. There was little opportunity for them to practice the very special skills involved in the joint telemedicine consultations, and this, we later discovered, led to some major confusion and discordance about the respective roles of the GPs and the consultants. Whereas in a normal clinical situation, one would actively encourage feedback from those using this service, with subsequent modification of practice, in the trial, this was specifically disallowed.

Because this was a trial, there were inevitably large numbers of forms and questionnaires to fill in. This constituted a significant additional workload for the participating clinicians, and the patients found themselves being asked to fill in three separate sets of questionnaires: one at entry to the trial, a second immediately after the index consultation, and the final set six months after recruitment. It is a great tribute to patients and clinicians alike that the trial came so successfully to conclusion and that the overall questionnaire response rate exceeded 70 percent.

What We Found

What we had hoped to find was a replication of the findings of the Dutch studies on joint consultation, with reductions in the numbers of patients being retained in the outpatient system and much better and more effective use of test investigations and treatment. What actually happened was more or less the converse. Patients in the virtual outreach group were overall more likely to be offered a follow-up appointment, odds ratio 1.52 (95 percent confidence interval [CI] 1.27 to 1.82, $p < 0.001$) (Wallace and others, 2002). Significant differences in effects were observed between the two sites ($p = 0.009$) and across different specialties ($p < 0.001$). Virtual outreach increased the offers of follow-up appointments more in Shrewsbury than in London, and more in ENT and orthopedics than in the other specialties. Fewer tests and investigations were ordered in the virtual outreach group, by an average of 0.79 per patient (95 percent CI 0.37 to 1.21 per patient, $p < 0.001$).

In the six-month period following the index consultation, there were no significant differences overall in number of contacts with general practice, outpatient visits, accident and emergency contacts, inpatient stays, day surgery, and inpatient procedures or prescriptions between the randomized groups. Tests of interaction showed evidence of differences in effects by specialty for number of tests and investigations ($p = 0.01$) and outpatient visits ($p = 0.007$). They indicated that virtual outreach decreased the number of tests and investigations, particularly in patients referred to gastroenterology, and increased the number of outpatient visits, particularly in those referred to orthopedics. Patient satisfaction was greater after a virtual outreach consultation than after a standard outpatient consultation (mean difference 0.33 scale points, 95 percent CI 0.23 to 0.43, $p < 0.001$), with no heterogeneity between specialties or sites. However, patient enablement after the index consultation, and the physical and psychological scores of the SF12 for adults and the scores on the Child Health Questionnaire for children under age sixteen, did not differ between the randomized groups at six months follow-up. Overall, six-month National Health Service (NHS) costs were greater for the virtual outreach consultations than for conventional outpatients: £724 and £625 per patient, respectively (difference in means £99 [95% CI £10 to £187], $p = 0.03$). The index consultation accounted for this excess. Cost and time savings to patients were found (difference in mean total patient cost £8 [95% CI £5 to £10], $p < 0.0001$). Estimated productivity losses were also less (difference in mean cost £11 [95% CI £10 to £12], $p < 0.0001$) in the virtual outreach group.

It appeared that for a substantial proportion of patients seen in virtual outreach, the specialists did not feel confident enough in the findings of their GP colleagues and required the patient to come for a repeat consultation in the hospital outpatient clinic. This was more commonly found in the surgical specialties than in the medical specialties, and probably reflected a real need to have direct contact with the patients, (as, for example, in the case of ENT surgery, where direct visualization of the ear or the throat was often required). However, there was also a lot of variation between specialists in the two sites, suggesting that it may equally have been the personal characteristics of the specialists and their ability to deal with uncertainty.

In terms of the downstream effects, the reductions in tests and investigations tended to be in the simpler investigations, and so the cost savings were rather limited. Interestingly, there was no evidence of a reduction in subsequent contact with the general practitioners, which we had anticipated. This was all the more important because although the actual consultation time of around ten minutes was the same in both the joint teleconsultation and the ordinary outpatient appointment, the GPs were found to be spending an average total of nearly thirty minutes in the joint teleconsultation, because of the time needed at the beginning to set up the equipment and to explain its functioning to the patients and at the end to pick up and clarify the issues raised by the specialist during the consultation.

The increase in patient satisfaction with joint teleconsultations was marked (Figure 18.2). The patients clearly liked the novelty, and in addition appreciated the punctuality of the consultation and the fact that they took place in the GP's office rather than in the hospital. In addition, they found the level of communication better and clearly enjoyed having two physicians for the price of one.

When we interviewed the GPs, the hospital specialists, and the patients who had participated in the trial, we found some interesting issues. There clearly were very different expectations about the roles of the GP and hospital specialists in the so-called triadic consultations. Many of the hospital specialists said that they rather hoped that the GPs would act like junior doctors and give them a full account of the patient's history and examination findings. The GPs, for their part, did not wish to undertake this role and were keen either to let the patients speak for themselves or to take an active role as the patient's advocate. This seems to have led to quite a lot of confusion and on occasion to the GP's taking an almost entirely passive role. There was also difference of opinion about the opportunities for learning. The GPs on the whole said that they did learn from many of the consultations, but the specialists were much less positive about this aspect of the work. If anything, they said that they at least were able to put names to faces, where before they had been dealing with letters from GPs whom they had often never met.

Project Status

The GPs and specialists did a remarkable job during the trial, many of them under considerable time pressures and sometimes against their own better judgment. We

FIGURE 18.2. RESPONSES TO OVERALL PATIENT SATISFACTION BY RANDOMIZED GROUP.

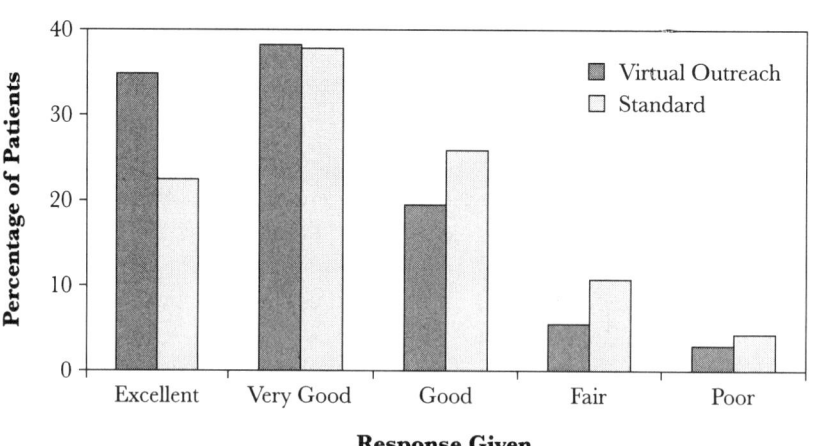

recruited over and above the number of patients for the trial, and only one clinician in each group dropped out. However, at the end of the eighteen-month recruitment phase, the clinicians were faced with the difficult decision of whether to continue with the virtual outreach service, this time without the constraints of the trial but with the significant additional burden of fairly substantial ISDN costs. There was some fairly active discussion in both the rural and urban arms of the trial; in the end, both groups agreed that they could not continue their subscriptions, and as a result the service ceased to function in both centers.

The trial itself has been widely acclaimed as a landmark study, and its results have been published in highly respectable medical journals (Wallace and others, 2002; Jacklin and others, 2003). A great deal has been learned about the workings of virtual outreach and its potential benefits and significant shortcomings. Major lessons have been learned about how these (and other) technologies need to be introduced into health care systems, and have also published on this issue.

Some of they key practical issues around teleconsultations follow:

• The involvement of all three parties in the consultation has the potential to change the dynamic and allow better levels of communication. For this to occur, all three parties have to understand the "rules of engagement and conduct"; this may require training for both the GP and specialist.

- Not all cases are suitable for teleconsultation. Those where physical examination or investigation is a vital prerequisite for decision making or there are serious questions of malignancy are unlikely to benefit from teleconsultation.
- Teleconsultation may be especially helpful for patients who have difficulty in articulating their views and concerns. The GP can assist with this.
- Teleconsultations require special coordination. Administrative systems have to be set up and staffed appropriately, and all three parties must be prepared to attend on time. Such constraints can place major burdens on already overstretched systems.

As for the overall commissioning of telemedicine services, it is clear that this requires a composite of preconditions to be fulfilled in order to enable appropriate applications to be identified and installed in such a way as to meet the real needs of consumers and providers of health care services as they are intended. In the final analysis, failure of the virtual outreach trial to demonstrate clinical or economic benefits or to achieve normalization was due as much to the difficulties that the professionals had in rethinking and reengineering their clinical practice as to the technical problems posed by the information and communication technologies or the trial design. These are important lessons, and it behooves all of those involved in the development of e-health and telemedicine applications to take them seriously.

Discussion Questions

1. What are the key issues to be addressed prior to commissioning a virtual outreach service?
2. What management issues need to be considered during commissioning?
3. What do the outcomes regarding patient satisfaction indicate about this model of care?
4. Why were patients in the virtual outreach group more likely to be offered a follow-up appointment?
5. Is the care model employed in the virtual outreach clinic effective and appropriate in the long term?

References

Jacklin, P., and others. "Virtual Outreach: An Economic Evaluation of Joint Teleconsultations for Patients Referred by Their General Practitioner for a Specialist Opinion." *British Medical Journal*, 2003, *327*, 84–88.

Vierhout, W.P.M., and others. "Effectiveness of Joint Consultation Sessions of General Practitioners and Orthopaedic Surgeons for Locomotor-System Disorders." *Lancet*, 1995, *346*, 990–994.

Vlek, J.F.M. "Cardialogue; Joint Consultations of General Practitioners and Cardiologists in a Primary Care Setting." Thesis, University of Maastricht, 2000.

Wallace, P., and others. "Joint Teleconsultations (Virtual Outreach) Versus Standard Outpatients Appointments for Patients Referred by Their General Practitioner for a Specialist Opinion: A Randomised Trial." *Lancet*, 2002, *359*, 1961–1968.

CHAPTER NINETEEN

THE FINANCIAL SIDE
OF A TELE-ONCOLOGY PRACTICE

Gary C. Doolittle, Ashley Spaulding, Ryan Spaulding

Providing medical care using telemedicine to patients with cancer in rural Kansas began in 1995 when the University of Kansas Medical Center's (KUMC) tele-oncology project connected a KUMC oncologist with a rural medical center in the central part of the state. After establishing the initial clinic in Hays, a second telemedicine clinic was developed in Horton, Kansas, two years later. Telemedicine technology enables the oncologist to remain at KUMC in Kansas City, Kansas, and examine patients in Hays, approximately 266 miles from KUMC, and Horton, which is located in the northeast corner of the state, approximately 81 miles from KUMC. A team of professionals—the KUMC oncologist, on-site nurses, administrative personnel, and technical support staff—collaborates to provide periodic on-site services in addition to the services provided telemedically.

The tele-oncology project began in response to a lack of cancer specialists in rural Kansas towns, a shortage felt by many small towns across the United States. Using available telemedicine technology, patients with cancer in areas without oncologists are able to receive vital treatment on a regular basis (Figure 19.1). Telemedicine is not intended to replace traditional face-to-face health care services, but it does offer underserved populations the opportunity to obtain quality medical care in a convenient and timely manner. In addition to increasing patient access to the health care system, tele-oncology practices have generally been well received by patients (Allen and Hayes, 1995; Mair, Whitten, May, and Doolittle,

2000). Although some patients have expressed concerns about tele-oncology clinics, such as not seeing the doctor in person and not being comfortable with a nurse performing certain aspects of the physical examination, most rural patients understand the utility of telemedicine services and value enhanced access to specialist care (Mair, Whitten, May, and Doolittle, 2000).

The desire to continue providing such telemedicine services to rural Kansas towns led to the need to assess the financial components associated with this service. While improving access to health care for rural patients is one thing, providing this care in an economically reasonable manner is another. Essentially, the livelihood of every tele-oncology practice—of every telemedicine practice, for that matter—is fundamentally rooted in the economic viability of the service.

Conducting a Tele-Oncology Cost Analysis

Several studies have examined patient and provider perceptions of tele-oncology practices (Allen and Hayes, 1995; Allen and others, 1995; Kunkler and others, 1998; Mair, Whitten, May, and Doolittle, 2000); however, few researchers have analyzed costs associated with providing cancer care with telemedicine.

The oncology practices discussed here consist of telemedicine on-line visits and traditional face-to-face visits conducted in an outreach clinic setting. The goal of this cost analysis was to document expenses associated with tele-oncology visits in order to compare them with the costs associated with traditional oncology

**FIGURE 19.1. USING TELEMEDICINE TECHNOLOGY
TO PROVIDE CARE TO A RURAL PATIENT.**

care conducted in an outreach setting for two practices in Hays and Horton. A 1998 analysis measured costs for providing oncology services at only one facility (Hays Medical Center). Researchers used the same methods for measuring costs in the later analysis at both facilities (Doolittle and others, 1998). Everyone involved with the tele-oncology project was encouraged by the results of the more recent analysis: the costs of providing cancer care with telemedicine decreased from an average of just over $800 per consult reported in the original study (Doolittle and others, 1998) to $410 per consult in Hays and $629 per consult in Horton.

During the fiscal year 2000 analysis, eighty-three patients seen in Hays for oncology care generated 242 face-to-face visits and 121 tele-oncology visits. Also during that time, thirty-two patients in Horton produced 75 face-to-face visits and 70 tele-oncology visits. The costs associated with providing services for each facility were tabulated. On-site clinic expenses included air and car travel, secretarial and scheduling personnel, fax and phone, office rent, physician contract, nursing staff, nursing and hospital administrative expenses, billing costs, transcription, clinic room and equipment, equipment depreciation, and supplies. Telemedicine clinic expenses included the cost of the telemedicine room, telemedicine equipment, telecommunication line charges, technical personnel, and miscellaneous supplies. Tables 19.1 and 19.2 offer a more detailed look at how costs per visit were calculated for each facility. The tables break down costs attributed to KUMC and to Hays and Horton, respectively; they then calculate cost per visit by dividing the total costs by the total number of visits.

Cost Analysis Challenges

Perhaps the biggest challenge encountered while conducting the cost analysis was obtaining financial figures from so many different health care systems and personnel groups. When working with an academic medical center (which comprises four separate fiscal entities itself) and two private hospital systems, it becomes quite

TABLE 19.1. HAYS PRACTICE COSTS.

	On-Site	Telemedicine
University of Kansas Medical Center costs	$16,001	$6,177
Site costs	116,179	43,487
Total costs	132,180	49,664
Total visits	242	121
Cost per visit	$546	$410

TABLE 19.2. HORTON PRACTICE COSTS.

	On-Site and Telemedicine
University of Kansas Medical Center costs	$45,125
Site costs	46,020
Total costs	91,145
Total visits	145 (75 in-person, 70 telemedicine)
Cost per visit	$629

a challenge to determine who is paying for what expenses. Furthermore, there were different levels of sophistication when tracking expenses electronically. The oncologist was based at an academic medical center; consequently, in order to track expenses related to physician time, researchers had to ascertain which elements of care were funded by the academic center (school of medicine, the physicians' practice corporation, and the hospital) and which were borne by the rural health care systems.

After understanding funding lines, the next step of collaborating with different fiscal and different political institutions to obtain actual cost figures was even more challenging. We learned that in order to bring so many different groups to the table, it is essential that those people responsible for assisting with the analysis have an interest in understanding the purpose for and the intended outcomes of conducting the cost study.

What the Cost Analysis Taught Us

Providing telemedicine services is expensive. Financial feasibility is not something easily obtained in a specialty telemedicine clinic of any kind. It is, however, something to continue working toward. Here are the lessons learned from conducting a cost analysis of the Kansas tele-oncology project:

• *While the average cost per tele-oncology visit is high, it has decreased significantly in the past several years.* Although the costs of providing cancer care using telemedicine to Hays and Horton are $410 and $629, respectively, those figures illustrate a significant reduction from the $800 average cost per consult in Hays in 1998 (Doolittle and others, 1998). As the two practices continue to grow and ways to cut costs are elucidated further, we anticipate that the costs associated with providing tele-oncology services will continue to decline. Finally, while costs for outreach visits and telemedicine visits for the Horton site were comparable, it is important to point out that providing in-person visits for the Hays site was more expensive than providing services using telemedicine (see Table 19.1).

• *Cost is closely tied to system use; many expenses associated with telemedicine relate to personnel rather than technology.* As with any other technology, the cost of telemedicine equipment has steadily declined over the past several years as it has become more widely used. However, the costs associated with telemedicine personnel have not decreased over time. It is therefore necessary to begin looking at project personnel as a next step in potential cost reduction. The roles and responsibilities of individuals involved with the tele-oncology project in Kansas should be reevaluated in an effort to decrease expenses—at the same time providing quality care—as we continue to work toward an economically sensible model.

• *Successfully conducting a cost analysis of a tele-oncology practice is largely dependent on the personnel involved with the analysis.* Because one of the fundamental challenges associated with conducting a cost analysis is the ability to bring different systems of people together in collaboration with one another, it is imperative to have personnel involved with the analysis who are genuinely interested in understanding the project from a business perspective. Many individuals were instrumental in pulling together numbers for both analyses described in this chapter. The director of oncology services, the tele-oncology nurse, the office manager, and the telemedicine coordinator at the Hays site all participated in the analysis by gathering numbers related to the telemedicine project. Horton's chief financial officer and tele-oncology nurse were responsible for providing KUMC researchers with their cost figures, and the assistant director of telemedicine, along with the oncology services office manager at KUMC, helped collect data at the Kansas City site. The desire these contributors had to learn about conducting a cost analysis and to determine whether tele-oncology makes sense from a financial framework ensured the ultimate success of conducting the analysis.

• *Tele-oncology is not just about money; it is about providing a much-needed service.* To many, the intangible components of offering tele-oncology services to patients in rural Kansas outweigh the associated costs. The nature of cancer makes it a family problem; it is a condition that touches the lives of everyone around the patient, and as such, health care providers must create ways to treat the entire family. They must accommodate family members and caregivers as much as possible, and they must attempt to relieve the burden placed on both groups whenever feasible as well. While tele-oncology makes it possible for patients to receive much-needed care and treatment at home in their own communities without the need to travel, it also helps health care providers accommodate family members and other caregivers. Tele-oncology offers family members and other caregivers the ability to take part in clinic visits without having to miss work or spend time away from their own nuclear families.

Since the Kansas tele-oncology project began in 1995, we have seen costs decline, have determined that personnel requirements may be reduced in order to recognize further cost reductions, have learned that a successful cost analysis is driven by a team that is truly interested in understanding the business side of telemedicine, and have noted that while tele-oncology visits are typically expensive, there are many intangible benefits for cancer patients and their families.

The Future of Tele-Oncology in Kansas

While the Horton, Kansas, tele-oncology practice has not quite reached the point financially that the Hays practice has attained, it is approaching success in terms of economic feasibility. It is important to point out that the expenses listed for each practice are offset by the revenue generated for the hospital system when patients remain in their local communities (laboratory fees, X-rays, chemotherapy administration charges). At this time, the KUMC oncologist continues to see patients in Hays and Horton using telemedicine as well as on-site because each local community has determined that the benefit outweighs the costs when it comes to the care of cancer patients. Researchers at KUMC, in collaboration with partnering rural sites, continue to look for ways to decrease the costs of providing these essential services.

To build on the cost analyses described in this chapter, KUMC tele-oncology researchers are developing a protocol for conducting a cost-benefit analysis of the project. This study is examining how the costs associated with providing oncology care using telemedicine relate to the benefits realized by patients who receive telemedical services. The twenty-five-item Therapy-Related Symptom Checklist (Williams and others, 2001) will be used to assess the quality of life of cancer patients who participate in the Kansas tele-oncology project. Quality of life will in turn be used to measure the benefits associated with the project. We hope this upcoming cost-benefit study will demonstrate that while telemedicine currently is a more expensive way than traditional visits to provide oncology care, it offers several important benefits to the patients who use the technology. In future years, we hope to develop a cost model that justifies the tele-oncology practice from an economic perspective as well.

Discussion Questions

1. Do the costs associated with maintaining a tele-oncology practice outweigh the potential benefits realized by rural cancer patients?
2. If you were a hospital administrator who was asked to evaluate the costs associated with a tele-oncology practice at your facility, how would you do so?
3. What ways can you conceive for reducing the costs associated with providing care to cancer patients using telemedicine?

References

Allen, A., and Hayes, J. "Patient Satisfaction with Teleoncology: A Pilot Study." *Telemedicine Journal*, 1995, *1*(1), 41–46.

Allen, A., and others. "A Pilot Study of Physician Acceptance of Tele-Oncology." *Journal of Telemedicine and Telecare*, 1995, *1*(1), 34–37.

Doolittle, G. C., and others. "A Cost Measurement Study for a Tele-Oncology Practice." *Journal of Telemedicine and Telecare*, 1998, *4*, 84–88.

Kunkler, J. H., and others. "A Pilot Study of Tele-Oncology in Scotland." *Journal of Telemedicine and Telecare*, 1998, *4*(2), 113–119.

Mair, F., Whitten, P., May, C., and Doolittle, G. C. "Patients' Perceptions of a Telemedicine Specialty Clinic." *Journal of Telemedicine and Telecare*, 2000, *6(1)*, 36–40.

Williams, P. D., and others. "Treatment Type and Symptom Severity Among Oncology Patients by Self-Report." *International Journal of Nursing Studies*, 2001, *38*, 359–367.

PART FIVE

EDUCATION

Education is what survives when what has been learned has been forgotten.

B. F. SKINNER

CHAPTER TWENTY

THE ROLE OF THE INTERNET IN PROSTATE CANCER SURVIVORS' ILLNESS NARRATIVES

Michael Irvin Arrington

Prostate cancer is a disease with an impact on men's identities, relationships, and sex lives (Arrington, 2000b). Men's narrative accounts of their prostate cancer experiences reflect the stigma of the cancer label, the uncertainty that accompanies diagnosis and treatment, attendant changes in marital and family relationships, and confirmed or modified definitions of appropriate sexual behavior (Arrington, 2000a, 2002, 2003). Upon diagnosis, men seek information to help them countermand the stigma of cancer and the fears of side effects such as incontinence and erectile dysfunction.

Extant research has used narrative analysis to examine survivors' postillness stories of identity and relationships (Arrington, 2000a). Further reflection reveals that technology, especially the Internet, can play a substantial role in the stories of prostate cancer survivors. Health-related sites such as webMD.com and cancer.org (the official site of the American Cancer Society) provide information that can lessen uncertainty for newly diagnosed men. On-line support groups can serve as an informational and emotional support forum in which the lack of face-to-face contact makes personal disclosure less threatening and stigmatizing. It comes as no surprise, then, that approximately one-third of the prostate cancer survivors I have interviewed acknowledged the Internet as a site (pun intended) of informational and emotional support. Some of the men used the site as their only source of formal support, while others combined it with support from other sources.

The following three composite narratives illustrate the range of Internet use among the prostate cancer survivors I have interviewed for various research projects examining the sources of information and support for men diagnosed with prostate cancer. The cases present the experiences of one survivor who did not use the Internet, one who gathered information on-line, and one who used the Internet as a source of information and emotional support.

Case One: Mr. Allen

Well, I had been pretty healthy for most of my life. I don't have the stamina of a marathon runner or the strength of a bodybuilder, but I did what I could to stay in fairly good shape. But about six months ago, I began to notice an increase in my urination frequency, especially at night. I could no longer sleep through the night without waking up once—and usually at least twice—to go to the bathroom. I didn't say anything about it for a while. I just kept crawling out of bed each night, as quietly as possible, trying not to wake my wife. After a couple of weeks, though, my wife suggested that I make an appointment with our family doctor.

To be honest, I thought it was no big deal—just one of those marks of getting older. My physician, on the other hand, was highly concerned, especially after he conducted a physical exam and found that my prostate was larger than normal. She gave me the name of a urologist and suggested that I see him for a prostate specific antigen (PSA) test. At the time, I was rather embarrassed to admit that I didn't even know what "PSA" stood for. I made the appointment and underwent some tests at the urologist's office. A few days later, I received a call from the doctor's office, asking me to visit the office again. Of course, I then knew that something wasn't right. No one ever minds telling you good news over the phone. And before I knew it, there I was, sitting in the doctor's office again as he explained to me that I had cancerous cells in my prostate.

Oh my goodness, I thought. *Cancer.* I hate that word. Almost as much as I hated the thought of telling my wife about my diagnosis. In fact, I don't know which I feared more: the possibility of dying of cancer or the task of telling my wife I had cancer. The doctor talked for a few more minutes about treatment options and said that my situation wasn't as bleak as it likely seemed to me. To tell you the truth, though, I hardly even remember that conversation. I wasn't thinking about hormones or surgery or any of the other terms I vaguely remember from the doctor's conversation. I wasn't even thinking about obtaining a second opinion. I just wanted to get home and find a way to break the news to my wife.

It took me a day or two to get over the initial shock and to decide whether to tell my daughter. My wife and I agreed not to bother her with the news yet. She recently married and moved to another state, and we did not want to worry her. I was relieved that my wife agreed; besides, I would have had no idea of how to tell our daughter. It dawned on me that I knew next to nothing about prostate cancer—or "prostrate cancer," as I referred to it until the urologist corrected me. Not only did I know little about prostate ca—, um, the disease, but I had no idea what the disease would do to me. How would this experience affect these things that I held dear? If something went wrong, in what position would I leave my wife? How would this affect me sexually? How would all of these matters affect me as a person? Would I become bitter? Would the disease leave me debilitated and victimized? Would I spend the final days of my life as a burden to someone? These were not the kinds of questions I usually discussed with my doctor—or with anyone else, for that matter.

I needed to find some answers, so I started reading everything I could find. In the newest and largest bookstore in town, I scanned the health section, hoping to find a book about my situation. Instead, I found about thirty. Half of them were written by doctors who claimed to have discovered a cure for the disease; the other half were written by men who claimed to have beaten the disease. My tight budget would only allow me to purchase a few books, so I bought two from the former list and one of the survivors' stories.

The first two books taught me a great deal about the disease—some medical terms I had never heard before, various treatment options, and explanation of what PSA actually stands for. At the same time, though, parts of the books seemed too good to be true. One claimed that some nutrient in tomatoes could cure the disease. In the second book, the miracle cure was something called saw palmetto. During my next office visit, I asked my doctor about the books, but he was not convinced that either espoused "cure" was effective. He was glad, however, that I had done some reading about ways to treat the disease. We discussed the matter together before deciding on a prostatectomy, and I'm glad I was able to understand his comments.

Case Two: Mr. Bartlett

After the doctor told me about my prostate, the first thing I felt was anxiety. You know, what does this mean for me in the future? How much longer will I live? How will this affect relationships with my wife and children? My wife and I have five children. The youngest and only girl, a registered nurse, is thirty. I always call her whenever I have questions about medical matters, even after seeing a doctor. My doctor is very knowledgeable, but he has so little time to talk with me that I always leave his office with unanswered (and unasked) questions.

My family is the greatest blessing I have ever been given, but I wanted to find the answers on my own. I guess I'm the kind of a person who prefers to do my own research. I'm a visual person; I learn best by reading, by seeing things. So when I learned that my PSA score was higher than normal, I decided to search for information about prostate cancer. Aside from the occasional story on the evening news, and that time when a character on my favorite television show had the disease in a story line, I never gave much thought to my prostate. After the PSA test, though, I had to make up for lost time. I read everything I could find on prostate cancer. After reading some customer reviews, I ordered a few books from my favorite on-line bookstore. I also used the Web to look for recent research on prostate cancer. I never realized there were so many medical journals out there, each one dealing with a different health topic. While I pondered treatment options, I read one book and Internet site after another until I reached the verge of pathological investigation. I knew I needed to make a decision soon, but too much information made the decision as difficult as (if not more difficult than) it would have been with the little information I received from my physician.

While perusing the bulletin board at church one Sunday, I noticed an announcement about a group that was meeting to discuss prostate cancer. *Why not?* I figured. The next week, I attended the group meeting and learned lots of information that confirmed my personal findings. After reading about enough treatment options to make my head spin, it was helpful to talk with other men who had undergone these procedures. The group facilitator, a young physician who was relatively new in town, also contributed information to the group discussion, even though he had not been diagnosed with the disease. In addition to the information I received, I felt a great deal of support there from other people who had the same sense of curiosity about how to handle the diagnosis and treat the disease.

I attended a few more monthly meetings, sharing information and asking for advice until I opted to undergo radiation therapy. To be honest, I had little use for the group after my treatment. The group focuses on pretreatment issues—defining important terms, discovering treatment options, etc.—to the exclusion of the post-treatment questions that few people mentioned at the meetings. My story doesn't end with my treatment. So where do I go now? What can I expect after treatment? Will I be incontinent? Impotent? What do I tell my wife? How will this illness continue to affect me?

Case Three: Mr. Carpenter

One of the most helpful things that I came across early on in my reading was that there were four values that I needed to understand. First was the value of knowing as much as I could about the enemy, meaning the cancer itself. I needed to know this disease and how it functioned in every way: what it looked like on slides, every bit of information I could get my hands on.

Second was the value of knowing my allies. By that, I mean my wife, my family, and the other people I could call on when I was emotionally caught up in the issues related to my mortality.

The third value lay in knowing myself—in knowing how my body and my life were changing. So many questions plagued me: Do I know what's happening to me? Do I understand how this illness will change my sexual experiences? Have I placed too high a value on my sex life? Are there other things in life that should be more important to me?

The fourth value was the importance of knowing my resources. You see, this is my story, but I am not alone in my battle against prostate cancer. I am blessed with more resources than I ever knew I had, and, to my surprise, one of my most powerful resources has been my computer.

My story started some time ago. For over a year, I was going to the bathroom frequently at night. I was getting up five or six times every evening, often waking my wife. Anyway, the university cancer center distributed printed advertisements for free PSA testing. My wife saw it first and suggested I go in for an exam, so I did. When the doctor told me that my score was 9.5, I didn't know whether to be relieved or worried. Finally, after an awkward pause, "You'd better get yourself a urologist and do something about it." I did so without even discussing it with my wife.

But *Do what?* I wondered. Fortunately, I was learning how to use the computer our daughter bought us for our anniversary. In fact, I used the computer every day, whether to play games, read the news, or send messages to the kids. One day, instead of e-mailing my children, I surfed the Web, using a search engine to find Web sites about prostate cancer. I was simultaneously saddened and relieved to know that I was not alone in my experience; many men discussed their own experiences on personal Web pages. Other sites had a more professional look; these sites usually were the pages of well-known organizations such as the American Cancer Society or the National Cancer Institute. Other sites, such as the National Prostate Cancer Coalition, advocated for funding for prostate cancer research. All of these sites included valuable information. In a short time, I felt like an expert on the disease.

A few weeks later, I underwent what the doctors call a radical prostatectomy. In common language, a surgeon removed my prostate. Before my diagnosis, I had no idea that the prostate was such an important part of sexual function. Shortly after treatment, however, I was all too aware that I lost much of my sex drive and sexual function. Despite the surgeon's preprocedural disclaimer, I never imagined that I would be . . . well, impotent. And I never imagined that I would have to discuss the matter with my wife.

One day, out of curiosity, I entered "prostate" and "impotent" into a search engine. The computer responded with a lengthy list of on-line news groups and chatrooms. As I examined each site, I was overwhelmed with information, but not the kind of information I was accustomed to reading. Instead, the chatrooms included men's questions and answers about the ways in which prostate cancer changed who they were—as fathers, grandfathers, brothers, husbands, lovers, and sexual beings. I read each entry as though I had never seen anything like it before—because, to be honest, I hadn't. I read about new patients' disbelief after hearing the diagnosis. One man worried that his wife would leave him if his surgery left him impotent. Another patient worried whether he would have to quit his job because of incontinence. I even read men's conversations about posttreatment sex (and, in some cases, the lack thereof), a topic I previously had been unable to address with my wife. When she came home from the grocery store that evening, my wife and I openly (albeit awkwardly) talked about who we were before the cancer and who we could become in its aftermath.

Discussion Questions

1. Why might prostate cancer survivors feel more comfortable going on-line for information about prostate cancer and related matters than they would feel when seeking support in face-to-face contexts?
2. If you were designing a Web site or an on-line support group about prostate cancer, what elements would you regard as necessary for the site or group to be successful? How would you address these needs?
3. If you were researching the utility of on-line prostate cancer information and support groups, on which variables might you want to focus? How would you design such a study?
4. What advantages do on-line information and support groups hold over a face-to-face support group?
5. What advantages does a face-to-face support group hold over an on-line group?
6. If your father or grandfather were diagnosed with prostate cancer, would you expect him to go on-line for information and support? Would you want him to go on-line?

References

Arrington, M. I. "Sexuality, Society, and Senior Citizens: An Analysis of Sex Talk Among Prostate Cancer Support Group Members." *Sexuality and Culture,* 2000a, *4*(4), 45–74.

Arrington, M. I. "Thinking Inside the Box: On Identity, Sexuality, Prostate Cancer, and Social Support." *Journal of Aging and Identity,* 2000b, *5,* 151–158.

Arrington, M. I. "Recreating Ourselves: Stigma, Identity Changes, and Narrative Reconstruction Among Prostate Cancer Survivors." Unpublished doctoral dissertation, University of South Florida, 2002.

Arrington, M. I. "'I Don't Want to Be an Artificial Man': Narrative Reconstruction of Sexuality Among Prostate Cancer Survivors." *Sexuality and Culture,* 2003, *7*(2), 30–58.

CHAPTER TWENTY-ONE

SUCCESSFUL WEB SITE CONSTRUCTION AND MANAGEMENT

Harnessing the Skill and Enthusiasm of Volunteers

Marlene M. Maheu, Joseph P. McMenamin

Health education takes many forms, including information disseminated to the public. SelfhelpMagazine (http://selfhelpmagazine.com) is one of the first privately developed mental health Web sites on the Internet. The on-line magazine was first published (under the name of *Practical Psychology Magazine*) on November 1, 1994, and has ranked as one of the world's top ten mental health Web sites ever since. SelfhelpMagazine (SHM) averages over 120,000 unique monthly visitors from 103 countries worldwide. It does not offer direct access to clinicians for professional service of any type. Instead, it was developed to translate scientific information into plain English for a worldwide readership. SHM is accessible twenty-four hours a day. This format is only one of many large and creative endeavors offered by mental health practitioners exploring how to advance their professions and deliver information using the power and reach of the Net. From the beginning, SHM has been an educational publication, aiming to help consumers understand and cope with issues ranging from mental illness through social and emotional problems. The successful engagement of volunteers has kept costs down; nevertheless, this approach has its own unique set of problems and requires supervision and coordination.

The volunteer-based peer-reviewed Web site holds a rich selection of approximately 825 short articles contributed by hundreds of credentialed mental health professionals. Mental health is still a young and growing field, and controversies abound even among trained professionals. The authors whose works are featured may disagree with each other from time to time and with the editors, but readers are given a divergent point of view and asked for their own opinions regarding the usefulness of each article. In addition, with forty discussion forums, the Web site supports one of the largest and most active on-line communities. By combining professionalism, a user-friendly presentation, and community building forums while avoiding blatant commercialism, SHM has become one of the most respected and frequently linked-to mental health Web sites.

Perhaps in part because of the success and prominence of SHM, mental health professionals are requesting accurate information about the development of professional Web sites for various telehealth purposes. This chapter outlines the approach employed by one such site, SelfhelpMagazine.

Managing Costs by Working with a Volunteer Staff

The features and traffic on the SHM Web site rival those of Web sites built by companies with million-dollar budgets. Yet with careful planning and management of resources, it has cost less than $10,000 to develop and operate the site for almost a decade. Most of these costs have been for hosting fees, that is, the cost of renting space and support services through a commercial Web service provider. Although SHM receives some support from sponsors and advertisers, its content, construction, and maintenance have relied principally on the contributions of over three hundred volunteer professionals. These unpaid mental health professionals, Web site developers, and artists may benefit from experience and exposure, but they seem motivated mostly by a desire to serve the public. Contributors also sign agreements that describe their responsibilities and give ownership of their work to Pioneer Development Resources, Inc., which owns SHM. Volunteers have come from three groups.

The first group consists of Web developers. SHM regularly recruits Web development volunteers by advertising in programmers' e-mail discussion lists, Web sites devoted to Web masters and managers, and the SHM newsletter. Most new recruits are now found by current or former volunteers, who regularly suggest that new developers gain experience by joining the magazine's staff. The design and programming staff has evolved to consist of an average of thirty active members at any given time, forming a management team with five levels of promotion available to any incoming intern. All Web developer volunteers share weekly reports that foster a sense of community among staff members. In fact, various groups have banned together to accomplish larger projects and nickname themselves to denote their special bond (for example, "Webring team" or "graphics team").

The second group of volunteers includes artists, most of whom have volunteered their graphics after visiting SHM. Others were contacted by volunteers or by the editor in chief to ask permission to reproduce their work in the magazine. Most such contributors are motivated by their own altruism, as well as the opportunity to be associated with a large-scale, successful Web site that might help them increase traffic to and interest in their work. This method of enhancing the visual aspects of the Web site has worked extremely well: all artists approached to date have agreed to contribute their work.

The third volunteer group consists of an ever growing number of mental health professionals who write and review articles. Although recruitment efforts in the mid-1990s were made every four to six months by sending requests to various professional e-mail listservs, articles now arrive from new and previous authors every month in the mailbox of the editor in chief from a link at the bottom of SHM's Web pages. Press releases summarizing published clinical research outcomes are received from number of credible professional associations, and also used as the basis for new articles when specialized information is requested by readers or when traffic in the magazine suggests that readers are seeking information on a particular topic. All contributions are peer reviewed and carefully edited by the managing editor before publication.

Initially authors were encouraged to add their e-mail addresses or Web site addresses to articles they authored, but it soon became apparent that this practice might all too easily lead to personal and professional e-mail communication between reader and author. If in the mind of the reader a "professional relationship" were to be developed and something were to go wrong in that relationship, someone might claim that the magazine (as well as the entire volunteer staff) was responsible for being the "referral source." This might create liability for the online magazine. Therefore, the practice of giving direct electronic access to authors was stopped. The magazine does allow traditional contact information, telephone number and street address, as published in an author's biographical statement for each article.

SelfhelpMagazine Content

Originally, the magazine published articles according to the standards set by print publication for consumers, that is, without references. It has now evolved to follow standards in place for on-line health care publications. New contributions must have at least one reference that is not written by the same author. More references are better. Articles must also be written in basic English, that is, written at a sixth-grade reading level. Cross-cultural sensitivity is essential as well, since readers from 105 countries gather information from this Web site.

Although some reprints and artwork are obtained with permission from other Web sites and publications, most of the material in SHM is original and specifically written for its readership. Only a few new articles are selected every month to augment the existing library of approximately 825 articles, divided into twenty departments. Departments have changed over the years, but Exhibit 21.1 outlines the departments as currently designated that seem to draw the most readers.

The articles convey varied science-based perspectives on psychological issues and usually include guidelines for working on problems. Readers are advised that in a number of areas of psychology, controversy surrounds certain professional beliefs and practices. Readers are asked to rate each article for usefulness, ease of reading, and overall quality. A number of professionals who read the on-line magazine have reported that they print out articles and give them to their patients because of the ease of understanding the material.

One of SHM's most significant contributions to the mental health community is the vast number of discussion forums operated in-house. The discussion forums generate a remarkable amount of traffic, averaging seven thousand unique visitors per day. Members from around the world participate in these forums, which provide support for those with social and emotional problems from cross-cultural perspectives from around the world. Support is offered by the community by giving and receiving responses to questions posed by anonymous users. Despite this anonymity, participants can elect to have e-mail responses sent directly to their e-mail boxes when their messages are answered. Users freely give their e-mail addresses to SHM. The site's privacy policy is not to resell or release e-mail addresses of community members to third parties.

SHM discussion forums are not directly mediated or moderated before messages appear on-line. Many users are regular contributors (daily, weekly, or monthly) and know each other by their "handles," that is, names they have given themselves in the SHM Forum. Other users drop in occasionally, make a few comments or

EXHIBIT 21.1. MOST POPULAR ARTICLE DEPARTMENTS IN SELFHELPMAGAZINE.

Aging and Aging Parents	Gay/Lesbian/Bi/Trans	Relationships
Alcohol, Nicotine and	Health	Seasonal Articles
Other Drugs	Internet Psychology	Sex and Lust
Children's Behavior	Loss and Bereavement	Spirituality
Chronic Illness	Meditation, Guided	Sports and Performance
Cultural Competence	Fantasies and Other	Teens
Cyber-affairs	Stress Reducers	Traumatic Stress
Depression and Anxiety	Men	Women
Divorce	Parenting	Work
Dreams and Dreaming	Personal Growth	Readers' Articles
Eating Disorders	Psychotherapy	

leave a question, and wait for an e-mail to notify them that they have received a response. Because the discussion forums have been part of SHM since 1996, former participants nostalgically stop in to see old friends, give the community a personal update, ask another question, or simply read what others have written.

An advantage of an in-house discussion forum, as opposed to an e-mail listserv discussion group or a large news group, is that in-house discussion forums can more readily enforce a code of conduct (http://www.selfhelpmagazine.com/conduct.html) and a service agreement (http://www.selfhelpmagazine.com/serviceagreement. html) that assist users in maintaining the tone and tenor of the community. Forum members are informed that they can post anonymously and inappropriate responses will be removed by staff members as soon as possible.

It is clearly stated that professionals associated with the Web site will not answer consumer questions and that users are to proceed at their own risk with any advice they obtain from others who post in a discussion forum. SHM disclaims intending to or creating a professional-patient relationship. Nonlicensed volunteers comb through the discussion forums on a regular basis and delete all posts that violate any aspect of the code of conduct.

SelfhelpMagazine Newsletter

SHM publishes a newsletter that is sent to over sixty-five hundred recipients worldwide by e-mail. The newsletter typically carries one or two articles in their entirety. While other publications have moved from this format to simply listing titles and brief summaries of articles, SHM has maintained its niche as a publisher of relevant mental health articles in e-mail without reliance on the Web site. This allows the readership to forward through e-mail an entire article to friends and family who may be limited to e-mail in their access to the Internet. Links to other articles by the same author or along the same themes are also included. The SHM Newsletter features links to several discussion forums, an advertising department for the magazine's continual search for new volunteers, book listings, and a sponsor message and link to the sponsor's Web site. One must specifically make a request to receive the SHM Newsletter (http://www.selfhelpmagazine.com/ subscrib.html). Sponsors are plainly identified at the top of every newsletter.

SelfhelpMagazine has taken a number of forms since 1994, owing primarily to the creativity and generosity of its volunteer staff, and the interactivity the magazine enjoys with its readership. SHM has become and remains one of the largest and most active mental health Web sites on-line. The details of its internal function will serve as a guide to those who are interested in developing Web sites for their particular telehealth services.

Discussion Questions

1. What are the pros and cons of employing a volunteer workforce to maintain a health-related Web site?
2. If you ran a Web site such as this and found it necessary to fire an intern who proved ill suited to the job, how would you do it? What risks would you run?
3. What unique challenges does this on-line magazine face as a result of an international audience?
4. Discuss the relative advantages and disadvantages of an in-house discussion forum as opposed to an e-mail list serve discussion group or a large news group.
5. Who should judge the suitability of the content on the Web site in regard to profanity, sexual explicitness, and slander?

CHAPTER TWENTY-TWO

MULTIMEDIA EDUCATION FOR GESTATIONAL DIABETES PATIENTS

Deborah C. Glik, Sally F. Shaw, Gloria M. Chinea, Amy Myerson

The growing epidemic of diabetes in the developed world is also affecting pregnant women. Gestational diabetes mellitus (GDM), or diabetes during pregnancy, is one of the most common health problems affecting pregnant women and is on the increase. In the United States, 135,000 pregnant women are diagnosed with GDM each year. The incidence of this condition is greater among Native Americans and African Americans, and highest among Hispanics, reportedly affecting up to 10 percent of pregnancies.

Broadly defined, GDM is a carbohydrate intolerance with variable degrees of severity identified during pregnancy. The symptoms and management are similar to diabetes type 2, but because it occurs during pregnancy, this condition puts both mother and child at risk. GDM can cause complications of pregnancy and childbirth, birth defects, increased incidence of stillbirth, and increased risk for diabetes and obesity among children born to diabetic women. With prenatal care, including strict monitoring and self-regulation of diet and blood sugar levels and compliance with necessary insulin regimens, the risks associated with this condition can be greatly reduced.

It is common practice to mount health education interventions during pregnancy to ensure that women change or reduce their risk behaviors. However, successful health education programs within clinical settings can be labor intensive, and for pregnant women they are time limited. Proper control of GDM entails intensive education, monitoring of blood glucose levels, and vigilance on the part of both mothers and clinical staff. Women are typically diagnosed at twenty-four to twenty-eight weeks of pregnancy and must quickly learn to control their diabetes within a short ten- to twelve-week window. A great deal of the burden lies with the mother, who must check her blood sugar levels, adjust her diet and exercise level, go through routine testing, and learn a great deal of information about her condition in a very short time. Ethnic minority women at most risk may not have access to such programs. Appropriate materials in print or video form for often low-literacy, non-English-speaking populations may be lacking. There is also increased caregiver burden, as managing GDM means increased surveillance and counseling on the part of providers.

The Beginnings of Healthy Beginnings

In 1997, a collaboration was formed between researchers at the University of California, Los Angeles (UCLA) School of Public Health and the educational and OB/GYN and Medicine departments at St. John's Regional Medical Center (SJRMC) and St. John's Pleasant Valley Hospital (SJPVH) to discuss the need to develop a tool that would provide standardized gestational diabetes education to GDM patients in the short amount of time before childbirth, as well as reduce the burden on health care providers and improve patient-provider interactions. Multimedia, educational CD-ROMs appeared to be the option that would meet the needs of the health care providers and their GDM patients. That year, UCLA and SJRMC/SJPVH began planning and developing a multimedia educational program for women who have GDM, particularly low-income Hispanic women.

SJRMC/SJPVH had already created the Healthy Beginnings program, an educational intervention program that delivered comprehensive perinatal services care program for high-risk women. This program uses bilingual health educators to conduct health education classes and nutritional counseling. Despite its success, the "Healthy Beginnings" program was labor intensive and dependent on the availability of bilingual and bicultural health care workers. Moreover, the program was not standardized in a format that could be shared with other facilities, thus making it difficult to communicate to other off-site facilities that may have wanted to adopt the program. The solution was the development of an interactive computer-based multimedia educational CD-ROM developed in both English and Spanish. The UCLA/SJRMC team adapted the Healthy Beginnings curriculum and created a CD-ROM to be used by low-literacy populations and to supplement the intensive education and case management of SJRMC patients.

The Healthy Beginnings curriculum and computer-based multimedia program are based on theoretical concepts from the health belief model (Becker, 1974) and the social learning theory (Bandura, 1982). The health belief model posits that improvements in patients' perceptions of risk, relative costs and benefits of actions, as well as overcoming barriers to action will increase initiation and maintenance of behavioral compliance with treatment guidelines (Becker, 1974). Elements of the program that are guided by social learning theory include an emphasis on skill building, behavior modeling, goal setting, and increasing self-efficacy.

Computer-Assisted Education

Recent advances in computer technology are being integrated into the clinical setting to increase patient behavioral adherence and reduce the burden on health providers. The use of computer-assisted instruction has the potential to provide patients with information in a manner that lets the patients control the amount and rate of information provided (Robinson, 1989; Science Panel on Interactive Communication and Health, 1999). Through the use of computer graphics, computer animation, and other multimedia techniques, understandable information is available to the patient. Multimedia-based programs decrease the need for reading required by print-based materials and make the information more accessible for those with low literacy levels. Narrated soundtracks allow the information to be translated into other languages such as Spanish (Mercer and Sweeney, 1995; Sweeney and Skiba, 1995). In addition, computer programs that use touch screen technology and are enriched with audiovisual aids and graphical animation can be effectively used to educate and teach skills to individuals with low literacy as well as those of varied ethnicity (Kinzie, Schorling, and Siegel, 1993; Kohlmeier, Mendz, and Miller, 1997; Mercer and Sweeney, 1995). Point-and-click technology, while not as easy as touch screen technology, provides a less expensive alternative. By using the computer to present information to patients in a standardized, reproducible format, staff time needed to conduct basic health education can be reduced, thereby increasing efficiency and reducing costs in the delivery of health care services (Farris, Stoupa, Mendenhall, and Mazzuca, 1995; Kahn, 1993; Sechrest and Henry, 1996; Tomita, Takabayashi, and Honda, 1995). Until now, no computer programs have been available for women with or at risk of GDM.

CD-ROM Development: Problems and Solutions

Prior to creating the CD-ROM, we spent a great deal of time conducting formative research and organizing information on gestational diabetes. A series of data-gathering tasks were carried out to understand the information needs of the patients, as well as the information priorities of the staff, verify the accuracy of the information, and address the literacy levels of clients. This included library research, key informant interviews, patient observations, and videotaping of ongoing classes.

The Healthy Beginnings multimedia educational CD-ROM is based on six distinct modules of content that complies with GDM clinical practice guidelines: the diagnosis of GDM, monitoring blood glucose levels, diet and exercise, insulin injection, medical complications, and postpartum care. Each module contains graphics with narration, embedded messages, quizzes, a glossary, and minimal text. The modules emphasize behavioral changes in diet, exercise, self-testing behaviors, health care utilization, and medication. These behavioral changes align with the standards of care for gestational diabetes patients.

The user-friendly CD-ROM uses Macromedia Flash software and contains minimal text, graphics, and narrative, with point-and-click technology and audiovisual capacity. It also includes a glossary to enhance an interactive environment. The instructions and educational material are represented with color-coded, multishaped, and animated pictographs. This format is based on the assumption that it is easier for individuals with lower literacy to recognize colors, shapes, and sounds rather than text. Each module is designed to run, on average, twenty minutes, to cover the important information that the patient needs to know to manage her GDM and reinforce the information through graphics, animations, narrative, and quizzes.

One of the elements we were very concerned about was keeping patient interest in the software program over the six modules. To keep the reader engaged, storytelling techniques have been used successfully in a number of health communications formats over the past few years—in videos; soap operas; and photo novellas, a format that is like a comic book except that the characters may be either drawn in graphic form or photographed styles (Glik and others, 1998). Thus, we wrote into the script a human interest story that complements the different messages of the chapters. We introduced a young woman, Rosa, and her husband, Juan, who become the story protagonists. The script follows Rosa over the course of her pregnancy: her attempts to get her blood sugar under control; the stress that she feels in trying to comply with all the demands of her treatment regimen; how she mobilizes a support network; her fears and concerns for her health; and finally, the delivery of a healthy baby.

In creating the program script, not only did the content have to flow logically from one subject to the next, but the program had to allow for linkages to be made between modules so that users can browse through the program. Each "page" contains multiple layers, such as narrative, graphic, sound, links to other pages, and icons on which to click. Thus, we needed to use storyboard techniques, similar to video and film production, to achieve this flow.

Finally, because the audience is relatively low literacy, some of the text on screen was replaced by narrative. Also, the content of the drawings, including characters, clothing style, background, and contextual cues, was made culturally appropriate.

Testing Effectiveness

A study was conducted to evaluate the effectiveness of this multimedia CD-ROM among pregnant, low-literate Hispanic women in Ventura County, California, from 2000 to 2002. Funding was provided by the National March of Dimes, a national organization that focuses on the prevention of birth defects and the promotion of healthy babies. In this randomized, controlled trial, all participants, who were newly diagnosed GDM patients, received standard education and case management. The treatment group participants received an additional educational component in the form of the gestational diabetes CD-ROM. Changes in self-perceptions, attitudes, and knowledge about gestational diabetes were assessed. Preliminary results showed greater increases in knowledge, attitudes, and self-efficacy for those exposed to the CD-ROM than those not exposed to the CD-ROM.

Revising the CD-ROM

Based on the widespread acceptance of the CD-ROM by providers and Hispanic/Latina women patients from our effectiveness study, as well as inquiries from other groups, we concluded that there is a need for a standardized educational product on this topic for other high-risk populations. The Southern California Chapter of the March of Dimes interest in the program led it to provide more funding. The CD was updated in 2004 (http://www.diabetesduringpregnancy.org).

Since the original development of the CD-ROM occurred from 1998 to—2000, the first step has been to investigate current prevention and treatment methods for GDM and update content of the GDM interactive curriculum (CD-ROM). Key informant interviews were conducted with a physician and a health educator from SJRMC/SJPVH who interact with GDM patients. The original scripts were reviewed for grammatical errors and then revised based on information provided in these interviews. When these revisions were completed, the text was submitted for review to the same physician and diabetes educator. The narrative text was reviewed for content accuracy and cultural sensitivity.

One of the problems with the original GDM multimedia CD-ROM was the large amount of on-screen text. To create a more interactive educational curriculum to which users can relate and be more involved with, graphics were created to replace some of the wordy on-screen text. Rather than have the user read on the screen what is already being said in the audio, graphics appear in place of the text to stimulate the user and to be more comprehensible for low-literate populations.

In addition, the original CD-ROM contained graphics that were cartoonish in nature, particularly the characters, such as Rosa, the main character, and the secondary characters: Juan (her husband), the doctor, the nurse, the health educator, and the lab technician. For the revised CD-ROM, new characters were created that possessed more real features that the users can relate to. Five new main characters of multiple race/ethnicities were created to represent Rose, which the user can choose from to follow through the modules (Figure 22.1).

For the CD-ROM to be more interactive and stimulating, not only should the characters be more realistic; they also be of a race/ethnicity that users can identify with. A user who can choose a character that she can identify with relates more to the situation that the character encounters in the storyline. To facilitate this tailoring of the program to the person using it, the main character's name has been changed from Rosa to the more generic Rose, which can be used for the diverse ethnic and racial groups portrayed. The new characters were tested for appropriateness and cultural sensitivity among a small sample of participants of varying race/ethnicities from SJMRC/SJPVH and UCLA.

A new interface was also created. The general layout of the original interface was kept the same, as was the coloring. In terms of the main menu, the computer programmer removed redundant chapter numbers from the original multimedia CD-ROM and consolidated quiz information. Furthermore, check marks were created, indicating which chapters or quizzes have been completed by the user. A drop-down menu on the bottom right was designed to include English, Spanish, and any other languages to be incorporated in the future. Changes to the interface include a progress bar, so that clients can see graphically how far they have to go in a chapter, and updated arrows, among other buttons, for a cleaner and more visible look. A new "blackboard" background was created for the chapter interface (see Figure 22.2). Further changes to the interface may be encountered with each update from the computer programmer.

Lessons Learned

The development and implementation of this service have offered lessons for a wide range of issues.

FIGURE 22.1. ORIGINAL AND NEW CHARACTERS
FOR THE GESTATIONAL DIABETES MULTIMEDIA CD-ROM.

Original
(Rosa)

Rose 1

Rose 2

Rose 3

Rose 4

Rose 5

Original
(John)

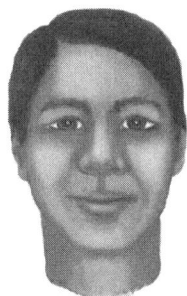

John

FIGURE 22.2. NEW MAIN MENU AND CHAPTER INTERFACES
FOR THE GESTATIONAL DIABETES MULTIMEDIA CD-ROM.

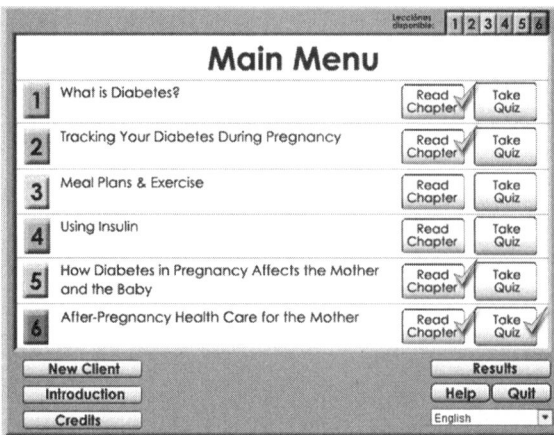

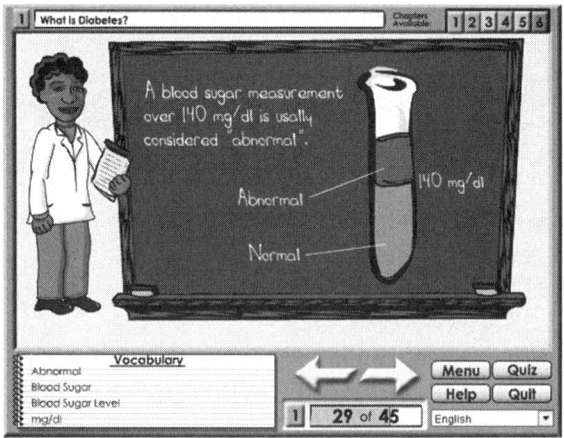

Content

When developing health education content, the focus should be on the essential topics that are needed for the desired behavior change. The actionable messages should be positioned first in the curriculum, followed by consequences and risks. Quizzes or assessments reinforce messages. Avoiding last-minute revisions will keep production on schedule.

Time and Money

During the planning stage, sufficient time must be allowed for script development, review, and revisions, as well as computer programming and graphics development for the CD-ROM. Adequate funding is essential during program planning. It is important to factor in technical costs, such as recording studio rental fees, voice-over actors, and recording equipment rental fees, as well as CD-ROM duplication, packaging, printing, and mailing costs.

Feedback from the Audience

An important step in health curriculum development is pretesting the material. To ensure that the curriculum will meet the needs of the target audience and the health care provider's needs, feedback can be acquired from a sample of the target audience, which should include all members of racial and ethnic groups, if applicable, in the sample population.

Utilization

When creating an educational multimedia program, user-friendliness is the key. Designing an educational multimedia CD-ROM that is easy to navigate will be helpful for low-literacy populations and is also a good selling point for dissemination of the product on a wider scale.

Discussion Questions

1. Incorporating computer-assisted education within the clinical setting can be an innovative strategy in the delivery of health messages. What may be the benefits of supplementing standard health education with an educational multimedia CD-ROM? What may be the drawbacks?
2. Traditional health care has been the standard for many years. How would you encourage provider acceptance of the use of computer-assisted health education?

3. What are other ways computer technology can assist low-literacy populations in disease management and prevention?

4. Tailoring messages for a target population is essential in developing curriculum. What other populations can you think of for which tailoring messages is important? How would you tailor your message?

5. What other settings can you think of in which computer-assisted education can be useful?

6. How would you design a computer-assisted program?

References

Bandura, A. "The Assessment and Predictive Generality of Self-Percepts of Efficacy." *Journal of Behavioral Therapy and Experimental Psychology,* 1982, *13*(3), 195–199.

Becker, M. H. "The Health Belief Model and Personal Health Behavior." *Health Education Monographs,* 1974, *2,* 324–508.

Farris, N., Stoupa, R., Mendenhall, J., and Mazzuca, K. "A Computerized Diabetes Education Module for Documenting Patient Outcomes." *Computers in Nursing,* 1995, *12*(6), 272–276.

Glik, D., and others. "Health Education Goes to Hollywood: Working with Daytime and Prime Time Television for Immunization Education." *Journal of Health Communication,* 1998, *3,* 263–282.

Kahn, G. "Computer-Based Patient Education: A Progress Report." *M.D. Computing,* 1993, *10*(2), 93–99.

Kinzie, M., Schorling, J., and Siegel, M. "Prenatal Alcohol Education for Low-Income Women with Interactive Multimedia." *Patient Education and Counseling,* 1993, *21,* 51–61.

Kohlmeier, L., Mendz, M., and Miller, M. "Computer Assisted Self Interviewing: A Multimedia Approach to Dietary Assessment." *American Society for Clinical Nutrition,* 1997, *65,* 1275s–1281s.

Mercer, Z., and Sweeney, N. M. "Developing Patient Education Programs with Multimedia Technology Incorporating Patient Feedback into Program Design." *Medinfo,* 1995, *8*(2), 1186–1189.

Robinson, T. N. "Community Health Behavior Change Through Computer Network Health Promotion: Preliminary Findings from Stanford Health Net." *Computer Methods and Programs in Biomedicine,* 1989, *30* (2-3), 137–144.

Science Panel on Interactive Communication and Health. *Wired for Health and Well-Being: The Emergence of Interactive Health Communication.* Washington, D.C.: U.S. Government Printing Office, 1999.

Sechrest, R. C., and Henry, D. J. "Computer-Based Patient Education: Observations on Effective Communication in the Clinical Setting." *Journal of Biocommunication,* 1996, *23*(1), 8–12.

Sweeney, M. A., and Skiba, D. "Combing Telecommunications and Interactive Multimedia Health Information on the Electronic Superhighway." *Medinfo 95 Proceedings,* 1995, 1524–1527.

Tomita, M., Takabayashi, K., and Honda, M. "Computer Assisted Instruction on Multimedia Environment for Patients." *Medinfo,* 1995, *8,* 1192.

CHAPTER TWENTY-THREE

NEW PARADIGMS FOR CONTINUING EDUCATION

Training Providers How to Use Technology

Thomas S. Nesbitt, Thu P. Tran, Jana Katz

Information and telecommunication technology offers new ways of delivering services to remote or isolated populations. Over the past fifteen years, telemedicine (TM) has been expanding at a rapid pace. Developed as a way to improve access to medical specialists in rural areas, many health care facilities are turning to telemedicine to help meet the needs of this underserved population ("Telemedicine," 2002). In addition, technology is being used for teleconferencing and continuing medical education for practitioners who are far from major urban areas and teaching hospitals. Although the spectrum of telemedicine applications has been in development for several decades, its use continues to expand and diversify. This is particularly true in California, where the large quantity of consultations and programs have added significantly to the growth of distance medicine (Grigsby and Brown, 1999).

The integration of telecommunication technology into the health care delivery system can be challenging and requires training and support. Specifically, the complexity of telemedicine systems can be an impediment to their use (Yamamoto, Toma, and Bell, 2001), and lack of training is frequently cited as a barrier to telemedicine within the medical literature (Blignault and Kennedy, 1999; Barry, Reid, Ibbotson, and Bower, 2000; Walker and Whetton, 2002). There are approximately ten telemedicine training programs available in the United States and Canada (http://tie2.telemed.org/telemed101/training.asp). Recognizing the importance of training in providing excellent telemedicine services, the

University of California provides a center where practitioners and administrators can develop the skills and knowledge needed to enhance the quality of health care in their communities.

The Program: The Telemedicine Learning Center

The Telemedicine Learning Center is a unique training program incorporating didactic sessions with hands-on experience to give participants the tools they need to run successful telemedicine programs.

Educational Foundation of the Telemedicine Learning Center

The Telemedicine Learning Center (TLC) at the University of California, Davis (UC Davis), uses a variety of educational models in its training curriculum. These include adult education, learning theory, and train-the-trainer models. Adult education research has shown that the process has more relevance in adult training and that instruction should follow incorporate resource provision or facilitation instead of pure lecturing. Role-playing, self-evaluation, simulations, and case studies are found to be the most effective (Kearsley, 1996). Furthermore, continuing medical education (CME) research has shown that problem-based learning has a significant impact on the practice behavior of CME attendees and is also strongly received and even enjoyed by a majority of participants (Zeitz, 1999). In addition, the need to instill collaboration and interaction into CME curricula is important (Abrahamson and others, 1999; Johnson and others, 2000).

Moreover, adult learners are motivated by such factors as professional advancement, the desire to learn to serve others better, and meeting external expectations (Cantor, 1992). The TLC is one of only a few telemedicine training centers that offer CME credit. CME accreditation certifies that the training provided is credible and promotes professional development. And by offering Category I credit from the American Medical Association's defined accredited providers, the training provides benefits for many types of practitioners, including nurses and social workers.

The TLC Teaching Model and Learning Environment

UC Davis launched the TLC in October 1999 with the purpose of enhancing the quality and use of telemedicine and telehealth statewide. The original concept focused on providing training for multidisciplinary teams, including physicians, administrators, and site coordinators. With this purpose in mind and with the learning theories described above as a foundation, the TLC curriculum was designed using a multi-instructional approach incorporating didactic sessions, group discussion, and hands-on training over the course of three days. The TLC philosophy views hands-on experience as the cornerstone of excellent training. Such education provides participants with the confidence that they can build their own telemedicine programs and the awareness that it will take time to establish a successful program. In addition, TLC participants learn the value of multidisciplinary collaboration in developing their programs.

An important part of the TLC curriculum is the involvement of clinical specialists from the UC Davis Health System. Clinicians who use the telemedicine system to see patients in remote rural areas are invited to discuss their experiences with TLC participants. Based on the composition of the group participating, the TLC staff is able to customize the training. For example, if many of the participants are from a mental health organization, a psychiatrist may be invited as the clinician specialist.

A facility designated specifically for telemedicine learning allows the classroom to be designed for lecture sessions and hands-on training and optimizes the simulated TM consulting experience. The learning center's space is fully customized with state-of-the-art telemedicine laboratories that allow participants to replicate actual TM consultations from both the consultant and patient perspectives. The room design incorporates simulated specialist and patient exam suites with viewing windows that face the main meeting room. Participants can view both the consultant and patient sides to a clinical consultation.

The curriculum is designed to allow participants to observe a clinical consultation, practice the skills themselves, and complete a mock consultation on their own. This progression from observation to practice increases participants' confidence in their ability to return to their home sites and provide clinical telemedicine services. Other hands-on components of the TLC curriculum are the opportunity to trouble-shoot actual equipment problems and connect to another location using the home health telemedicine equipment.

The Curriculum in Detail

TLC instructors developed a curriculum that employed multiple instructional tools in addition to the lecture format.

The first day of the three-day course is an executive overview. The didactic portion of the agenda includes general synopses of the current status of telemedicine, equipment and telecommunications, legal and regulatory issues, staff roles, implementation issues, and program sustainability planning. Participants also watch a telemedicine video consult demonstration between a primary care and specialty site.

The second day of TLC training presents more detailed information about clinical, operational, and technical considerations. Participants learn the basics of the video-based system and the medical peripherals, such as the general exam camera and fiber-optic nasopharyngoscope, and then get more hands-on experience during an interactive consult and a demonstration of home health technology. Participants tour the UC Davis Consult Suite. They then have the option to select an operational track or a technical track. Those who select the operational track learn about clinic operations, such as clinician presentation issues, tools for running a smooth-flowing clinic, and patient presentation. Those in the technical track learn more about telecommunications, procedures for the technical aspects of a telemedicine program, conducting a technical needs assessment, and the system components.

On the third day of training, the UC Davis technical staff leads a more general discussion on conducting equipment searches and working with vendors, troubleshooting and maintenance, and room design issues. In addition, technical track participants learn specific skills for troubleshooting technical problems that may occur, while the operational track students participate in a live video conversation with a remote site coordinator and learn about program evaluation and research. The instruction aims to broaden the understanding of how telecommunications can be used in health care telemedicine consultations by introducing the participants to other applications, such as distance education. To apply the knowledge learned, attendees participate in the "exit challenge": a final hands-on session designed to evaluate participants' performance in various scenarios they may encounter in their home communities.

Program Funding

The TLC is funded by a grant from The California Endowment (a foundation that aims to improve health care in California) through the California Telehealth and Telemedicine Center (CTTC), an organization formed in 1999 to facilitate the development of infrastructure that supports technology in health care delivery. CTTC funds are used to expand telemedicine applications, evaluate telemedicine programs, and provide training for grantees to support the development of successful telemedicine programs.

Tuition

The majority of TLC participants are California residents because significant tuition savings are offered to California-based organizations. There is no charge to organizations meeting the following criteria: (1) provides at least 75 percent of care to underserved or indigent populations, has a limited operating budget, is community based with strong local input, and is located in California. Reduced fees are available to other California-based institutions with nonprofit status. Organizations from other states are charged full tuition but have chosen to attend the TLC because of the unique curriculum offered. The fees received from these institutions contribute to the TLC's sustainability model.

Participant Profile

To date, seventeen three-day TLC sessions have been held, with 526 participants from California and other states, including Florida, Hawaii, Missouri, Oregon, and Washington. Participants also have come from Palau, Brazil, and Saipan for telemedicine training. In addition, five one-day executive overview sessions have been held, with fifty-nine participants. Overall, the majority of participants were from rural communities; 14 percent of the participants were medical doctors, 21 percent were registered nurses, and approximately 6 percent were allied health professionals (for example, medical social worker, licensed vocational nurse, and radiology technician).

Evaluation Methodology and Outcomes

Project managers included a data collection strategy to evaluate the quality and outcomes of the training services.

Curriculum Evaluation

All participants complete a preattendance inventory, which is designed to collect information about the health care facilities for which the participants work, the status of telemedicine at those facilities, the telecommunications infrastructure existing at their facilities, and the skills participants expect to gain from telemedicine training. This information is used to tailor the TLC curriculum to meet the individual needs and interests of the participants and their organizations.

After completing each day of training, participants evaluate the individual segments on the following criteria: relevance of information, knowledge of the speaker, presentation style and skills, value of handouts and audiovisuals, and overall evaluation of session. The evaluation surveys assess the overall program for the day on items such as relevance of the topics to their organization's needs, level of interaction between speakers and participants, format of the program, learning environment, and organization of the day's activities. Finally, participants rate the extent to which the day's curriculum increased their understanding of key technical, clinical, and operational issues related to telemedicine and how well the day's program met their own expectations. Open-ended comments are elicited in each of the daily training surveys as well.

Between three and six months following TLC training, an external evaluator contacts participants to complete a voluntary posttraining impact survey. The goals of the survey are twofold: (1) to assess the extent to which participants have been able to use what they learned during the training and (2) to develop informed judgments on the extent to which training prepared participants to meet real-world challenges of using telecommunication-based technologies in their practice or workplace.

Participant Feedback

Participants gave high ratings to the following major issues: topic relevance, meeting of expectations, increase in understanding, and learning environment (Figure 23.1). Evaluation results have been very high since the program was launched and also increased over time to "extremely high." One early improvement that was based on participant evaluation was the development of the mock telemedicine consultation session. Early feedback indicated that participants wanted to "watch a real session." Given patient confidentiality constraints, the instructors opted to perform a scripted session that illustrated appropriate telemedicine patient care techniques and also allowed participants to experience typical audio and video quality of a session.

General participant feedback showed that the TLC curriculum was most beneficial for sites on the verge of implementation. Not only were the skills attained important, but also the confidence gained from practicing these skills before actually using them. In addition, the executive overview was found to be beneficial for strategic and program planning, and the technical overview sessions were surprisingly well received by nontechnical staff. For these persons, more extensive knowledge of the technology may have helped to buoy overall confidence.

Overall, respondents were highly satisfied with the methods used to cover these multiple topics. The highest satisfaction ratings were consistently for the "hands-on sessions on the use of video-based technologies" and "tele-technology room design." These topics were rated as having the most impact on participants' work. The lowest mean satisfaction survey ratings of any training area are for the topics of "evaluating one's program" and "risk management and liability." These two topics are important to all programs but tend to be a core responsibility of fewer participants.

FIGURE 23.1. PARTICIPANT FEEDBACK ON THE TELEMEDICINE LEARNING CENTER CURRICULUM.

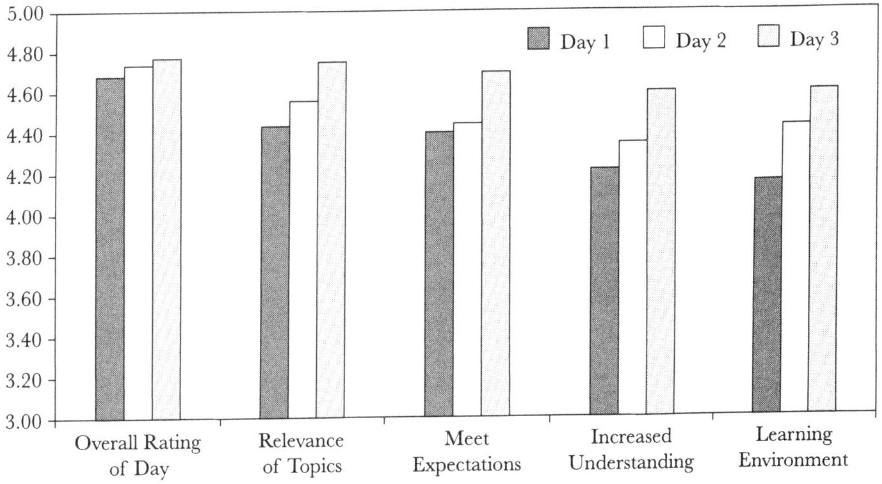

Note: Based on a five-point Likert scale, with 1 = poor and 5 = excellent.

Reflecting a frequently occurring theme, participants identified program sustainability and financial planning as the foremost topics requiring continued training. Participants expressing interest in additional training on a particular topic were given references on where to seek assistance, with a majority indicating plans to seek help.

Future Direction for Telemedicine Training

The blend of problem-based learning with didactic sessions at the TLC has proven to be a successful model, with participant satisfaction improving over time. In the future, the TLC plans to record presentations that will be made available on the Internet and on CD and also to create model forms that will aid telemedicine operation (for example, patient informed-consent and referral forms). In addition, the TLC plans to offer specific training for advanced site coordinators (with one or more years of experience) on various issues, including operational strategies and regulatory and legal updates; clinical focus areas such as psychiatry, critical care, and dermatology; and advanced technical staff in the areas of teleconferencing, trouble-shooting, and telecommunications. In partnership with CTTC, plans are being evaluated to create a TLC module based in southern California with a focus on store-and-forward telemedicine or home telecare.

Since telemedicine standards are still emerging, established telemedicine programs have a responsibility to participate in this process. Training, which is a commonly used indicator of quality, is anticipated to be a component of review by accrediting bodies in the future. This will require credible telemedicine training programs that are capable of certifying that staff can implement and operate quality programs. Thus, the future of telemedicine training will continue to mature.

Discussion Questions

1. What are some training standards and guidelines that every telemedicine training program should meet?
2. How does the Telemedicine Learning Center curriculum compare to your experience with continuing education courses? What are the similarities and differences?
3. What other issues regarding continuing education has the Telemedicine Learning Center not addressed? How should they be?
4. Can the curriculum at the Telemedicine Learning Center be applied to other types of continuing medical education or education in general? If so, how?
5. Do you believe splitting the participants into two tracks hinders the overall understanding of telemedicine implementation? If so, how?

References

Abrahamson, S., and others. "Continuing Medical Education for Life: Eight Principles." *Academic Medicine*, 1999, *74*(12), 1288–1294.

Barry, N., Reid, M., Ibbotson, T., and Bower, D. J. "Telemedicine Diffusion in Scotland: Training and Technical Support Issues." *British Journal of Health care Computing and Information Management*, 2000, *17*(5), 20–22.

Blignault, I., and Kennedy, C. "Training for Telemedicine." *Journal of Telemedicine and Telecare*, 1999, *5*(Suppl. 1), S1:112–S1:114.

Cantor, J. A. *Delivering Instruction to Adult Learners.* Toronto: Wall and Emerson, 1992.

Grigsby, B., and Brown, N. "The State of Telemedicine." *Artificial Organs*, 1999, *23*(12), 1129–1131.

Johnson, R. L., and others. "Final Report of the FOPE II Education of the Pediatrician Workgroup." *Pediatrics*, 2000, *106*(5), 1175–1198.

Kearsley, G. "Explorations in Learning and Instruction: The Theory into Practice Database." 1996. [http://www.biztrek.com.au/personal/print/tip.pdf].

"Telemedicine: Part of the IT Revolution." *Futuretech,* Feb. 8, 2002.

Walker, J., and Whetton, S. "The Diffusion of Innovation: Factors Influencing the Uptake of Telehealth." *Journal of Telemedicine and Telecare,* 2002, *8*(Suppl. 3), S3:73-S3:75.

Yamamoto, L. G., Toma, C. S., and Bell, C. K. "Telemedicine in a Box: Overcoming Complexity and High-Cost Telemedicine Barriers Using Self-Contained Videoconferencing Units." *Pediatric Emergency Care,* 2001, *17*(4), 289–292.

Zeitz, H. J. "Problem Based Learning: Development of a New Strategy for Effective Continuing Medical Education." *Allergy and Asthma Proceedings,* 1999, *20*(5), 317–321.

CHAPTER TWENTY-FOUR

TELEHEALTH IN CYBERSPACE

Virtual Reality for Distance Learning in Health Education and Training

Dale C. Alverson, Stanley M. Saiki Jr., Thomas P. Caudell

Two medical students, one from New Mexico and one from Hawaii, come upon a car crash victim lying on the ground and bleeding near an overturned vehicle. Frantically, they attempt to determine the extent of the victim's injuries. The victim is rapidly turning blue and convulsing. Working as a team, the students begin managing a series of life-threatening problems but, tragically, their patient dies at the scene. "What went wrong?" They discuss the series of events and determine the problem and appropriate solution. "If only we could try again. Can we try again?" they ask. Suddenly the clock turns back, they correct their mistakes and now the patient survives! A miracle? A dream? Science fiction? No, this is a virtual reality simulation, where making mistakes helps students learn. Even more incredible, one student is physically located in New Mexico and the other in Hawaii, separated by thousands of miles, but working and learning collaboratively in virtual cyberspace.

There have been explosive developments and innovations in advanced computing, visualization, virtual environments, and Internet2, the next generation of

The project described was partially supported by grant 4H2ATM00057–03–03 from the Office for the Advancement of Telehealth, Health Resources and Services Administration, U.S. Department of Health and Human Services. Its contents are solely the responsibility of the authors and do not necessarily represent the official views of the Health Resources and Services Administration.

Internet networking, which provides high-speed, broadband connectivity between universities and national laboratories and enables rapid multicenter exchange of large quantities of multimedia data, along with voice and video information, independent of the commodity Internet and its current congestion. Internet2 provides the network infrastructure that supports the multimedia multicasting of the access grid that facilitates the simultaneous multiple site interaction in virtual reality environments. These developments provide tools for revolutionary applications for collaborative problem solving, integration of new knowledge, and experiential learning, independent of distance. The advanced distributed communications high-speed networks, such as Internet2, provide the opportunity for knowledge sharing and collaboration in interactive virtual environments. Combined, they create the concept of telehealth in cyberspace.

The incredible rate in the increase of human knowledge creates challenges to learning (Issenberg and McGaghie, 1999; Issenberg and others, 1999, 2002). Consequently, technology must be developed to facilitate the shift occurring in science and education from developing the ability to remember and repeat information to developing the ability to find information and use it in a timely, effective, and appropriate manner (Simon, 1996).

In addressing a learning concept, Winn (1993) makes a distinction between simulation and reification. The purpose of simulation is to represent real-world objects as accurately as possible. Reification is the process whereby phenomena that cannot be directly perceived and experienced in the real world are given qualities of concrete objects that can be perceived and interacted with in a virtual learning environment (Winn, 1993). For example, global representations, large populations or groups of individuals, community-based settings, organs, and cellular or molecular objects are among the reification possibilities. Entering virtual worlds and simulations where there normally cannot be typical or repetitive interaction, or which cannot be easily visualized, is particularly useful because it allows the user to form a three-dimensional (3D) mental model, which allows for better understanding (Dalgarno, 2001, 2002). The developments in Project TOUCH (Telehealth Outreach for Unified Community Health) employ many of these advances in information technology to reify basic clinical concepts, promote student group interactions, and enhance medical practice, problem solving, and management.

The scope of the project focuses on four major areas of scientific research and development, which will be closely integrated: (1) new approaches to learning, knowledge transfer, and attaining competence; (2) novel developments in information technologies, which integrate simulations and virtual reification of basic and complex concepts; (3) distribution of these methods over the Internet2 access grid for collaborative learning and remote access; and (4) application of innovative approaches to evaluating the impact of these approaches on enhancement of learning, knowledge transfer, and competence attainment.

Project Description

The foundation for the current efforts builds on our work over several years of development and research with simulations and education processes embedded in virtual reality environments and collaborative services, artificial intelligence, and experiential active learning. Project TOUCH (Jacobs and others, 2003; Caudell and others, 2003; Lozanoff and others, 2003) started in August 2000 as a collaborative effort between the University of New Mexico (UNM) and University of Hawaii (UH) and their associated high-performance computing centers. As a multiyear program, Project TOUCH is designed to demonstrate the feasibility of employing advanced computing methods, such as virtual reality, to enhance education in a problem-based learning format (Kaufman and others, 1989; Anderson, 1991; Bereiter and Scardamalia, 2000), currently being used in the curriculum in the two schools. We are applying specific clinical cases (initially brain injury) as models and deploying to remote sites and associated workstations over the Next Generation Internet2 Access Grid (http://www-fp.mcs.anl.gov/fl/ Access Grid/). Equally important, we are attempting to objectively evaluate the impact of these advanced technologies on actual learning.

The team has extensive background in information and scientific visualization and virtual environments, high-performance computing simulation, cognitive sciences and knowledge structures, basic medical sciences and education, and human subject evaluation. In order to enhance experiential learning coupled with novel applications of developing innovation in information and computing technology, the project attempts to create a greater sense of reality in order to better comprehend relevant basic medical principles and complex concepts using virtual reality and 3D graphical simulations integrated and applied to study cases. These virtual simulations also create a safe environment to practice, make mistakes, exercise knowledge, be assessed, gain confidence, overcome uncertainty, and ultimately effectively transfer concepts and skills from simulation to practice and applied problem solving.

Project TOUCH uses a collaborative immersive environment based on the open source visualization and virtual reality environment development tool called Flatland created at UNM (Caudell and others, 2003). Flatland is a modular system that allows run-time configuration of functional modules into potentially complex applications. The entire virtual world, visual display format, body tracking configurations, locomotion metaphors, and all application functionality are dynamically loaded one on top of another, like a Lego toy, to build Flatland systems.

Flatland is designed to make use of any position-tracking technology. A tracker is a measurement device that can, in real time, monitor the position and orientation of multiple receiver devices in space, relative to a transmitter device. In the standard Flatland configuration, trackers are used to locate handheld wands and track the position of the user's head. User interaction is a central component of Flatland.

The TOUCH system is composed of three Flatland application modules loaded into the standard Flatland environment: the virtual patient environment, the rule-based artificial intelligence (AI), and the access grid remote camera. The virtual patient environment consists, for the case under study, of a car accident scene along with a cliff and an emergency room setting (Figure 24.1).

The system is driven by a virtual reality system operator, who uses the computer monitor to keep track of the user's activities, assisting with virtual body position movements when necessary. The immersed user interacts with the virtual patient through a joy wand, equipped with a six degree of freedom tracking system, buttons, and a trigger. The wand's representation in the environment is a virtual human hand. The user may pick up and place objects by moving the virtual hand and pulling the wand's trigger (Figure 24.2).

Fundamental to the TOUCH system is the AI module for Flatland. The AI system contains the knowledge of domain experts and knowledge of how objects interact. Time is a special state of the system that is not directly modified by the AI but whose rate is controlled by an adjustable clock. Since the rate of inference within the AI is controlled by this clock, the operator is able to speed up, slow down, or stop the action controlled by the AI. The independent camera viewpoint application, the access grid remote camera, captures images from the Flatland environment and transmits them over the access grid for viewing at remote sites. Figure 24.3 provides a view of the studio, screen and student user using the TOUCH system during one of the experimental sessions. The screen shows a mixture of live video images of the students participating in the learning session, and

FIGURE 24.1. THE VIRTUAL PATIENT WITH A BLOOD PRESSURE CUFF, NECK BRACE, AND HEAD BANDAGE.

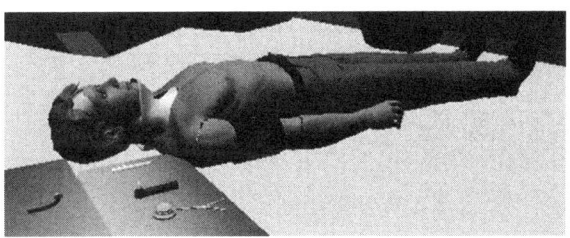

FIGURE 24.2. SCHEMATIC DEPICTION OF THE PATIENT SIMULATOR INPUT AND OUTPUT SYSTEM.

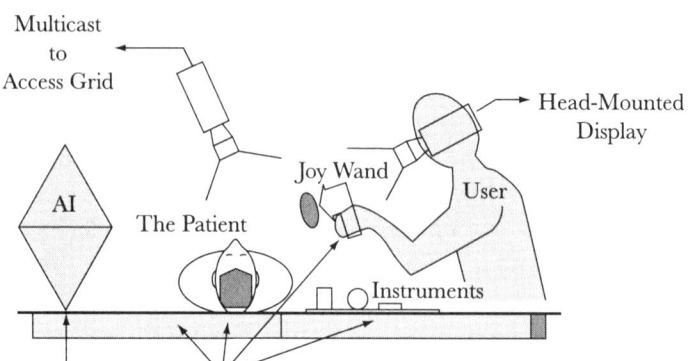

the remote camera view of the virtual environment as seen by the immersed student (upper right corner of the screen). The small dark-colored box over the user's head is part of the tracking system. The student holds a joy wand in his right hand. The operator is seen below the center of the screen.

The access grid remote camera can move around within Flatland to any position. Multiple cameras may be launched simultaneously and separately moved for multiview transmission.

Project Evaluation

The initial experimental evidence from this project confirmed convincingly the feasibility of using the case designed for TOUCH and associated technologies to conduct a problem-based learning tutorial with second-year medical students from two institutions using the access grid and virtual reality, in combination or separately, and has demonstrated essential principles noted in recent reviews of simulations (Issenberg and others, 1999, 2002). Medical students in the TOUCH tutorials were accepting and willing to engage in use of these technologies in their medical education experiences. They enjoyed working with similar-level students from other institutions. Several substantive processes occurred in each tutorial, including hypothesizing from a set of facts and connecting clinical science to the case.

In additional studies, we have used fourth-year medical students in the virtual reality environment participating collaboratively in problem solving and manag-

FIGURE 24.3. THE STUDIO, SCREEN, AND STUDENT USER
USING THE TOUCH SCREEN.

ing of a simulated patient with a closed-head injury. Using separate virtual reality workstations, two students participated simultaneously fully immersed in the virtual environment. The participants divided tasks and used handoff of virtual tools, functioning as a team (Figure 24.4).

When a poor outcome was realized, the students would pause to discuss the problem, attempt to determine the reason for the negative reaction of the virtual patient, and strategize a new approach. They were then allowed to repeat the scenario until the appropriate response occurred. Students stated that opportunities to make mistakes and repeat actions in the virtual reality simulation were extremely helpful in learning and remembering specific principles and gave them confidence their performance would be improved in a similar real-life situation. Virtual reality simulation created higher performance expectations and some anxiety among users. Students stated that virtual reality orientation was adequate, but they needed time to adapt and practice in order to improve efficiency.

As part of a proof of concept, we also demonstrated the ability to have multiple fully immersed participants engage in interactive collaboration within the virtual reality environment between the University of Western Australia in Perth and the University of New Mexico in Albuquerque, nearly ten thousand miles apart with no discernable time lag. Participants passed objects to one another within the virtual environment, quickly adapting to the team environment.

FIGURE 24.4. STUDENTS WORKING AS A TEAM IN THE VIRTUAL REALITY ENVIRONMENT DESPITE PHYSICAL SEPARATION OVER DISTANCE.

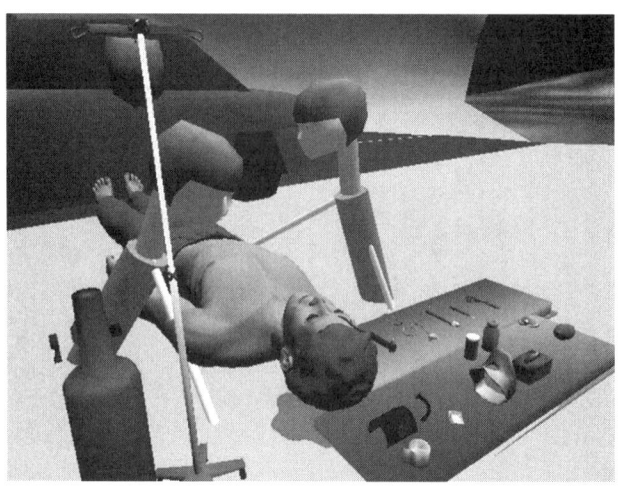

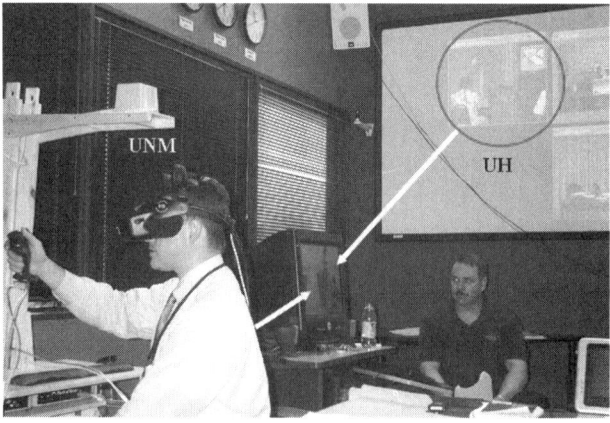

Bringing people together as virtual teams for interactive medical education, experiential learning, and collaborative training, independent of distance, provides a platform for distributed just-in-time training in which the learner can safely make mistakes and better understand the principles involved. It also offers the potential as a performance assessment and credentialing platform (Satava and Jones, 1999). Further validation is necessary to determine the potential value of the distributed virtual reality simulations and should entail training participants to competence in using these tools (Champion and Higgins, 2000). Ziv, Wolpe, Small, and Glick (2003) also make a compelling argument of the need to develop further simulation-based medical education as an ethical imperative to ensure optimal treatment, patient safety, and well-being.

Project Problems, Lessons Learned, and Solutions

Project TOUCH is a challenging, exploratory, and complex interdisciplinary effort that combines advanced information technology, education processes and concepts, and advanced performance and evaluation methods from many disciplines at several institutions. There is a need for flexibility, open discussion, and constructive critique as the project dynamically evolves. The UNM-UH team has three years of experience conducting an advanced information technology program in telemedicine with similar but more basic objectives.

Project Administration and Management Challenges

The program has been administered through the UNM Center for Telehealth, Health Sciences Center, which has ample experience administering federal research and development projects, as well as service activities across the state. A management team provides oversight management for the project and is drawn from the administrators and team leaders from UNM and UH. Key to success has been the employment of a full-time project coordinator who works closely with the investigators, staff, and subcontractors and assists in monitoring project progress, time lines, and deliverables; addressing obstacles; managing the budget; and producing reports.

Project Organization

We have designed a program that conducts the project in terms of tasks conducted over four phases. The proposed three research task teams and their efforts—education, information technology research, and evaluation—are coordinated by the management team. Meetings of teams as well as plenary meetings are held weekly using the access grid and other information and collaborative technology. We have an external advisory committee to counsel the program. The committee meets twice a year to review program progress objectively and is composed of experts from across the country with expertise in technology, education, and evaluation. We have included a provision for subject matter experts as needed, drawn from within our institutions and others. Subcontractors for various aspects of work also contribute to the program. In the future, international participants will participate over the access grid; their participation provides faculty and students an excellent opportunity for exchange of information, model development, and collaborative learning.

Program Phases

Phase 1, concept development, has the goals of developing the learning environment concepts and applications. The second phase, prototype testing and learning evaluation, emphasizes tests and experiments to ensure that the applications replicate the real-world environments, situations, and rules as closely as possible. In particular, this phase validates the functions of the immersive environment, learning applications, and learning outcomes evaluation. Field testing is conducted at selected schools of medicine in the third phase. Phase 4, curriculum and training program integration, which is still in the future, will complete production, dissemination, and technical support of the project. The goal is the fully supported distribution of the virtual interactive learning environment to schools of medicine for integration into their curriculum.

Conclusions and Future Plans

Further application of these advanced computing methods in a distributed, interactive manner offers the opportunity for access to medical education and training independent of distance and can assist in obtaining and applying new knowledge in ways that can sustain and improve understanding and performance in the rapidly expanding health arena, placing telehealth in cyberspace. Anticipated impacts of this project include:

- Enhancing efficiency in the learning process needed to transfer gained knowledge to problem solving and application of skills
- Achieving reification of complex, abstract concepts, otherwise difficult to comprehend and learn, so that they can be applied more effectively to real-life problems and appropriate management

- Determining the minimal degree of fidelity and realism required to achieve the learning goals, knowledge transfer, and attainment of competence
- Providing safe environments to practice, make mistakes, learn by doing, and gain confidence with guided feedback for transition to real-world applications
- Improving retention of knowledge and skills, as well as continued quality improvement
- Providing objective methods for performance assessment
- Promoting group learning, communication, and cooperation
- Creating a distributed environment for virtual interaction and access, independent of distance, and thus reaching audiences that are geographically dispersed more efficiently and effectively, just-in time, where distance and location are barriers to participation
- Developing an open source modular form of these developments that fosters flexibility and continuous improvements

A key aspect of the project is to create, as needed, educator-developed customized learning scenarios. We propose to create a high-level visual programming language to dynamically assemble simulations, rules bases, and graphical, aural, and haptic components into a functional Flatland system. The creation of a library of simulations that can be accessed on demand and appropriate to a given set of learning or training goals and objectives needs to be created in order to fully realize the value of these tools.

Virtual reality simulation is one application in the educational and training tool kit that can complement several other learning modalities. Experiential simulations for learning may be most helpful to certain students. Each modality needs to be evaluated and applied in a manner that is complementary to other methods and best suits the learning preferences and needs of individual students and disciplines.

For the continuation of this project, we are starting with the advanced features of the existing TOUCH application and then incorporating the keystone reification features of continuous semantic zooming, as well as a number of significant enhancements. These include a modular visual programming system for rapid configuration of new virtual learning scenarios, interfaces to the Web and databases, complete import interfaces to commercial 3D modeling and animation tools, advanced sound and speech interfaces, and the integration of force feedback (technologies that allow the user to have a sense of touch, resistance to, or contact with objects within the virtual reality environment) as a new sensorial modality. This technical program, in addition to the key simulation and reification question, gives rise to several questions as we implement various enhancements: the relationships between human performance measures in virtual environments as a function of the characteristics of the technologies and interfaces, the perceived usability of the virtual reality application by educators, the effect of continuous immersion and control over the environment by students, and the effects of haptics, speech, and sound on measures of comprehension.

As the project looks forward to adequate development and proof of concept, the potential for widespread dissemination and transition to market becomes feasible. Issues of general use, marketing, and sustainability will need to be addressed. In addition, intellectual property requires ongoing discussion and agreement, particularly in a multidisciplinary, multi-institutional environment. Many of the tools being developed are available as open source in order to make them widely available and to facilitate further development and future applications of the technologies employed.

We are proposing to create a virtual international, interinstitutional, and interdisciplinary classroom and laboratory for learning and research in information technology using Internet2 for collaboration. This virtual learning and research collaboratory would address a wide spectrum of interdisciplinary domains in information technology, computer science, human interaction with technology, cognitive psychology, education, and graphic or musical arts. The program would engage students at all levels in developing interest and skills in science, technology, engineering, and math in order to foster the development of the next generation of experts in the complementary fields. A problem-based, case-based learning approach would be used to make the learning of important basic and complex principles relevant to learners from the interdisciplinary information technology science domains involved. Faculty will serve as leaders of "learning families," sharing their expertise. Using Internet2, the program provides a forum for international, interinstitutional, and interdisciplinary collaborative education and research in information technology science independent of distance. Overall, this proposed program can create a virtual collaboratory for teaching, learning, and innovation in information technology, science, engineering, and mathematical science and research.

Discussion Questions

1. What are the potential values of virtual reality simulations?
2. What is the value of distributed interactive virtual environments?
3. How should these tools be validated, verified, and evaluated?
4. Specifically, how do we evaluate the impact on learning, training, and ultimate performance?
5. How should these tools be integrated into health educational curricula and training programs? What are the chances of general adoption?
6. What is the potential for use in performance and competence assessment?

7. How do we solve the challenges and derive the values of interdisciplinary, interinstitutional collaboration in research, development, and education?

References

Anderson, A. "Conversion to Problem-Based Learning in Fifteen Months." In D. Boud and G. Feletti (eds.), *The Challenge of Problem Based Learning.* New York: St. Martin's Press, 1991.

Bereiter, C., and Scardamalia, M. "Commentary on Part I: Process and Product in Problem-Based Learning (PBL) Research." In D. H. Evensen and C. E. Hmelo (eds.), *Problem-Based Learning: A Research Perspective on Learning Interactions.* Mahwah, N.J.: Erlbaum, 2000.

Caudell, T. P., and others. "A Virtual Patient Simulator for Distributed Collaborative Medical Education." *Anatomical Record (Part B),* 2003, *270B,* 16–22.

Champion, H. R., and Higgins, G. A. *Meta-Analysis and Planning of SIMTRAUMA: Medical Simulation for Combat Trauma Training.* Higgins, Ga.: Telemedicine and Advanced Technology Research Center, U.S. Army, 2000.

Dalgarno, B. "Interpretations of Constructivism and Consequences for Computer Assisted Learning." *British Journal of Educational Technology,* 2001, *32,* 183–194.

Dalgarno, B. "The Potential of 3D Virtual Learning Environments: A Constructivist Analysis." 2002. [http://www.usq.edu.au/electpub/e-jist/docs/Vol5%20No2/Dalgarno%20-%20Final.pdf].

Issenberg, S. B., and McGaghie, W. C. "Assessing Knowledge and Skills in the Health Profession: A Continuum of Simulation Fidelity." In A. Tekian and others (eds.), *Innovative Simulations for Assessing Professional Competence: From Paper-and-Pencil to Virtual Reality.* Chicago: University of Illinois at Chicago, Department of Medical Education, 1999.

Issenberg, S. B., and others. "Simulation Technology for Health Care Professional Skills Training and Assessment." *JAMA,* 1999, *282,* 861–866.

Issenberg, S. B., and others. "Effectiveness of a Cardiology Review Course for Internal Medicine Residents Using Simulation Technology and Deliberate Practice." *Teaching and Learning in Medicine,* 2002, *14*(4), 223–228.

Jacobs, J., and others. "Integration of Advanced Technologies to Enhance Problem-Based Learning over Distance: Project TOUCH." *Anatomical Record (Part B),* 2003, *270B,* 16–22.

Kaufman, A., and others. "The New Mexico Experiment: Educational Innovation and Institutional Change." *Academic Medicine,* 1989, *64,* 285–294.

Lozanoff, S., and others. "Anatomy and the Access Grid: Exploiting Plastinated Brain Sections for use in Distributed Medical Education." *Anatomical Record (Part B),* 2003, *270B,* 16–22.

Satava, R. M., and Jones, S. B. "The Future Is Now: Virtual Reality Technologies." In A. Tekian and others (eds.), *Innovative Simulations for Assessing Professional Competence: From Paper-and-Pencil to Virtual Reality.* Chicago: University of Illinois at Chicago, Department of Medical Education, 1999.

Simon, H. A. "Observations on the Sciences of Science Learning." Paper prepared for the Committee on Developments in the Science of Learning for the Sciences of Science Learning: An Interdisciplinary Discussion, Department of Psychology, Carnegie Mellon University, 1996.

Winn, W. D. *A Conceptual Basis for Educational Applications of Virtual Reality.* Seattle: Human
    Interface Technology Laboratory, University of Washington, 1993.

Winn, W. D. "Learning in Virtual Environments: A Theoretical Framework and Considera-
    tions for Design." *Education Media International,* 1999, *36,* 271–279.

Ziv, A., Wolpe, P. R., Small, S. D., and Glick, S. "Simulation-Based Medical Education:
    An Ethical Imperative." *Academic Medicine,* 2003, *78,* 783–788.

CHAPTER TWENTY-FIVE

THE SEEDS PROJECT

From Health Care Information System to Innovative Educational Strategy

Judith J. Warren, Katherine A. Fletcher, Helen R. Connors, Anita Ground, Charlotte Weaver

Imagine a world in which students enter a clinical learning laboratory, using a cutting-edge clinical information system (CIS) for the purpose of planning, managing, and evaluating virtual client care with other interdisciplinary team members. These students, working as a team, are able to savor the fruits of their labor as the case evolves over the semester. Some virtual clients may experience additional problems and complications due to omissions in care, while others experience efficient, effective, quality health care services. As they learn, these students practice critical decision-making skills and interdisciplinary care management in an environment that will do no harm. This is all made possible through SEEDS (Simulated Electronic hEalth Delivery System) using a live-application CIS with virtual patients within a virtual health care delivery system.

History of the SEEDS Project

SEEDS was launched in fall 2001 at the University of Kansas School of Nursing after approximately eighteen months of preplanning to establish the infrastructure and contract negotiations. It is a jointly funded partnership between the University of Kansas School of Nursing and Cerner Corporation, representing a pioneering event for education and for the health care information technology industry. It marks the first time that a live production designed for care delivery is being used in a simulated way for teaching nursing students curriculum content. SEEDS required that a virtual health care organization be created: acute care hospital, outpatient clinics, mental health facility, public health clinics, school-based clinics, health fairs, and home care services.

Overview of the SEEDS Project

The CIS used in SEEDS is designed for a traditional acute, inpatient health care organization and adapted to meet the curriculum needs for acute care and community settings. Courses were analyzed for the potential of using a CIS as a teaching-learning strategy. The CIS has components that reflect the nursing process. This process (similar to the problem-solving process) is fundamental to teaching nursing. The steps of the nursing process along with the CIS components are as follows:

1. Patient assessments are documented in narrative clinical notes or on forms with structured data entry using a standardized terminology.
2. Nursing diagnoses are entered on the patient's problem list as well as medical diagnoses.
3. Patient goals are determined and then entered in clinical notes.
4. Nursing interventions can be selected from a multidisciplinary order entry screen or entered in a clinical note.
5. Evaluations are made from viewing the patient data on a flow sheet and making comparisons over time.

   A patient care plan results as each of these features is completed.

Critical Thinking Seminars

Foundations in Nursing is a first-semester course emphasizing nursing process, care planning, documentation, and critical thinking using lecture, clinical experiences, and small group seminars. Case studies of virtual patients are analyzed, and then assessment documentation and care planning are entered in the CIS. Students use the CIS interactively while in seminar. The instructor is able to project the work of the students on a screen and give immediate feedback as students practice this skill. The documents are saved and may be retrieved later for review by both instructor and students.

Client Assessment and Clinical Techniques, two other first-semester courses, provide learning opportunities in (1) physical examination skills and patient findings documentation and (2) performing clinical procedures with accompanying documentation. Screens have been designed to support these activities through structured charting with reference text that directs the student to useful Web site documents that present the evidence supporting the approach to documentation and provide a glossary for unfamiliar terms. As the students perform the required skills demonstrating competency, they are required to document their findings in the CIS, providing appropriate repetition to reinforce the new knowledge and skill.

Information Technology in Healthcare is another first-semester course that employs SEEDS. Students learn about electronic health records, functionality of clinical information systems, and requirements for patient confidentiality and data security. Having a CIS to explore and discuss these issues makes these potentially dry topics gain reality and importance in the delivery of patient care.

Care Planning in Clinical Courses

Clinical courses are composed of lectures and clinical experiences in health care agencies. The major evidence of student achievement in mastering the nuances of theory and critical thinking skills is the nursing care plan. This care planning activity translates into documentation of patient responses, identification of nursing diagnoses, and generation of orders for nursing interventions in electronic patient records that practicing nurses use. To ensure the students are able to participate in CIS efforts and health information management activities required in health care organizations after they graduate, the graded care plans for Nursing of Adults, Nursing of Children, and Mental Health Nursing are completed within the academic CIS. Students enter assessment data for their assigned patient and then complete a care plan. This care planning activity is a standard educational requirement for all nursing students. While the clinical data reside in a secure server that meets Health Insurance Portability and Accountability Act of 1996 requirements, we also deidentify all clinical data, teaching the students data protection requirements.

Lessons Learned

The theoretical framework for this innovative education project is Rogers's diffusion of innovation (1995), which describes the communication process by which innovations spread within a social system. Innovations that were perceived by individuals as having a greater advantage, that is, more compatibility with the organization's values and past experiences, had a degree to which they could experiment with it, had results that were visible to others, and were less complex to understand were adopted more rapidly than other innovations (Rogers, 1995).

Perceived Attributes of the Innovation

To enhance the adoption of an innovation, it is important that all of the stake-holders feel that they have something to gain from promotion of this innovation. An equitable partnership such as this project requires attention to the issue of intellectual property and copyrights. A formal contract was negotiated between the two partners to explicate the relationship and ownership issues before engaging in the partnership.

Academic freedom has been a pinnacle in the teaching environment of university systems. There was a concern that implementation of a CIS such as this would interfere with the faculty's style of teaching. Contrary to fears, the system became another valuable tool that supported rather than impeded their teaching styles. The faculty used the CIS to promote individual as well as group learning using a wide variety of teaching strategies that promoted critical thinking, such as discussion, storytelling, role playing, and case studies.

Convenience of CIS access also became an issue that affected the acceptance of this innovation. Students may return to the School of Nursing for classes only one or two days a week. This makes completing clinical assignments in a timely manner in the school's training lab difficult, if not impossible. In an effort to mitigate this situation, CIS access was installed in the university's learning lab. A third access portal, the Internet, was also added.

Type of Innovation Decision

Authority and collective decisions were employed in the project. The dean made the authoritative decision to engage in the partnership and implement the use of a CIS in the curriculum. When committing to a project where the impact is unknown, support of executive administration is essential. This project has had unwavering support for the top administrators on both sides of the partnership since the beginning. As the project developed, the decision making changed to collective decision making, with the project director, information technology staff, and faculty members deciding how to adapt the CIS and integrate nursing informatics in the curriculum.

Communication Channels

Strategic planning with course coordinators concerning whether SEEDS should be used in each course, and if so, how SEEDS could be used in each, needs to occur in an ongoing systematic fashion. As the faculty used the system for student projects, they discovered that the traditional ways of grading were obsolete. New grading rubrics had to be configured for the CIS. As the clinical system was used, the faculty also found that the students developed a thirst for data. The case studies and other instructional strategies had to be reconstructed to allow many more data items. Nurses in practice are challenged to use the data to formulate information into knowledge that will improve health care for all clients (Chastain, 2003). Using the CIS helped students to achieve outcomes that were more closely aligned to what is expected in practicing nurses.

Training of faculty and students to use the CIS has relied on class, manuals, and directions in syllabi and one-to-one instruction from an experienced user. Faculty members receive training on the system prior to using it in their courses. Each faculty member has the CIS on his or her office computer to facilitate practice in a safe environment and evaluate student efforts. Students are taught how to use the CIS by the faculty during the seminars in the Foundations course (one of the first nursing courses). The focus is not on learning a specific piece of software, but on learning nursing process and how to use data and information in making clinical judgments.

Finally, the process of implementing new functionality and maintaining the CIS presents a challenge. System upgrades require considerable attention to the amount of time needed for application and integration testing. Every function and form of the application used for data entry, care planning, and student learning must be tested for each role. A system upgrade must be planned around the academic calendar.

Extent of Change Agents' Promotion Efforts

SEEDS was implemented first as a small trial that involved the information technology staff, several Cerner associates, 3 faculty members, 34 students, and the project director. On completion of the trial, a full implementation was rolled out to 120 students and 15 faculty members in the second year of the project. Because of this initial trial, minimal fine tuning was needed to ensure a successful implementation across the curriculum.

Outcomes of this project are being evaluated on several levels and include qualitative, quantitative, and cost analysis techniques. Specific evaluation measures being used are course evaluations of performance and satisfaction, students' perception of the use of technology on the best practices in education, direct observation and videotape of student interactions with SEEDS to examine the impact of technology on teaching and learning practices, and focus groups with faculty and students. Finally, cost analysis data are being collected to determine cost and return on investment. The SEEDS on-line survey is developed from the Flashlight Program Current Student Inventory and is designed to assess specific best practices in education (Chickering and Ehrmann, 1996). The items selected for this study address the effects of CIS on five major areas of learning: critical thinking, student-student interaction, rapid feedback, efficient use of time, and application to real world.

Future of SEEDS

SEEDS is an exciting innovative curriculum project that challenges students to develop information management and critical thinking skills and faculty to develop teaching strategies that take advantage of this unique technology. SEEDS provides the structure to implement an evidence-based, academic CIS fully supporting the students' ability to practice nursing in today's health care environment.

Discussion Questions

1. The SEEDS project is a creative partnership between a school of nursing and a business. How does this partnership change your thinking about innovation in education?
2. Suggest other partnerships that could be used to enhance the learning of students and better prepare them for the future health care system.
3. Using Rogers's model of diffusion of innovation as a guide, hypothesize problems you might encounter in your institution when implementing a project such as SEEDS.
4. If you were considering implementing SEEDS or a similar program at your school, what organizational strategies would you employ?
5. If you were designing an evaluation for a program such as SEEDS, what outcomes would you select to study? Discuss various designs and methods for the evaluation.
6. How might you reengineer the teaching-learning process to maximize the impact of SEEDS or a similar project on student outcomes?

References

Chastain, A. R. "Nursing Informatics: Past, Present and Future." *Tennessee Nurse*, 2003, *66*(1), 8–10.

Chickering, A. W., and Ehrmann, S. "Implementing the Seven Principles: Technology as Lever." *AAHE Bulletin*, 1996, *49*, 3–6. [http://www.tltgroup.org/programs/seven.html].

Rogers, E. M. *Diffusion of Innovations.* (4th ed.) New York: Free Press, 1995.

PART SIX
___

UNIQUE APPLICATIONS
___

You cannot depend on your eyes when imagination is out of focus.

MARK TWAIN

CHAPTER TWENTY-SIX

BRINGING CARE HOME TO THE RURAL ELDERLY

Clinician and Patient Satisfaction with Telehealth Communication

Carma L. Bylund, Bonnie Wakefield, Jane E. Morse, Annette M. Ray

Projected population increases in older persons over the next decade make elder care one of the most pressing public health issues for the twenty-first century. This is particularly true in rural areas, where extended family members who previously lived nearby and provided informal caregiving have moved away, leaving elderly individuals isolated and in need of assistance. Thus, the rural elderly, particularly the oldest old (eighty-five years and older), are at risk for limited access to needed health care services (Buckwalter and others, 2002). Furthermore, approximately 43 percent of all U.S. residents will spend some time in a nursing home during their life (Kemper and Murtaugh, 1991). Relatively few physicians routinely make patient care visits in nursing homes, so these frail elderly individuals must frequently travel to receive specialty services. Thus, a major potential benefit of telehealth in home settings and long-term care (LTC) is greater and timelier access to specialized health care services that may not be available within the community or facility where the patient resides.

Telehealth applications may have particular relevance for the Veterans Affairs (VA) system. In particular, issues of travel time and distance to Veterans

This work has been funded in part by grants from the Department of Veterans Affairs Health Services Research and Development Service to Bonnie Wakefield (DEV 97–012; RCD 99–311–1; ARCD 99–311–1; NRI 99–345–1).

Affairs Medical Centers (VAMCs) for veterans is a concern (U.S. Government Accounting Office, 1995). Telehealth applications have the potential to assist the VA in meeting these concerns. This is especially true in a state such as Iowa, with the highest proportion of citizens over age eighty-five in the country, a high percentage of rural-dwelling elderly, and harsh travel conditions in the winter months. Veterans suffer from high rates of chronic illness, making access to health care services crucial.

A program of research at the Iowa City VAMC has evaluated the provision of services using interactive video to veterans in their home setting, whether in personal residences or LTC facilities (Figure 26.1). In evaluating these projects, issues of provider and patient satisfaction are paramount. If providers and patients are not comfortable with these services, it would be difficult to claim success. In the following, we present several case studies that demonstrate telehealth projects implemented by researchers at the VAMC.

Chronic Wound Assessments

Owen Williams, a sixty-eight-year-old veteran, lives at a state-owned LTC facility in rural Iowa. He has suffered from diabetes for nearly twenty years and recently has begun to have complications of foot ulcers. These wounds have been managed to the extent possible by the nursing staff at the care facility, but because of the impaired circulation in Mr. Williams's lower extremities due to peripheral vascular disease, the staff needs expert advice to manage these wounds in the proper way. Although recently

FIGURE 26.1. PATIENT RECEIVING TELEHEALTH SERVICES.

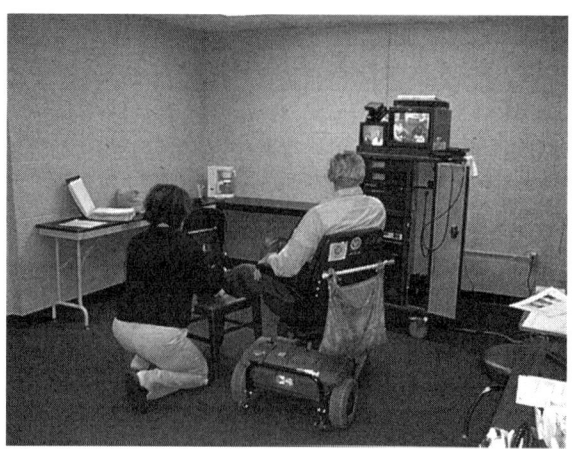

a nurse with expertise in chronic wound management from the university, eighty-five miles away, has been able to work with Williams, the distance makes it difficult for him to get the type of wound care he needs on a regular basis. Because of this, he has wounds that are not healing properly, causing him a great deal of discomfort.

Owen Williams represents the many elderly people who have experienced lack of timely access to experts in wound care, especially those living at home or in LTC facilities. Chronic wounds, such as pressure ulcers, diabetic foot ulcers, venous ulcers, and arterial ulcers, are a common problem among older persons. Proper management of chronic wounds requires frequent, routine monitoring in order to optimize healing and ensure early recognition of impending complications. Researchers at the University of Iowa College of Nursing and the Iowa City VAMC tested an application of telehealth to help elderly patients like Williams receive better care for their wounds more frequently. Although the technology of transmitting still pictures of wounds from patient to consultant sites had been used previously, interactive video technology was less well established. The potential was great, but it was not yet clear if interactive video technology, specifically the Tele Doc system, was a satisfactory and effective replacement for in-person visits. The Tele Doc is a mobile high-end telemedicine cart with high-resolution monitor, electronic stethoscope, exam light and camera source, remote camera controls, and backlit box for transmitting X-rays. Connection speeds on this unit range from 384 to 1,152 Kbps.

This project evaluated the implementation of a nurse-managed telehealth chronic wound clinic for residents of one LTC facility. Prior to implementation of the clinic, the wound consultant from the College of Nursing was making a 170-mile round trip to the LTC facility to consult with facility staff on the management of chronic wounds. Because of the distance, the consultant's trips to the facility were irregular. The objectives for implementing the telehealth chronic wound clinic included reducing travel costs and time for the consultant and timelier follow-up for patients. Data were collected from patients at the LTC facility, seven primary nurses and one skin care nurse at the LTC facility, and two consultant nurses providing telehealth wound assessment. Analyses compared on-site and telehealth assessments for thirteen individual wound consultations. Inter-rater reliability for nine different wound characteristics ranged from 54 to 100 percent; eight wound characteristics had an inter-rater reliability considered acceptable at 75 percent or higher (Gardner and others, 2001). The cost of telehealth wound consultations was estimated to be $92.80 for each twenty-minute consultation (Specht, Wakefield, and Flanagan, 2001).

Satisfaction of both the nurses and the LTC residents with the telehealth clinic compared to in-person assessments were favorable (Johnson-Mekota and others, 2001). The residents found the telehealth consultation to be as good as the in-person assessment, although patients noted some difficulty hearing and seeing the telehealth consultant. Nurses were equally satisfied with both the telehealth and in-person consultations and felt both consultation modes were a productive use of their time and skills.

Williams now meets with a nurse expert in wound care management weekly through the Tele Doc system to manage his foot ulcers. As time has passed, he has become more comfortable with using the system; a recently installed larger monitor has made it easier for him to see the nurse. He has developed a good rapport with the nurse, and they are able to communicate effectively using this system. Because nursing staff at the LTC facility are directly involved with the consultation process, they are more aware of important assessment parameters and the treatment plan. Most important, Williams's foot ulcers are healing well, and he now has increased mobility.

Physician Specialty Services in Long-Term Care

Marvin Johnson, age eighty-two, has lived for the past five years at the Iowa Veterans Home, a 758-bed state home that provides LTC services. When he first came to live at the home, he was suffering from a seizure disorder. Although the seizures are being managed, the disorder is becoming more serious, and Johnson has developed recurrent urinary tract infections. Because of this, he needs care from specialists in neurology and urology.

To get the care he needs, Johnson has to take either a four-hour round trip to the Iowa City VAMC or a ninety-minute round trip to the Des Moines VAMC. Then he spends even more time each visit waiting at the VAMC, as several veterans from the home go on the same day for visits scheduled at different times. Thus, he and the others often spend eight hours away from the home each time they need to have a visit with a specialist that takes no more than fifteen to twenty minutes. This is strenuous for Johnson, given his health status, and is sometimes a difficult trip for all given the hazardous driving conditions of winter.

Johnson symbolizes the hundreds of Iowa elderly veterans who need specialty care on a regular basis. This study evaluated the provision of specialty physician clinic visits using interactive video to elderly residents, like Johnson, of a large multilevel LTC setting. If it was successful, these telehealth applications could lead to substantial savings of time and improved care for patients. Researchers were interested if the veterans home residents, specialty physicians, and nurses would find visits using interactive video satisfactory and effective.

Specifically, researchers assessed patient, physician, and nurse satisfaction with the visit and outcomes of the consultation (Wakefield, Buresh, Flanagan, and Kienzle, 2004). Data were collected on seventy-six individual patient consultations, which involved twelve physicians, over a period of eight months. Most consultations (97 percent) were follow-up visits in urology, neurology, cardiology, and general surgery clinics. The most frequent outcome was a change in treatment plan with the patient remaining at the LTC setting (38 percent) or no change in treatment (34 percent). Thus, in nearly three-quarters of the consultations, the medical issue was able to be resolved using interactive television. Physicians' ratings of the telehealth consultations were generally positive:

- 78 percent rated the consultations as good to excellent for usefulness in developing a diagnosis
- 87 percent gave good to excellent ratings for usefulness in developing a treatment plan
- 79 percent gave good to excellent ratings for quality of transmission
- 86 percent gave good to excellent ratings for satisfaction with the consult format

Similarly, patients' acceptance of telehealth services was also high:

- 72 percent of patients were satisfied with the consult format (8 percent were neutral, 6 percent were somewhat dissatisfied, and 14 percent did not respond to this question).
- Uniformly (100 percent), patients believed the specialist understood their problem, and 92 percent felt it was easier to get medical care with telehealth.

In addition, all participating nurses at the remote site believed the telehealth consultation was a good use of their time and skills.

Today, telehealth specialty clinics are scheduled for selected specialties where efficiencies can be achieved by using interactive video. These include clinics with a high volume of patients at the remote site (such as urology) and those clinics for which the physician traveled to the LTC facility (rather than the patients coming to the clinic). Telehealth visits are also used on an as-needed basis, that is, when a patient needs to be seen sooner than a scheduled clinic visit, or for patients who present challenging travel circumstances, such as those with spinal cord injuries.

Follow-Up Care After Hospital Discharge for Congestive Heart Failure Patients

Charles Parker, a seventy-two-year-old retired insurance salesman and Korean War veteran, tells friends and acquaintances, "I wouldn't be alive today if not for Millie." They have been married nearly fifty years, and for the past ten of those years, Millie's role as caregiver for Charles has been significant. Besides having diabetes, Charles also suffers from chronic obstructive pulmonary disease (COPD) and has been oxygen dependent for the last six years. When Charles was diagnosed with congestive heart failure (CHF) a year ago, Millie was overwhelmed. Could she help him to manage this too? Charles had reached the point where nearly any activity was difficult. His breathing was quite labored, he often looked uncomfortable, and he had to have a commode next to his chair because he was unable to walk the distance to the bathroom.

As represented by Charles Parker, one of the most common reasons for patients age sixty-five and over to be hospitalized is CHF (Rich, 1997), and frequent readmissions are common (Wray and others, 1997). Home-based interventions can prevent up to 50 percent unplanned readmissions of CHF patients (Rich and others, 1995; Stewart, Vandenbroek, Pearson, and Horowitz, 1999). Such visits can help patients avoid the discomfort and inconvenience of travel, clinic waiting rooms, and feelings of isolation (Campion, 1997). Despite these benefits, home-based interventions can be difficult to deliver because they are staff intensive, time-consuming, poorly reimbursed, and unsafe to provide in some neighborhoods (Campion, 1997). In addition, patients who use VA health care services often live long distances from the facility, and many live in rural areas, creating barriers for VA-based home care providers. Telehealth technologies can potentially circumvent these logistical difficulties and offer support for isolated rural caregivers as well (Buckwalter and others, 2002).

A current study being conducted at the Iowa City VAMC is testing the efficacy of telehealth interventions for CHF patients like Parker. The study is a randomized, controlled trial comparing telephone and videophone care to a control group, who have regular face-to-face clinic visits. This four-year study will evaluate patient and clinician satisfaction as well as the efficacy and cost-effectiveness of these technologies in reducing hospital admissions and improving symptom management and quality of life. Although we do not have data to share yet, we can offer some anecdotal ways in which these telehealth applications are making a difference in patients' lives.

During Charles's last visit to the hospital for CHF, he and Millie agreed to be a part of a telehealth study that would allow them to interact with a nurse from their home over a videophone. The first week they visited with the nurse over this telephone three times, and then visited once a week for three months. When the project assistant came to set up the videophone, Charles and Millie insisted that it be set up so that both could see and be seen by the nurse. During visits, Millie often gave information about Charles's medications and nutrition that was important for the nurse. Charles made great progress during the three months of telehealth visits. By the end of the three months, his mobility level had increased to the point that he could get to the bathroom if needed. Charles's nurse commented that she was able to see his progression as they interacted over the videophone during the three months.

Charles was not the only one who benefited from the telehealth program. Millie's burden as the caregiver was relieved by having someone to validate what she was doing and give her support.

Lessons Learned

Some general lessons about telehealth may be extended to other populations aside from the rural elderly:

- It may take time to attain clinician and patient satisfaction. Our anecdotal evidence indicated that as participants (both staff and patients) learned how to use the equipment over time, their satisfaction with the telehealth clinic improved.
- Engaging the cooperation of all parties is essential for telehealth success. For instance, we found that the cooperation of the specialty nurse case managers in Iowa City was critical for arranging specialty clinics. Some nurse case managers were tentative when first approached about arranging telehealth clinic consultations, but agreed to collaborate with the research assistant in gaining buy-in from the respective physician staff.
- It is critical to understand the reluctance of physicians to use telehealth unless they see a direct benefit, such as time savings, improved interaction with patients, or increased access to services, all of which might factor into the levels of satisfaction they have with it. There is value in enlisting patients favorable to the technology to encourage use by physicians. Providing hands-on support for providers so they do not have to operate equipment during the consultation process is also important to enlisting their support. Indeed, the benefit to the clinician for using telehealth may also play a role in the frequency of its use. For example, telehealth specialty clinics were used more frequently by physicians from the Des Moines VAMC than from the Iowa City VAMC. This is likely because, prior to this study, physicians from the Des Moines VAMC were traveling *to* the LTC facility to conduct clinics (approximately a two-hour round trip drive for the physicians once per month), whereas LTC facility patients were transported to Iowa City for specialty clinic follow-up.

Conclusion

The current evidence on home-based telehealth shows generally good results on clinician-patient satisfaction but mixed results in terms of other outcomes (Balas and others, 1997; Currell, Urquhart, Wainwright, and Lewis, 2001; Hersh and others, 2001; Mair and Whitten, 2000). Patient satisfaction is high, but studies are descriptive and reasons that patients like (or do not like) home telehealth have not been explored. Providers are more resistant to using the technology, for reasons that have not been elucidated. There are few telehealth-specific outcome measures available to evaluate the efficacy of these technologies. In addition to further investigation into the reasons patients and clinicians are satisfied or not satisfied with home telehealth, the future research agenda must address which populations will profit most from home telehealth and how much telehealth is needed. For example, Charles Parker is the type of patient who might benefit from repeated telehealth visits, while others may need just a few weeks to get them on the right track. A limitation of the studies presented here is that they primarily involve male patients. Further research ought to examine the appropriate matching of patient need to technology; use larger sample sizes to make definitive statements regarding the efficacy of the home-based application; identify potential patient safety issues; describe the mechanism of effect, such as why home telehealth works; and elucidate the organizational infrastructure needed to support telehealth services.

Discussion Questions

1. What types of systems and subsystems were these telehealth cases embedded in?
2. In what ways might this technology change patient-provider communication (and thus affect satisfaction)?
3. Should providers and patients who are uncomfortable with telehealth application be encouraged to try them? Or should researchers and health care providers accept that telehealth will not be an option for some people?
4. What other types of telehealth applications may be useful to this population?

References

Balas, E. A., and others. "Electronic Communication with Patients: Evaluation of Distance Medicine Technology." *JAMA*, 1997, *278*, 152–159.

Buckwalter, K. C., and others. "Telehealth for Elders and Their Caregivers in Rural Communities." *Family and Community Health*, 2002, *25*(3), 31–40.

Campion, E. W. "Can House Calls Survive?" *New England Journal of Medicine*, 1997, *337*, 1840–1841.

Currell, R., Urquhart, C., Wainwright, P., and Lewis, R. "Telemedicine versus Face to Face Patient Care: Effects on Professional Practice and Health Care Outcomes." *Cochrane Library*, no. 4, 2001.

Gardner, S., and others. "How Accurate Are Chronic Wound Assessments Using Interactive Video Technology?" *Journal of Gerontological Nursing*, 2001, *27*, 15–20.

Hersh, W., and others. "Clinical Outcomes Resulting from Telemedicine Interventions: A Systematic Review." *BMC Medical Informatics and Decision Making*, 2001, *1*(5). [http://www.biomedcentral.com/1472-6947/1/5].

Kemper P., and Murtaugh C. M. "Lifetime Use of Nursing Home Care." *New England Journal of Medicine,*" 1991, *324*, 595–600.

Johnson-Mekota, J., and others. "A Nursing Application of Telecommunications: Measurement of Satisfaction for Patients and Providers." *Journal of Gerontological Nursing*, 2001, *27*, 28–33.

Mair, F., and Whitten, P. "Systematic Review of Studies of Patient Satisfaction with Telemedicine." *British Medical Journal*, 2000, *320*, 1517–1520.

Rich, M. W. "Epidemiology, Pathophysiology, and Etiology of Chronic Heart Failure in Older Adults." *Journal of the American Geriatrics Society*, 1997, *45*, 968–974.

Rich, M. W., and others. "A Multidisciplinary Intervention to Prevent the Readmission of Elderly Patients with Chronic Heart Failure." *New England Journal of Medicine*, 1995, *333*, 1190–1195.

Specht, J., Wakefield, B., and Flanagan, J. "Evaluating the Cost of One Telehealth Application Connecting an Acute and Long Term Care Setting." *Journal of Gerontological Nursing*, 2001, *27*, 34–39.

Stewart, S., Vandenbroek, A. J., Pearson, S., and Horowitz, J. D. "Prolonged Beneficial Effects of a Home-Based Intervention on Unplanned Readmissions and Mortality Among Patients with Chronic Heart Failure." *Archives of Internal Medicine*, 1999, *159*, 257–261.

U.S. Government Accounting Office. *VA Health Care: How Distance from VA Facilities Affects Veterans' Use of VA Services.* Washington, D.C.: U.S. Government Printing Office, 1995.

Wakefield, B., Buresh, K., Flanagan, J., and Kienzle, M. "Interactive Video Specialty Consultations in Long-Term Care." *Journal of the American Geriatrics Society*, 2004, *52*(5), 789–793.

Wray, N., and others. "Application of an Analytic Model to Early Readmission Rates Within the Department of Veterans Affairs. " *Medical Care*, 1997, *35*, 768–781.

CHAPTER TWENTY-SEVEN

SYSTEMWIDE ROLLOUT OF DOCTOR-PATIENT SECURE WEB MESSAGING

The University of California, Davis, Virtual Care Experience

Eric M. Liederman, Eric M. Zimmerman, Marcos A. Athanasoulis, Margaret A. C. Young

Health care has frequently been cited as a latecomer in embracing information technologies to improved business processes and streamlining communication between trading partners. This lag is particularly notable in the most important relationship in health care: the doctor-patient relationship. Those interested in deploying new information technologies to secure communication pathways have had few published models from which to design a successful program. This case study examines the successful pilot implantation of a Web-based patient messaging service within the University of California Davis Health System (UCDHS).

Background

Recent surveys have found that 67 to 78 percent of adults with Internet access in the United States would like to communicate with their own physician on-line (Harris Interactive, 2002, 2003; Lenhart and others, 2003). These consumers want to communicate electronically with their doctor's office to schedule appointments, refill medication, obtain test results, and receive medical advice from a nurse or doctor (Harris Interactive, 2003). For these reasons, the Institute of Medicine (2003) has included electronic doctor-patient communication among its proposed core features of an electronic health record.

Despite latent consumer demand and potential for clinical benefit, few patients are able to communicate on-line with their doctors today. Indeed, fewer than one in five physicians use any form of e-mail with their patients, a figure that has remained flat over the past year (Manhattan Research, 2003), despite rapid growth in physician use of the Internet during that same period for both personal and professional use.

When introduced to the idea of electronically communicating with their patients, physicians at the UCDHS expressed what may be commonly held concerns. They feared being inundated with patient messages and inappropriate messaging by patients, which they feared would lead to an increase in the amount of time they would spend on uncompensated care.

Web Messaging versus E-mail

In an effort to overcome these barriers in its design for a virtual care pilot project, UCDHS elected to use a secure Web messaging service from RelayHealth Corporation rather than standard e-mail. Web messaging differs from e-mail in several important ways.

Privacy, Security, and Access Control

Web-based messaging provides an additional layer of security beyond regular e-mail. Messages are stored behind firewalls on a secure server, and all transmissions are encrypted in a manner similar to on-line financial transactions. Patient access can be limited to those who have been seen in person in the practice. Privacy can be improved through secure Web site sign-in names and passwords. Either party (doctor or patient) may discontinue the on-line communication relationship at any time, mitigating physician concerns about overuse or inappropriate use by certain patients.

Clinical Structure, Content, and Workflow

Unlike e-mail, Web messaging enables communications from patients to be automatically categorized and routed to the most appropriate person in the practice based on customizable rules in the software. Appointment requests can route to the scheduler, medication refill requests to the appropriate staff nurse, billing inquiries to the accounting office, and requests for on-line clinical care or advice to a triage nurse or the patient's own doctor. Requests for clinical advice (called "WebVisits" within RelayHealth) take advantage of algorithm-driven clinical interviews conducted on-line to inform treatment decisions and advice.

Physicians can tailor their response to a WebVisit interview sent by a patient using medically reviewed, guidelines-based content, attach relevant patient education materials, and, if appropriate, prescribe on-line for the patient, all from within the messaging service. Patients can access the on-line treatment advice as well as on-line educational materials attached by the physician and can route the electronic prescriptions or refills to their pharmacy of choice.

Charging and Reimbursement

E-mail lacks the facility for physicians to be compensated for clinical advice and care support rendered on behalf of their patients. In contrast, the RelayHealth Web messaging service gives physicians the option to assess patient fees for consultations conducted on-line and handles both patient eligibility checking and submission of claims to participating health plans.

Program Overview

In late 2000 and early 2001, the UCDHS formed a committee to research patient demand for e-health services. The greater Sacramento area is a highly competitive medical marketplace with a sizable number of technology firms and computer-savvy consumers. Interest and investment in Internet-based services of all kinds was very high, and UC Davis leaders were aware that some of its competitors were moving beyond static Web pages to provide more on-line services to patients and partners.

The committee then investigated how to offer such a service and determined that the use of regular e-mail would be highly problematic. Guidelines on how to communicate with patients on-line safely and effectively appeared to preclude the use of e-mail (Kunkler, 2001). The committee's concerns were amplified by concern over the coming publication of the Health Insurance Portability and Accountability Act of 1996 Privacy Rule. These concerns led the committee to look at alternative Web messaging solutions instead of at e-mail.

By 2001, UC Davis, like many other health systems, was moving philosophically from a strategy of building its own information systems to purchasing systems. It looked at the vendor marketplace and ultimately selected RelayHealth, which appealed to committee members for several reasons. First, the user interface seemed easy to use and intuitively designed. Second, the business model, in which insurers reimburse for on-line clinical consultations (WebVisits), paralleled the current in-office fee-for-service model and seemed likely to succeed with payers, providers, and patients. Third, the array of on-line tools, including electronic prescribing, interactive patient interviews, and note templating, was attractive.

Once the committee had selected a vendor, discussions began with health system leaders. Site visits were made to several early adopter physicians using the selected Web messaging system. Although these physicians uniformly reported success and satisfaction with the system, no large provider organizations had as yet implemented the service, so UC Davis leadership decided to undertake a pilot test at one primary care clinic and conduct a structured evaluation before proceeding with a large-scale implementation.

To prepare for the pilot, policies and procedures had to be created. This process, which required half a year, involved ambulatory care administration, in-house counsel, and risk management. Starting with national guidelines (Kunkler, 2001; Prady, Norris, and Lester, 2001), a one-page patient information sheet was developed to communicate these policies and clearly describe the responsibilities of patients, providers, and staff in the use of secure Web messaging. Patients were allowed to self-register on-line, since Web messaging was seen as analogous to telephone communication, and patients were not required to come to the office to register to phone their provider. The only tasks left were to select the pilot site, the pilot start date, protocols for message routing and handling, and how to market to patients.

Program Implementation

The health system leadership decided that the best place to initially deploy on-line doctor-patient communication services would be in the system's primary care network (PCN), which consists of twelve community-based clinics serving the greater Sacramento area. Of these twelve clinics, the Folsom clinic emerged as the logical pilot site because physicians in that clinic were known to be technologically savvy, the clinic staff had good management, and they were generally open to new ideas and initiatives. In addition, the socioeconomic status of the Folsom clinic patient population matched the general demographics of Internet users, suggesting that a sizable portion of patients were already on-line.

A second meeting was held with clinic physicians and staff in August 2001 to design the message routing and workflow for the clinic. The selected vendor service enabled the clinic to customize messaging routing and response roles using a workflow engine within the software. Responsibility for triaging and answering each message type was mapped out in simple flowchart form. Initially, the clinic chose to mirror workflow for phone messages to minimize impact on the clinic staff. The message routing rules, along with basic demographic and credential information for all of the physicians and staff, was supplied to the vendor, and an on-line representation of the clinic was mapped into the software.

On-site training was conducted during November 2001 to take advantage of a period with lower visit volume and fewer staff vacations. All of the staff and providers received a half-hour of didactic instruction on the service and then spent the following hour gaining hands-on skill by responding to sample fictitious patient messages using the Web messaging service. A RelayHealth trainer visited the clinic two weeks and four weeks after the initial training to answer individual questions and provide follow-on training and support as needed.

Two weeks after the training, a subset of clinic patients were mailed an informational letter about the new communication service and invited to register on-line. Approximately 50 patients registered. Brochures and posters were also posted in the waiting area announcing the new service. In March, the mailing was repeated to all patients who had been seen in the previous year, which resulted in another 275 patients registering to communicate with their doctor on-line.

Overall Pilot Program Results

Project and health system leaders considered the pilot implementation of the Web-based messaging system a success. Most users were satisfied, found the system easy to use, and thought it improved communication and was better than using the telephone for nonurgent patient-provider communications. Use was commensurate with the level of patient enrollment. Small use spikes were seen in response to program outreach efforts, such as mass mailings to all patients eligible to communicate with their physician on-line. By administering quantifiable surveys throughout the pilot, UCDHS was able to tune the service to address and avoid potential problems and pitfalls. Areas that needed improvement included clinician response times to patient messages and staff perception of an increased workload.

Patient Enrollment

Enrollment varied, with one provider having fewer than 10 patients and one provider having over 250 patients. The mean number of patients enrolled per provider was 115 at the end of the study period. Enrollment (and messaging) increased after each of two mass mailings. Physicians who discussed the service directly with their patients had the highest number of enrolled patients by the end of the study period. Enrollment rates were consistent with initial pilot expectations.

Broader Rollout

Following the successful pilot program at the Folsom clinic, the UCDHS leadership decided to expand doctor-patient Web messaging to its other PCN community clinics in Sacramento and three surrounding counties. To accomplish this goal, a project plan and time line were created.

During this same period, UCDHS ambulatory care administration was about to embark on a six-month rolling implementation of open access scheduling at each of the PCN clinics. This scheduling initiative, which involved converting every physician's practice to allow the same-day scheduling of most patients, was determined to be complementary to the secure Web messaging initiative. Both projects were perceived to improve patient access. As a result, each clinic was scheduled go live with patient Web messaging as it completed its conversion to open access scheduling. The first site went live in May 2002 and the last in November 2002.

Lessons Learned

Experiences from this project pointed to five specific lessons from which to draw:

- *Expect patients to like the service more than the staff and providers do.* There is a significant amount of patient demand for on-line communication with doctor and clinic for messaging. Patients using the service are self-selected and are already comfortable with on-line activities such as shopping, and as a result they do not need training. These self-selected patients represent the left side of the adoption curve (innovators and early adopters), while providers and staff represent the entire adoption curve. A "one-size-fits-all" training for providers and staff is not enough. To ensure a successful initiative, do regular review of utilization and employ tactics to give special attention to resisters. Offering one-on-one training and engaging opinion leaders to carry the message helps with resisters. Strong health system leadership also helps.
- *Pilot the service prior to deployment.* The successful pilot greatly increased the probability of success by demonstrating that success is possible and by creating a cohort of internal advocates.
- *Secure Web messaging may improve productivity.* Early data suggest that messaging does not hurt, and may improve, productivity. This was an important lesson for providers, who expressed an almost universal fear that electronic access would result in a tidal wave of patient messages. Patients for the most part are judicious in their use of on-line messaging with their health care providers.
- *Offer a full suite of communication services.* Patient messaging by itself is useful but becomes more powerful when combined with features such as electronic routing

of prescriptions to pharmacies and structured on-line patient interviews, resulting in better information and documentation for doctors. These helpful features improved provider and staff efficiency.

• *Reimbursement matters.* The follow-up focus groups identified that the providers want to be paid to perform clinical patient services on-line. The providers saw Web messaging as clinical work and felt they should be paid for this service. This finding corroborates recent national surveys. Fortunately, a growing number of insurers and employers are beginning to offer reimbursement for services like the Relay Health WebVisit.

Discussion Questions

1. What are the characteristics of an effective, secure doctor-patient on-line communication program?
2. What are specific benefits to patients, practices, and health systems?
3. What are some of the main barriers to successful implementation of a technology initiative within a medical group?
4. Describe some of the strategies that can be used to overcome these barriers to adoption.
5. Discuss future opportunities for on-line communication to improve care processes.

References

Harris Interactive. "Patient/Physician On-line Communication: Many Patients Want It, Would Pay for It, and It Would Influence Their Choice of Doctors and Health Plans." *Harris Interactive News,* 2002, *10*(8). [http://www.harrisinteractive.com].

Harris Interactive. "Those with Internet Access to Continue to Grow But at a Slower Rate." Harris Poll, Mar. 14, 2003. [http://www.harrisinteractive.com].

Institute of Medicine. *Key Capabilities of an Electronic Health Record.* Washington, D.C.: National Academies Press, 2003. [http://books.nap.edu/html/ehr/NI000427.pdf].

Kunkler T. "Legal Issues and Unsolicited E-Mail." *MD Net Guide,* 2001, *3*(2), 18–22.

Lenhart, A., and others. "The Ever Shifting Internet Population: A New Look at Internet Access and the Digital Divide." Mar. 14, 2003. [http://www.pewinternet.org/reports/toc.asp?Report=88].

Manhattan Research. *Taking the Pulse: Physicians and Emerging Information Technology.* June 24, 2003.

Prady, S. L., Norris, D., and Lester, J. E. "Expanding the Guidelines for Electronic Communication with Patients." *Journal of American Medical Informatics Association,* 2001, *8*(4), 344–348.

CHAPTER TWENTY-EIGHT

LOW-VISION REACHING OUT THROUGH TELEMEDICINE

The Process of Implementing One Ophthalmic Subspecialty

Jade S. Schiffman, Gina G. Wong, Rosa A. Tang

As the population of the United States continues to age, an increasing number of patients will be affected by ocular conditions that will cause visual loss. In patients over seventy years of age, the third leading cause of disability requiring assistance is visual loss (Warnecke, 2003). Age-related macular degeneration (ARMD), glaucoma, diabetes, and other eye conditions are more prevalent in the elderly and are the leading cause of blindness in the United States (First-Gov, 2002). ARMD affects 5 percent of the U.S. population, but in patients over age sixty-five, it affects 20 percent (Brody, Roch-Levecq, and Gamst, 2002). As the population continues to age, a growing number of people will be affected. Rural Texas has a large number of visually impaired individuals who are underserved. A barrier to low-vision service is a lack of low-vision services or transportation to get services (Pollard, Simpson, Lamoureux, and Keeffe, 2003).

The University of Houston College of Optometry (UHCO), University Eye Institute (UEI) in Houston, Texas, has a low vision clinic with access to low vision specialists. A Texas Infrastructure Fund Board (TIF) grant was awarded to UEI in 1999 to establish a pilot program for telemedical eye care to rural and urban underserved sites in Texas. The grant provided funding for purchasing telemedicine equipment, peripheral devices, and telecommunication lines. Protocols and consent forms were developed and approved by institutional committees or institutional review boards. A combination of store-and-forward and videoconferencing technology was employed for the low vision consultations. Once established, the telemedicine low-vision consultations could be self-sustaining because Medicare will reimburse for telemedicine if there is a real-time encounter and if the site is rural and underserved. In the following, we describe the process taken to implement one subspecialized telemedicine program.

Acquiring the Infrastructure

Tele-ophthalmology is image intensive, so the telemedicine system, peripheral devices, and telecommunication lines used must support this. Good image resolution allows the consultant to diagnose at a level as close to an office visit as possible. Fundus digital images may be 640 X 480 to 2000 X 2000 (Tang and Schiffman, 2001). For our project, we required video and audio clips of parts of the exam as well as fundus photos and the paper exam findings. Therefore, we needed peripheral devices such as automatic document feeder (ADF)/flat bed image scanner, nonmydriatic retinal camera, microphone, printer, and video camcorder with tripod. Our camcorder had infrared (nightshot) capability, which allows imaging of pupils in a dark room. Mobility was important so a desktop unit with flat screen liquid crystal display monitor was mounted on a sleek cart with an ADF/image scanner, video camcorder, microphone, and speakers (Figure 28.1). The telemedicine system readily allowed capture and organized data storage into electronic patient image files. It allowed connection using a number of different telecommunication methods so we were also able to connect with regular telephone service if necessary.

Choosing a telemedicine software and hardware system requires review of its telemedicine capabilities, costs, and level of security and encryption. Because telemedicine consultations are similar to actual patient office visits, integration of the patient's telemedicine visit data with the office's medical records system was important to us. After extensive review of various telemedicine systems, we chose a system that allowed integration of complete medical record software with a store-and-forward system with video and audio clip capture and storage capability, and face-to-face or teleconferencing. We could access the telemedicine patient file from our office electronic medical record as well as access it directly from the telemedicine software. Store-and-forward capability allows large files to be transmitted at any time using any bandwidth, and a paging and e-mail system alerted the consultant to the available consult data. The telemedicine software could be placed on the consultant's computer so the medical data could be reviewed from home or office rather than going to the telemedicine room. The consultant could type up a consult note or record an audio dictation note, which could be sent from home to the remote site. In addition to hardware and software costs, there are many other fees.

FIGURE 28.1. SYSTEM FOR TELE-OPHTHALMOLOGY.

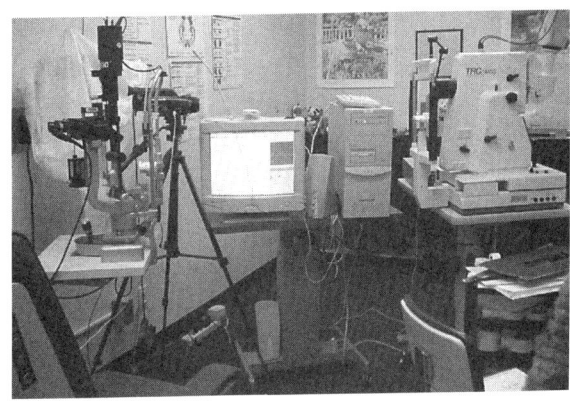

A

B

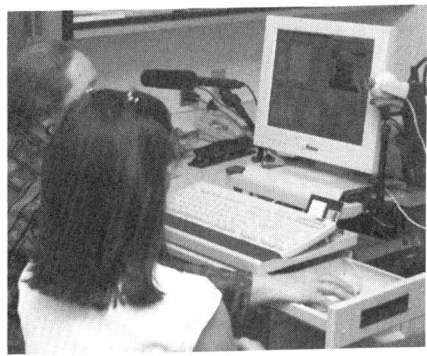

C

Note: (A) Example of peripheral devices that can be attached to the telemedicine system. Left to right: slit lamp, video camcorder, monitor with desktop computer telemedicine unit, Topcon nonmydriatic camera, and low-vision equipment in mobile drawers. (B, C) Desktop telemedicine system with flat screen liquid crystal display monitor and scanner on the mobile cart.

Health Insurance Portability and Accountability Compliance Issues

The Health Insurance Portability and Accountability Act of 1996 (HIPAA) was developed for administrative simplification in electronic billing and medical record transactions. It was set up to guard the privacy of patient medical and billing information during electronic transfers, but it now applies to the confidentiality of medical records in general. Protected health information is "any individually identifiable health information transmitted by or maintained in electronic media or any other form or media" (Goldberg, 2002). HIPAA establishes guidelines to ensure data integrity, security, confidentiality, and safety in all medical records. It provides guidelines to prevent unauthorized use and disclosure of protected health information (PHI). It applies to telemedicine systems and all personnel who are in contact with the patient and PHI.

Our telemedicine system contained different security access levels, password protection, and encryption of data. All data entered are time and date stamped when created and by whom. Software tracks who has accessed, created, and modified the patient file or episode. An automatic data backup system was developed and backup data was stored at a separate secure site. Confidentiality forms must be developed and signed by all personnel involved in the telemedicine encounter. Any health care providers, ancillary personnel, video camera operators, and vendors such as the telemedicine vendors need to sign an HIPAA confidentiality form or business associate agreements. The patients are given a copy of HIPAA guidelines and must sign a form acknowledging this. Anyone who may see or deal with patient medical information, even for billing and insurance purposes, needs to sign the confidentiality form.

Consent Forms and Clinical Privileges

We developed a consent form for the project that was approved by the university's human subjects committee and the local hospital. The hospital also developed an additional consent form. Ideally, a general telemedicine consent form can be created that allows all medical specialties access to telemedicine services; however, some institutions are still fixed in the idea that consent forms can be created only for a specific research project. Due to institutional constraints, it took months of revisions to create what became a three- to four-page consent form. Consent forms should be only one to two pages long if possible and address benefits and risks and potential billing charges. Because telemedicine was new to the local hospital, it needed time to develop administrative rules and protocols. Often the hospital wants examples of other telemedicine programs and their protocols. All telemedicine consulting and participating remote presenters were required to apply for privileges at the hospital and had active licenses in the state. These necessary consents and privileges can be a lengthy obstacle.

Low-Vision Telemedicine

We met with the local ophthalmologist and optometrist, who welcomed the idea of low-vision telemedicine consults. The local hospital was also happy to get infrastructure to set up its own telemedicine capability. Potentially, telemedicine could be used for other specialty consults in the hospital. Most hospital administrators tried to help facilitate the project when administrative issues arose. The university's low-vision consultants worked with us to establish the data required to prescribe the appropriate optical devices for each patient. Together, we developed a flow sheet of exam data required and how the information should be obtained (Exhibit 28.1). Ideally, remote site presenters (such as nonophthalmic personnel or optometric student) could use the guide to perform the remote exam to send to the consultant for analysis.

Patients were referred for telemedicine low-vision services by the local ophthalmologist and optometrist. There are four steps in this telemedicine low-vision consultation:

1. On-site eye care provider exam (preconsultation)
2. Low-vision protocol sent to the consultant (store and forward),
3. Consultant review of information and recommendations sent to remote site
4. On-line videoconference consultation

After the low-vision referral is made, the patient consent is signed, and previous eye care exam records are obtained and scanned into the telemedicine software. A low-vision evaluation is scheduled with the remote site examiner, who was an optometrist. A hospital information technology person assigned to the telemedicine project helped to capture nonmydriatic retinal images and exam video and audio clips and enter the required data into the telemedicine electronic file.

Patient Episode

One patient referred had decreased vision from a recent stroke and was not realistic in his goals. He wanted to be able to drive again and declined suggestions for any optical devices. This patient was educated on scheduling an appointment with a driver's visual and physical rehabilitation program that is available in Houston.

EXHIBIT 28.1. PROTOCOL FOR VIDEO AND AUDIO CLIP FOR LOW-VISION REMOTE EXAMINATION.

	Patient	Chart Needed	Light On (Room or Near Light)	Camera Focus
1	Distance visual acuity	Feinbloom	On	On patient's face-eyes
2	Telescope _2.2x for distance	Feinbloom	On	Face close up
3	Telescope 4x_ for distance	Feinbloom	On	Face close up
4	Near-vision acuity with bifocal, if has them	Single letter (OD and OS) and paragraph (OU) chart allow patient to hold chart	Near light on paragraph chart or single letter chart	@ 45 side view. View of both patient's face while reading and chart
5	Near-vision acuity with near-optical device +5.00D over subjective refraction	Paragraph: If patient is unable to obtain a paragraph acuity, check VA with single letter chart	Near light on	Side view of patient holding near chart, reading lowest line. Can read easily and lowest line read with difficulty
6	Near-visual acuity with near-optical device +10.00D over subjective refraction	Paragraph or single letter chart	Near light on	Side view of patient holding near chart, reading lowest line. Can read easily and lowest line read with difficulty
7	Amsler grid each eye OD, OS and OU – ask patient to find 'centre dot', hold it and draw defects in vision around fixation	Amsler grid	Amsler grid	Zoom in on patient eye movements

Examiner Audio	Patient Audio	Camera Light On/Focus
1 Announce patients lowest VA read with difficulty or easily in snellen, for example, 10/20	Reading acuity chart lowest line	On/auto or manual
2 Announce patients lowest VA read with difficulty or easily	Reading acuity chart lowest line	On/auto or manual
3 Announce patients lowest VA read with difficulty or easily	Reading acuity chart lowest line	On/auto or manual
4 Announce patients lowest VA read with difficulty or easily in M notation at what distance, for example, 2M at 30cm	Reading acuity chart lowest line	On/auto or manual
5 Announce patients lowest VA read with difficulty or easily in M notation at what distance, for example, 1M at 5cm	Reading acuity chart lowest line	On/auto or manual
6 Announce patients lowest VA read with difficulty or easily in M notation at what distance, for example, 0.4M at 5cm	Reading acuity chart lowest line	On/auto or manual
7 Announce if patient viewing eccentrically and describe abnormality found	Reading acuity chart lowest line	On/auto or manual

If patient can obtain a distance acuity of 20/40 or better than 10/20 with the 2.2x FDTS, skip the 4x telescope demonstration
If patient obtains a near acuity (paragraph) of 1M or better with the +5 D lens over his or her distance correction, skip the +10D demonstration

Images that are needed

1. Fundus picture of each eye with Topcon nonmydriatic camera

2. Visual fields

3. Amsler grid

4. Low-vision exam form

5. Low-vision history form

6. Consent form

Another patient was legally blind from macular degeneration. He wanted to be able to read again and to see his grandson play baseball or help his wife spot signs in the distance. The remote optometrist and information technology person obtained video clips and exam data following the protocol. This was entered into the patient's electronic record and time and date stamped. Data entered together are saved as an "episode," or visit. Each episode displays thumbnails of the available documents, images, and video or audio data available for viewing (Figure 28.2). After review of this store-and-forward data, the consultant sent recommendations for the patient's visual goals. During the second visit, the patient tried the suggested near and distance devices. Magnifiers allowed him to read again, and a telescope improved his distance vision. Filters recommended to increase contrast and cut glare were tried and found to be helpful. A real-time video connection was made with the consultant, and the patient and his wife were introduced to the consultant. A questionnaire was administered after the exam, and the patient was very happy with the low-vision telemedicine project.

Telemedicine Reimbursement

Medicaid in Texas and nineteen other states recognizes telemedicine teleconsultations for reimbursement to both the originating remote site and the consult site, but it requires a real-time video teleconference with the consultant. Store-and-forward telemedicine consultations are not usually reimbursed. Texas allows reimbursement of physician consultants and health care personnel who are remote site presenters. Because our low-vision consultations originated from a rural underserved region (rural health professional shortage area) and in a hospital, the encounter could be billed for the consultation as well as a fee for the use of a hospital facility. Telemedicine reimbursement uses the same consultation codes as medical examinations, or a telemedicine modifier may be added to the code.

Conclusion

Telemedicine consults can benefit patients who otherwise would have no access to low-vision and visual rehabilitation. Patients requiring low-vision consultation would not have to travel to enhance their remaining vision. This project ended when the grant ended because it was not yet self-sustaining. The TIF board grant paid only for the cost of telemedicine infrastructure and did not allow any payment for personnel to support the telemedicine project. Personnel from the institutions therefore had telemedicine added onto their current work responsibilities.

FIGURE 28.2. PATIENT ELECTRONIC EPISODE.

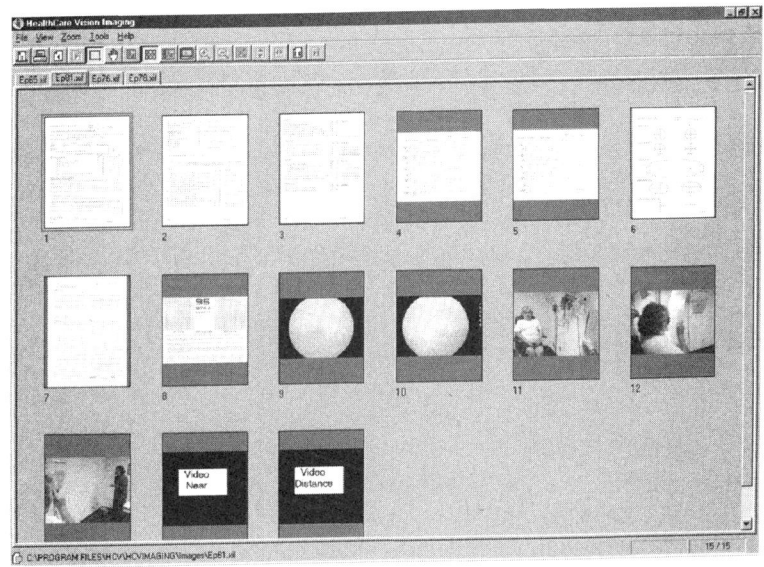

A

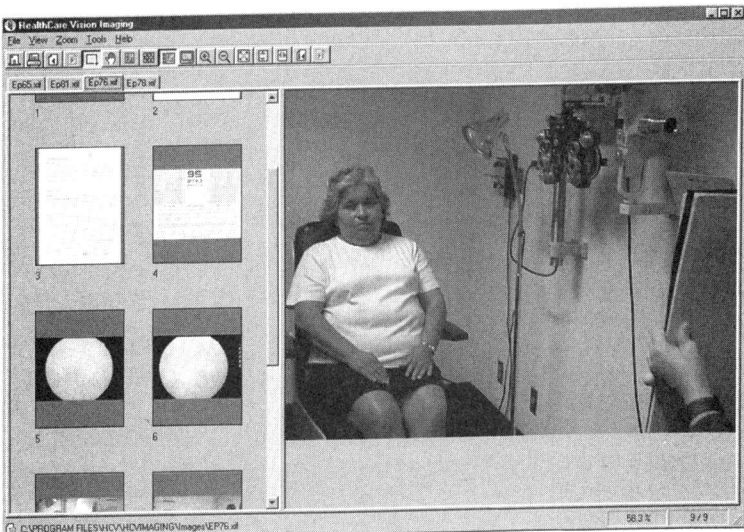

B

Note: (A) Patient electronic file episode shows thumbnails of documents available for viewing in the telemedicine software. (B) The chosen image or video is shown in the large view.

This was difficult for the personnel involved even if they wanted to help implement the project. Rarely was the work load decreased enough in the remote sites for the clinicians to feel that it was not interrupting normal operations.

Telemedicine low vision can be self-sustaining from insurance and Medicare reimbursement and cost of low-vision optical devices. Once the low-vision telemedicine project was established, we hoped that telemedicine would be available for other medical specialties at the rural hospital. With telemedicine available to more services, the project could have been more quickly self-sustaining before the grant ended. Indeed, we learned that telemedicine can help rural and underserved populations, although implementation can be difficult.

Discussion Questions

1. In considering hardware and software telemedicine options, what do you need to look for?
2. What do you need to find out from institutions that will be involved in the telemedicine consultations or encounters?
3. What do you need to know about HIPAA and confidentiality? About human subject or institutional review boards and consent forms?
4. Does your state recognize telemedicine consultations?
5. What type of accreditation or licensing is required for your state (or states)?
6. Will the institution's telemedicine personnel have a decrease in current work load to help implement telemedicine?
7. Does the telemedicine grant help pay for personnel as well as infrastructure?

References

Brody, B. L., Roch-Levecq, A., and Gamst, A. C. "Self-Management of Age-Related Macular Degeneration and Quality of Life: A Randomized Controlled Trial," *Archive of Ophthalmology*, 2002, *120*, 1477–1483.

FirstGov. "More Americans Facing Blindness Than Ever Before by National Eye Institute and Prevent Blindness." Mar. 20, 2002. [http://www.seniors.gov/articles/0602/blindness.htm].

Goldberg, A. S. "Alan S. Goldberg's Law Technology and Change Homepage." Oct. 9, 2002. [http://hipaalawyer.com].

Pollard, T. L., Simpson, J. A., Lamoureux, E. L., and Keeffe, J. E. "Barriers to Accessing Low Vision Services." *Ophthalmic Physiologic Optometry*, 2003, *23*(4), 321–327.

Tang, R. A., and Schiffman, J. S. "Tele-Ophthalmology May Improve the Ability to Manage Eye-Care Challenges." *Business Briefing: Next Generation of Healthcare*, Oct. 2001, pp. 1–4.

Warnecke P. "A Caregiver's Eye on Elders with Low Vision." *Caring*, Jan. 22, 2003, pp. 12–15.

CHAPTER TWENTY-NINE

INTERNET-BASED SPECIALTY CONSULTATIONS

A Study of Adoption Challenges

Paul Heinzelmann, Joseph Kvedar

Since 1995, Partners Telemedicine, a joint initiative of Brigham and Women's Hospital and Massachusetts General Hospital, has been enabling access to its medical specialists through information and communication technologies. With a vision that health care decision making should be rapid and delivered to the point of need, Partners Telemedicine has extended the reach of these four thousand specialists through over nine thousand specialty consultations.

Consultations using the Internet began in 2001 through the Partners Online Specialty Consultations (POSC) Web portal, and as of September 2003, 182 were completed. Through POSC, a patient's medical information is sent directly from the provider to a medical specialist at one of several Harvard-affiliated centers of excellence, including Brigham and Women's Hospital, Massachusetts General Hospital, and the Dana-Farber/Partners Cancer Care Center. Clinically relevant information such as medical histories, labs, electrocardiogram, X-rays, and CT scans are sent securely over the Internet or by traditional fax, phone, or mail. A telemedicine coordinator oversees information and communication flow among POSC users. Either patients or their physicians may initiate a POSC consultation, but specialist feedback is always returned directly to the patient's local provider, keeping the patient-provider relationship intact.

A recent retrospective study of outcomes demonstrated that POSC specialists provided new diagnoses in 5 percent of cases, and offered alternative treatment recommendations in 90 percent of cases. Turnaround time for the receipt of a specialist opinion by the provider also decreased from 19 to 6.8 working days when compared to traditional consultation (Kedar and others, 2003). Noteworthy is that 90 percent of consults were for ongoing care of cancer patients.

Addressing Health Care Inequities

Internet-based consultation ultimately aims to improve problems in the existing health care delivery model. There is clear evidence that accessible, high-quality, and cost-effective health care is not equitably allocated on either a national or global scale. In the United States, this includes underuse and misuse of resources, long wait times to access medical specialists, significant geographical practice variability, and poor adherence to established standards of care, where only 54 percent of Americans receive the evidence-based recommendations for screening and basic care of acute and chronic conditions (McGlynn, 2003). Continuing discourse is needed on how Internet technologies can increase health care quality, access to health care, health education, and cost-effectiveness, all while preserving the sanctity of the patient-provider relationship.

Partners Telemedicine aims to impact the following areas of health care delivery by leveraging the Internet through POSC:

> *Access:* POSC operates through a secure Web portal to create readily available access to specialists at recognized centers of excellence affiliated with the Harvard Medical School.
>
> *Quality:* By enabling rapid transfer of medical expertise from centers of excellence, deficits associated with geographical variability in quality can be mitigated. Faster implementation of the most appropriate care reflects a higher level of quality.
>
> *Cost-effectiveness and cost-benefit:* As a cost-saving alternative, Internet-based consultation preserves the benefit of accessing a high level of medical expertise without the costs of travel.

Partners Telemedicine has easily recruited medical specialists for POSC and receives referrals from multiple sources, resulting in an increasing volume overall. However, despite initial encouraging predictions from an independent consulting firm, the volume of POSC consults initiated directly from patients registering on the Web site has fallen short of expectations. A review of data from the POSC server from July 1, 2001, through September 30, 2003, reveals that

2,098 patients and 744 referring physicians registered on the Web site, but only 174 actual cases resulted. This represents only 8.3 percent of the patients who registered. And of 10,380 unique visitors to the POSC Web site in the three-month period of July 1 through September 30, 2003, only 18 became actual cases. We have since attempted to understand the reasons for this slower-than-expected adoption and to develop strategies to promote adoption and to develop strategies to promote adoption among patients and providers.

Strategies to Promote Adoption

Grigsby (2002) describes four levels for understanding adoption and diffusion of telemedicine: economic, societal, institutional, and individual. We use these levels to describe our experience at Partners, outline lessons learned, and provide future direction of the initiatives.

Economic Level

This level refers to the productivity of using Internet technology as an alternate means of providing medical services and can be quantified in terms such as cost-effectiveness, cost-benefit, and return on investment. Internet-based consultation disrupts the economic status quo by introducing the following.

Unsubstantiated Cost-Benefit. There remains a strong potential for Internet-based telemedicine to offer a cost-effective alternative to traditional specialist care and acts as a driver among innovators and early adopters. Mounting evidence for cost-effectiveness is accruing gradually; however, few long-term studies have provided well-documented evidence of this (Whitten and others, 2002). Services through the POSC model are undoubtedly less expensive for most when considering the costs of transportation, housing, and associated opportunity costs of traveling to Boston for a face-to-face specialist consultation. Typical costs to a patient range from $225 to $750 depending on the number of specialists involved in the case. To further demonstrate the cost-effectiveness of Internet-based consultation, Partners Telemedicine continues to invest in research that examines economic factors.

Beneficial But Nonreimbursable Transactions. By its nature, Internet-based communication enables increased dialogue between patients, providers, and specialists that is value-adding but not routinely reimbursed. As a result, only patients who are willing to pay out of pocket drive the demand for Internet-based consultation.

Partners Telemedicine has addressed this issue by developing payment agreements with several Fortune 100 companies. Through this mechanism, POSC services are provided to over 300,000 employees as part of their health benefits package, removing out-of-pocket cost as a barrier. It is too early to tell what the impact on adoption will be, but increased volume is anticipated.

Societal Level

This level refers to the norms and expectations within society that are imposed by governments and health care systems. According to the 2001 Institute of Medicine report, large-scale changes within society ultimately must occur to improve health care quality and should include integration of information technology and the introduction of new reimbursement schemes to finance these innovations. Not surprising, the findings of a recent study also suggested that physicians who perceived professional and social responsibilities regarding adoption of telehealth in their clinical practice had a stronger intention to use this technology (Gagnon and others, 2003). The following are some of the modifications that Internet-based consultation introduces into an already highly structured and regulated system and which users must ultimately accept before large-scale adoption occurs.

Modified Roles and Social Networks. Through Internet-based consultation, patients themselves may more easily initiate consultation with a specialist, and provider-specialist interactions become more accessible. If used in ways that equally support the individual roles of patients, providers, and specialists with minimal disruption, the Internet may empower all of these parties as it improves health care delivery through more efficient use of human resources.

The patient-provider relationship however, remains an accepted and highly valued part of the American health care tradition and is founded and fostered through personal, face-to-face meetings. Disrupting the expectations associated with established social roles can create tension. For example, within the growing managed care delivery model, Internet-based consultation may be perceived as a threat to the primary care provider's role as gatekeeper, where unchecked access to specialists may mistakenly be viewed as excessive or unnecessary.

To promote the relative advantages with minimal disruption of the status quo, POSC requires collaboration with a local provider to preserve the mutually valued patient-provider relationship. Notably, this is unlike other sponsored Internet-based consultations that put the onus entirely on the patient and risk severing patient-provider partnerships.

Access That Is Independent of Time and Place. Internet-based communication can be real time like a telephone conversation, but is typically (as with POSC) asynchronous and more akin to voice mail or e-mail messaging. As such, it allows for specialist collaboration that is more convenient by minimizing the need for coordinating the schedules of the patient, provider, and specialist.

Through POSC, Partners Telemedicine challenges the traditional standard of face-to-face consultation by enlisting a cadre of medical specialists who are willing to break with tradition and provide their services in this innovative way.

Technology-Enabled Patient Care. Communication technologies may improve quality of care through reinforcement of evidence-based standards and timely access to specialist expertise. As an analogy, consider the telephone. Despite its limitations, it is estimated that one-sixth of ambulatory care visits have now been replaced by telephone communication (Darkins and Cary, 2000). What now seems commonplace took years to become widely adopted due to its initial disruptive nature, and it is likely that a similar barrier must be overcome for the more sophisticated technology of Internet-based consultation. Partners Telemedicine addresses these issues by striving for simplicity and usability within the POSC Web site.

Institutional Level

This is the level of the health care organization, hospital, or clinic that functions within the larger health care system. Internet-based consultation can alter existing institutional norms by modifying intra- and interorganizational relationships.

Internet communication holds certain advantages that allow and promote collaboration and networking within and between organizations. To the innovative health care CEO, virtual organizations become possible, where geographical borders or time zones do not bind members, and competition is based more on quality and cost. In addition, subgroups may more easily form that avoid the political and bureaucratic complexity of a large centralized organization while preserving the economy of scale associated with increased operational efficiency (Hu, Liu Sheng, and Wei, 1996).

Traditional referral patterns, however, often rely on predictable specialist resources within a geographically defined region such as managed care health networks or affiliations with certain health care facilities or organizations. Internet-based consultation may threaten health care organizations and their affiliated specialist groups that have relied on the usual system of referral for their patient base.

Partners Telemedicine is unique in that it operates as a division within the larger Partners Health care system, an affiliation that allows it to introduce innovation more easily. Partners Telemedicine has actively gained the endorsement of influential individuals with rare talents. John Glaser is a classic example of an opinion leader who serves as vice president and chief information officer of Partners Health Care and has recognized the value of telemedicine as a way to improve the efficiency of this health care corporation.

Individual Level

This is the most basic unit of adoption and is shaped by knowledge, attitudes, and behaviors. Adoption of new behaviors are required by the patient, the provider, and the specialist if Internet-based consultation is to be integrated successfully.

The Internet catalyzes knowledge transfer between individuals and simultaneously generates novel educational opportunities relevant to the immediate experience of caring for a patient. In contrast, the usual method of specialist feedback involves a mailed letter from the specialist to the primary provider. Typically taking weeks, it usually includes the specialist's opinion and may include new diagnostic or treatment recommendations. Although it follows no established format to guarantee quality and fails to provide a timely educational opportunity, it does not require that the specialist enter data into a computerized template. Internet-based consultation therefore requires the assimilation of new behaviors for knowledge transfer and a new set of expectations by both the specialist and the local provider. Finally, it may alter specialist referral sources that are based on interpersonal relationships between providers and specialists.

Partners Telemedicine has capitalized on the relative advantage of using the Internet by producing a more standardized specialist report and enabling faster turnaround time and faster implementation of the most appropriate care. We believe that this translates into improved outcomes and improved quality.

At present, the demand for POSC is primarily patient driven and has seen its greatest use in a group of individuals with similar characteristics: cancer patients. By appreciating the role of what Rogers (1995) refers to as homophilous groups (individuals with binding similarities), POSC seeks to develop a strategy to increase adoption by targeting other groups of similar individuals (for instance, disease-specific support groups).

Conclusion

Through POSC, Partners Telemedicine is providing global access to the medical specialists of Harvard-affiliated centers of excellence. Despite attempts to build on the relative advantages of this approach, adoption of this technology has been slow. Meanwhile, outcomes research strives to validate the potential benefits. Challenges remain at the economic, societal, institutional, and individual levels before the chasm to widespread adoption is bridged. Incorporating the observations of marketing theorists and focusing on promotion of the relative advantages of Internet-based consultation has served as a strategy to address these challenges.

Discussion Questions

1. List several possible limitations to providing Internet-based consultation in response to a sudden large increase in demand by patients.
2. What communications channels might best be used to inform and persuade providers to consider participating in Internet-based consultation?
3. Are there any risks or benefits associated with using the Internet for health care that are particularly important to you?
4. Identify which adopter category best represents your attitude toward Internet-based consultation and why: innovator, early adopter, early majority, late majority, or laggard.

References

Darkins, A. W., and Cary, M. A. *Telemedicine and Telehealth: Principles, Policies, Performance, and Pitfalls.* New York: Springer, 2000.

Gagnon, M. P., and others. "An Adaptation of the Theory of Interpersonal Behaviour to the Study of Telemedicine Adoption by Physicians." *International Journal of Medical Information,* 2003, *71*(2–3), 103–115.

Grigsby, J. "The Diffusion of Telemedicine." *Telemedicine Journal and e-Health,* 2002, *8*(1), 79–94.

Hu, P. J., Liu Sheng, O. R., and Wei, C. *A Framework for Investigating Impacts of Telemedicine.* Waco, Tex.: Baylor University, 1996.

Institute of Medicine. *Crossing the Quality Chasm: A New Health System for the Twenty-First Century.* Washington, D.C.: National Academy Press, 2001.

Kedar, I., and others. "Internet Based Consultations to Transfer Knowledge for Patients Requiring Specialized Care: Retrospective Case Review." *British Medical Journal,* 2003, *326,* 696–699.

McGlynn, E. A. "The Quality of Health Care Delivered to Adults in the United States." *New England Journal of Medicine,* 2003, *348,* 2635–2645.

Rogers, E. M. *The Diffusion of Innovations.* (4th ed.) New York: Free Press, 1995.

Whitten, P., and others. "Systematic Review of Cost Effectiveness Studies of Telemedicine Interventions." *British Medical Journal,* 2002, *324,* 1434–1437.

CHAPTER THIRTY

TELEREHABILITATION

A Harvest of Multidisciplinary Services

Cynthia Scheideman-Miller

The INTEGRIS telerehabilitation project began when the Choctaw Memorial Hospital, a small, rural hospital in Hugo, Oklahoma, wanted to help local students receive speech therapy. Since then, the project has grown and blossomed from a one site and one discipline into a multidisciplinary program with services delivered to very diverse population at a variety of sites. Over thirty-five hundred telerehabilitation encounters were made in the first four years of the rural telemedicine program and led the way to the expansion of telerehabilitation applications and into other areas of health care.

Preparing the Ground

Rehabilitation is sometimes required following injury, but it is also sometimes compulsory for some public school students. Schools are federally mandated under the Individuals with Disabilities Education Act to supply services as needed for their students with disabilities. However, rural schools, especially smaller and more remote schools, find that securing services such as speech therapy is a yearly and often fruitless endeavor. In addition, if services are secured, it is frequently at a much higher cost than their metropolitan counterparts.

Telerehabilitation, or telerehab for short, was seen as a potential alternative for securing needed services. Telerehab is the clinical application of consultative, preventative, diagnostic, and therapeutic therapy using two-way interactive audiovisual linkage. It is performed in real time, versus a store-and-forward method. It is becoming an option for rural residents to access needed therapy services in their own community.

INTEGRIS Health, an Oklahoma-based and -operated health care system, realized that information technology was a progressive way to support rural providers and better fulfill its mission to improve the health of the communities that it served. It received a rural telemedicine grant from the Office for the Advancement of Telehealth under the Human Resources and Services in 1997. A rural Oklahoma hospital that was part of this grant was approached by the project director about the potential of using its videoconferencing equipment for speech therapy. The local telemedicine coordinator found a large demand for speech therapy in the local school.

Since little information could be found on telerehabilitation, it was decided to conduct a prepilot study at the hospital to gather information and reassure school personnel and parents that the students were getting proper therapy. Satisfaction with using telemedicine for speech therapy as well as clinical outcome data was gathered. Satisfaction was high in all groups, with therapists slightly less enthusiastic since they said they would always prefer being able to touch the patient, if only as a positive reinforcement. The surprising outcome to the prepilot was a noticeable improvement after only five weeks in the cognitive domains of social interaction, problem solving, and memory.

The use of teletherapy was so well received by the parents, children, and therapists involved that the school board approved a year-long project, but using telemedicine equipment at the school itself. Telerehab was used first to supplement the school pathologist, supplying therapy to students that exceeded her legal caseload. Speech teletherapy has since been used for multiple schools as far as 327 miles from Oklahoma City to supplement an on-site therapist or serve as the sole source of speech therapy for the school.

Planting the Seeds

Well-placed champions for telerehabilitation programs and projects were needed who were willing to think in novel ways and accept a certain level of risk. Early spokespersons and adopters must be advocates for the field, not only to other professionals but also to state and federal legislators. One critical role for administrative champions is to advocate for third-party reimbursement for services to help ensure long-term sustainability for telerehab programs after grant funds are spent. Clinician champions exude expertise and credibility to their peers, making skeptics more open to new approaches.

Trying to coax a physical therapist to consider telemedicine proved to be ineffective, so the clinician champion used her influence to get one therapist's boss to pressure him to at least look at what the clinician and telemedicine project director were talking about. The therapist finally agreed when a former inpatient of his was to be the patient using telemedicine. This patient and his spouse agreed to travel the 60 miles to receive physical therapy services at a rural hospital with videoconferencing capabilities rather than the 236-mile round trip to Oklahoma City.

A videoconference was set up during the session. The rural physical therapist working with the patient was proficient with orthopedic therapy but had little experience with patients following stroke. The metro physical therapist, who specialized in therapy following neurological insult, watched the session and after a few minutes became excited at the potential he saw.

The Right Tool for the Right Job

It was quickly recognized that the difficult logistics of arranging telerehabilitation sessions would quickly kill the budding program if they were not addressed. The therapists themselves chose to forgo some video quality in favor of easier scheduling and working with the patient in the ideal environment, the patient's home. One of the major events that helped shape the INTEGRIS telerehab program was the introduction of technology using plain old telephone services (POTS). The introduction of POTS technology eliminated almost all of the scheduling problems.

The first units used in the home required the patient's television and phone to work. They were cumbersome to set up, the patient had to remain a certain distance from the television to remain in focus, and the video quality was fairly poor. Fortunately, technology has improved, and although the quality of video is still less than optimal, movement is smoother and picture quality is clearer even when the patient moves across the room. Therapists tested several videophones, but only one passed the speech and language pathologists' scrutiny. The pathologists had to be able to see fine motor motion such as tongue movement to conduct therapy, and this was not possible with most of the POTS based technology. The easy use of the videophone helped to increase the use of teletherapy and made it possible to serve patients all across Oklahoma.

Weeds and Pests: Discussion of Challenges and Their Solutions

In farming, the most expert cultivation and loving care of crops can fall to the mercy of nature. Sometimes, as in hail, nothing can save the crop, but hail insurance is one way to help prevent the loss of the farm. Preparation for problems that occur, and invariably they do, was the approach taken with the INTEGRIS telerehab program. Problems the INTEGRIS telerehab program has experienced in its growth and development fall into three main categories: clinical, administrative, and consumer.

Clinical

Telemedicine and telehealth has been around in various forms for several years, but it is still not widely known or incorporated into everyday medical practice. As a result, the majority of the first year of the Telerehab program was spent educating clinicians, administrators, third-party payers, patients, and caregivers on what telerehabilitation is and how it could be beneficial. Education regarding telerehab was in the form of booths, continuing medical education meetings, one-on-one demonstrations, brochures, publications, cable TV interviews, and eventually marketing in the newspaper and medical minute spots on television. Acceptance of this new idea is still being developed, though the "play station generation" seems to embrace it more quickly than older health care providers, who are less comfortable with technology.

Administrative

One of the challenges to any program is how to show revenue and cost savings to justify having it. The two primary populations for telerehabilitation in Oklahoma proved to be school-based or Medicare and Medicaid groups. State legislation allowed for telemedicine reimbursement for telerehabilitation in Oklahoma. Most of the children receiving speech teletherapy were in low-income, high-need areas and enrolled in Medicaid. A meeting with the Oklahoma Healthcare Authority, the administrators of Medicaid in the state, took place prior to implementing the telespeech program. At their direction, the schools contracted with INTEGRIS Health for services, and the school submitted the proper Medicaid paperwork filled out by the therapist for reimbursement.

Medicare does not yet reimburse for telerehabilitation encounters, so these patients primarily receive services as part of a federal demonstration grant. The school program is now self-sustaining, but the home-based program will probably have a limited life span unless Medicare reimbursement is secured.

Several meetings had to occur with accounting, risk management, legal, and therapy administration before a billing mechanism was put in place to bill for tele-rehab. Again, most of the meetings centered around education of the different departments on what telerehab is, third-party payer reimbursement and nonreimbursement status for telemedicine, and where the services were being supplied from.

Consumer

Initially, placing a camera unit between the telephone and television to connect to a specialist was unnerving for some people. Some would not move the equipment even to clean for fear of "messing something up." Using videophones has lessened the fear of technology, but it still exists, especially in more rural areas with limited exposure to technology. An advisory council made up of representatives from several rural sites helped write the script for a video to educate the public on what telemedicine is and how it is being used in their community, and also to allay the fears of the patients and their caregivers.

Watch the Markets: Revenue and Cost Savings

Any rehabilitation program—traditional or telerehabilitation—has to have financial benefit to the program supplying the services to be sustainable for the long term. Sustainability does not always equate profitability, especially in early stages of a program. Eventually, however, profit must be achieved for most programs to be continued. Diversifying sources of revenue, much like diversification of an investment portfolio, is a logical strategy. Contracting with a captive population like schools is an example of a stable revenue stream with a lower margin of profit, with the more traditional fee-for-service reimbursement as an example of an intermittent funding source with a higher profit margin. Finally, all aspects of financial benefits to a provider must be considered. Financial benefits to a program can include revenues or cost savings, or a combination of both.

Cost Savings

Telemedicine enables better use of limited resources. For example, therapists who specialize in working with people following neurological insult would not be fully used in a rural area. They would need to serve other counties as well to maximize their expertise. Geographical distances would reduce the therapists' productive time. Telerehab can be used for several therapy services, enabling the therapist to spend more time working with patients and less time traveling.

Gardening Hints: Lesson Learned

The INTEGRIS Health telerehabilitation program has been developed through four years of trial and error. Some helpful hints to those wishing to start a telerehabilitation program include these:

- A traditional face-to-face session should be conducted with the patient and designated caregiver or support person.
- Patients who are medically stable and motivated are the best candidates for telerehab.
- If a caregiver is needed for teletherapy, it is essential that this person be physically able to help, want to help, and able to follow audiovisual instruction.
- It is helpful for experienced teletherapists to train new therapists how to conduct a session. A major part is being able to verbalize what would normally have been demonstrated by touch. Physical therapists have been known to practically jump through the screen wanting to put their hands on the patients before controlling the urge and rethink how to approach the session.
- Educate and reeducate on what telerehabilitation is and what its strengths and limitations are. Physical therapy in particular is hard to visualize.
- Work with insurance companies, school administration, and hospital billing systems prior to starting the program.
- Develop the program from the ground up but have administrative support from the top.

The Harvest Is In: Time to Plan for the Next Crop: Update on the Project

The INTEGRIS telerehabilitation program first and foremost was developed out of an identified need for rehabilitation services in rural areas. It began as a seed from an existing infrastructure, turned into an individualized project, and is now maturing into a full program. The school speech teletherapy program has reached sufficient numbers that it is self-sustaining and keeping two speech therapists busy during the school year. The focus was originally on only rural patients at rural facilities receiving care from providers at metropolitan facilities. As it has matured, the program produced side roots in the form of other projects at INTEGRIS. One such root is a grant project that supplies vocational rehabilitation services to Native Americans. Using the technology in their home community has allowed for greater cultural sensitivity and a higher success rate. The technology is used in this grant not only for vocational services but also for other therapy services if needed to bring clients to a level that they are employable.

Future changes include sites and services. Underserved metropolitan areas are being considered since barriers to health care exist in those areas also. Rural sites are beginning to use telemedicine and telehealth applications to better serve their areas for primary or subspecialty care such as physician consults, wound care, hospice, congestive heart failure monitoring, and mental and school health. New services and sites are always being considered and reviewed for the long-range plan. The model is evolving as technology, consumer, and provider acceptance and reimbursement components change.

Discussion Questions

1. Is telerehabilitation applicable to all conditions and populations requiring rehabilitation?
2. Provide some suggestions for overcoming the ingrained independence and suspicion of outsiders in rural culture.
3. What services not listed in the chapter would be appropriate for telerehabilitation application? What are the limitations of these services (for example, logistical, reimbursement, technological, cultural)?
4. What extenders should be included at the patient site to optimize sessions and limit risk of injury? (Diagnosis, level of competence, and discipline used will need to be defined.)
5. What steps could be taken now to lessen resistance to change that providers and insurers consistently exhibit?

PART SEVEN

TECHNOLOGY

The best way to predict the future is to invent it.

ALAN KAY

CHAPTER THIRTY-ONE

SUSTAINABLE SECURITY

Building Virus and Vulnerability Management into an Organization's Culture

C. Scott Blanchette, David T. Noll

The summer of 2003 will be remembered as a disruptive period in the annals of computing. Entities suffered significant periods of downtime and poor performance. Malicious code, designed to exploit vulnerabilities in Microsoft's complex operating systems, placed information systems at risk for prolonged periods of time. Derivations of the original exploit forced information technology departments to respond to continually changing threats. The total cost of these events will continue to be calculated for some time to come, but conservative efforts suggest the cumulative loss will be in the billions of dollars.

What remains striking is not the breadth and depth of impact, but more fundamentally the damage caused by relatively simple code. Malicious software developed to exploit Microsoft operating system vulnerabilities was neither complex to develop nor difficult to propagate. In addition, Microsoft published a series of patches for these vulnerabilities many weeks before the first significant outbreak, suggesting the solution to the problem was available long before the first system went down. Although this was not an isolated milestone in computing history, the extent of damage suggests that there is significant room for improvement in global virus and vulnerability management efforts.

Developing and maintaining a robust security architecture, including efforts around virus and vulnerability management, is a critical and often overlooked component of sustainable computing. Viruses, worms, and other forms of malicious code render information systems unavailable or unreliable. This unpredictable state, perhaps more than any other, is the greatest threat to providers who rely on information systems more than any other data source when providing care.

The emergence of federal and state legislation, including the Health Insurance Portability and Accountability Act of 1996 and California Senate Bill 1386, mandates improved controls over information systems and places security and privacy in a highly visible medium. This case study is intended to provide background on the state of health care information systems security, challenges to implementing security in an academic medical center setting, and a series of recommendations to ensure that future information systems are sustainable.

Background

Health care information systems, as an industry, have traditionally lacked appropriate information system controls. Historically, security served as an afterthought, and many of today's hospital computing environments suggest that security was not considered at all. While delivering the functionality needed by end users, this approach yielded an environment that is highly susceptible to malicious code and vulnerable to periods of poor performance and downtime. Compounding these challenges are contemporary cost pressures across health care to manage capital spending while simultaneously compensating for historical control deficiencies.

Academic medical centers add a layer of complexity to the challenge of positively controlling and accounting for sensitive information. These institutions possess a wealth of research capabilities that contribute to the administration of leading-edge medicine. Translational medicine, while serving as a differentiator, creates a risk management challenge. Academic medical centers must constantly strive to balance the needs of the researcher or the provider against those federal and state requirements that seek to limit the propagation of information.

In the summer of 2003, Blaster, Welchia, SoBig, and derivations of these computing plagues hit companies across the globe. Environments rich in information technologies suffered from periods of downtime and poor performance. The result of a simple series of exploits yielded extensive damage to information systems. Microsoft and security vendors produced patches for these vulnerabilities and communicated their existence through traditional channels. However, the number and frequency of operating system patches over the course of a concise period of time made testing, implementation, and version control a challenge.

The Challenge

Responding to the challenge of security is a multitiered, comprehensive effort. The term *defense-in-depth* articulates the layers of security that contribute to a security architecture. Building a robust series of obstacles to unauthorized activity ensures that sensitive data become prohibitively time-consuming to exploit. The creation of a secure computing environment is not an all-or-nothing proposition. It should be viewed as a continual risk assessment and risk management effort that seeks to balance the business needs of the enterprise with the level of acceptable risk the enterprise can tolerate. Lynda Applegate, a recognized professor and leader in the world of corporate information systems, suggested, "Perfect security is unattainable at any price. The key need is to determine the point of diminishing returns for an organization's particular mission and geography" (Applegate and others, 1999, p. 410).

Compounding this challenge is the constant battle between application, operating system, and networking vendors attempting to deliver functionality to the end user and malefactors who seek to disrupt that delivery. The ability to manage risk for health care practitioners effectively, the single group in a hospital setting that requires data the most, is a central component to the ultimate success or failure of an information technology team.

At the heart of any successful implementation is education and communication. This is even more critical in the often misunderstood world of information security. Senior management should be properly educated on the benefits of a security initiative and its value. Perhaps more common, funding may be sacrificed for more easily understood efforts. Central to education is the conduct of a comprehensive risk assessment that allows decision makers to understand security risks in both a qualitative and a quantitative manner.

Christopher King, a security practitioner and leader within the world of security architecture, indicated, "The success and effectiveness of an information security program is largely dependent upon the support of senior management and the security function's location in the organizational hierarchy. Both financial and political support is needed from senior management" (King and others, 2001, p. 74). Central to King's argument is the recognition that successful virus and vulnerability management relies as much on the ability to generate funding and support as it does on the technical ability to mitigate information systems risk.

Building Blocks for Sustainable Security

There are a number of critical enablers to the successful execution of a virus and vulnerability management program. Without these enablers, any organization will have tremendous difficulty achieving even the most basic levels of protection against viruses, worms, and other forms of malicious code. Successful organizations that are rich in information resources dedicate significant resources to fully realizing each of these infrastructure foundation elements:

Homogeneous computing infrastructure. Derivations from a baseline environment make support for that environment, especially support for desktop computing, exponentially more difficult. A standardized computing platform that is centrally managed and maintained yields significant dividends when defending against systems threats.

Controls for ingress and egress points. Without the ability to control traffic both inbound and outbound, computing environments become susceptible to outbreaks of viruses or worms. This capability is most often enabled through the implementation and maintenance of a secure firewall.

Virus and vulnerability management support. Support from a reputable security vendor that provides near real-time access to vulnerability data is critical. The difference between formalized support and ad hoc support can often make the difference between immunity or containment or an enterprise-wide outbreak. While many organizations have built this capability internally, it is more frequently the case that the resources required to realize this capability will be found in an organization dedicated to this business process.

Test environment. The establishment and maintenance of a test environment that reflects the actual computing infrastructure is crucial to the rapid and successful testing of solutions. This is particularly critical in health care computing, as health care applications historically do not respond well to generic operating-system-level patches. The lack of a standardized computing platform across the environment compounds testing difficulties and makes the establishment of a test environment more costly.

Centralized administration. To achieve a credible level of accuracy in the constantly evolving world of virus and vulnerability management, it is crucial to have the ability to manage and monitor this activity centrally. Without this capability, organizations will divert resources to manual patch management efforts and lose both accuracy and opportunities for economies of scale.

Knowledge management. Understanding the environment is an often overlooked component of the complete virus and vulnerability management life cycle. The ability to aggregate and analyze vulnerability data efficiently saves countless hours and yields significant dividends.

These enablers are by no means comprehensive. There are numerous alternatives that will contribute to successful virus and vulnerability management. Management teams should identify these components as being the critical elements required to build subsequent systems protection efforts. Without this foundation, investments in more advanced security capabilities would yield dividends but fail to realize their full potential.

Methodology for Sustainable Security

To implement and sustain a sound security posture within any organization, a defined, repeatable process is critical for success. This process should include virus and vulnerability management in each phase of the systems development life cycle. The following five phases are representative of the systems life cycle, with a particular emphasis on virus and vulnerability management within each:

- *Security management.* The appropriate decision-making data points should be developed to ensure that virus and vulnerability management efforts are prioritized in the appropriate context. Senior management must be educated on the necessity of incorporating virus and vulnerability management efforts in the systems development and operation, and they must be provided the quantitative data necessary to underscore its importance. In addition, security policies, procedures, and implementation methodologies must include virus and vulnerability management as a core process.
- *Security engineering.* The implementation of security controls throughout the systems development life cycle is a precursor to subsequent success. Virus and vulnerability management capabilities included in systems design and development efforts are statistically more successful than similar efforts to retroengineer a similar solution after a system has been fielded. Virus and vulnerability management engineering must be aligned with methodologies promoted by the program management office to ensure that efforts are clearly defined and repeatable.
- *Security operations.* Virus and vulnerability management should be an integral part of daily computing operations and operations support. Dedicated resources should focus on maintaining the health of the computing environment, which includes virus and vulnerability maintenance. Support from a vendor that delivers dedicated vulnerability management services provides customers with focused results and preserves fiscal resources.
- *Security monitoring and response.* Understanding the health of the computing environment is no different from clinical processes employed by providers with their patients. It is critical to monitor and manage the health of information systems continuously to ensure that potential outbreaks are identified, contained, and remediated in a timely manner.
- *Security audit.* Auditors and information system professionals historically have uneasy relationships. The uncomfortable nature of this relationship causes many organizations to miss an opportunity to make significant improvements in information systems security. Security management should embrace the audit

relationship and view this as an opportunity to identify areas across the computing environment that are vulnerable and require attention. Malicious code activity in summer 2003 heightened senior management awareness of infrastructure security issues. Security audits serve as a third-party resource to underscore the importance of building and maintaining a robust security architecture.

The process is both linear and cyclical. Linearity ensures that efforts are migrated from one phase to another with consistency of message, methodology, and priority. Cyclical efforts are designed to ensure that data points collected in a security audit are incorporated into subsequent management efforts in the first phase. In addition to the development and implementation of a sound methodology, tight integration with other IT functions is critical. For example, inclusion of the security methodology into the formalized systems development life cycle promoted by a program management office ensures that consistently defined controls are implemented at the appropriate points. Integration with information technology operations ensures that virus and vulnerability management efforts are included across the enterprise in multiple computing environments.

The complex nature of modern computing suggests there will always be threats to information systems and the availability of data. Operating systems are too complex in nature and developed too rapidly to exhaust all possible avenues of potential exploit. However, there are a number of actions that any health care enterprise can take to reduce its risk posture to a manageable level. Focused efforts around virus and vulnerability management can yield dividends for enterprises that cannot afford to have information systems unavailable. This focus, when applied appropriately, will allow hospitals to manage the delicate balance between risk and caution and ultimately allow providers to have information when and where they need it.

Discussion Questions

1. What steps can be taken to improve understanding of virus and vulnerability management? Who should be the target audience?
2. How do you best quantify or qualify the importance of virus and vulnerability management efforts? Who is the best person to champion the communication of this message? Within an organization, who can best influence the outcome of investment decisions?
3. In a hospital setting, what systems are most important to ensure availability? What systems are least important? What data elements can you not afford to place at risk?

4. How would you align virus and vulnerability management activities to other health care information technology functions? Who are the stakeholders, and who should lead vulnerability management efforts?

References

Applegate, L. M., and others. *Corporate Information Systems Management: Text and Cases.* (5th ed.) New York: McGraw-Hill/Irwin, 1999.

King, C., and others. *Security Architecture: Design, Deployment and Operations.* New York: Osborne McGraw-Hill, 2001.

CHAPTER THIRTY-TWO

DESIGNING TECHNOLOGY

A Case of Vendor and Provider Partnership

Audrey Kinsella, Kim Lee, Brenda Ecken

Home telehealth is moving distinctly from frontier status in home care service delivery to becoming a mainstream choice as an accepted adjunct to conventional home care skilled visits. Using home telehealth has been given impetus from many fronts, owing to circumstances such as an impending nationwide nursing shortage; Medicare's Prospective Payment System for care (and other insurers' capitated systems), which requires improved or maintained patient health outcomes to be documented (Sienkiewicz, 2000); and a burgeoning elderly population, projected to reach 66 million by 2030, with many living with multiple chronic diseases and needing frequent reinforcement of their self-care routines (U.S. Bureau of the Census, 1996; Institute on Aging, 1996). Although home health telecare appears to offer a solution to providing less costly in-person contact and more off-site assistance to these more needy patients (Kinsella, 2003a), there are few standard, detailed guidelines to assist home health agencies in planning and creating quality home telehealth programs (Kinsella, 2003b).

This chapter describes the home telehealth program preparation undertaken by one large home health agency in rural Pennsylvania. The focus is on the agency's work with a commercial telehealth equipment provider to customize a telehealth solution for its elderly and rural population.

The Home Nursing Agency

The Home Nursing Agency (HNA) in Altoona, Pennsylvania, services an extensive geographical territory of patients located in nine counties in western Pennsylvania. It is one of thirty-one home health agencies sharing in a landmark $750,000 congressional earmark of the Omnibus Appropriations Bill to the Pennsylvania Homecare Association from the U.S. Department of Health and Human Services for initiating home telehealth during 2002–2004. A specific goal of the grant is addressing the challenges of the projected nursing shortages in the next twenty years and preparing to care for the growing ranks of needy elderly populations who live at home and prefer to receive their care there. Pennsylvania has the second largest population of elderly people in the United States, and 40 percent of its nurses are age forty-five or over (Pennsylvania State Nursing Association, 2002).

The HNA's executives recognized that a home telehealth program could provide benefits such as improving nurse recruitment and retention, providing market differentiation, enhancing clinical and business processes, and encouraging patients to become active participants in managing their diseases. Therefore, decision makers at the HNA decided to approach telehealth as a business strategy rather than simply an installation of technology. Building on the opportunity provided by the grant, the agency invested additional funds and established its in-house telehealth program team.

At the inception of the grant in September 2002, no one at the HNA had had direct experience in telehealth. The team therefore set out to understand telehealth applications, identify their opportunity to make improvements, and then define requirements for the program as well as for the technology that would support it. The program was to be integrated into the business strategy and the business and clinical processes and provide the benefits envisioned by the executive team.

Locating a Technology Partner

Early on in the home telehealth planning process, the HNA had to locate and secure a vendor to get the right fit between product and patient—that is, a vendor that could customize a solution for the agency's elderly and rural population.

Prior to choosing a vendor, the HNA project planners had identified patient groups who could benefit from more frequent nursing contact and chose patients living with newly diagnosed congestive heart failure (CHF) as its first telehealth demonstration group. Previous studies have shown that patients living with CHF have had success with telehealth contact (Kinsella, 2003a). Having tele-assistance with daily control of their weight and eating patterns, including sodium reduction, can make demonstrable strides in terms of maintained (or improved) patient health outcomes. At the HNA's program, the interventions were aimed toward a one-year goal of preventing hospitalizations.

After focused investigation of commercial products, the majority of the planning staff knew that they wanted a solution that would meet the specific needs of the initial pilot population but would also support a variety of patient populations and could scale to handle a growing number of patients who would be monitored. But rather than simply purchase multifunctional workstations, the HNA team wanted the vendor to collaborate with them and assist them in the definition and implementation of their program. ViTel Net of McLean, Virginia, was selected as the technology partner.

Working with the Vendor

The ViTel Net MedVizer system, which has a history of use in hospital settings, is a customizable workstation with peripheral devices integrated as required. The product has recently been targeted for home care use.

Once the vendor was chosen, its staff of software engineers, home telehealth designers, and a nurse with training in telehealth worked closely with the HNA team. Between September 2002 and May 2003, this new team met regularly and clarified the technical requirements, conducted design reviews, provided training to the nursing staff, field-tested the custom applications, and obtained feedback to revise the solution.

One example of a change made as a result of collaboration was the addition of a "Practice" button on the user interface. Recognizing that use of the home devices would be new and perhaps disconcerting to some elderly patients, a "practice" capability was installed on the workstation. Patients could capture their vital sign data with each of the peripherals in practice sessions and so become familiar and comfortable with using the system.

Another example involved the company's removal of a step that patients had found confusing. Patients were instructed to follow a routine of taking their vital signs and then answering on-screen questions about their condition. A button marked "Save Vitals" needed to be pressed to send their vital signs; however, patients would routinely press the "Questions" button instead. The engineers' solution was to remove the Questions button and allow the Questions screen to appear as soon as patients pressed the Save Vitals button.

The on-screen health status questions were also customized. HNA staff designed the questions in a conversational tone to be nonthreatening and to reinforce the patient teaching provided by the nurse.

These easy-to-use touch screens used in the home units provide a manageable way for patients to interact with the equipment and answer the questions.

Making the equipment suitable for the typical rural home and the technically inexperienced patient was equally key in the planning for the HNA's project. The idea of working with the givens of the lone light bulb in the rural living room and the black rotary phone affixed to the kitchen wall were only some of the very basic starting points to implementing home telehealth. The nursing agency's nurses alerted the designers to the often-poor condition of phone jacks and outlets in rural homes of their patients and sometimes inconsistent phone line service. After six months of planning, piloting, and modifying their customized solution, the agency has moved from its initial concept to one that is currently in place at the HNA central offices and in patients' homes.

Results

The HNA is well on its way to managing the problem of dealing with a rural and isolated population of elderly patients who need increased contact. It now has a customized, easy-to-use system for its patients. The approach of involving agency nurses in telehealth solution and telehealth workstation capability development is important for making telehealth work at this agency. In addition, with the telecare units being used in areas where access to medical facilities is limited, local physicians report being very pleased that this technology can bring health care to rural Pennsylvania and assist in the monitoring of disease states. This is a noteworthy milestone: the telehealth program is moving from being simply a demonstration project to being viewed as a needed adjunct to providing quality patient care.

Conclusion

Using this disciplined planning and implementation approach required more effort and time than simply installing technology. This study has introduced a new way for home nursing agencies to make the conventional home care visit electronic—by working closely with the vendor to produce a more targeted home telehealth product. Furthermore, the agency's nurses designed contact questions written simply enough that patients would readily understand (they had heard them before) and answer so that nurses would know about patients' progress and respond appropriately. These home telenurses are operating at a distance but not in the dark. With telehealth, they have the opportunity to assist their patients' needs regardless of patients' location.

Projected nursing shortages boding more limited services and the projected increase of elderly populations in the United States have important ramifications, particularly for patients living in rural areas, where access to in-person health care services has typically always been more difficult and may become less frequent. The development work at the HNA provides an instructive example of clinicians using home telehealth to target machine and communications to reach out to their elderly, challenging, and rural home care patients.

Discussion Questions

1. Are grants key to starting a successful home telehealth program?
2. Is providing home health telecare different in rural areas of the United States compared to telecare provided in urban centers?
3. What are some of the issues involved in home health agencies' choosing not to use home telehealth?
4. Is it appropriate for Medicare patients to receive home health telecare?
5. If a full-scale workstation can replicate conventional nursing visits, why should customization be needed?

References

Institute on Aging, University of California, San Francisco. *Chronic Care in America: A Twenty-First Century Challenge.* Princeton, N.J.: Robert Wood Johnson Foundation, 1996.

Kinsella, A. "Success Stories in Home Telehealth." In A. Kinsella (ed.), *Home Telehealthcare: Process, Policy, and Procedures.* Kensington, Md.: Information for Tomorrow, 2003a.

Kinsella, A. "Telehealth Delivery Guidelines: Working with Multiple Compasses." *Telehealth Practice Report,* 2003b, *7*(6), 8–10.

Pennsylvania State Nursing Association. "Pennsylvania Nursing Shortage Leadership Platform." 2002. [http://www.psna.org/HotIssues/platform.htm].

Sienkiewicz, J. I. "Answers to Frequently Asked Questions About the Proposed Home Care Prospective Payment System." *Home Health Care Nurse,* 2000, *18*(5), 323–330.

U.S. Bureau of the Census. *Sixty-Five Plus in the U.S.* Washington, D.C.: U.S. Government Printing Office, 1996.

CHAPTER THIRTY-THREE

BEHIND THE APPLICATIONS

Making Technology Transparent

Sally R. Davis, Pamela Whitten

Applications and technology rely on one another for their existence: one has no purpose in the absence of the other. Programs are most successful when this relationship achieves a balance that allows applications to be prominent. A transparent technology foundation allows the focus to be on service delivery, thus increasing the likelihood that telehealth will be incorporated into routine business functions. However, achieving the goal of transparent technologies in a health setting is not easy. It requires strategic planning, flexibility, and a little luck. This case is the story of how a telemedicine program in Michigan's Upper Peninsula achieved the goal of transparency.

Telehealth at Marquette General Health System

Michigan's Upper Peninsula (UP) is one of the northernmost sections of the Midwest. The UP's fifteen counties are surrounded by three of the Great Lakes and are connected to the Lower Peninsula by the five-mile span of the Mackinac Bridge. The peninsula contains 33 percent of Michigan's landmass yet represents only 3 percent of the state's population. Annual snowfalls in the region can reach over three hundred inches, occasionally closing roads into the area's largest city of Marquette (population nineteen thousand). Access to tertiary health care often means travel times of two or three hours over two-lane roads. A drive across the peninsula from west to east takes six hours, and travel to quaternary health care in lower Michigan averages eighteen travel hours round trip. The harsh winter climate, long stretches of desolation between communities, and frequent encounters with wildlife increase the hazards of travel for specialty care. The UP represents a region ripe for the use of communication technologies to augment delivery of health services.

In 1994, telehealth in the UP began from the seed of an idea that sprouted within the education department at the regional referral center: Marquette General Health System (MGHS). The initial emphasis on professional education quickly diversified to include administrative meetings and community applications. Clinical consultations and home telecare developed soon after, with significant growth beginning in 2000. Store-and-forward applications have evolved from the original teleradiology based on telephone service to include telepathology, telecardiology, and picture archiving and communication systems. Today, the Upper Peninsula Telehealth Network (UPTN) has grown to a twenty-eight-site, seventy-system network providing seven thousand connections annually.

The UPTN represents a grassroots model of telehealth built on relationships among independent health care organizations and maximization of the talents of local personnel. MGHS provides hub services for the network that include technical assistance, centralized scheduling, bridging services, and the vast majority of programming. Sites include community hospitals, rural health clinics, physician offices, Native American health centers, and behavioral health offices.

Technology Selection and Deployment Strategies

Four factors drove the decisions regarding technological solutions: the potential and cost of the hardware and telecommunications, transmission flexibility, equipment adaptability, and organizational issues.

Connectivity, Affordability, and Site Independence

The development of telehealth services in the region was influenced significantly by the grassroots initiation of the network. In the absence of regionwide management or strategic planning, each site needed practical reasons to join the network. With minimal proof of concept and without replicable models throughout the country, sites also needed an affordable method to introduce the technology.

The concept of site independence became a key feature of the UPTN and helped build trust among the independent organizations. The MGHS hub site assisted smaller hospitals in acquiring grant funding for equipment in a show of genuine support for sustained health care in the local communities. Planners set out to ensure that each site was able to connect to other locations independent of a centralized office. Each site was, and still is, responsible for its transmission costs, and no formal network dues are charged. This model differs from many other telehealth networks that are built on dedicated networks with connections to the outside world only through the hub site.

The quest for connectivity and site independence required a solution with direct-dial connectivity and standards-based systems. Both T-1 (a dedicated digital transmission link with a capacity of 1.544 Mbps) and integrated switched digital network (ISDN), a switched digital transmission link, services were considered for network transmission. Discounts through the Federal Communication Commission Universal Service program were not yet available, and T-1s, at approximately $1,400 per month, were determined to exceed the financial tolerance of the end sites at that time

The network was the first customer of ISDN service in the region in 1995. Limited ISDN availability allowed negotiated arrangements for foreign exchange dial-up service. All sites had basic rate ISDN (128 Kbps) service foreign exchange into the Centrex system at the hub site. Although the monthly charges were significant ($250 to $600 per month), the arrangement encouraged frequent use and allowed sites to direct-dial within the network and outside the network.

Equipment for the first seven videoconferencing systems was selected in 1994 through a request for proposals. An out-of-state objective consultant joined local technical and programming personnel in the assessment of the bids. PictureTel 4000 ZXs were chosen for their superiority in low bandwidth, and many of these systems have remained in service for ten years.

The UPTN was testing the waters with low bandwidth when many other programs were operating at full T-1 capacity. Early ISDN was not always reliable, but it was tolerated because the technology was new. Tolerance declined as videoconferencing became routine for meetings and educational programming. Many sites were able to justify the cost of additional ISDN service to bring their capability up to 384 Kbps for clinical applications. Other programs around the country were also searching for the balance between cost and capability, and general consensus developed for 384 Kbps as an acceptable and cost-effective standard for clinical applications.

The focus on connectivity, affordability, and site independence was vital to building a sustainable network in the UP region. Sites recognized their ability and responsibility to drive the technology in a direction that fit their community needs. It set the stage for local commitment in transmission costs while building economies of scale in applications.

Flexibility in Transmission and Location

By the late 1990s, the UPTN had outgrown its bridging capacity (the process of multipoint control unit equipment that serves to link one videoconference site with others), and users were frustrated with the limited availability of systems. Those who were conducting clinical consultations were showing less tolerance for low bandwidth and for the necessity of using conference rooms for patient encounters. The network needed to expand its capacity and increase the convenience to the clinical users.

As the videoconferencing network was evolving, so was the MGHS regionwide health information network that offers a cafeteria plan of services to the region's health care organizations. The information technology department at MGHS manages more than four thousand desktop computers, a thousand network devices, and one hundred different applications. The regionwide health information network provided a solution that catapulted videoconferencing in the UP into the next era.

Internet protocol (IP) videoconferencing was initiated in 2000 using existing T-1 lines and an Accord MG 100 multipoint control unit (bridge) that merged ISDN service and IP protocol. Pilot implementation on the chief executive officer's desktop, followed by a neurologist's PC, proved an immediate success with quality, reliability, and security. Over the next two years, the number of systems on the network more than tripled, with installations of this easy and practical solution continuing at a steady pace.

The addition of IP technology has provided many advantages to the UPTN, including:

Flexibility in location of equipment provided the convenience needed for clinical applications. Videoconferencing can be easily installed on a consulting practitioner's desktop with minimal expense. This factor significantly increased the number of clinical applications because the technology is adapted to the practitioner and his or her practice routine. At the patient end, IP equipment can be moved wherever the patient (and a data jack) is located. As wireless technology has become more widely available, the flexibility in point-of-care location has increased.

Flexibility in transmission through the integration of IP and ISDN provided transmission options and backward compatibility with older equipment. Some systems operate on both transmission modes. Options include direct dial to other similar systems (IP or ISDN) and connection between IP and ISDN through the bridge. As always, ISDN systems have direct-dial capability to other ISDN systems around the globe. IP systems connect outside the wide area network without compromising security by dialing the bridge and using the bridge's ISDN service.

Economies of scale were achieved using the current health information network T-1 lines. Administrators view transmission for the health information network as a necessary utility, whereas separate telehealth ISDN service would be a stand-alone expense. The move to IP has ensured the long-term sustainability of telehealth solutions.

Integration of applications became evident during a proof-of-concept demonstration for emergency telestroke. The consulting practitioner was able to videoconference with the patient and emergency room practitioner while viewing the CT scan on the same computer screen.

Redundancy of service has improved with the transmission options and the overall increase in the number of systems. While reliability of transmission has greatly improved in recent years, pockets of the UPTN are still vulnerable to quality and priority-of-service issues. The growth in the number of systems due to IP availability provides options when multiple requests are received for a site. Denial of requests due to limited availability has been eliminated.

Adaptability

As the UPTN continues its quest to create new efficiencies, we recognize that we are changing the culture of the health care business. The early years elicited reactions of, "I'm not getting in front of that TV!" Later reactions became, "What do you mean there's not a system available?" Recent years have provided user requests and demands that challenge creativity. How well telehealth programs adapt to requests for new directions will determine the degree to which this industry is viewed as a solution to evolving health care challenges.

The progression of telehealth applications has begun to move faster than we had dared hope. Where we once pushed users to try the technology, we are now striving to catch up with the influx of ideas. Our most valuable resources for adapting to new issues and applications have come from local resources and network partners. Table 33.1 presents some of the adaptations the UPTN made during 2003. Most have resulted from user and potential user inquiries.

Organizational Aspects

Nurturing the technology aspect of a telehealth program is a lot like parenting. There are philosophies to choose from, research results to consider, recognized experts to consult, and models to follow. There are even advice columnists (through listservs) and critics who will tell you what you did wrong. And as all parents know, when it comes to implementation, there is much you have to figure out on your own. Each program, community, and services are unlike any other.

TABLE 33.1. EXAMPLES OF UPPER PENINSULA TELEHEALTH NETWORK ADAPTATIONS.

Issue	Solution
Scheduling of clinical consults was time-consuming and prone to human errors. The system that worked during the development of clinical applications was no longer practical with the increasing number of consults.	An electronic scheduling system was developed for clinical consultations. The scheduling system allows users to submit electronic requests through Lotus Notes or the Web. The requests are received by e-mail at the appropriate locations. The hub site staff and the site coordinators have the ability to accept or decline each request, recommend alternative dates or times, and cancel or reschedule patients as needed. This system is being expanded to include routine requests for education events and administrative meetings.
Preparation of family practice residents for rural practice was determined to be unrealistic. Although Marquette General is classified as a rural facility, the tertiary medical center environment does not prepare physicians for the reality of practice in remote communities.	Remote precepting was established that allows a third-year resident to practice full time in a community of six thousand while being precepted by family practice faculty at Marquette General Hospital. Approval for off-site precepting from the National Residency Review Committee for Family Practice was obtained prior to implementation. Technology-supported rural rotations allow first- and second-year residents to experience rural practice without disrupting their didactic requirements or the continuity of care for their established Marquette patients. This solution is the equivalent of reverse consultation for patients. The patient is located at the regional referral center and is seen by his or her physician (resident) in the rural community using telemedicine. A wireless Tandberg Intern is used in Marquette at the patient site. The resident on rotation in the rural community connects using a laptop with Polycom Via Video that can be plugged into any data port within the rural clinic.
Training for nurse anesthetists was costly. A shortage of Certified Registered Nurse Anesthetists was addressed in 2001 through the initiation of a distance-learning program between Marquette General Health System and Beaumont Medical Center in Detroit. As	Installation of a dedicated T-1 between the two organizations reduced the cost to less than $1,200 per month. While this sounds simplistic, unique complexities led an IT staff person to exclaim, "This is by far the oddest T-1 I've ever ordered!" Adding remote camera control to the systems allowed the savvier videoconferencing students in Marquette to control their view of the primary classroom in Detroit.

the program expanded, long distance ISDN costs were often exceeding $5,000 per month.	
Extended lengths of stay can be costly to the hospital.	Activities occurred to coordinate with discharge planners to identify patients whose length of stay can be shortened though the use of telehealth technology, or whose health could be maintained with the assistance of telehealth technology to avoid hospitalization. In one case, a patient had nonreimbursable costs of $111,291 over four admissions. In addition, the hospital had spent considerable money to return her to her home and make it accessible. A home telecare system was installed in her home when it was evident that her health was once again declining. A family practice physician now conducts monthly unreimbursed home visits using American Telecare equipment.

All telehealth programs will have some common objectives in technology investments. These are generally identified in terms of reliability, interoperability, economy, and security. During the ten-year UPTN history, additional underpinnings of long- and short-term decision making have been identified that can serve as lessons learned for programs in development. One of the underpinnings is that technology decisions cannot be made in isolation of organizational, relational, and structural aspects of health systems.

A number of key organizational issues were important in selecting technologies for the region. First, it was important to assess the values of the network partners. Most often these values are unwritten and unspoken, and thus a depth of knowledge and understanding of the partners is important. For the UP, an open, switched network provided the site independence and connectivity that was vital to the organizational relationships at the time.

Second, it was key to link technology solutions to community needs and organizational goals and objectives. Where one community lacked obstetrical services, we matched equipment capabilities with supportive services for monthly specialty clinics. Where a community wanted to ensure timely echocardiogram readings during the absence of the local cardiologist, we developed a store-and-forward solution that brought the images to him in another community. At the regional referral center, we worked with program directors to identify ways in which technology could enhance the achievement of outreach objectives for the centers of excellence. By tying equipment capability to specific service and organizational goals, administrators and practitioners began to view telehealth as a solution to real issues. Along the way, we acknowledged that the equipment and transmission often work well, but the processes for communicating and scheduling do not. Working directly with office managers of the specialty practices provided insight into technology solutions to mitigate barriers.

Finally, we continually advocated for the development of practical solutions in the use of technology. Several times we halted projects in midstream to ask whether we were seeking a problem to fit a chosen technology instead of identifying a technology solution to a legitimate problem. Asking what problem we were trying to solve, and what impact that issue had on the organizations, helped to stay focused on practicality. For example, remote readings of pediatric echocardiograms brought us through the evolution of three solutions before finding the one with the right fit. Each new application should be viewed as a unique technology question with a customized solution rather than fitting the application to current equipment and transmission. Selected technologies should adjust to the practice and the culture.

Conclusion

Telehealth is often described as "disruptive" technology. This implies that use of the technology requires a thought process and skill set separate from what is routine. Working toward transparency in technology solutions allows the practitioners, health care staff, organizations, and communities to make the transition to a culture that includes telehealth as the norm. How will we know when we have achieved full technological transparency? We will have reached this threshold the day telehealth departments become extinct and tracking the number of telehealth events is not only unimportant but also impossible.

Discussion Questions

1. Which is more important: the technology or the applications being delivered?
2. Is it possible to achieve the level of transparent technology in a health setting?
3. Compare and contrast the four criteria employed by MGHS in the selection and deployment of technology: potential and cost, flexibility, adaptability, and organizational issues.
4. Who, in a health organization, should be in charge of developing a technology selection and implementation strategy?
5. Why are communication technologies often described as disruptive in the health setting?

PART EIGHT

POLICY

*I make a fortune from criticizing the government and then hand it over to the
government in taxes to keep it going.*

GEORGE BERNARD SHAW

CHAPTER THIRTY-FOUR

POLICY AND THE ORIGINS OF THE ARIZONA STATEWIDE TELEMEDICINE PROGRAM

Ronald S. Weinstein, Gail Barker, Sandy Beinar, Michael Holcomb, Elizabeth A. Krupinski, Ana Maria Lopez, Alison Hughes, Richard A. McNeely

In 1996, Arizona legislators were faced with inequitable delivery of medical care among the state's rural communities, its prison populations, and its numerous tribal nations. The statewide Arizona Telemedicine Program was established to address this issue as well as concerns about the rising costs of health care. The program developed a virtual organization that currently connects forty-one health care organizations under a single administrative umbrella, offering a wide variety of telemedicine and telenursing services. In 2003, over eighty thousand tele-diagnoses and teleconsultations were provided in cardiology, dermatology, neurology, pathology, psychiatry, radiology, rheumatology, and other specialties. In addition, the program delivers distance education, runs a technology assessment service, and conducts research.

Policy Overview: Political Environment

To create a statewide telemedicine program, legislators in Arizona had to resolve a basic philosophical policy issue regarding the appropriate role of the state in health

We gratefully acknowledge Beth Newburger for helpful discussions on policy issues and for suggestions and Kris Erps and Mary Weinstein for editorial assistance.

care delivery. If the state had responsibility to provide medical care in rural communities and state-run facilities, then the traditionally conservative legislature faced questions of funding medical care for any and all state residents. Its members also had to question their role in creating long-term delivery solutions and deciding issues relating to the appropriate sources of authority for such a system.

The following description of the creation and implementation of the Arizona Telemedicine Program tells the story of how the statewide system addresses these significant policy decisions. The seven-year-old system provides a model for other states that are considering similar solutions for the successful delivery of health care.

Stages of Development of a Telemedicine Program

Multispecialty telemedicine programs can be examined in terms of their specific activities at different stages of program development:

Stage 1: Preparation—the accumulation of factors that create a favorable environment for telemedicine, needs assessments, pilot projects, and planning

Stage 2: Commencement—funding, division of authority, recruiting leaders and assigning responsibility, and policy development

Stage 3: Early start-up—infrastructure build-out, procurement, and branding decisions

Stage 4: Late start-up: ramp-up—market introduction and initial telemedicine services

Stage 5: Achievement—documentation of standards of care; user and provider satisfaction studies; design of an evaluation system, implementation, and analyses; and introduction of additional specialties

Stage 6: Sustainability—conversion from a demonstration project to a long-term or permanent health care delivery system

A telemedicine program's commencement (stage 2) can be fast under certain circumstances. Due to the fluidity of the situation, this stage can present extraordinary opportunities for innovation if the key decision makers are prepared to seize the moment and are driven by a sense of urgency.

Stage 1: Preparation

In 1994, Robert Burns, chair of the Appropriations Committee of the Arizona State House of Representatives, heard a presentation on telemedicine by a pioneer in the field, Jay Sanders, and visited the statewide telemedicine program in

Georgia. Burns was impressed that telemedicine might provide solutions to several chronic health care delivery problems in Arizona (J. Lee, personal communication, 1996). After the trip, he encouraged the leadership at the Arizona Health Sciences Center in Tucson, which houses the state's only college of medicine, to develop planning documents for a statewide telemedicine pilot project and began looking for opportunities for the legislature to fund the project (Vuturo and McNeely, 1994; Hughes and others, 1995).

The founding director of the Arizona Telemedicine Program, Ronald S. Weinstein, is also chair of the Department of Pathology at the University of Arizona College of Medicine. The new program would be administratively assigned to the Department of Pathology, although the program would provide teleconsultations in many subspecialties of medicine (Weinstein and Bloom, 1990).

A brief discussion of the implications of the policies has been added where specified below. Two policy implications come out of Stage 1.

- Telemedicine is becoming recognized as an important channel for health care delivery.
- Telemedicine can be integrated into the ongoing operations of a clinical department.

Stage 2: Commencement

Events moved rapidly for the program once the Arizona state budget was passed in 1996. The state legislature allocated $1.2 million per year for a three-year, eight-site telemedicine pilot project to test the efficacy of doing telemedicine in Arizona. Participants were to be geographically dispersed, independent health care organizations. Initial sites would include a state prison, a hospital on one of Arizona's twenty Indian reservations, and six other rural medical centers. The program would be administered by the Arizona Health Sciences Center. The enabling legislation named the project the Arizona Rural Telemedicine Network.

From the outset, the director had concerns about the program as it was being structured and shared them with the vice president for health sciences (who also served as the dean of the College of Medicine) as well as with legislative leaders. First, sustainability seemed problematic because the program was receiving term-limited funding to support some of the rural telemedicine sites. Second, the College of Medicine's in-patient facility, University Medical Center in Tucson, was a competitor with other health care systems critical to the success of the project. Third, the project was narrowly focused and needed to be immediately expanded through the addition of other components, including a technology assessment program and a training center. And fourth, it was agreed that the authority for a statewide telemedicine program should emanate from a level higher than the Arizona Health Sciences Center.

Within a week, while the situation was still fluid, the director presented the vice president for health sciences with two concepts for the program. Plan A called for the creation of a hub-and-spoke telemedicine pilot program. All telecommunications would be point-to-point, between the Arizona Health Sciences Center in Tucson and individual spoke sites (rural sites). Spoke sites would not have spoke-to-spoke linkages. Plan A was embodied in the enabling legislation that funded the program.

Plan B went beyond the scope of the legislative mandate. It envisioned a statewide, all-provider multiorganization telemedicine virtual organization, to be named the Arizona Telemedicine Program. University faculty physicians would not be exclusive providers of telemedicine services, and traditional clinical referral patterns would be maintained wherever possible. A new invention was a quasi-governmental body that would provide advice, guidance, and foresight in developing a long-term strategic plan for effective implementation and monitoring of the new program. This would be structured not as a statutory committee but rather as a voluntary advisory council. The body would be named the Arizona Telemedicine Council and would be cochaired by leaders of the House of Representatives and Senate of the Arizona state legislature. The blue-ribbon Arizona Telemedicine Council would include legislative, state agency, and public members. The program would have a direct reporting relationship to the Arizona Telemedicine Council. As envisioned, the Arizona Telemedicine Council would become a permanent entity and the overarching authority for telemedicine in Arizona. It would also serve as the official bridge between the legislature and the program.

Also described in plan B, a first order of business for the Arizona Telemedicine Council would be to create a telemedicine and telehealth policy action plan (*telehealth* is a broader term covering nonphysician health care services using telecommunications, such as telenursing). The Arizona Telemedicine Council would take responsibility for policy development in areas of special interest to the state legislature.

In addition to its advisory and policy development roles, the Arizona Telemedicine Council would develop special expertise on issues related to the creation of a statewide health care information network and the joining together of independent heath care organizations in a way that would make it possible for patients to move seamlessly between health care providers with their health-related information.

The vice president for health sciences and legislative leaders immediately approved plan B. The legislature's original name for the program, Arizona Rural Telemedicine Network, was relegated to describing the telecommunications infrastructure of the program.

Two policy implications come out of stage 2:

- Statewide programs based on information technologies and telecommunications may especially benefit from deriving their authority at the level of a state legislature.
- Novel structures, such as the Arizona Telemedicine Council, can serve as overarching authorities for regional multiorganization health care programs that span geographical boundaries and multiple jurisdictions.

Stage 3: Early Start-Up

In its early start-up stage, the program identified two immediate challenges: to develop and implement a regional telecommunications strategy for telehealth in Arizona and to develop and implement a strategy for creating telemedicine equipment standards and standard operating procedures for all of Arizona.

Two policy implications come from stage 3:

- A telemedicine program can be designated as the primary driver for extending a broadband telecommunications infrastructure to geographically underserved populations.
- Interoperability and scalability are of paramount importance to the success of sustainable multiorganization telemedicine and telehealth networks.

At this point, the program faced two challenges.

Challenge 1: A Statewide Health Care Telecommunications System. In 1996, it was incorrectly assumed that telecommunication companies operating in Arizona would become willing vendors. However, linkages, if and when available, would be very expensive (up to $63,000 per year for a single point-to-point T-1 connection). Delivery dates for T-1 lines were often unreliable. Due to the unfavorable telecommunications climate in Arizona, the program was forced to rethink its telecommunications strategy. As a statewide enterprise, the program had two options for telecommunications: to take in-house the design, installation, and operations of the program's telecommunications infrastructure or, alternatively, to scale back the goals for the program.

By 1998, the program developed an innovative solution that brought control of the installation and operations of the telecommunications infrastructure in-house and simultaneously addressed other objectives as well. After failing to partner with the telecommunications companies, the decision was made to restructure the program and create a novel regional telemedicine consortium, including a telecommunications network component (McNeill, Weinstein, and Ovitt, 1999; McNeill, Barker, and McElroy, 2001). Certain resources, such as the telecommunications infrastructure, network access, and training, would be shared.

The program's engineering staff, all of them university employees, designed a scalable T-1/ATM (asynchronous transfer mode) broadband telecommunication system. (ATM is a commonly used telecommunication backbone that uses short cells or packets to transport information and then reassemble them at their final destination.) These engineers operate the network infrastructure. Currently, this private health care telecommunications collaborative extends broadband connectivity to over seventy-seven sites in Arizona, Nevada, Utah, and New Mexico (Figure 34.1).

The following policy implication stems from this challenge:

• A state-administered program can devise entrepreneurial solutions to intractable problems such as inadequate rural telecommunications infrastructure.

Challenge 2: Statewide Telemedicine Interoperability. In Arizona, the program facilitates the promotion of statewide telemedicine interoperability and the adoption of uniform standard operating procedures and best practice guidelines by independent health care organizations throughout the state. Standards are adopted as the result of ongoing assessment and evaluation procedures:

Facility planning. The program's facility design and vendor selection service plays a critical role in the implementation of interoperable telemedicine clinics throughout the region. An initial goal was to have all full-service telemedicine clinics in the state equipped with interoperable equipment and to use a standardized room design. In large measure, this has been accomplished.

Telemedicine applications. The program serves as a clearinghouse for telemedicine and telehealth applications (for example, telecardiology and teledermatology) for the state. For individual applications, such as teledermatology, technology assessments are carried out by the program's clinical investigators, and when it is deemed necessary, clinical research projects are funded and implemented. This information is shared with health care organizations throughout the state.

Telemedicine training. The program offers one- and two-day courses on telemedicine, free of charge, for all health care organizations in Arizona. These courses provide a unique opportunity for the presentation of key concepts, including the importance of interoperability of facilities.

Telemedicine clinic operations. The program develops and issues standard operating procedures, clinical practice protocols, and best practice guidelines for

FIGURE 34.1. ARIZONA TELEMEDICINE NETWORK.

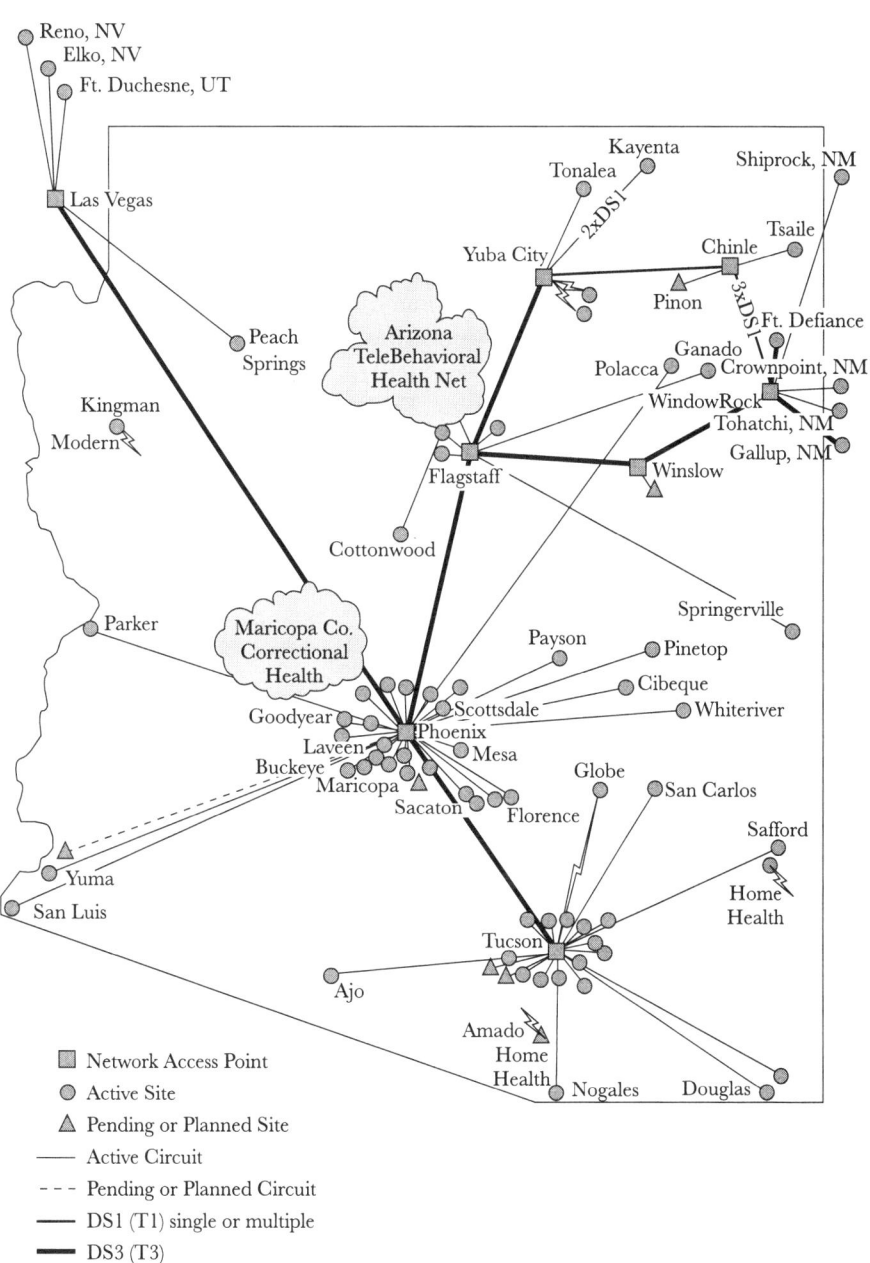

Reno, NV
Elko, NV
Ft. Duchesne, UT

Las Vegas

Kayenta
Tonalea
Shiprock, NM

Yuba City
2xDS1
Chinle
Tsaile

Peach Springs
Arizona TeleBehavioral Health Net
Pinon
3xDS1
Ft. Defiance

Kingman
Modern
Ganado
Polacca
Crownpoint, NM

WindowRock
Tohatchi, NM
Gallup, NM

Flagstaff
Winslow

Cottonwood

Springerville

Parker
Maricopa Co. Correctional Health
Payson
Pinetop

Cibeque
Whiteriver

Goodyear
Scottsdale
Phoenix
Laveen
Mesa
Globe
San Carlos

Buckeye
Maricopa
Sacaton
Florence

Safford

Home Health

Yuma
San Luis

Tucson

Ajo

Amado
Home Health
Nogales
Douglas

☐ Network Access Point
○ Active Site
△ Pending or Planned Site
— Active Circuit
- - - Pending or Planned Circuit
— DS1 (T1) single or multiple
— DS3 (T3)

telemedicine facilities throughout the state. Currently, relatively few health care organizations have the resources and expertise to generate their own telemedicine standard operating procedures and guidelines.

Grants. The program writes grants and contracts that have an impact on the development of interoperability standards. Forty-two grants and contracts for the program or its affiliates, totaling over $12 million have been funded over the last seven years.

Two policy implications stem from this challenge:

- A multipronged approach is effective for creating telemedicine facility inter-operability standards and a shared telecommunications infrastructure.
- Policies should encourage obtaining supplemental funding from extramural sources such as granting agencies and foundations. A benefit of centralized grant writing is the promotion of uniform telemedicine standards and guidelines within the region.

Stages 4, 5, and 6

A ubiquitous evaluation system is now in place that makes possible ongoing analysis of system utilization volumes at macro and micro levels. Thousands of patients at rural health care facilities have benefited from timely access to a broad range of medical specialists without leaving their communities. Many of the institutions participating in the program regard telemedicine as a permanent health care delivery system.

Management and Maintenance Issues

In Arizona, the administrative placement of the state-sponsored telemedicine program at the Arizona Health Sciences Center by the state legislature made sense but presented risks. First, reporting relationships in academic health centers are often complex and burdensome. Second, university culture does not necessarily favor strong leadership that may be essential to the success of a telemedicine program. Third, a university medical center has many competing self-interests. And fourth, community-based organizations may feel uncomfortable with the idea of having university administrators in charge of a new statewide health care program.

In Arizona, implementation of the statewide telemedicine program was simplified and rendered manageable when leaders of the Arizona legislature's Joint Legislative Budget Committee became involved in the affairs of the Arizona Telemedicine Program, to a degree beyond traditional roles for Arizona legislators. It showed that the legislature was thinking ahead to what next-generation health care enterprises might look like in the future. Had the role of overarching authority for the program been assumed by another state administrative unit, such as the Arizona Health Sciences Center or the Arizona Department of Health Services, the outcomes might have been different. It is likely that the program would have been narrower in scope and would have had difficulty achieving the critical mass of activities necessary for survival.

Two policy implications stem from this challenge:

- Authority management can be a key to success for a multiorganization telemedicine and telehealth program.
- The division of policymaking authority among various participants enhances the development of a sense of a shared mission.

Linking Creation and Policy

Ideally, the aims and enabling policies for a new telemedicine program should emerge at the time of the program's creation. In Arizona, there was a brief window of opportunity for innovators, government leaders, policymakers, health care executives, and educators to create an information technology-based paradigm shift in the health care delivery system in the state. A comprehensive package, consisting of eight telemedicine and telehealth policies for the state, was expeditiously drafted by the program director and the vice president for health sciences at the Arizona Health Sciences Center, and approved by state legislative leaders within weeks of notification of funding of the program. The policy decisions were:

- To have as a goal the creation of a single multiservice telemedicine program
- To establish a program governance framework with an overarching authority structure to support the unique missions of a telemedicine organization
- To operate the program as a virtual organization that would be inclusive and create incentives for all health care organizations to participate in a single telemedicine program
- To provide access to the program's telecommunications infrastructure for all legitimate health care organizations
- To encourage the development of interoperability of all telemedicine facilities
- To develop an open staff model for participation of telephysicians as service providers for multiple health care organizations
- To promote best practice guidelines that are evidence based and supported by clinical research

- To have the state legislature encourage all state agencies, including the Arizona Department of Corrections and the Arizona Department of Health Services, to participate in the program.

The eight telemedicine policies were approved by legislative leaders as a package and made the greatest sense when viewed as components of a unified vision for telemedicine in Arizona. It is likely that approval of these policies would have been difficult to obtain in a piecemeal fashion at a later date, especially once individual health care organizations began to implement independent telemedicine programs. Instead, these eight cardinal policies now serve as the foundation for a rapidly expanding and sustainable regional telemedicine program.

These policies provide the foundation for future and ongoing telemedicine initiatives to be integrated under a unified vision to serve as the basis for the development, adoption, and implementation of an interrelated set of policies. Without this vision, telemedicine efforts would likely become fragmented, undermining these broader efforts to provide an interoperable statewide network. Furthermore, policy development should be grounded in well-defined outcome expectations for health care, ensuring that enhancing health services remains the primary focus of all telemedicine initiatives.

Discussion Questions

1. What actions were taken in Arizona to implement a set of policies aimed at minimizing the number of autonomous telemedicine networks in the state?
2. Which activities of Arizona's telemedicine policy support the concept of statewide telemedicine facility interoperability. Which activities promote this concept? What are the major benefits of the telemedicine interoperability policy for the state?
3. What are the pros and cons of having the Arizona Telemedicine Program take on the responsibility of selecting state-supported telemedicine clinic sites? Why would legislative officials choose to delegate this responsibility? What policies would affect site selection?
4. What policies would encourage independent health care organizations to become members of a statewide telemedicine consortium?

References

Hughes, A., and others. *Rural Telemedicine Demonstration Project.* Tucson: Arizona Health Sciences Center, 1995.

McNeill, K. M., Barker, G., and McElroy, J. "Experience Using an ASP Model to Expand a State-Initiated Telemedicine Program." In *Proceedings of the Fifteenth IEEE Symposium on Computer Assisted Radiology and Surgery*. 2001.

McNeill, K. M., Weinstein, R. S., and Ovitt, T. W. "Project Nightingale: A Geographically Distributed, Multi-Organizational Integrated Telemedicine Network Infrastructure." In *Proceedings of the Thirteenth IEEE Symposium on Computer Assisted Radiology and Surgery*. 1999.

Vuturo, A. F., and McNeely, R. A. *Current Status of Educational Informational Outreach Technologies and Expanding These Technologies to Support AHCS's Growing Outreach Mission*. Tucson: Arizona Health Sciences Center, 1994.

Weinstein, R. S., and Bloom, K. J. "The Pathologist as Information Specialist." *Human Pathology*, 1990, *21*, 4–6.

CHAPTER THIRTY-FIVE

THE LONG AND WINDING ROAD TO MEDICARE REIMBURSEMENT

Joseph A. Tracy, Karen E. Edison

Our large representative democracy is slow and cumbersome at times. It takes input from a wide range of stakeholders before any significant policy change occurs, helping to diminish the inevitable unintended consequences. The key to successful policy change is the involvement of knowledgeable stakeholders. Medicare reimbursement for telehealth care is a perfect example of this.

In 1999, a doctor could bill Medicare for a patient visit performed using telehealth only if that doctor split the fee and sent 25 percent of it back to the referring health care provider. If the same doctor did the same for a patient he or she saw in person, the doctor would be committing a federal crime. This reimbursement requirement was one of a host of problems associated with the first wave of Medicare reimbursement for telehealth.

Balanced Budget Act of 1997

Telehealth began a major expansion in the early 1990s with the help of an influx of federal grant dollars from the U.S. Departments of Health and Human Services, Commerce, and Agriculture. However, although these agencies provided the needed funding to develop telehealth pilot projects throughout the country, the lack of reimbursement for services provided using telehealth threatened to bring telehealth to a standstill. If physicians and other providers could not be paid for delivering health care services using telehealth, then it was unlikely that they would provide such services free of charge on an ongoing basis.

In an effort to remedy this reimbursement problem for telehealth, the Balanced Budget Act (BBA) of 1997 contained language that would be the first step toward reimbursing telehealth services beginning in January 1999. The BBA allowed physicians who examine Medicare beneficiaries to provide consultation services using telehealth and to receive payment for their services. Unfortunately, the language was put together hastily, without much input from the telehealth field, and it was flawed from both a legal and regulatory standpoint.

The Centers for Medicare and Medicaid Services (CMS), previously known as Health Care Financing Administration, had guidelines based on the BBA that allowed for payment of consultation codes only and eliminated the participation of a variety of other health care providers using telehealth. Eligible beneficiaries had to live in an area with a shortage of primary care providers. This made little sense, as telehealth was most commonly used to provide needed specialty services to rural areas in order to support the local primary care providers and help them feel less isolated. Payment for any telecommunications line charges or facility fees was prohibited. The law also went a step further to say that Medicare beneficiaries could not be billed for such charges.

The most illogical aspect of the reimbursement legislation and regulation had to do with the fee split. Regulations required that the fee be split between the consulting and referring practitioners 75-25 percent. Because this was a violation of the federal antikickback statute if done for a patient seen in person, most telehealth providers had no desire to send 25 percent of the fee back to the referring provider. The federal tax implications were also unclear. Would the consulting physician need to generate a 1099 form for each referring provider annually? The administrative burden of tracking this fee split rested squarely on the shoulders of the consulting physician.

Providers eligible for this reimbursement included only physicians, physician assistants, nurse practitioners, nurse midwives, and clinical nurse specialists. This eliminated many other providers who use telehealth to care for patients. Psychologists were one of the obvious examples. The law also required a specific type of "telepresenter." This person had to be the referring primary care physician, physician assistant, or nurse practitioner; in fact, most telehealth patients were seen with a licensed practical nurse or a registered nurse in the room with the patient. Finally, payment was allowed only for real-time live interactive clinical encounters.

In spite of these problems, the BBA legislation and the resultant CMS regulations were the first major step toward telehealth reimbursement in the Medicare program. Telehealth providers and program directors knew, however, that more work was needed. With the problems clearly identified, the telehealth community went to work in search of both legislative and regulatory change. This activity was aided greatly by the use of the Internet and the management of an active nationwide listserv of interested parties.

Benefits Improvement and Protection Act of 2000

Just prior to the implementation of the Medicare reimbursement rules for telehealth, the Southern Governors' Association (SGA) created the Taskforce on Medical Technology. One of the charges of this task force was to examine reimbursement issues related to Medicare and Medicaid. A reimbursement subcommittee was started and was chaired by Weldon Webb, associate dean for external affairs at the University of Missouri. The work of this committee would eventually work its way into Senate bill 2505, and most of it would eventually be passed into law as part of the Medicare, Medicaid, and State Children's Health Insurance Program (SCHIP) Benefits Improvement and Protection Act of 2000 (BIPA).

The SGA also analyzed several federal bills that were also being introduced in the 106th Congress to deal with the problems associated with the Medicare reimbursement laws and regulations. All of these bills had both positive and negative aspects, but a more comprehensive bill was needed.

While the SGA reimbursement task force was working diligently on recommendations in the spring and summer of 1999, a new development happened in June 1999. That was the selection of Karen Edison, a physician, as one of six Robert Wood Johnson Health Policy Fellows for the 1999–2000 year. Edison chose to work in the office of Senator Jim Jeffords (R-Vermont), who chaired the Senate Health, Education, Labor and Pensions Committee and was a senior member of the Senate Finance Committee, which oversees CMS and the Medicare program. The most significant part of Edison's placement was that she had practiced teledermatology at the University of Missouri and the Harry S Truman Memorial Veterans Hospital for approximately four years prior to receiving this fellowship. Edison was a champion of telehealth and wanted to see improvement in the Medicare telehealth reimbursement laws and regulations put forth in the BBA.

In September and October 1999, the University of Missouri conducted the first of two national assessments of telehealth encounters designed to understand the numbers of telehealth encounters being reimbursed by Medicare (Tracy, McClosky Armstrong, Sprang, and Burgiss, 1999). The assessment gathered use and billing information from programs across the country to show that telehealth services were being provided to Medicare beneficiaries even if they were not being billed. This was undertaken due to concern that the lack of claims submitted to Medicare would translate into CMS having very little data to present to Congress or to support future changes to the telehealth reimbursement language. In fact, if CMS was not receiving claims because they had no chance of being paid, then CMS could easily make the argument to Congress that telehealth activity was minimal at best because nobody was billing for it.

In September 1999, the SGA held its annual meeting and released its report, *From Promise to Practice—Improving Life in the South through Telemedicine.* The initial reimbursement language was widely circulated but fell short of being sent to Congress as a formal resolution from the SGA in 1999.

The SGA report recommended that Congress eliminate the 25 percent/75 percent fee split, reimburse any provider currently covered under the Medicare program, provide some reimbursement to the patient site to cover overhead costs, essentially eliminate the telepresenter requirement, and provide reimbursement for patients in all rural counties and for emergency care in any location if no alternative exists. The SGA report also recommended that home telehealth services be included in payment for home health providers and that store-and-forward technologies be reimbursed.

In October 1999, the Center for Telemedicine Law (CTL) hosted the National Conference on Legal and Policy Developments. As part of that meeting, a panel of telehealth professionals discussed the problems associated with the BBA. This panel told both legislators and legislative staff that the current reimbursement rules were not working: claims were not being submitted. As a result, CMS would have little information to report to Congress.

Starting in January 2000, efforts to change the telehealth laws and regulations began to heat up. Edison met with the University of Missouri Telehealth staff members Joe Tracy, Barry Kling, and Susan Becklenberg to begin crafting language that would eventually become Senate bill 2505. Using the information derived from this meeting, Edison worked with her mentor, Paul Harrington, Senator Jeffords's health policy director, to craft the Telehealth Improvement and Modernization Act of 2000. Senator Jeffords was interested in this effort, primarily because Vermont's academic medical center, Fletcher Allen Health Care, had an active telehealth program throughout Vermont and upper New York State. This proposed legislation was introduced by Senator Jeffords on May 4, 2000, with bipartisan cosponsors. It would change the telehealth reimbursement laws and regulations by fixing most of the problems created in BBA.

Over five months, Edison met with health staff in many key offices in the Senate and House explaining the bill and relating her experiences caring for patients using telehealth technology. Jennifer Bell, a speech therapist, was an intern at the time in the Health, Education, Labor and Pensions Committee office. She accompanied Edison on several of these educational visits on the Hill and became interested in the fate of this telehealth legislation. Bob Waters from the Center for Telemedicine Law (CTL) provided Edison with much expert advice through-out the entire process. Support for the bill picked up steam at the American Telemedicine Association (ATA) meeting in late May 2000. There were presenta-tion and networking sessions regarding this bill and how to promote it.

In early June 2000, a group of eight telehealth directors gathered in North Carolina to discuss this bill in detail and to determine a strategy that could be used across the country to advocate for its passage. This group included Sam Burgiss (University of Tennessee), Donna Hammack (Good Samaritan Health System, Nebraska), Shari Freuh (St. Alexius Medical Center, North Dakota), Joe Tracy (University of Missouri), Thelma McClosky Armstrong (Deaconess Hospital, Montana), Rob Sprang (University of Kentucky), Nina Antoniotti (Marshfield Clinic, Wisconsin), and Susan Gustke (East Carolina University). These individ-uals had been working together as grantees of the federal Office for the Ad-vancement of Telehealth (OAT) since the mid-1990s. During the meeting, these telehealth directors consulted with Bob Waters, counsel for the CTL and Edi-son. During that consultation, it was determined that two things needed to be done before July 15, 2000. One was to readminister the assessment of telehealth en-counters conducted by the University of Missouri and the second was to develop a single point of contact (SPOC) within each state. The job of the SPOC was to represent and communicate important issues to other telehealth programs within their state, comment on proposed legislative changes, and provide recommenda-tions for change. This group of eight telehealth directors had approximately thirty days to accomplish both tasks.

Within the thirty-day window, the group managed to identify SPOCs in forty states and readminister the assessment. Twenty-one programs responded and reported that collectively, 4,424 telehealth encounters had occurred between July 1, 1999, and December 31, 1999. Only 261 (6 percent) of these encounters would have been eligible for reimbursement given the regulatory constraints. Medicare cases accounted for 779 of the 4,424 encounters; however, only 107 of those were billed. (One vertically integrated telehealth network alone accounted for 66 percent of those billings.) These data clearly indicated that the reimburse-ment rules were not working.

The Resolution Regarding Medicare Reimbursement of Telehealth Services

On July 10, 2000, the SGA sent A Resolution Regarding Medicare Reimburse-ment of Telehealth Services to Congress. For everyone working on the reim-bursement issue across the country, the content of the resolution was of no surprise.

It contained and supported all of the points that were part of Senate bill 2505. Although this resolution was expected in September 1999, the release in July 2000 was, in hindsight, timely for the telehealth community.

The effort to keep the provisions of Senate bill 2505 moving forward was coordinated by the eight telehealth directors who met in North Carolina, the SPOCs (the grassroots), the American Telemedicine Association, the Center for Telemedicine Law, and the Association of Telemedicine Service Providers (ATSP). Edison continued working the bill in the Senate and was successful in having the House introduce a companion (similar) bill through Representative John Thune (R–South Dakota). Jennifer Bell, the intern in Senator Jeffords's office who worked with Edison on this legislation, had taken the position of health legislative assistant to Representative Thune. Given the rural nature of South Dakota, she was easily able to interest her boss in this legislation, and he became a champion of telehealth in the House. During this time, the results of the University of Missouri assessment were disseminated widely so that everyone working together throughout the country had the same information from which they could communicate to their legislators.

An important telehealth demonstration at the Avera McKennan Hospital and University Health Center in Sioux Falls, South Dakota, was conducted on August 14, 2000. Mary DeVany, the manager of the Avera McKennan Telehealth Network, demonstrated the power of telehealth to Representative Bill Thomas (R–California), chairman of the Health Subcommittee of Ways and Means, Representative Thune, and Representative Jim Ramstad (R-Minnesota). Thomas was in a powerful position in regard to the future passage or failure of the language contained in Senate bill 2505. The demonstration went well, and DeVany, who was well versed on Senate bill 2505, the SGA resolution, and the results of the utilization and payer assessment, was in a position to communicate that information firsthand to the three legislators, one of whom was in a key position of power.

On September 7, 2000, the House Commerce Committee's Subcommittee on Health and the Environment convened a hearing to address the concerns regarding Medicare reimbursement of telehealth services. The members heard from Robert Berenson of CMS, a panel of telehealth professionals providing telehealth services, and a young patient benefiting from telehealth. This hearing brought several things to light that proved beyond a doubt that the existing Medicare reimbursement scheme for telehealth was not working. The telehealth community and nation learned that between January 1, 1999, and the second quarter of 2000, only 298 Medicare claims relating to telehealth services had been paid by CMS. The members heard that the fee-sharing requirement, if administered for traditional face-to-face care, would be a federal crime. They clearly heard that telehealth delivered far more direct patient care services than consultations and that the current laws and regulations arbitrarily denied many Americans living in rural areas the right to have access to telehealth services. And, perhaps most important, they heard from the mother of a young child, who without telehealth access would have had to choose between making ends meet financially or traveling hundreds of miles to the University of Virginia on a regular basis for her child to receive care. Yet the appropriate care her child was receiving using telehealth was being done pro bono because reimbursement for the service was not a reality.

Senate bill 2505 had enough support to be passed on to the Congressional Budget Office (CBO) for scoring (pricing). It is CBO's job to put a price tag on bills that are moving forward for a vote. The support of Finance chairman William Roth (R–Delaware) and the majority health staff of the Finance Committee was key to ensuring that leadership in the Senate asked for a score for this relatively small piece of legislation. When telehealth bills were scored prior to 2000, CBO typically turned to CMS for advice. Unfortunately for the telehealth community, CMS repeatedly told CBO that telehealth would open the floodgates to health care access and cost billions of dollars. As a result, prior telehealth reimbursement bills were scored so high they had no chance of being considered any further by Congress. Most of these bills were scored at $1 billion.

In September 2000, CBO had a little more information to use than in prior years. First, during the summer of 2000, a workshop was held at the Center for Telemedicine Law to develop a scoring methodology for CBO to use when considering bills related to telehealth reimbursement. This process was aided by the work of a former CBO analyst and by Bob Waters at CTL. Second, CBO was given a copy of *Medicare Reimbursement for Telehealth: An Assessment of Telehealth Encounters*, which was completed in July 2000 (Tracy, McClosky Armstrong, Sprang, and Burgiss, 2000). In the scoring process, a CBO analyst called Joe Tracy, the executive director of telehealth at the University of Missouri who had led the assessment effort. This analyst had questions: the data she was reviewing in the assessment were inconsistent with what she was being told by CMS. Tracy answered all of this analyst's questions and made the point that the assessment contained information on more than four thousand telehealth cases over a sixth-month period versus any information she was receiving from CMS, which had only 298 cases in its database over an eighteen-month period. Also, Edison asked for and was granted a meeting with the CBO analyst. It was clear that CBO wanted to give the legislation a fair assessment.

The power of the assessment information coupled with the scoring methodology developed in the CTL workshop helped lead to Senate bill 2505's receiving a reasonably cheap price tag by federal standards: $150 million over five years. The bill had a chance of passage, but only if the language could attach itself to a larger Medicare bill moving forward.

During the fall of 2000, the language contained in Senate bill 2505 was modified in conference and rolled into House Resolution (HR) 5661: the Medicare, Medicaid, and SCHIP Benefits Improvement and Protection Act (BIPA) of 2000. This was the legislative vehicle that the telehealth community was looking for.

Unfortunately, not everything that Senate bill 2505 asked for made it to HR 5661. The final package was the result of a negotiation among the Senate Finance, House Commerce, and House Ways and Means committees. Ways and Means Health Subcommittee chairman Bill Thomas took a hard line against several provisions in the language. Members and staff from both the House and the Senate fought valiantly and were successful in preserving about 80 percent of Senate bill 2505. They were aided greatly by the use of the nationwide telehealth listserv managed by Joe Tracy. When a question arose during the negotiations, Edison would call him and say, for instance, "I need examples of patients cared for without a telepresenter, and I need them now!" Tracy would get the word out on the listserv and within an hour would have the information.

HR 5661 was incorporated by reference in the conference report to HR 4577, the Consolidated Appropriations Act 2001, which became Public Law 106–554 on December 21, 2000. On that date, Medicare reimbursement for telehealth encounters was significantly changed. (For details, see HCFA Program Memorandum Intermediaries/Carriers, May 1, 2001, Transmittal AB-01–69.) The changes were implemented on October 1, 2001.

Conclusion

Accomplishing a significant change in any type of policy requires that the key stakeholders get involved. Support must come from many places. The most important voice, however, is the voice of the constituent because legislators constantly think about getting reelected. Nevertheless, they want to do the right thing for their constituents. They are pulled, however, in many directions and cannot be expert on every topic. They must rely heavily on trusted experts to help them craft good policy. Those of us who are affected by changes in policy must serve as those trusted experts.

It takes a coordinated group effort to accomplish this sort of task and much patience. Policy work can be slow and frustrating, but the rewards are great. It helps to have good data and a good anecdote. (The testimony of the little girl's mother at the Commerce hearing is a good example of such an anecdote.) Good policy tends to rise to the top of the debate, and sometimes timing is everything. In this case, the right people were in the right place at the right time, and the impact of the effort was a better reimbursement landscape for telehealth across the United States.

The telehealth community had endured a long but successful effort to improve telehealth reimbursement policy in the Medicare program. Many individuals and organizations played an important role in the process by communicating a common reimbursement message to Congress. Having a listserv that enabled everyone at the grassroots level to work together on this issue, coupled with having the right people in the right place in Washington, D.C., resulted in a positive reimbursement outcome for telehealth.

Discussion Questions

1. Why would Senate bill 2505 have requested that store-and-forward activities be reimbursed only for federal demonstration projects operating in Alaska and Hawaii?
2. Why didn't all of the recommended actions in Senate bill 2505 roll over into HR 5661?
3. Although it was not addressed in Senate bill 2505, is it still illegal to bill Medicare beneficiaries for facility or telecommunication charges associated with telehealth?
4. Which changes to the Balanced Budget Act required legislative action for change, and which could be changed by the Centers for Medicare and Medicaid Services in its rule making?
5. How does one contact and best present information to legislators?
6. What is the most important thing one can do to give a legislator or a legislative staff member a thorough understanding of telehealth?

References

Southern Governors' Association. *From Promise to Practice—Improving Life in the South Through Telemedicine* Washington, D.C.: U.S. Government Printing Office, 1999.

Tracy J., McClosky Armstrong T., Sprang R., and Burgiss, S. "Medicare Reimbursement for Telehealth—An Assessment of Telehealth Encounters—January 1, 1999–June 30, 1999." Oct. 1999. [www.telehealth.muhealth.org].

Tracy J., McClosky Armstrong T., Sprang R., and Burgiss, S. "Medicare Reimbursement for Telehealth—An Assessment of Telehealth Encounters—July 1, 1999–December 31, 1999." July 2000. [www.telehealth.muhealth.org].

CHAPTER THIRTY-SIX

ADDRESSING BARRIERS TO ACCESS FOR UNINSURED IN WESTERN NEW YORK STATE

WNYhelpnet.ORG

Thomas Hugh Feeley, Denise M. Rizzo, Jeannine M. Osborne

Nearly 42 million citizens of the United States (approximately 16 percent of the population) lack basic health insurance coverage as of 2001 (Covering the Uninsured, 2003). Consider also that the United States spent $1.4 trillion on health care in 2001. New York, the third most populated state in the country, with over 20 million residents, has an unemployment rate of 16.4 percent (U.S. Bureau of the Census, 2003). It is worth noting that over 80 percent of uninsured U.S. residents come from full-time and part-time working families, and the majority of the uninsured work in service industries or in small businesses. Taken together, the unemployment rate and the number of those employed without basic health insurance, the challenges before health care policymakers and health management organizations are many, and they may even get progressively worse before they get better, at least in New York State.

People who lack basic health insurance are more likely to go without preventive care and treatment for chronic conditions and thus are sicker than other patients when they finally see a physician. Emergency rooms have become the surrogate primary care physicians for the uninsured, which places added stress on the health care system as the whole. The Erie County Medical Center (2003) in Buffalo, New York, reports providing emergent care for over thirteen thousand uninsured patients in 2001.

The need for state, federal, and private foundation funding to address the problem of the uninsured cannot be overstated. Many of the solutions, we argue, can be accomplished through health informatics programs and initiatives, specifically in the area of information management (for example, who is uninsured, programs for uninsured).

Toward a Local Solution

The Community Health Network (CHN) of western New York (Figure 36.1) held a regional summit in the spring of 2000 with the objective of prioritizing the most vital and emergent health concerns in the region. From these discussions, access to health care and reducing the number of uninsured were identified as the top priorities. A CHN access committee was formed and assigned the task of addressing the issue of access to health care and health insurance immediately after the regional summit. After several virtual and live meetings, two stakeholders, the University at Buffalo Department of Family Medicine and the Uninsured Trust Fund Coalition, emerged as leaders for these initiatives.

Two project objectives for the access committee were quickly outlined: (1) extend and expand the community-supported insurance coverage for the working uninsured, and (2) design a Web site to warehouse, organize, and simplify existing services for the uninsured. The second objective is the focus of this chapter. It became evident that there were myriad services available in the Buffalo and western New York communities for the uninsured, but there was no central repository or database for provider locations and service information—information critical for both the uninsured and for caseworkers, who were charged with linking the uninsured and indigent with cost-free or sliding-fee services.

A necessary first step toward meeting the objectives of the access committee was obtaining funding to support project activities and to subsidize insurance premiums for the working uninsured. Toward this end, the University at Buffalo Department of Family Medicine applied for and received funding for the project on behalf of the alliance and coalition from the Community Access Program (CAP) administered through the U.S. Department of Health and Human Services Health Resources Administration. The grant award was for $1.04 million, and most of the grant was used for setting up the infrastructure to administer the Uninsured Connections Network (UCN), the tentative title given to the Web site. This award announcement was in late 2001.

Identifying a Web-Based Solution

Two major findings were consistent across these focus groups and both observations confirmed the committee's expectations. First, the idea of a central Web site for services was widely supported, and, second, a central "one-stop shopping" Web

FIGURE 36.1. THE WESTERN NEW YORK STATE REGION.

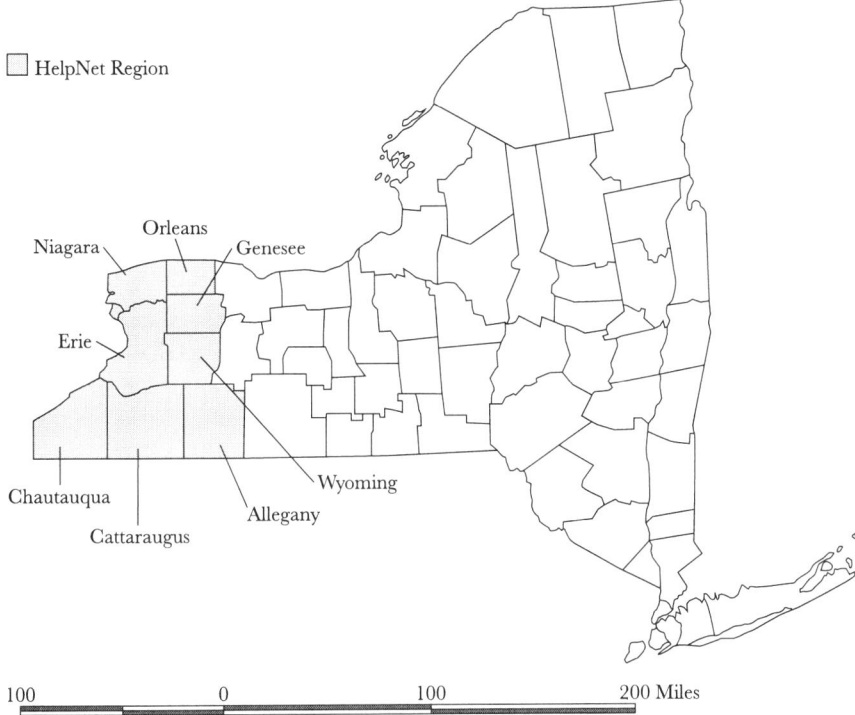

site was greatly needed across the regions to facilitate access to available programs and services. The name of this Web site was changed to WNYhelpnet.ORG. Its goal was to provide a central directory for health and human services for the estimated 200,000 western New York residents who lack basic health insurance.

The Web site would allow end users to systematically link the underserved to the nearest available service provider. The Web-based directory of services was originally designed for health and human service professionals who serve as caseworkers for the uninsured, almost all of whom, it was known, had Internet access at their work site. It is important to note that the helpnet is the first regionwide effort of its kind to consolidate many small directories into one comprehensive database. Included on the site are agency and program names, description of services, hours of service, and eligibility requirements. The site is open to community organizations and the general public, and no fee or charge is associated with the site.

After much planning, much anticipation, and intensive problem solving regarding information technology issues, the helpnet went on-line in April 2002. To advertise the helpnet, letters and user guides were sent to more than fifty-three hundred health service professionals and organizations.

About the Site

The site is linked off the HealthforAll (www.healthforall.org) main Web page or can be accessed directly (it is also now linked off several other hospital and health services sites). The home page provides introductory information about the help-net and queries users to log in, register, or list an agency site, as the case may be. The search index page allows users to search by keyword or by search categories, and allows searches to be limited by county. Programs and services include de-scriptive information (address, contact information, available services), eligibility information (referral needed, insurance accepted, sliding fee), and often directions linked from Mapquest (www.mapquest.com).

Initial Results

As of June 3, 2003, there were 413 total registered users of the helpnet: 271 full ac-cess users and 142 guest users. It is important to note that these numbers reflect the first twelve months of helpnet use from May 2002 to May 2003. Most users (50.2 percent of 223 users reported) heard about the helpnet from the initial mailing sent from HealthforAll staff in August 2002. Another 33 percent of full access users learned of the helpnet from social networks—word-of-mouth or from coworkers.

Table 36.1 lists the number of monthly and average daily hits, sessions, and page views. For the first six months of the project, the helpnet averaged between thirty-eight and fifty-four individual sessions per day, and each session typically re-quested three to six page views.

Perhaps the most telling information is related to category use, that is, the cat-egories or services that are most queried by caseworkers and individuals. Table 36.2 outlines these data by full access and guest users. The top five most commonly queried categories are free/low-cost/sliding fee, children/youth/teen services, mental health and counseling, family services, and Medicaid.

Challenges in Meeting Project Objectives

Health programs designed to improve the status quo are rife with challenges, and how an organization or project team is able to deal with challenges and adapt often determines success or failure. The first real challenge was focus. Solving the unin-

TABLE 36.1. WNYHELPNET.ORG USER STATISTICS, DECEMBER 2002–MAY 2003.

Date	Average Daily Hits[a]	Average Daily Sessions[b]	Average Daily Page Views[c]	Average Page Views by Session[d]
December 2002	1,098.45	37.90	177.42	4.68
January 2003	1,398.90	54.16	223.23	4.12
February 2003	1,129.54	36.07	185.54	6.14
March 2003	1,432.13	46.23	260.94	5.64
April 2003	1,386.53	49.33	194.87	3.95
May 2003	1,213.61	46.00	155.68	3.38

[a]Based on the total number of monthly hits divided by thirty, with a hit defined as any request for data.

[b]Individual sessions or single uses per month divided by thirty.

[c]Number of Web page requests per month divided by thirty.

[d]Computed by dividing average daily page views by average daily sessions.

sured problem in western New York is a lofty and unrealistic challenge, and it is often too easy to identify problems and shortcomings in the health care system and economy in upstate New York. The challenge was to create and lead with a singularly focused project that could be accomplished within a relatively short window of time (two to three years) on a fixed budget. This challenge in our estimation was more than met with the WNYhelpnet.ORG project and HealthforAll of Western New York Incorporated, the umbrella organization that developed and maintains the helpnet.

The second challenge was Internet technology (IT) problems in developing the helpnet Web site. Specifically, the project team underestimated the IT costs (originally estimated at $120,000) and expertise required of IT consultants. The second issue related to IT was the decision to use a consultant rather than hire a project manager for the Web site. The solutions were straightforward but financially costly. Clearly, knowledge of the health services landscape and the needs of the client population was necessary (and lacking) for designing the Web site. Money from other project activities—approximately $50,000—had to be cut to accommodate the IT costs. HealthforAll found it difficult to engage an IT consultant who had little knowledge of the health and human service field. Clearly future projects would benefit from coproject directors who together have expertise in IT and health and human services.

A third challenge, still unresolved, is determining and measuring project success. Certainly, having data showing health and human service personnel using

TABLE 36.2. WNYHELPNET.ORG CATEGORY USE BY USER STATUS.

Helpnet Category	Log Count (Percentage) for Full Access Users	Log Count (Percentage) for Guest Access Users
Free/low cost/sliding fee	4,660 (14)	27 (10)
Children/youth/teen services	2,928 (9)	0 (0)
Mental health and counseling	2,385 (7)	10 (4)
Family services	2,322 (7)	2 (1)
Medicaid	1,883 (6)	9 (3)
Accessibility and disability	1816 (5)	6 (2)
Housing and shelter	1,517 (5)	9 (3)
Women's services	1,510 (4)	11 (4)
Education and prevention	1,452 (4)	7 (2)
Senior services	1,447 (4)	12 (4)
Financial services	1,322 (4)	2 (1)
Addiction and recovery	1,278 (4)	17 (6)
Abuse and violence	1,098 (3)	19 (7)
Men's services	1,028 (3)	5 (2)
Homeless	1,007 (3)	2 (1)
Food and nutrition	678 (2)	9 (3)
Legal and mediation	513 (2)	2 (1)
End of life	507 (2)	2 (1)
Clothing	501 (2)	0 (0)
Employment	406 (1)	14 (5)
Veterans	403 (1)	0 (0)
HIV/AIDS	352 (1)	5 (2)

Note: Only the twenty-two most frequented categories are listed.

the Web site is encouraging but still an indirect measure of success. Impact measures might include actual delivery and utilization of services to western New York uninsured residents. Moreover, was the service on the Web site indispensable? That is, in the absence of the helpnet, would the end user have found the health service information? An important activity to benchmark success might include a random sample of helpnet consumers on both the process and impact of the WNYhelpnet.ORG. Was the electronic database easy to use and helpful in finding critical health and human service information? Was it successful in addressing the needs of end users? The project should have greater outreach than it currently does in western New York. With an estimated 126,000 uninsured adults in western New York as of 2000 (Family Medicine Research Institute, 2000), it would appear that the project and the Web site can serve more of the western New York residents than it currently does. Recall that the helpnet has but 432 registered users, although most of these users (63 percent) are social and caseworkers who serve multiple clients each day. Perhaps more vigilant and targeted advertising would better diffuse the benefits of the WNYhelpnet.ORG.

A fourth challenge is adapting the current system to accommodate more "guest users" who are not health and human service personnel. The original intent of the helpnet was to assist caseworkers who counsel the indigent of western New York. Through focus groups, it was decided to target professionals who link the uninsured to services—those who are more likely than the uninsured to have access to computers. Additional community collaborations have indicated that through the use of computers at schools, libraries, and eventually public kiosks, the uninsured could be empowered to look for helping services.

A fifth challenge is the perceived conflict of interest among agencies that provide overlapping services with respect to health insurance and human service information. While moving forward with the project initiatives of the helpnet, we learned of organizations that offered services similar to the charge of the helpnet. Specifically, there were information and referral agencies (I&Rs) that provided, over the telephone, the phone numbers and address information of helping services to consumers in a particular county. The challenge faced from I&Rs' duplicative services was twofold. First, these individuals felt threatened by HealthforAll and its overlapping services. The second challenge was to create a unique and more comprehensive program that improves on the current I&R efforts.

The helpnet is unique in that it is fully computerized, and its database of health care service providers is far more comprehensive than any individual I&R database in western New York. The helpnet is also a free service, whereas many I&Rs charge for some of their database information (for example, directories and disks), as these I&Rs depend on such revenue to operate.

Efforts have been successful to integrate the helpnet's efforts with those of I&Rs in each of the eight counties. As an example, each I&R now is responsible for the information on the helpnet in its geographical area; thus, I&Rs essentially "own" an area of the Web site to update and maintain. In turn, individual I&Rs have access to adjacent county information in western New York. Clearly, regional buy-in from I&Rs and health service organizations is essential in moving forward and in future grant efforts to expand the helpnet.

Project Update and Future Plans

The current plans are to make the helpnet accessible in the field for the typical caseworker. A recent needs assessment survey of a sample of thirty caseworkers and peer advocates has greatly informed our future planning. Seventy-seven percent of those surveyed reported that either "most of the time" or "every time," they refer clients to agencies, programs, or services, and 80 percent of caseworkers reported that "some of the time" or "most of the time," they are unable to locate the appropriate referral service information for the client.

The recent needs assessment and anecdotal evidence from social workers indicates a possible time and media lag between when a caseworker counsels the individual and when she or he is able to cull up the requisite information from the helpnet Web site. Consider that, on average, 55 percent of clients are seen outside the office where computers and the Internet are not readily accessible. To remedy this, our project team is proposing to make the helpnet portable with personal digital assistants (PDAs). Our needs assessment posed the question, "How valuable would a hand-held device (PDA) or laptop with referral information be when you are assisting clients away from the office." Eighty-seven percent reported this medium would be either "very valuable" or "extremely valuable."

HealthforAll and the WNYhelpnet.ORG must work hard to sustain itself financially and programmatically. Program and service information must be updated routinely and accurately, and this requires vigilance and conscientious support staff, who are often paid just above minimum wage. The Web site must also be adapted to the changing health care environment, especially with more patients over time directly accessing the site on their own.

The next phase will focus on helping hospitals identify all the services offered within their system and proving the value of the helpnet to hospital administrators. A full-time hospital liaison has been employed to sell the helpnet as a valuable resource for hospitals and physician groups as an internal resource for hospital staff to use to identify locations within their own system for patients to obtain follow-up services recommended at the time they are discharged.

Financially, HealthforAll, the helpnet's parent organization, must sustain funding from Robert Wood Johnson, the Health Resources Services Administration, community grantors, and possible future contracts. Advertising the value of the health service information provided on the helpnet is another planned activity for the planning group. The needs of the uninsured are many, and the demographics of this population make advertising and marketing challenging, as many of the uninsured work atypical hours and often hold more than one job to provide for their families. A critical part of the outreach effort is for HealthforAll, in cooperation with its community partners, to sponsor kiosks or public Internet access (for example, located in community centers or libraries) stations to those who may not own personal computers.

Discussion Questions

1. What was the main problem the WNYhelpnet.ORG attempted to address in its project objectives?
2. Choose two challenges the helpnet project team confronted during the de-

velopment of the Web site. How did the team deal with the challenge, and what could it have done differently?

3. Understanding the objectives of the helpnet, what other plans or activities might help the project staff work toward these objectives? Consider cost, support staff, and feasibility in your answer.

4. What other methods using Internet technology might be used to address the uninsured problem in the United States?

5. If you were a representative of an organization that sponsored grant money to support the helpnet, how would you determine the overall effectiveness of the helpnet? What specific measures and data would you like to see? What challenges (both practically, logistically, and otherwise) would challenge evaluation of the helpnet?

References

Covering the Uninsured. "Fact Sheets." 2003. [http://www.coveringtheuninsured.org/factsheets].

Erie County Medical Center. *Annual Report for 2001*. 2003.

Family Medicine Research Institute. *A Needs Assessment of Western New York Uninsured*. Buffalo: Department of Family Medicine, State University of New York at Buffalo, 2000.

U.S. Bureau of the Census. "Census Statistics." 2003. [http://www.census.gov].

CHAPTER THIRTY-SEVEN

USING COMPUTER TECHNOLOGIES TO PROVIDE RELEVANT CANCER INFORMATION TO VULNERABLE POPULATIONS

The NCI Digital Divide Pilot Projects

Gary L. Kreps, David H. Gustafson, Peter Salovey, Rosemarie Slevin Perocchia, Wayne Wilbright, Mary Anne Bright, Cathy Muha, Carol C. Diamond

In 2001, the National Cancer Institute (NCI) supported the development of four new demonstration research programs to examine new strategies for narrowing the digital divide that limits access to relevant cancer information. The NCI awarded close to $1 million to help develop these four innovative research projects to increase understanding about how to narrow the digital divide that exists among many underserved populations in accessing and using information about cancer on the Internet.

The awards were an effort of NCI's Cancer Information Service (CIS) to work collaboratively with regional cancer control groups and organizations to test new strategies designed to improve cancer communications in underserved communities. The CIS is a national program supported by the NCI to provide the American public with answers to questions they might have about cancer. The CIS has three components: a national toll-free telephone network (1–800–4-CANCER), as well as an informative set of Internet-based Web pages and specialized cancer information and treatment search engines available through www.cancer.gov: the CIS Partnership Program, which helps bring cancer information to people who do not traditionally seek health information or may have difficulties doing so because of educational, financial, or language barriers, and the CIS Research Program, which studies the most effective ways to communicate health information in order to help people adopt healthier behaviors.

By working in concert with the Digital Divide Pilot Projects, the CIS hoped to learn how to better reach diverse and underserved audiences of people who need relevant health information and support. The pilot projects also served to support the communication research and the community partnership programs that CIS has developed to help extend and refine its information services to vulnerable populations.

The NCI is a federal agency, part of the U.S. Department of Health and Human Services. It is the largest of more than twenty major research institutes within the National Institutes of Health (NIH). The mission of the NIH is to improve the health of the American public by increasing understanding of the processes underlying human health and by developing new and relevant knowledge about prevention, detection, diagnosis, and treatment of disease. A major objective of the NCI, in particular, is to significantly reduce the national burden caused by cancers by generating new knowledge about cancer prevention and control. To achieve these goals, the NCI has developed an ambitious program of cancer research.

The NCI is authorized by the National Cancer Act of 1971 to not only generate new scientific knowledge about cancer prevention, detection, and treatment, but to communicate relevant new knowledge learned about cancer to health care consumers, providers, researchers, policymakers, and the American public in general. In this regard, the NCI has made a large and ambitious commitment to cancer communications research and outreach. In fact, it identified cancer communications as one of its priority areas for investment, an area of extraordinary opportunity (Kreps, 2003). The research and development program described in this chapter is part of this extraordinary opportunity in cancer communications. It was designed to learn how to communicate effectively through new communication technologies with several hard-to-reach groups of people in the United States who are most vulnerable to the lethal effects of cancer. These research projects, called the Digital Divide Pilot Projects, developed and tested new strategies for providing different poor and underserved groups of people with access to the latest and most accurate information about cancer prevention, control, and treatment (Kreps, 2002). This kind of investment in health information dissemination research is important; the unique strategies developed in these research projects helped to overcome communication barriers that may have limited access to and use of health information.

Data Gathered and Methodology

The following four innovative demonstration research projects were conducted in collaboration with the CIS to identify effective new strategies for providing access to relevant cancer information to underserved populations.

The CHESS Program

A University of Wisconsin–based research group, in collaboration with two NCI Cancer Information Service regional offices, one in Wisconsin and the other in Detroit, developed a multiyear demonstration research project to test the feasibility of working in collaboration with the CIS Network to disseminate an integrated online cancer communication system, the Computerized Health Education and Support System (CHESS), to underserved women recently diagnosed with breast cancer (Gustafson and others, 2001). This project was funded in partnership with the Markle Foundation, and the combined funding allowed the researchers to extend the original NCI-funded project and increase subject enrollment. The CHESS information system is a unique computer-based support program that provides users with multiple information options (for example, on cancer information, reference materials, support groups, and journaling). This project was a pilot test of a new information dissemination strategy to provide underserved cancer patients with access to an Internet-based version of the CHESS system to provide them with high-quality breast cancer information and support. Results from this study tested the ability of disseminating the CHESS system broadly using the Internet and positioned the NCI and other organizations with cancer information services to develop innovative information dissemination strategies to reduce the digital divide among those facing cancer. If successful, this could serve as a model for a nationwide dissemination of Internet-based cancer information and support to the underserved.

In past studies, CHESS was found to have positive effects with high levels of use by test group members (Gustafson and others, 1999). However, until now, the CHESS system software was installed as part of the computers used by respondents in previous studies. This application uses Internet delivery of CHESS to a widely dispersed population of users to see if the system could have broader applications and dissemination potential with geographically distant audiences of potential users. A unique feature of this Digital Divide Pilot Project (DDPP) study is the comparison of adoption and use of the CHESS system using Internet delivery by low-income women in rural Wisconsin and urban Detroit to better understand the unique information needs of these different underserved populations. (The Wisconsin women recruited for this study are primarily white, and the Detroit-based women in the study are black, providing an interesting comparison of system use across race.) Results of this study suggest that Internet delivery of CHESS worked well with both populations of women, leading to strong adoption and system use in rural Wisconsin and urban Detroit. Outcome measures showed that the system had positive effects on user satisfaction, well-being, support, and adjustment to living with cancer. The fact that system adoption, use, and satisfaction were consistently strong across the Wisconsin and Detroit populations suggests that the system works well for women from different racial and geographical backgrounds.

CancerInfoNet: A Harlem-based Program

The New York regional CIS office, in collaboration with researchers at the Memorial Sloan-Kettering Cancer Center in New York, conducted an innovative community partnership intervention program designed to teach both consumers and health care providers in Harlem, New York, about on-line cancer resources, basic Internet skills, and credible cancer Web sites (Perocchia and Rapkin, 2001). They conducted computer-based training workshops in English and Spanish using CancerInfoNet.org, a Web site created by the research team specifically for the project, to teach strategies for accessing health information on-line to target populations consisting of lower-income minority (primarily black and Hispanic) group members. These workshops were conducted at a network of community organizations that served as both technology access sites and training centers.

A unique feature of this project was the use of established community organizations as delivery sites for information dissemination, including nonprofit support organizations, a hospital setting, and a corporate technology center. These organizations provided points of access for technology training and information searching. This demonstration project provides an important model for how macrosocial community interventions can be used to help overcome the digital divide by ensuring that medically underserved populations have access to the same information and array of on-line tools as the rest of the population. This project provided an opportunity to develop and test tools to deliver cancer information. Results from this study demonstrate increased access to and use of relevant cancer information among target groups. In addition, the project indicated that participants, initially uncomfortable with computer use, became more comfortable using on-line resources and more aware of places in the community to access computers. An increased knowledge of cancer information Web sites, increased confidence in making judgments about the reliability and appropriateness of the sites, and increased willingness to discuss Internet information sources with patients and their family members were reported among health professionals.

The LUCI Program

Researchers at the Louisiana State University Medical School, in collaboration with the Mid-South regional CIS office, developed an innovative multidimensional strategy to overcome the digital divide for low-literacy elderly senior center participants in Louisiana (Wilbright and others, 2001). This project uses a train-the-trainer program, a computer education program, installation of computer and Internet resources in state-operated senior centers, and an innovative narrative-based computerized multimedia information translation application (interface) for improving the dissemination of cancer information. The implementation of this interface, which is called the Low-literacy User Cancer Information Interface (LUCI), uses multimedia technologies for overcoming literacy-based barriers to computer use and the acquisition of cancer information. To engage seniors unfamiliar with computer and Internet usage, LUCI presents information in a multimedia narrative format, similar to a televised soap opera, that does not rely on reading or computer literacy.

Results have indicated that the LUCI application is popular with the senior citizens and is easy for them to use. However, outcome measures have failed to demonstrate significant increases in health promotion knowledge and activity among the seniors. Perhaps longer exposure to the LUCI intervention is warranted. This project illustrates innovative strategies for reaching low-literacy audiences in senior centers and clinics that have the potential for broad application. The challenge is to find the best applications of this communication strategy and the most opportune sites for program delivery.

The Head Start Program

The New England regional Cancer Information Service office, in collaboration with researchers from the Department of Psychology at Yale University, developed an important community intervention project that established community technology centers at two Head Start early childhood education programs to provide access to health information to low-income families (Salovey and others, 2001). In this innovative project, Head Start staff members were trained as technology coaches to deliver computer-training courses to parents and other community members who earned free, refurbished, Internet-ready computers to take home by completing the training program. The unique focus in this project on the family as a unit of analysis, based on the Head Start program model, provided a rich multigenerational approach to computer skills development and use.

This project, like the Harlem project, provides a provocative model for using established community resources to educate underserved populations and bridge the digital divide in access to health information. Results suggest strong acceptance of the program within the Head Start system, as well as positive outcome influences on computer skills, health information access, and information use. There is great potential to develop similar technology centers in other Head Start programs, as well as in a number of different community organizations, to help bridge the digital divide and provide underserved families with both access to and the skills to use relevant health information.

Cancer and Vulnerable Populations

Many of the people who are most at risk of dying from cancer are members of underserved populations (populations that generally comprise individuals who are often of low socioeconomic status, possess low levels of literacy, are elderly, are members of ethnic minority groups, or have limited formal education). These underserved and vulnerable populations often have limited access to relevant health information, especially information widely available over the Internet (Science Panel on Interactive Communication and Health, 1999). They are also subject to serious disparities in health care and generally have much higher rates of morbidity and mortality due to serious health threats than the rest of the public, especially from cancers (Institute of Medicine, 1999). New strategies and policies need to be developed to help these underserved populations access relevant health information and use such information to make informed health-related decisions about seeking appropriate health care and support, resisting avoidable and significant health risks, and promoting their health.

The pattern of limited access to relevant health information is a global issue. It occurs wherever there are pockets of poverty, illiteracy, and social disenfranchisement. Limited access to health information is a significant problem in the United States and also an issue in many other countries. Health and health care are universal issues that affect all people, and relevant health information is a critical resource that empowers people to make good decisions to enhance their health and well-being.

Health information is essential in health care and health promotion because it provides both direction and rationale for guiding strategic health behaviors, treatments, and decisions (Kreps, 2001). The digital divide has been identified as a special problem in health care that can lead to significant disparities in care. Many studies show that certain minority groups, as well as low-income, low-education populations in the United States, suffer a disproportionate cancer burden and have limited access to electronic information about health (Institute of Medicine, 1999). However, too little is known about different disenfranchised groups' interests in, access to, and abilities to use health information.

The U.S. Department of Commerce and other groups have documented the digital divide that separates those who have access to computer technology and the vast storehouse of information available through the World Wide Web from those who lack access. A recent White House report (U.S. White House, 2000) indicates the gap between people who have access to the latest information age tools and those who do not is widening, and the digital divide is growing along racial and ethnic lines. This White House report suggested several steps intended to break down the digital divide. One of the goals is to make access to computers and the Internet as universal as the telephone is today. The 2010 *Healthy People* report for the first time has a section on health communications, with goals for access to health communication and computer-mediated health information (U.S. Department of Health and Human Services, 2000). The digital divide is a special problem in health care. Many of the characteristics that identify those on the have-not side of the digital divide also characterize those who suffer the negative effects of health disparities: people with less education, low income, and ethnic minorities. While information and knowledge are not guarantees of good health care decisions and adherence to recommended health behaviors, there is ample evidence that they contribute to them. Currently, substantial barriers prevent major segments of the population from seeking and using on-line health information.

Lessons Learned

Each of the four digital divide pilot projects supported by the NCI developed provocative new community strategies for providing underserved groups of people with access to relevant computer-based information about cancer. There is great opportunity to expand and sustain these interventions to provide additional underserved populations with relevant health information. There may be some opportunities to combine aspects of these different projects for application in different contexts. Lessons learned from these projects can be fruitfully applied in many other settings to narrow the digital divide and reduce health disparities. These funded projects attempt to increase understanding of why barriers to information and knowledge exist and use the information gleaned from these pilot projects to design programs that can lead to better health care decisions and adherence to recommended health behaviors. These pilot projects will serve as models for larger-scale efforts. Similar efforts to narrow health disparities by bridging the digital divide will help empower underserved health care consumers to make informed health care decisions, seek the best possible health care, and enhance their quality of life. The results of these Digital Divide Pilot Projects should be interpreted and applied to develop new programs and policies for providing relevant health information to all segments of modern society.

Discussion Questions

1. Why is it an important health promotion goal to provide poor and other underprivileged people with access to health information?
2. What are some of the advantages and disadvantages of using computer-mediated channels of communication for health information dissemination?
3. Describe some of the unique health communication strategies employed by each of the Digital Divide Pilot Projects to increase the access to and use of relevant health information by underserved and vulnerable groups of people.
4. Identify the health communication strategies used that you think were most successful, and explain why they worked effectively.
5. How transportable are the communication strategies used in each of the Digital Divide Pilot Projects from the settings where they were developed to other settings and populations? Describe some settings where communication strategies might work well and settings where they are unlikely to be effective.
5. How can lessons learned from these projects be fruitfully applied in other settings to narrow the digital divide and reduce health disparities?

References

Gustafson, D. H., and others. "Impact of a Patient-Centered, Computer-Based Health Information/Support System." *American Journal of Preventive Medicine*, 1999, *16*(1), 1–9.

Gustafson, D. H., and others. "Assessing Costs and Outcomes of Providing Computer Support to Under-Served Women with Breast Cancer: A Work in Progress." *Electronic Journal of Communication/La Revue Electronique de Communication*, 2001, *11*(3 & 4). [http://www.cios.org/www/ejc/v11n3.htm].

Institute of Medicine. *The Unequal Burden of Cancer: An Assessment of NIH Research and Programs for Ethnic Minorities and the Medically Underserved*. Washington, D.C.: National Academy of Sciences, 1999.

Kreps, G. L. "The Evolution and Advancement of Health Communication Inquiry." In W. B. Gudykunst (ed.), *Communication Yearbook 24*. Thousand Oaks, Calif.: Sage, 2001.

Kreps, G. L. "Enhancing Access to Relevant Health Information." In R. Carveth, S. B. Kretchmer, and D. Schuler (eds.), *Shaping the Network Society: Patterns for Participation, Action, and Change*. Palo Alto, Calif.: Computer Professionals for Social Responsibility, 2002.

Kreps, G. L. "The Impact of Communication on Cancer Risk, Incidence, Morbidity, Mortality, and Quality of Life." *Health Communication*, 2003, *15*(2), 163–171.

Perocchia, R., and Rapkin, B. "Bridging the Digital Divide Project: Providing Access to Cancer Information through the Internet." *Electronic Journal of Communication/La Revue Electronique de Communication*, 2001, *11*(3 & 4). [http://www.cios.org/www/ejc/v11n3.htm].

Salovey, P., and others. "Developing Computer Proficiency Among Head Start Parents: An In-Progress Case Study of a New England CIS Digital Divide Project." *Electronic Journal of Communication/La Revue Electronique de Communication*, 2001, *11*(3 & 4). [http://www.cios.org/www/ejc/v11n3.htm].

Science Panel on Interactive Communication and Health. *Wired for Health and Well-Being: The Emergence of Interactive Health Communication.* Washington, D.C.: U.S. Department of Health and Human Services, U.S. Government Printing Office, 1999.

U.S. Department of Health and Human Services. *Healthy People 2010*: Washington, D.C.: U.S. Government Printing Office, 2000.

U.S. White House. "White House Proposal: From Digital Divide to Digital Opportunity." 2000. [www.whitehouse.gov/WH/New/digitaldivide].

Wilbright, W. A., and others. "Toward Overcoming the Digital Divide for the Dissemination of Early Detection Cancer Information." *Electronic Journal of Communication/La Revue Electronique de Communication*, 2001, *11*(3 & 4). [http://www.cios.org/www/ejc/v11n3.htm].

CHAPTER THIRTY-EIGHT

BRIDGING THE DIGITAL DIVIDE

Lessons from the Health InterNetwork India

Joan Dzenowagis, Andrew Pleasant, Shyama Kuruvilla

Information and communication technologies (ICT), including the Internet, are often depicted as bridges to better governance, enhanced economies, and improved health (Digital Opportunities Task Force, 2003). However, details on how these bridges can be successfully constructed remain the exception rather than the norm (Wade, 2002). Nevertheless, the technologies are broadly promoted as an engine for national development (Digital Opportunities Task Force, 2003; Wade, 2002; International Telecommunication Union, 2002). In this context, United Nations Secretary General Kofi Annan launched the Health InterNetwork in September 2000 as part of the Millennium Action Plan "as a concrete demonstration of how we can build bridges over digital divides" through innovative partnerships (United Nations, 2000). The initiative proposed to install computers and Internet connectivity at thousands of hospitals and health centers in developing countries to provide up-to-date health information. The private sector committed to providing the millions of dollars required, but the dot-com bubble of the 1990s burst before the project could get off the ground, and the promised funding never materialized.

This chapter is based in large part on an article published in the *British Medical Journal* and is published with the kind permission of the journal (Kuruvilla and others, 2004).

The challenge of improving the flow of timely, relevant, and reliable information for health nevertheless remained, and the World Health Organization (WHO) decided to proceed with the initiative. WHO consulted on the Health InterNetwork (HIN) concept with U.N. agencies, technical experts, nongovernmental organizations, and national governments, resulting in a strategy to implement and evaluate a series of pilot projects to inform the eventual scaling up of the overall initiative. This strategy was also thought to be more feasible given that focused projects were a better fit with the approach of funding agencies than were large-scale, infrastructure development initiatives. The HIN pilot projects would focus on key aspects of the digital divide in health: connectivity, content, capacity building, and policy (Health InterNetwork, 2003).

Within that framework, an early Health InterNetwork pilot to improve access to scientific publications for researchers in developing countries quickly became a larger initiative when, seizing the opportunity to move beyond a limited pilot, a range of partners came together to form the Health InterNetwork Access to Research Initiative (HINARI). Coordinated by WHO and the BMJ, today HINARI provides public health institutions in 113 countries free or low-cost access to over twenty-three hundred biomedical journals from more than forty of the world's major publishers (Aronson, 2002; Smith, 2003).

A second pilot, Health InterNetwork India (HIN India), was developed to document and analyze the process of establishing and using connectivity to support public health services. This chapter discusses the lessons from the pilot based on the project evaluation and drawing on the experience of staff, participants, collaborators, and volunteers.

Mapping the Digital Divide

One of the first steps in planning the Health InterNetwork was to develop a framework to guide the initiative. The phrase *digital divide* often refers to unequal Internet access in and between countries (Table 38.1). The digital divide, however, represents more than the inability to access the Internet physically. Access to computers and connectivity does not guarantee that individuals and societies will benefit from their use. Diffusion and meaningful uptake of the Internet and related technologies require specific skills and resources, and their presence or absence tends to reflect existing social divides (Wade, 2002; International Telecommunications Union, 2002; Lessig, 2001). Issues related to the ownership and management of the infrastructure, technology, and content also contribute to the divide (Wade, 2002; Lessig, 2001).

For the Health InterNetwork, the effort to bridge the digital divide focuses on four main components:

TABLE 38.1. ESTIMATED INTERNET ACCESS, 2002.

Region	Number of Internet Users (million)	Total Population	Estimated Internet Access
World	605.6	More than 6 billion	10%
Canada and United States	182.67	316 million	58
Europe with Commonwealth of Independent States	190.91	727 million	26
Latin America	33.35	520 million	7
Asia/Pacific	187.24	3.7 billion	5
Africa	6.31	795 million	Less than 1

Sources: International Telecommunication Union (2002): United Nations Conference on Trade and Development (2003); NUA (2002); United Nations Population Division (2002).

- Connectivity: facilitating information access and use through ICT
- Content: providing timely, relevant, and high-quality information
- Capacity building: developing skills in ICT management and use
- Policy: lowering the barriers to ICT integration into public health practice

HIN India: Background

India was selected as the site for the first Health InterNetwork pilot project because the priority public health programs, together with the availability of resources and skills, provided an opportunity to test the process of establishing and using connectivity to support public health services. An explicit goal of HIN India was to proceed in partnership with local organizations, coordinated through the office of the WHO representative to India. This approach was intended to ensure relevance and sustainability of the efforts. Partners (nearly forty in total) included national and state government departments, local U.N. agency offices, nongovernmental organizations, research institutions, health service facilities, universities, and the private sector (Health InterNetwork, 2003).

India's health system is complex, and a wide range of agencies provides health care in the country. Primary and secondary health care is available through a network of government subcenters, primary health centers (PHC), community (rural) health centers, and district hospitals (Table 38.2). Tertiary health care is provided through government medical college hospitals and specialized institutions. Government health services are free or highly subsidized. There is a rapidly growing private health care sector alongside traditional systems of medicine, as well as major public health programs organized by international agencies (Gouri-Devi, Satishchandra, and Gururaj, 2003).

TABLE 38.2. INDIAN GOVERNMENT HEALTH SERVICE FACILITIES.

Type of Facility	Population Served per Facility	National Total
Government subcenter	10,000	150,000
Primary health center	30,000–50,000	23,000
Community health center	100,000	2,750
District hospitals	1.5–2 million	600

Source: Gourie-Devi, Satishchandra, and Gururaj, 2003.

Based on project objectives and in consultation with country partners, HIN India focused on selected primary health centers, community health centers, and medical colleges in the states of Karnataka and Orissa. The two states were chosen based on the contrast in health and socioeconomic status (Table 38.3), national government priorities, and other considerations, including the presence of identified project champions (National Family Health Survey, 2000; Registrar General and Census Commissioner, 2001; United Nations Development Programme, India, 2001). Concentrating on two national priority public health programs—tuberculosis and tobacco control—further focused the pilot. Project sites thus also included institutions for tuberculosis and tobacco research in Bombay, Chennai, Bangalore, and Delhi (Health InterNetwork, 2003).

During the pilot, HIN India established or expanded connectivity at the project sites to improve the flow of information and communication for public health services. From some perspectives, the digital divide was bridged when the computers and Internet connectivity were installed, but at the sites themselves, the divide became tangible when challenges to using the technology emerged. In the following sections, we highlight key lessons from the pilot for the main components of the HIN initiative: connectivity, content, capacity building, and policy.

Connectivity

The pilot project demonstrated that it is feasible and useful to provide computers and Internet connectivity even in remote settings. Six months were allocated to establish connectivity, but the process took over a year at some sites. The inadequacy of basic infrastructure and services such as reliable electricity supply and functioning telephone lines presents a considerable challenge to establishing, using, and maintaining the connections. An additional challenge in establishing connectivity was establishing new processes and linkages beyond the health sector, including with electricity and telephone service providers and government administrative departments.

At the pilot sites, HIN India assessments reviewed the physical settings as well as information and communication needs. A generic package was developed to

TABLE 38.3. KEY COMPARISONS BETWEEN KARNATAKA AND ORISSA, INDIA.

Selected Indicators	Karnataka	Orissa	India
Population (millions)	52.3	36.0	1002.1
Population: Percentage urban	34	14	27
Life expectancy at birth	63.6	54.8	59.4
Under-five mortality rate	69.8	104.4	94.9
Population served per government doctor	13,536	64,178	NA
Literacy rate (%)	67.04	63.61	65.38
Per capita net domestic product, 1999–2000	16,343 rupees (US$353)	9,162 rupees (US$198)	17,039 rupees (US$368)

Source: National Family Health Survey (2000); Registrar General and Census Commissioner, India (2001); United Nations Development Programme India (2001).

meet hardware and connectivity requirements, and computers and Internet connectivity were installed or upgraded. The installations consisted of electrical and telephone connections, a desktop computer, printer, scanner, and Internet service provider (ISP) subscription at an average cost of US$2,750 per site (Health InterNetwork, 2003).

HIN aims to move beyond the approach of using ICT for development to encouraging the development of ICT for use. Information and communication technologies are used in the context of different needs, cultures, and resource environments. Promoting models developed for high-income countries could stifle development or hinder deployment of more relevant and sustainable models for lower-income countries (Wade, 2002). In India, technologies such as wireless local loop, satellite connectivity, handheld computers, and solar-powered computer stations are available and should be considered as technology options. HIN India reviewed these options but was unable to fully test them in the context of a short-term pilot (Health InterNetwork, 2003).

Tools to improve the flow of health information were tested once connectivity was established. These included e-fax, geographic information systems, and e-mail consultation between PHC and specialist hospital doctors. Some participants experienced immediate benefits. For example, during the summer, a messenger from each PHC takes a daily heat stroke report to the district health office. Given the limited frequency of buses and time involved in travel, this could take the better part of a day. With e-fax, reporting is done almost instantaneously—as long as electricity and telephone lines are functioning.

Content

Computers intended for use by overburdened public health staff will remain unused unless there are real incentives, and access to relevant and timely content provides an important motivating factor. To ensure that useful content is available to health personnel, the Indian Council of Medical Research and HIN India, together with research institutes and government and nongovernmental public health agencies, established the National Health Information Collaboration (NHIC).

The NHIC objective is to facilitate electronic access to locally relevant content, including public health statistics, health program and policy documents, and national scientific publications such as the *Indian Journal of Tuberculosis*. Making content relevant for different audiences is a challenge for public health in general, and better access to existing content does not necessarily increase its utility (Health InterNetwork, 2003; Piotrow, Kincaid, Rimon, and Rinehart, 1997). For example, long technical reports may not be the most effective means of communicating with policymakers, and more content in local languages is essential for community health workers (Health InterNetwork, 2003).

Access to international scientific publications is also a challenge. In India, which is not part of the HINARI scheme (Aronson, 2002), one full-text journal article costs US$12 to obtain on-line or involves a wait of up to four months for a copy to be delivered by surface mail (Health InterNetwork, 2003). To improve access to full-text resources, HIN India facilitated a consortium for sharing journals on-line. In its first phase, a group of twenty-five medical colleges in Karnataka have access to the full text of 250 medical journals and an on-line system for requesting articles from the National Medical Library. The success in building this consortium is largely attributable to a local champion, the Rajiv Gandhi University of Health Sciences.

Capacity Building

Skills and resources to use and manage connectivity and content are essential to bridge the digital divide. HIN India provided training in computer and Internet skills to over three hundred public health staff and medical students by contracting with local training institutes in Karnataka and Orissa. Recognizing the value of computer literacy, one government official reported delaying staff promotions until they could demonstrate these skills.

Beyond the basics, effective use of computers and the Internet in public health work requires specific skills, and a concerted effort must be made to provide relevant training. For example, a goal of HIN India is to establish an electronic pipeline for public health data between field workers, health centers, and decision makers using tools such as handheld computers and geographic information systems. Electronic tools can facilitate the process, but for the data to be of value, the process should be well thought out, and the staff involved must have the requisite skills and knowledge.

Capacity is also required to manage the training of personnel and the sites themselves, including equipment maintenance and ISP costs. Through a local initiative, HIN Clubs were formed at two medical colleges in Orissa to address site management and resource issues. The clubs are managed by a committee of faculty and students and operate on a fee-for-access basis. In addition to generating resources, this strategy has promoted a strong sense of local involvement (Health InterNetwork, 2003).

HIN India demonstrated that local champions at all levels—from a PHC nurse who worked to excel at computer skills and was willing to teach other staff, to university faculty and government administrators who advocated for the project—can make a big difference. Identifying and supporting such champions is vital in promoting awareness and adoption at sites and for gaining support at higher levels.

Policy

Health information systems are critical for public health and require collaboration at all levels in order to function effectively, as was evident during the SARS outbreak (World Health Organization Multicentre Collaboration Network for SARS Diagnosis, 2003). Information and communication technologies can play a major role in strengthening these systems. As a public health officer in India pointed out, "Without computers and the Internet, we are fighting 21st century health problems with 19th century tools" (Health InterNetwork, 2003).

There are many barriers to ICT integration into public health practice, including cultural and political factors such as lack of coordination in ICT development activities, lack of incentives for cooperation across sectors and political levels, and entrenched bureaucratic procedures at all levels. HIN India illustrated the need for national and international coordination to optimize the use of limited ICT resources in health and related sectors. Strategies were explored at a workshop organized by WHO, the United Nations Development Programme, and the Orissa state government. A direct outcome was that a major donor reallocated resources in the state to provide training for health personnel instead of duplicating efforts to supply computer hardware (Health Internetwork, 2003).

HIN is founded on the principle of equitable access to information and tries to ensure that new technologies do not exacerbate sociocultural divides, so it is important to understand the settings and address gaps identified by local partners.

HIN India needs assessments showed that over 50 percent of private sector doctors had access to the Internet compared to fewer than 20 percent of government doctors. Researchers and administrators reported the highest access (75 percent). In all settings, professionals of higher rank are predominantly male (Health InterNetwork, 2003). HIN India site selection and equipment provision addressed these gaps to the extent feasible, for example, by providing computers and training to PHC and field staff and planning for computer installations in women's quarters at medical colleges. To further facilitate equitable use, open access software was used, and an effort was made to ensure that NHIC content is in the public domain.

HIN India was initially conceived as led by country partners with WHO India serving a coordinating role. However, the demands for efficiency in a short-term pilot project combined with the demands on location institutions made a strong leadership role by an agency like WHO almost inevitable. Finding the balance to ensure local ownership, control, and sustainability is an ongoing responsibility.

Conclusion

The Health InterNetwork shows that ICT can be adopted and used effectively in local and national public health practice. HIN India highlights challenges and opportunities in using information and communication technologies in public health, and further work should be done to evaluate impact and establish best practices. The analysis of HIN India suggests that an important foundation for bridging the digital divide is to ensure that connectivity, content, capacity building, and policy meet real needs. Information and communication technologies will not have a major impact without developing human resources and investing in basic infrastructure. For these technologies to truly benefit health, a foundation of effective public health practice is also essential. The Health InterNetwork shows that innovative partnerships can play a catalytic role in building concrete foundations for digital bridges in health.

Discussion Questions

1. If resources were limited, where would you focus your efforts—content, connectivity, or capacity building—and why?
2. Why is it important to undertake needs assessments before initiating a project? How should they be approached to get the best results?

3. What do you see as the advantages and disadvantages of working in partnerships with local partners?

4. What are the different dimensions of equitable access? What would be some additional means to ensure equitable access to information in the health sector? How could these be implemented?

5. If you were designing the next evaluation for this project, what would you identify as key areas to investigate further, and what would be the process?

References

Aronson, B. "WHO's Access to Research Initiative (HINARI)." *Health Information and Libraries Journal,* 2002, *19,* 164–165.

Digital Opportunities Task Force. "Addressing the Global Digital Divide. 2003." [http://www.dotforce.org].

Gourie-Devi, M., Satishchandra, P., and Gururaj, G. "Epilepsy Control Program in India: A District Model." *Epilepsia,* 2003, *44,* 58–62.

Health InterNetwork. "The Health InterNetwork India Pilot Project." 2003. [http://www.hin.org.in].

International Telecommunication Union. *World Telecommunications Development Report.* Geneva, Switzerland: International Telecommunication Union, 2002.

Kuruvilla, S., and others. "Digital Bridges Need Concrete Foundations: Lessons Learned from the Health InterNetwork, India." *British Medical Journal,* 2004, *328,* 1193–1196.

Lessig, L. *The Future of Ideas: The Faith of the Commons and a Connected World.* New York: Random House, 2001.

National Family Health Survey. "National Family Health Survey." 2000. [http://www.nfhsindia.org/data/india/statfind.pdf].

NUA. "How Many Online?". 2002. [http://www.nua.ie/surveys/how_many_online].

Piotrow, P. T., Kincaid, D. L., Rimon II, J. G., and Rinehart, W. *Health Communication, Lessons from Family Planning and Reproductive Health.* Westport, Conn.: Praeger, 1997.

Registrar General and Census Commissioner, India. *Census of India 2001.* 2001. [http://www.censusindia.net].

Smith, R. "Closing the Digital Divide." *British Medical Journal,* 2003, *326,* 238.

United Nations. *We the Peoples: The Role of the United Nations in the Twenty-First Century.* New York: United Nations, 2000. [http://www.un.org/millennium/sg/report].

United Nations Conference on Trade and Development. *ICT Development Indices.* New York: United Nations, 2003.

United Nations Development Programme India. "Inter-State Health Statistics." 2001. [http://www.undp.org.in/report/IDF98/idfthlth.htm].

United Nations Population Division. *World Population Prospects: The 2002 Revision.* New York: United Nations, 2002. [http://esa.un.org/unpp].

Wade, R. H. "Bridging the Digital Divide: New Route to Development or Dependency." *Global Governance,* 2002, *8,* 443–466.

World Health Organization Multicentre Collaboration Network for SARS Diagnosis. "A Multicentre Collaboration to Investigate the Cause of Severe Acute Respiratory Distress Syndrome." *Lancet,* 2003, *361,* 1730–1733.

NAME INDEX

A

Aarts, J., 71, 78
Abidi, S. S., 11, 18
Abrahamson, S., 204, 210
Alaoui, A., 118
Allen, A., 112, 117, 171, 172, 177
Alverson, D. C., 46, 212
Anderson, A., 214, 223
Anderson, J. G., 28, 29, 71, 78
Angus, R., 3
Annan, K., 337
Antezana, F., 139, 144
Antoniotti, N., 314
Applegate, L. M., 279, 283
Ariff, K. M., 11, 18
Armstrong, P., 30
Aronson, B., 338, 342, 345
Arora, N. K., 95, 99
Arrington, M. I., 181, 186
Athanasoulis, M. A., 244
Austin, C., 47, 57
Aydin, C. E., 23, 25, 28, 29

B

Baer, L., 130, 137
Bakke, B., 130, 137
Balas, E. A., 241, 242
Ball-Rokeach, S., 101, 104, 109
Bandura, A., 195, 202
Barker, G., 299, 303, 309
Barley, S. R., 25, 28
Baroudi, J. J., 23, 28
Barry, N., 203, 210
Bashshur, R. L., 143, 144
Bass, B., 59, 68
Becker, M. H., 194, 195, 202
Becklenberg, S., 313
Beffort, S., 46
Beinar, S., 299
Bell, C.K., 203, 211
Bell, J., 313, 315
Bereiter, C., 214, 223
Berenson, R., 315
Berland, G., 59, 68
bin Hashim, M. A., 11, 18
Blanchette, C. S., 277
Blignault, I., 203, 210
Block, P., 65, 68
Bloom, K. J., 301, 309
Blouin, A., 47, 49, 58
Boland, A., 3
Borchardt, S., 19, 28
Bower, D. J., 203, 210
Bradford, D., 59, 68
Braverman, H., 19, 28
Brenner, D. J., 19, 28
Bright, M. A., 328
Britton, B., 39, 45
Brody, B. L., 251, 260
Brown, N., 203, 210
Bruner, J., 95, 99
Buckwalter, K. C., 235, 240, 242
Buffett, W., 37
Burcham, C., 30
Buresh, K., 238, 243
Burgiss, S., 145, 312, 314, 316, 318
Burns, R., 300–301
Bylund, C. L., 235
Byrne, E., 47, 49, 58

C

Campbell, B. C., 23, 28
Cantor, J. A., 204, 210
Capella, J. N., 96, 99
Capewell, S., 3
Carlson, R., 151
Cary, M. A., 265, 267
Caudell, T. P., 212, 214, 223
Cegala, D., 119, 125

Cerda, G. M., 130, 137
Champion, E. W., 240, 242
Champion, H. R., 219, 223
Charlton, J., 4, 10
Chastain, A. R., 229, 231
Chen, R. J., 17, 18, 116
Chen, V., 105, 109, 117
Cheong, P. H., 101, 104, 109
Chetney, R., 39, 45
Chickering, A. W., 230, 231
Chinea, G. M., 193
Clemens, C. M., 111
Cohen, A., 59, 68
Collmann, J., 118
Conger, J., 59, 68
Connors, H. R., 225
Cook, N., 145
Counte, M. A., 23, 28
Cowain, T., 130, 137
Coye, M. J., 76, 78
Cronen, V. E., 96, 99
Cryer, L., 45
Cukor, P., 130, 137
Currell, R., 241, 242

D

Dahlin, M. P., 16, 18
Dalgarno, B., 213, 223
Darkins, A., 91, 265, 267
Davies, C., 6, 9
Davis, J., 111, 117
Davis, S. R., 284
Deitsch, S. E., 130, 137
Detmer, D. E., 69, 76, 78
Deuser, J., 39, 45
DeVany, M., 315
Diamond, C. C., 328
Dimmick, S. L., 145
Dooley, K., 71, 78
Doolittle, G. C., 111, 112, 117, 171, 172, 173, 174, 177
Dowling, A. F., Jr., 19, 28
Dzenowagis, J., 337

E

Ecken, B., 284
Eder, L. B., 19, 28
Edison, K. E., 310, 312, 313, 314, 315, 316, 317
Effertz, G., 46
Einstein, A., 127

Elford, R., 130, 137
Engelke, M., 39, 45
Engle, W. M., 16, 18
Erhmann, S., 230, 231
Erickson, R., 130, 137
Ermer, D., 130, 137

F

Fallows, D., 59, 68
Farris, N., 195, 202
Feeley, T. H., 319
Finch, T., 3, 80
Finnegan, J. R., 99
Fischer, P. J., 23, 28
Flanagan, J., 237, 238, 243
Fleming, D., 4, 10
Fletcher, K. A., 225
Fox, S., 59, 68
Freuh, S., 314
Frueh, B. C., 130, 137

G

Gagnon, M. P., 264, 267
Gamst, A. C., 251, 260
Gao, M., 47, 57
Gardner, S., 237, 242
Gerding, R., 30
Ghosh, G. J., 130, 137
Glaser, J., 266
Glick, S., 219, 224
Glik, D., 193, 195, 202
Glueckauf, R. L., 138, 144
Gold, W., 19, 29
Goldberg, A. S., 254, 260
Goldstein, J., 71, 72, 78
Goodwin, V., 59, 68
Gouldner, A. W., 96, 99
Gourie-Devi, M., 339, *340*, 345
Greenhalgh, T., 71, 79
Grigsby, B., 203, 210
Grigsby, J., 263, 267
Ground, A., 225
Gururaj, G., 339, *340*, 345
Gustafson, D. H., 328, 330, 335
Gustke, S., 314

H

Hailey, D., 47, 57
Hales, R. E., 130, 137
Hammack, D., 314

Harper, D. C., 138, 141, 142, 144
Harrington, P., 313
Harris, L. M., 91
Haycox, A., 3
Hayes, J., 171, 172, 177
Haytin, D. L., xviii, xxiii
Hebert, M. A., 47, 57
Heeks, R., 77, 78
Heinzelmann, P., 261
Henderson, J., 16, 18
Henry, D. J., 195, 202
Hersh, W., 130, 137, 241, 243
Hibbert, D., 3
Higgins, G. A., 219, 223
Hilty, D. M., 130, 137
Hirschheim, R. A., 19, 28
Holcomb, M., 299
Holsti, O. R., 120, 125
Honda, M., 195, 202
Horowitz, J. D., 240, 243
Hu, P. J., 265, 267
Hughes, A., 299, 301, 308
Humphreys, J., 59, 68

I

Ibbotson, T., 203, 210
Ibrahim, I., 11, 18
Issenberg, S. B., 213, 216, 223
Ives, B., 23, 28

J

Jacklin, P., 168, 169
Jacobs, J., 214, 223
Jeffords, J., 312, 313
Jennett, P. A., 47, 57
Jerant, A., 39, 45
Johnson, B., 19, 28
Johnson, R. L., 204, 210
Johnson-Mekota, J., 237, 243
Johnston, B., 39, 45
Jones, S. B., 219, 223

K

Kahn, G., 195, 202
Kaluzny, A. D., 19, 29
Kaplan, B, 71, 78
Karp, W. B., 139, 144
Katz, J., 19, 29, 203
Kaufman, A., 214, 223

Kautto, M., 30
Kay, A., 275
Kearsley, G., 204, 211
Kedar, I., 262, 267
Keeffe, J. E., 251, 260
Kellner-Rogers, M., 72, 79
Kemper, P., 235, 243
Kennedy, C., 203, 210
Kienzle, M., 238, 243
Kim, Y.-C., 104, 109, 110
Kincaid, D. L., 345
King, C., 279, 283
Kinnick, G. S., 151
Kinsella, A., 284, 286, 288
Kinzie, M., 195, 202
Kissinger, K., 19, 28
Kjerulff, K. A., 23, 28
Kling, B., 313
Kling, R., 19, 28
Kobb, R., 91, 98, 99
Kohlmeier, L., 195, 202
Korpman, R. A., 19, 29
Kouroubali, A., 69
Kreps, G., 91, 95, 99, 328, 329, 333, 335
Krupinski, E., 130, 137, 299
Kunkler, J. H., 172, 177
Kunkler, T., 246, 247, 250
Kvedar, J., 261

L

Lamoureux, E. L., 251, 260
Larsen, K.R.T., 72, 79
Leape, L. L., 152, 159
Lee, J., 301
Lee, K., 284
Lehman, S., 30
Lenhart, A., 244, 250
Lessig, L., 338, 345
Lester, J. E., 247, 250
Levine, B. A., 118
Lewis, P., 39, 45
Lewis, R., 241, 242
Liederman, E. M., 244
Lighter, D., 30
Lin, W. Y., 11, 18
Lincoln, T. L., 19, 29
Lindberg, D.A.B., 19, 29
Lindsey, J., 30
Liu Sheng, O. R., 265, 267
Logan, R. A., 19, 28
Lopez, A. D., 4, 10

Lopez, A. M., 299
Lorenzi, N. M., 72, 79
Lozanoff, S., 214, 223
Lucas, H., Jr., 23, 29
Lundsgaarde, H. P., 23, 28

M

Mahmud, K., 39, 45
Maheu, M. M., 187
Mair, F., 3, 80, 87, 171, 172, 177, 241, 243
Makoul, G., 95, 99
Manchanda, M., 130, 137
Manning, T., 19, 29
Markus, M. L., 19, 29
Matei, S., 102, 104, 109, 110
May, C., 3, 5, 6, 10, 69, 80, 81, 84, 87, 171, 172, 177
Mazzuca, K., 195, 202
McClosky Armstrong, T., 312, 314, 316, 318
McCormick, A., 4, 10
McElroy, J., 303, 309
McGaghie, W. C., 213, 223
McGlynn, E. A., 262, 267
McLaren, P. M., 130, 137
McLuhan, M., xvii, xxiii
McMenamin, J. P., 187
McNamara, C., xix, xxiii
McNeely, R. A., 299, 301, 309
McNeill, K. M., 303, 309
Mekhjian, H., 120, 125
Mendenhall, J., 195, 202
Mendz, M., 195, 202
Mercer, Z., 195, 202
Meyer, M. A., 98, 99
Miller, E. A., 130, 137
Miller, M., 195, 202
Miller, T. W., 130, 137
Mitchell, J., 130, 137
Morse, J., 235
Mort, M., 80, 84, 87
Moushui, M., 30
Muha, C., 328
Mun, S. K., 118
Mundy, D., 78
Murray, C.J.L., 4, 10
Murtaugh, C. M., 235, 243
Musharbash, S., 149
Myerson, A., 193

N

Nelson, E., 129
Neoh, K. H., 11, 18
Nesbitt, T., 39, 45, 130, 137, 203
Neumann, C., 47, 49, 58
Neustadtl, A., 118
Niederpruem, M., 30
Noll, D. T., 277
Norris, D., 247, 250

O

O'Connor, J., 3
Olson, M. H., 23, 28
Orphanoudakis, S., 69
Osborne, J. M., 319
Ostwald, M, 116, 117
Ovitt, T. W., 303, 309

P

Packer, C. L., 19, 29
Patterson, J., 59
Paul, N., 130, 137
Pearce, W. B., 116, 117
Pearson, S., 240, 243
Peel, V., 71, 78
Pellegrino, E., 77, 79
Pellissier, S., 47, 49, 58
Perocchia, R., 328, 331, 335
Pettigrew, A. M., 72, 79
Piotrow, P. T., 342, 345
Pleasant, A., 337
Plsek, P. E., 71, 78, 79, 95, 96
Pollard, T. L., 251, 260
Prady, S. L., 247, 250
Preston, A., 46
Pullara, F., 46, 57

R

Rahman, A., 39, 45
Rains, D., 39, 45
Ramstad, J., 315
Rapkin, B., 331, 335
Ray, A., 235
Reid, M., 203, 210
Rendon, M., 130, 137
Rice, R. E., 19, 25, 27, 28, 29
Rich, M. W., 240, 243
Rimon, J. G., II, 342, 345
Rinehart, W., 342, 345

Rizzo, D. M., 319
Roberts, C., 3
Robinson, J. D., 118
Robinson, T. N., 195, 202
Roch-Levecq, A., 251, 260
Rogers, E. M., 227, 231, 265, 267
Rognehaugh, R., 19, 29
Rosten, L., 89
Roth, W., 316
Roupe, M., 39, 45
Ryan, P., 91, 98, 99

S

Saiki, S. M., Jr., 212
Salazar, A., 78
Salloway, J. C., 23, 28
Salovey, P., 328, 332, 335
Sanders, J., 143, 144, 300
Santos, A. B., 130, 137
Satava, R. M., 219, 223
Satishchandra, P., 339, *340*, 345
Sauls, E., 39, 45
Scardamalia, M, 214, 223
Scheideman-Miller, C., 268
Schiffman, J. S., 251, 260
Schmidt, M., 49, 58
Schorling, J., 195, 202
Schulman, G., 59
Schultz, R. L., 23, 29
Sechrest, R. C., 195, 202
Shannon, G., 143, 144
Shaw, G. B., 297
Shaw, S. F., 193
Shea, S, 39, 45
Shyama, Kuruvilla, 337
Siegel, M., 195, 202
Sienkiewicz, J. I., 284, 288
Simon, H. A., 213, 223
Simpson, J. A., 251, 260
Sittig, D. F., 71, 79
Skiba, D., 195, 202
Skinner, B. F., 179
Slater, S., 39, 45
Slevin, D. P., 23, 29
Small, S. D., 219, 224
Smith, D. B., 19, 29
Smith, R., 338, 345
Sousa, K. H., 39, 45
Spaulding, A., 171
Spaulding, R., 171
Specht, J., 237, 243
Sprang, R., 312, 314, 316, 318
Stacey, R. D., 91, 96, 100

Starren, J., 39, 45
Steele, D. J., 23, 28
Stewart, S., 240, 243
Still, A., 45
Stoupa, R., 195, 202
Stratmann, W. C., 23, 28
Street, R. L., Jr., 19, 29
Stryker, S., 25, 29
Stumpf, S. H., 17, 18
Suhaimi, M., 11
Suleiman, A. B., 11, 18
Sweeney, M. A., 195, 202
Sweeney, N. M., 195, 202
Sypher, B. D., xviii, xxiii, 111

T

Tahir, M., 11
Takabayashi, K., 195, 202
Tang, R. A., 251, 260
Teng, C. L., 11, 18
Thomas, B., 315, 317
Thune, J., 315
Tohme, W. G., 118
Toma, C. S., 203, 211
Tomita, M., 195, 202
Tracy, J., 310, 312, 313, 314, 316, 317, 318
Tran, T. P., 203
Tsiknakis, M., 69
Tucker, C., 151
Turisco, F., 47, 49, 58
Turner, J. W., 118, 119, 126
Twain, M., 233

U

Urquhart, C., 241, 242

V

Vandenbroek, A. J., 240, 243
Vierhout, W.P.M., 161, 170
Vigil, K. Y., 30
Viswanath, K., 99
Vlek, J.F.M., 161, 170
Vuturo, A. F., 301, 309
Vygotsky, L., 95, 100

W

Wade, R. H., 337, 338, 341, 345
Wainwright, P., 241, 242
Wakefield, B., 235, 237, 238, 243

Walden, C., 45
Walker, J., 203, 211
Wallace, P., 81, 87, 160, 166, 168, 170
Warnecke, P., 251, 260
Warren, J., 225
Watcher, G., 16, 18
Waters, B., 313–314, 316
Watson, J. P., 130, 137
Wayne, J., 1
Weaver, C, 225
Webb, W., 312
Wei, C., 265, 267
Weick, K., 95, 100
Weinstein, R. S., 299, 301, 303, 309
Weiss, R., 151, 159
Wheatley, M. J., 72, 79
Wheeler, L., 39, 45
Wheeler, T., 139, 144
Whetton, S., 203, 211
Whitten, P., 171, 172, 177, 241, 243, 263, 267, 284
Whittington, J., 59, 68
Wilbright, W., 328, 332, 336
Wilkin, H. A., 101, 104, 109
Williams, P. D., 176, 177
Williams, T., 80, 84, 87
Wilmsen, P, 45
Wilson, T., 78, 79
Wilver, D., 39, 45
Winchester, J. F., 118
Winn, W. D., 213, 224
Wolpe, P. R., 219, 224
Wonderlich, S., 130, 137
Wong, G., 251
Wootton, R., 11
Wray, N., 240, 243
Wu, P., 129, 137

Y

Yadav, H., 11, 18
Yamamoto, L. G., 203, 211
Young, M.A.C., 244
Young, S., 39, 45
Yusof, K., 11, 18
Yusoff, Z., 11, 18

Z

Zalunardo, R. R., 17, 18
Zeitz, H. J., 204, 211
Zimmerman, E. M., 244
Ziv, A., 219, 224

SUBJECT INDEX

A

Academic medical centers, involvement of, complexity resulting from, 278, 306
Access committee, 320
Access, Internet, 338, *339*
Access to care, addressing, 262, 264–265, 319–326
Access to information, gap in. *See* Digital divide
Accreditation, 204, 210
Achievement stage, 300
Activity rates/usage. *See* Utilization
Adaptability, 293
Adaptations, network, example of, *294–295*
Adaptive systems, understanding, 96
Administrative challenges, 271–272
Adoption: of Internet-based specialty consultations, 261–267; of Internet-delivered health education system, 331
Adoption strategies, 263–266, 267
Adult education research, 204
Advanced site coordinators and

technical staff, specific training for, 209–210
Advisory board, appointing, reasons for, 66
Advisory committee, external, use of, 220
Advisory council, voluntary, 302
Affordability factor, 290–291
Age-related macular degeneration (ARMD), serving patients with, 251–260
American Cancer Society web site, 181, 185
American Medical Association, 204
American Psychiatric Association, 129, 133, 137
American TeleCare, 40, 42, 43
American Telemedicine Association (ATA), 314, 315
Anderson Schools of Management, University of New Mexico, 46
Annenberg School for Communication, University of Southern California, 102
Applications: clearinghouse for, 304; prominence of, making

technology transparent for, 289–296
Arizona Department of Corrections, 308
Arizona Department of Health Services, 307, 308
Arizona Health Sciences Center, 301, 302, 306, 307
Arizona Rural Telemedicine Network, 301–302
Arizona state legislature, 299–300, 302
Arizona Telemedicine Council, 302, 303
Arizona Telemedicine Program, policy issues in, addressing, 299–308
Artificial intelligence (AI), 215
Association of Telemedicine Service Providers (ATSP), 315
Audits, security, 281–282
Authoritative decision making, 228
Automated medication administration system, using, 151–158
Avera McKennan Hospital, 315
Avera McKennan Telehealth Network, 315

B

Balanced Budget Act of 1997
(BBA), 310–312, 313
Bar code labeling software, 155
Bar Code Medication Administra-
tion (BCMA) program, 151–158
Barriers to access, addressing, for
the uninsured, 319–326
Benefits Improvement and Protec-
tion Act of 2000 (BIPA),
312–314, 317
Best practices: educational, assess-
ing, 229–230; guidelines for,
statewide adoption of, 304, 306
Bilingual education, 194, 195, 198,
331
Black audience, low-income, com-
puter-based training for, 331
Blaster computing plague, 278
BMJ, 338
Books, health care, role of, 183, 184
Breast cancer patients, low-income,
providing cancer information
to, 330–331
Bridging capacity, 292
Bridging the digital divide, strategies for, in developing nations,
337–344
Brigham and Women's Hospital,
261
Britain. *See* United Kingdom
Broadening rollout, 249
Bureaucratic and entrepreneurial
management model, choosing
between, 60–62
Business case: considering a, 47–49;
for prison telehealth program,
49–57
Buy-in: ensuring, need for, 34;
nurse, addressing, 39–44;
regional, 325

C

California Endowment, 206
California Senate Bill 1386, 278
California Telehealth and Telemedicine Center (CTTC), 206, 210
Cancer: information on, providing,
328–334; managing symptoms
of, patient-provider dialogue for,
91–99; prostate, survivors of,

narratives by, 181–185; and vul-
nerable populations, 333–334
Cancer Information Service (CIS),
collaboration of, on digital
divide pilot projects, 328–334
CancerInfoNet program, 331
Capacity building, for bridging the
digital divide, 338, 342–343
Capitated payment systems, 284
Cardiac Connection, 40–41
Care planning activity, 227
Caregiver satisfaction, 112–115,
116, 142
Caregiver support, 116, 175–176,
241
Case management model of care,
42–43
Case-based co-management model
of care, 47
Case-based learning approach, 222
CD-ROM development, 195–197
CD-ROM revision, 197–198, *199*,
200
Center for Telehealth, University
of New Mexico, 46
Center for Telemedicine Law
(CTL), 313, 314, 315, 316
Centers for Medicare and Medicaid
Services (CMS), 311, 312, 313,
315, 316
Centralized administration, 280
Cerner Corporation, 225
Champions, role of: in bridging the
digital divide, 343; in home telehealth programs, 41, 42, 44; for
reimbursement policy change,
312, 315; in telemedicine programs, 34; in telerehabilitation
service, 269–270
Change: key factors influencing,
72–75; understanding, 71, 72
Change agents: influencing, 77;
promotion efforts of, extent of,
229–230
Change management: and self-
organization, 77–78; in teleconsulting network project, 16; in
teledermatology service, 84–85
Charging fees, Web messaging
service and, 246
CHESS program, 330–331
Chief operations officer (COO),
appointing, reason for, 66

Children: with depression, teletherapy for, determining effectiveness of, 129–136; with
disabilities, serving, in rural
area, 138–144; with orthopedic
conditions and burns, telemedicine program for, 30–35
Children and Families First Program, 102
Choctaw Memorial Hospital, 268
Chronic obstructive pulmonary disease (COPD), serving patients
with, 3–9
Chronic wound assessments, using
telehealth for, with elderly veterans, 236–236
CIS Network, 330
CIS Partnership Program, 328–
329
CIS Research Program, 329
Client Assessment course, 226–227
Clinic operations, developing standards for, 304, 306
Clinical challenges, 271
Clinical information system (CIS),
live-application, project using,
225–230
Clinical privileges, applying for, 255
Clinical Techniques course,
226–227
Clinical training, virtual, project
involving, 225–230
Code of conduct for on-line
forums, 191
Collaboration: in bridging the digital divide, 343; to conduct cost
analysis, 174, 175; on digital
divide pilot projects, 328, 330,
331, 332; instilling, in training
curriculum, 204, 205; for medication error reduction, 154–
155; and preserving patient-
provider relationship, 264; in
providing telehealth services,
241; with vendors for technology design, 286; in virtual reality distance learning project,
214, 216–217, 222; in Web-
based directory service for uninsured, 325
Collective decision making, 228
Colmery-O'Neil VAMC, 151,
156–157

Commencement stage, 300, 301–303

Commitment, 35, 67

Committee on the Quality of Health Care in America, 98

Communication: channels of, 228–229; context of, impact of, 104, 116, 118, 125; open, importance of, 67; poor levels of, frustration with, effect of, 160

Communication action context, 104

Communication behaviors, analysis of, 123–124

Communication infrastructure approach, 104–105

Communication infrastructure, diagnosing, to reach target audiences, 101–109

Community Access Program (CAP), 320

Community and Technology Program, University of Southern California, 102

Community collaborations, 325, 331, 332

Community Health Network (CHN), 320, *321*

Community needs and organizational goals, linking technology solutions to, 295–296

Complex adaptive systems, 71, 77, 95, 96

Complexity: involving academic medical centers, 278, 306; in medical records information system implementation, 26; in teledermatology service, 86; of telemedicine systems, 203; in virtual outreach project, 162

Complexity theory, 71–72

Computer-assisted education, aspects of, 195

Computer-based training for low-income populations, 330–333

Computerized Health Education and Support System (CHESS) program, 330–331

Computerized medical records information system, implementing: integration of, with telemedicine system, 252; social aspects of, 19–27

Computerized patient record, 93, *97*

Computing environment, understanding, 280, 281

Concept development, 220

Confidentiality of medical records, 254

Conflict, among management team members, 64–65

Congestive heart failure patients: follow-up care for, after hospital discharge, use of telehealth for, 239–240; newly diagnosed, preventing hospitalizations of, designing technology for, 285–287

Congressional Budget Office (CBO), 316

Connectivity: in bridging the digital divide, 338, 340–341; statewide, 304, *305*; and transparency, 290–291, 295

Consent: in crisis telehealth program, 146; in home telehealth program, 40; for low-vision telemedicine service, 251, 254–255; for teletherapy treating childhood depression, 134

Consolidated Appropriations Act 2001, 317

Consultations: joint, 160–161, 162, 163–165; on-line, charging and reimbursement for, 246, 247; and reporting, issue of, 57; triadic, 81. *See also* Teleconsultations

Consumer challenges, 272

Consumer satisfaction, 331

Content: of health information, and bridging the digital divide, 338, 342; of multimedia educational program, 201; of on-line magazine articles, 189–190

Content categorization, in Web-based messaging service, 245

Continual risk assessment and management, 279

Continuing education, new paradigms for, 203–210

Continuing medical education (CME) research and accreditation, 204

Contracts, writing, 306

Conversation topics during

provider-patient interactions, 120, *121*

Coordinating symptom management through dialogue, 92–97

Coordinators: network, 12, 15–16; project, 219; site, 140, 209–210

Cost analysis: of prison telehealth program, 55, *56*; of SEEDS project, 229; of tele-oncology practice, 172–176

Cost constraints, in virtual outreach project, 165

Cost figures, obtaining, for cost analysis, 174

Cost management strategy: crisis telehealth as, 145–149; Web site volunteers as, 188–189

Cost reduction: in tele-oncology, 174–175, 176; through computer-assisted education, 195

Cost savings: of crisis telehealth program, 147, 148, 149; data on, importance of, in business cases, 49; of home telehealth programs, 39, 98; of prison telehealth program, 55, *56*; of rural teleconsulting for disabled children, 142; of telerehabilitation, 272–273; of virtual outreach project, 166, 167

Cost-benefit analysis: of Internet-based specialty consultations, 262, 263; of tele-oncology, developing protocol for, 176

Cost-effectiveness: of Internet-based specialty consultations, 262, 263; of Shriners telemedicine program, 35

Costs: of bridging the digital divide, 341; of connection linkages, 303; of crisis telehealth program, 148; of elder care telehealth services, 237; health care, 4, 111, 319; of home telecare trial project, 5; of Internet-based specialty consultations, 263; of network transmission, 291; of prison telehealth program, 50, 52, *53*; of teleconsulting network project, 12, 16; of telehealth wound assessments, 237; of tele-oncology practice, 173, 174, 175; of virtual

Costs (*continued*)
outreach project, 166; of Web
site development and operation,
188; of Web-based directory
service, 323
Covering the Uninsured, 319, 327
Crete, Greece, health care information system in, 69–78
Crisis situations, patient perspective
on, 122
Crisis telehealth program, as cost
management strategy, 145–149
Critical thinking seminars, 226–227
Curriculum, 205–206
Curriculum evaluation, 207–209
Customization of equipment,
286–287
Customized learning scenarios,
educator-developed, creating,
221
Cyberspace, telehealth in, 212–222

D

Dana-Farber/Partners Cancer
Care, 261
Deaconess Hospital, Montana, 314
Decision makers, model for per-
suading, and finding new part-
ners, 46–57
Decision making: innovation, 228;
for sustainable security, 281
Defense-in-depth security, 278–
279
Department of Psychology, Yale
University, 332
Departmental interactions, 25
Depressed children, teletherapy for,
determining effectiveness of,
129–136
Dermatology patients, serving,
81–87
Des Moines VAMC, 241
Design, job, 25
Designing technology, vendor-
provider partnership for,
284–288
Detroit, underserved populations in,
providing cancer information
to, 330–331
Developing countries, bridging the
digital divide in, strategies for,
337–344

*Diagnostic and Statistical Manual of
Mental Disorders* (DSM-IV), 133,
135
Dialogue, research as, 91–99
Diffusion of innovation framework,
227
Digital divide: addressing, tech-
nologies for, with vulnerable
populations, 328–334; bridging,
strategies for, in developing
countries, 337–344
Digital Divide Pilot Projects
(DDPPs), 328–334
Digital Opportunities Task Force,
337, 345
Directory service, Web-based, creat-
ing, for the uninsured, 320–326
Disabled children, serving, in rural
area, 138–144
Disclaimers, 191
Discussion forums, on-line, 190–191
Disease management programs,
incorporating home telehealth
into, 39–44
Distance learning, use of virtual
reality for, 212–222
Diversifying revenue sources, 272
Doctors/physicians. *See Provider
entries*
Documentation, 7, 43, 284
Dot-com bubble, 337
Downtime, computer, 277, 278

E

Early start-up stage, 300, 303–306
East Carolina University, 314
Economic analysis. *See* Cost analysis
Economic level affecting adoption,
263–264
Economies of scale, achieving, 293
Education and training. *See specific
type*
Educational best practices, assess-
ing, 229–230
Educational intervention program,
multimedia, for gestational
diabetes patients, 193–201
Educational models, 204
Educational strategy, innovative,
SEEDS project as, 225–230
Educator-developed customized
learning scenarios, creating, 221

Efficacy trials, issues facing, 136
Elder care: telehealth communica-
tion in, 235–242; vendor-
provider partnership
for providing, 284–288
E-mail, limitations of, 245, 246
E-mail newsletter, 191
Emergency rooms, 319
Employee attitudes, toward medical
records information system,
23–24
Employee perceptions, 21–23
Employer-based payment, 264
Empowered Manager, The (Block), 65
Encryption, 245
End-of-life care, role of telehospice
in, 111–116
End-stage renal disease (ESRD)
management, patient-provider
interactions in, 119–125
English teledermatology service,
81–87
Enrollment, recruiting. *See* Recruit-
ment
Enterprise-wide outcomes knowledge base, 93, *97*
Entrepreneurial and bureaucratic
management model, choosing
between, 60–62
Environment, external, and health
care information system implementation, 75
Equipment installation. *See* Equipment setup and installation
Equipment location, flexibility in,
292
Equipment maintenance and troubleshooting, training in, 206
Equipment problems. *See* Technical
problems
Equipment setup and installation:
in elder care telehealth service,
240; in home telecare trial project, 7, 8; in home telehealth
program, 44; in teleconsulting
network project, 12, *13*; in telerehabilitation service, 270; for
teletherapy treating childhood
depression, 134; for transparency, 292; in virtual outreach
project, 167
Equipment upgrades, 8, 84, 114,
229, 238

Equipment usability, working with vendor for, 286–387

Equipment, using, training for. *See* Technical training

Erie County Medical Center, 319, 327

Errors, medication, reducing, using point-of-care for, 151–158

E-Start-Up Management Team, leadership issues facing, 59–68

Ethical imperative, 219

Ethical responsibility, 116

Ethnic and racial diversity, attention to, 198, 330–331

Ethnically targeted local media, 101, 105, 106, 108

Evaluation system, ubiquitous, 306

Evidence-based service, stressing, 84

Expenditures. *See* Costs

Experiential simulations, 221

External advisory committee, use of, 220

External environment, and health care information system implementation, 75

F

Facility planning, role of, in interoperability, 304

Family Medicine Research Institute, 324, 327

Fear of technology, addressing, 272

Federal Communication Commission Universal Service program, 291

Fee split, 310, 311, 313

Feedback loop, understanding, 95, 96

Field testing, 220

Firewalls, 245, 280

Firing a team member, controversy over, 64–65

First 5 LA (formerly Proposition 10), 102, 105, 108

FirstGov, 251, 260

Flashlight Program Current Student Inventory, 229–230

Flatland systems, 214–216, 221

Fletcher Allen Health Care, 313

Flexibility in transmission and location, 292

Focused project, creating, challenge of, 322–323

Follow-up appointments, offering, in virtual outreach project, 166

Follow-up care, use of telehealth for, with elderly veterans, 239–240

Fortune 100 companies, 264

Foundation for Research and Technology-Hellas (FORTH), 69, 73

Foundations in Nursing course, 226

From Promise to Practice—Improving Life in the South through Telemedicine (Southern Governor's Association), 313

Full-text resources, access to, improving, 342

Funding lines, understanding, for cost analysis, 174

Funding, securing: in crisis telehealth program, 148; for digital divide pilot projects, 328, 330; for e-start-up organization, 61; for home telecare trial, 5, 9; for home telehealth program design, 285; for low-vision telemedicine service, 251; for multimedia education program, 197, 201; for network connectivity, 290–291; for SEEDS project, 225; for statewide telemedicine program, 301; for teleconsulting network, 12; for teledermatology service, 82; for telemedicine training program, 206; for telerehabilitation service, 269, 271, 272; for the uninsured, need for, 319; for virtual outreach project, 161; for Web-based directory service, 320, 326

G

Gatekeeper role, 264

Gender and the digital divide, 344

General consultation protocol (GCP), developing, 140

Georgetown University Medical Center, 119

Gestational diabetes patients, multimedia education for, 193–201

Goal clarification, importance of, 67

Goals, organizational, and community needs, linking technology solutions to, 295–296

Good Samaritan Health System, Nebraska, 314

Government policy, influence of, 76

Grant funding: of crisis telehealth program, 148; federal, influx of, 310; of home telecare trial project, 3, 5, 9; of low-vision telemedicine service, 251, 258; for network connectivity, 290–291; of telemedicine training, 206; of telerehabilitation service, 269, 271; of Web-based directory service, 320

Grant writing, 306

Greece, health care information system in, 69–78

Greek Ministry of Health, 69, 75, 76

Greek primary care, 70–71

Guidelines, developing: for home telehealth program, 43; for low-vision telemedicine service, 255, *256–257*; for rural teleconsulting with disabled children, 140; for statewide telemedicine program, 304, 306; for Web messaging service, 247

H

Hardware and software, using, training for. *See* Technical training

Harlem-based program, providing cancer information through, 331

Harris Interactive, 244, 245, 250

Harry S. Truman Memorial Veterans Hospital, 312

Harvard Medical School affiliation, 261, 262

Head Start program, 332–333

Health belief model, concepts from, basing multimedia program on, 194–195

Health Care Financing Administration (HCFA). *See* Centers for Medicare and Medicaid Services (CMS)

Health care inequities, addressing, 262–263

Health care information sources, connecting to, studying, 104–109

Health care information system (HCIS), 69–78

Health disparities, efforts to narrow, 334

Health education and training, using virtual reality for, 212–222

Health, Education, Labor and Pensions Committee, 313

Health improvement, outcomes research and, primary elements of, 95

Health information, access to, gap in. *See* Digital divide

Health information dissemination, investment in, need for, 329

Health information systems, importance of, 343

Health Insurance Portability and Accountability Act of 1996 (HIPAA), 227, 246, 254, 278

Health InterNetwork Access to Research Initiative (HINARI), 338, 342

Health InterNetwork (HIN), 337, 338, 339, 340, 341, 342, 343, 344, 345

Health InterNetwork India (HIN India), 338–344

Health Resources Administration, U.S. Department of Health and Human Services, 320, 326

HealthforAll of Western New York Incorporated, 322, 323, 325, 326

Healthy Beginnings program, 193–201

Healthy People 2010 report, 334

Hierarchical management systems, altering, need for, 63

HIN clubs, 343

Hiring a team member, controversy over, 65

Hispanic audience: computer-based training for, on accessing on-line cancer information, 331; multimedia education intervention aimed at, 194–201; reaching,

diagnosing communication infrastructure for, 101–109

Home Nursing Agency (HNA), 285–288

Home telecare trial project, problems implementing, 3–9

Home telehealth design, vendor-provider partnership for, 284–288

Home telehealth disease management program, 39–44

Home telehealth, for elder care, 235–242

Homogeneous computing infrastructure, 280

Hospice patients, serving, 111–116

HYGEIAnet initiative, 69, *70*, 71, 75

I

Impact measures, need for, for Web site assessment, 323–324

Implementation plans, issue of, 76

India, bridging the digital divide in, efforts at, 338–344

Indian Council of Medical Research, 342

Indian government health system, 339, *340*

Indian Journal of Tuberculosis, 342

Individual level affecting adoption, 266

Individuals with Disabilities Education Act, 268

Inequities in health care, addressing, 262–263

Information: amount and rate of, patient control over, 195; cancer, providing relevant, 328–334; exchange in, increase in, 25; sources of, reflected in prostate cancer survivors' illness narratives, 181–185

Information and referral agencies (I&Rs), challenge faced from, 325

Information flow: improving, to bridge the digital divide, 341; and self-organization, 72, 73

Information systems: benefits of,, 71; clinical, live-application,

project using, 225–230; future potential of, 143; health care, 69–78; medical records, 19–27, 252; positive and negative aspects of, 19, 22–23; security of, sustainable, developing and maintaining, 277–282

Information Technology in Health-care course, 227

Informational dimension, patient satisfaction with, 119–120

Ingress and egress points, controls for, 280

In-house discussion forums, 190–191

Innovation: adoption of, enhancing, 228; diffusion of, framework for, 227

Innovation decision making, 228

Innovative educational strategy, SEEDS project as, 225–230

Institute of Computer Science, 69

Institute of Medicine, 98, 99, 151, 245, 250, 264, 267, 333, 335

Institute on Aging, 284, 288

Institutional level affecting adoption, 265–266

Intangible components, in tele-oncology, 175–176

Integration: of applications, evidence of, 293; need for, 34, 143, 158, 220, 264, 343; for virus and vulnerability management, 282

INTEGRIS Health telerehab program, 269, 270–274

Intellectual property, issues with, 222, 228

Interdisciplinary approach, 222

Intermittent funding source, 272

Internal Review Board (IRB), involvement of, 131, 134

International Telecommunications Union, 337, 338, *339*, 345

Internet access, 338, *339*

Internet access to information, gap in. *See* Digital divide

Internet connection patterns, in Hispanic community, 106–107, 108

Internet protocol (IP) technology, initiating, 292, 293

Internet, role of, in prostate cancer survivors' illness narratives, 181, 182, 184–185

Internet search engine, managing start-up of, leadership issues in, 59–68

Internet2, 212–213, 214, 222

Internet-based specialty consultations, adoption of, 261–267

Internet-delivered cancer information, providing access to, for underserved populations, 328–334

Interoperability, statewide, promotion of, 304, 306

Interpersonal symptom management system model, 97

Investments in technology, planning for, issue of, 47

Iowa: serving children with disabilities in, 138–144; serving the elderly in, 236–242

Iowa City Veterans Affairs Medical Center (VAMC), telehealth program for elder care at, 236–242

Iowa Communication Network, 139, 143–144

Iowa Institute for Social Services, 140

J

Job design, 25

Joint consultations: real-time, issues with, 160–161; virtual, 161, 162, 163–165

Joint Legislative Budget Committee, 306–307

Just-in-time training, 219

K

Kansas: telehospice program in, 112–116; tele-oncology project in, 171–176

Kansas University Medical Center (KUMC). See University of Kansas Medical Center (KUMC)

Karnataka, India, 340, *341*

Kendallwood Telehospice program, 112–116

Kickback statute, 311

Knowledge, attitudes, and behaviors, effect of, on adoption, 263

Knowledge management, 280

Knowledge, understanding, 95–96

L

Late start-up stage, 300

Leaders: selection of, 41; trust in, issue of, 64, 65, 66; types of, 63

Leadership issues: facing e-start-up management team, 59–68; in health care information system implementation, 73–74, 77

Leadership style, micromanagement, problems with, 62–64

Learning environment, in telemedicine training program, 204–205

Learning time, need for, 24–25, 74

Legislative funding, 285, 301

Legislative reimbursement policies, 310–318

Library of simulations, creating, need for, 221

Listserv, nationwide telehealth, 317

Literacy issues, 197, 201

Location flexibility, 292

Long-term sustainability, ensuring, 270, 272, 293

Los Angeles County Children's Planning Council, 102, 110

Los Angeles County Commission for Healthy Families and Children, 102, 105

Los Angeles County Department of Health, 102, 110

Louisiana State University Medical School, 332

Low-income populations, computer-based training for, 330–333

Low-literacy User Cancer Information Interface (LUCI), 332

Low-vision telemedicine service, process of implementing, 251–260

M

Malaysia, teleconsulting network project in, 11–17

Malaysian Ministry of Health, 12

Managed care, roles in, 264

Management team: e-start-up, leadership issues facing, 59–68; for virtual reality project, 219, 220

Managing: health care information system implementation, 76; statewide telemedicine program, 306–307; teledermatology service, 84–85. *See also specific types of management*

Manhattan Research, 245, 250

Manual medication administration systems, problems with, 152

Mapquest Web site, 322

Markle Foundation, 330

Marquette General Health System (MGHS), efforts in transparency at, 290–296

Marshfield Clinic, Wisconsin, 314

Massachusetts General Hospital, 261

Measures of success, needing, for Web site assessment, 323–324

Mechanistic systems, understanding, 96

Media connections, understanding, approach to, 104, 105–109

Mediated communication, effect of, 114, 116, 118

Medicaid reimbursement, 258, 271

Medical mistake rate, 151

Medical records information system: implementing, social aspects of, 19–27; integration of, with telemedicine system, 252

Medical student satisfaction, 217

Medical training, virtual, project involving, 212–222

Medicare reimbursement: changing policies on, 310–318; documentation requirements of, 284; for low-vision telemedicine service, 252, 260; for telerehabilitation service, 271–272

Medicare Reimbursement for Telehealth: An Assessment of Telehealth Encounters (Tracy, McClosky Armstrong, Sprang, and Burgiss), 316

Medication administration system, automated, using, 151–158

Memorial Sloan-Kettering Cancer Center, 331

Mental health Web site, construction and management of, 187–191

Messaging service, Web-based, provider-patient, systemwide rollout of, 244–250

Metamorphosis project, 102–109

Michigan, telehealth program in, working towards transparency, 289–296

Micromanagement, problems with, 62–64

Microsoft, 277, 278

Millennium Action Plan, 337

Ministry of Health, Malaysia, 16, 17

Mobile crisis team (MCT), 145, 146, 147, 149

Model of care, selection of, for home telehealth program, 42–43

Morbidity and mortality rates, 333

Multidisciplinary approach: for medication error reduction, 154–155; for telemedicine training program, 204–205; in telerehabilitation, 268–274

Multigenerational approach, 332

Multimedia education: for cancer information dissemination to low-literacy elderly, 332; for gestational diabetes patients, 193–201

Multisite trials, reason for, 136

N

National assessments of telehealth encounters, 312, 314

National Cancer Act of 1971, 329

National Cancer Institute (NCI), 92, 94, 185; digital divide pilot projects funded by, 328–334

National Conference on Legal and Policy Developments, 313

National Family Health Survey, 340, *341*, 345

National health care system, vision for, 98

National Health Information Collaboration (NHIC), 342, 344

National Health Service Executive, 3, 4, 10, 80, 87

National Health Service (NHS), 5, 166

National Hospice and Palliative Care Organization, 111, 117

National Institutes of Health (NIH), 329

National Library of Medicine, 119, 139

National March of Dimes, 197

National Medical Library, India, 342

National Prostate Cancer Coalition, 185

National teleconsulting network project, challenges launching, 11–17

Nationwide telehealth listserv, 317

Native Americans, supplying vocational rehabilitation services to, 274

Natural habitat, dynamic of, 95–96

Needs assessment: for bridging the digital divide, 344; for Web-based directory service, 325–326

Needs, community, and organizational goals, linking technology solutions to, 295–296

New Mexico Corrections Department (NMCD), 46, 47, *48*, 49–55, *56*

New Mexico Department of Health, 47

New Mexico, prison telehealth program in, 46–57

New York, uninsured in, addressing barriers to access for, 319–326

Next Generation Internet2 Access Grid, 212–213, 214, 222

NUA, *339*, 345

Nurse buy-in issues, overcoming, 39–44

Nurse-led telecare trial project, 3–9

Nurse-run teledermatology clinic, 83–86

Nursing process components, 226

Nursing shortage, 284

Nursing training, virtual, project involving, 225–230

O

Office for the Advancement of Telehealth (OAT), 148, 269, 314

Oklahoma, telerehabilitation project in, 268–274

Oklahoma Healthcare Authority, 271

Omnibus Appropriations Bill, 285

Oncology practice, financial aspects in, 171–177

Ongoing coordinated communication, 92

On-line communication, security and privacy of, 245

On-line consultations, charging and reimbursement for, 246, 247

On-line discussion forums, 190–191

On-line health care publication standards, 189

On-line services. *See Internet-based entries; Web-based entries*

On-line support groups, 181, 182, 184–185

Open access scheduling, 249

Open access software, 344

Open communication, importance of, 67

Open source tools, benefit of, 222

Operational track, 206

Ophthalmic subspecialty, process of implementing, 251–260

Organizational goals and community needs, linking technology solutions to, 295–296

Organizational politics, in teledermatology service, 82, 83, 86, 87

Organizational structures, 74, 82, 83, 84; problems with, 86, 87

Organizational values, assessing, 295

Orientation period, importance of, 67

Orissa, India, 340, *341*, 343

Outcomes knowledge base, enterprise-wide, 93, *97*

Outcomes research and health improvement, primary elements of, 95

Out-of-pocket payments, 263

Outpatient referral, alternative to, virtual outreach project as, 160–169

P

Paradoxes: in Greek public health care system, 73–74; in human interactions, 96; in medical records information system implementation, 25, 26

Parent satisfaction: with teleconsulting, 142; with telerehabilitation service, 269

Participation, recruiting. *See* Recruitment

Partnering for bridging the digital divide, 339

Partners, finding new, model for, and persuading decision makers, 46–57

Partners Health Care, 265–266

Partners Online Specialty Consultations (POSC) Web portal, 261–267

Partners Telemedicine, 261, 262, 263, 264, 265, 266

Patient behavior, 124–125

Patient electronic file episode, 258, *259*

Patient perspectives, 121–122

Patient records, computerized, 93, *97*

Patient resistance, 7

Patient satisfaction: with elder care telehealth services, 236, 237–238, 239, 240, 241; with home telehealth programs, 39; with low-vision telemedicine service, 258; with rural teleconsulting for disabled children, 140–141; with Shriners telemedicine program, 35; with teleconsultations, 119–120; with telehospice program, 112–115, 116; with tele-oncology service, 171–172; with telerehabilitation service, 269; with teletherapy, 130; with virtual outreach project, 166, 167, *168*; with Web-based messaging service, 248, 249

Patient support, 181–185, 330

Patient-provider dialogue for symptom management, 91–99

Patient-provider interactions during telemedicine, perceptions and realities of, 118–125

Patient-provider relationship, preserving, 261, 262, 264

Patient-provider Web messaging

service, systemwide rollout of, 244–250

Pediatric orthopedics and burn cases, telemedicine involving, 30–35

Pennsylvania Homecare Association, 285

Pennsylvania, home telehealth program design in, 284–288

Pennsylvania State Nursing Association, 285, 288

Perceptions: versus behavior, 124–125; employee, 21–23; issue of, 119–120; patient, 121–122; provider, 122–123, 264

Personal digital assistants (PDAs), 326

Personnel costs, looking at, 175

Personnel management, building capacity for, 343

Phased-in approach, 34, 53, 220

Philotimo, defined, 74

Physicians/doctors. *See Provider entries*

PictureTel, 291

Piloting before deployment, benefit of, 249

Pioneer Development Resources, 188

Point-of-care documentation system, 43

Point-of-care, using, to reduce medication errors, 151–158

Policies, changing, on Medicare reimbursement, 310–318

Policy decisions, statewide, 307–308

Policy issues: addressing, for statewide telemedicine program, 299–308; in bridging the digital divide, 338, 343–344; for medication administration system, 154–155

Political environment and policy, 299–300

Politics, organizational, in teledermatology service, 82, 83, 86, 87

Practical Psychology Magazine, 187

Practicality, focusing in, 296

Practice sessions, addition of, 286

Pregnancy, diabetes during, multimedia education for patients with, 193–201

Preparation stage, 300–301

Pricing (scoring) of telehealth bills, 316

Primary care information system implementation, 69–70, 72–78

Prison telehealth program, presenting business case for, 46–57

Privacy of on-line communication, 245, 246, 254

Privileges, clinical, applying for, 255

Problem-based learning, use of, 204, 216, 222

Process: clearly stating, 43, 67; for medication administration system, 154–155; in rural teleconsulting, for disabled children, *141*

Productivity issues, addressing: in home telehealth program, 44; in Web-based messaging service, 249

Professional resistance. *See Provider resistance*

Profit margins, 272

Program creation, linking policy and, 307

Program development, stages of, policy issues in, 300–306

Project administration and management, 219

Project for Excellence in Journalism, 105, 110

Project organization, 219–220

Project Phoenix program, provider-patient interactions in, 119–125

Project TOUCH (Telehealth Outreach for Unified Community Health), 213, 214–222

Prospective payment system, 284

Prostate cancer survivors' illness narratives, role of Internet in, 181–185

Protocols, developing. *See Guidelines, developing*

Prototype testing, 220

Provider behavior, 124–125

Provider perspectives, 122–123, 264

Provider relationships, reconfiguring, 86

Provider resistance: to automated medication administration system, 155; in crisis telehealth program, 149; disputing, 75;

Provider resistance (*continued*)
in home telecare trial project,
6, 7, 9; in home telehealth program, 44; to patient-provider
e-mail communication, 245;
reinforced by patient resistance,
7; understanding, 241; to Web-based messaging service, 249

Provider satisfaction: with automated medication system, 158;
with elder care telehealth services, 236, 237, 238, 239, 240,
242; factors in, 241; with health
care information system, 75;
with home telehealth programs,
39; with prison telehealth program, 57; with rural teleconsulting for disabled children,
140–141, 142; with teledermatology service, 81, 82, 83,
85–86; with telehealth for congestive heart failure patients,
287; with telemedicine training
program, 208–209; with telerehabilitation service, 269; with
teletherapy for childhood depression, 130; with virtual outreach project, 166–167; with
Web-based messaging service,
247, 248, 249

Provider-patient issues. *See Patient-provider entries*

Provider-specialist interactions,
accessibility of, 264

Provider-vendor partnership, for
serving rural areas, 284–288

Psychiatric crisis, telehealth program for, cost management in,
145–149

Public education about telemedicine, 272

Public Law 106-554, 317

Q

Quality: of care, addressing, 262,
265; of life, assessing, 176

R

Racial and ethnic diversity, attention to, 198, 330–331

Rajiv Gandhi University of Health
Sciences, 342

Randomized controlled trials, use
of: in elder care telehealth service, 240; for home telecare trial
project, 4–5; potential, for rural
telemedicine research,, 144; in
teledermatology service, 81,
82; in teletherapy for childhood
depression, 131–132, 135; for
virtual outreach project, 161,
162, 165

Real-time joint consultations, issues
with, 160–161

Recruitment: in home telecare trial
project, 6, 8–9; for Internet-based specialty consultations,
262; in teletherapy for childhood depression, 132, 133; in
virtual outreach project, 168;
of Web site volunteers, 188–189; for Web-based messaging
service, 248

Redundancy of service, improvement in, 293

Referral agencies, 325

Referrals: in crisis telehealth program, 146; in home telehealth
program, 43, 44; for Internet-based specialty consultations,
262, 265, 266; in low-vision
telemedicine service, 255; and
Medicare reimbursement, 310,
311; outpatient, alternative to,
311; outpatient, alternative to,
virtual outreach project as,
160–169; in teleconsulting network project, 14–15, 16; in
teletherapy for childhood
depression, 133; Web-based
directory providing, for the
uninsured, 321–326

Regional network infrastructure, 69,
70

Regional telemedicine consortium,
creating, 303

Registrar General and Census Commissioner, India, 340, *341*, 345

Rehabilitation, approach to, 268-274

Reification, 213, 221

Reimbursement: changing policies
on, 310–318; for Internet-based

specialty consultations,
263–264; for low-vision
telemedicine service, 252, 258,
260; requirements in, 284; for
telerehabilitation, 271–272;
Web messaging service and,
246, 247, 250

Relational dimension, satisfaction
with, 119–120

Relationship-centered health care
communities, developing, role
in, 116

RelayHealth Corporation, 245,
246, 248

Reliability of transmission,
improvement in, 293

Remote health care, role of, 139

Reporting: facilitation of, 75;
problem with, 57

Request for Proposal (RFP) process,
12

Research and Development National Health Service Health
Technologies Assessment initiative, 161

Research as dialogue, 91–99

Research protocol, 134

Research task teams, 219–220

Resistance, patient, 7

Resistance, provider/professional.
See Provider resistance

Resolution Regarding Medicare
Reimbursement of Telehealth
Services, 314–317

Retreats, for management teams, 66

Revenue: of crisis telehealth program, 148; sources of, diversifying, 272

Ridgeview Psychiatric Hospital and
Center, 146, 147, 149, 150

Risk assessment, continual, 279

Risk management, 6, 8, 278, 279

Robert Wood Johnson funding, 326

Robert Wood Johnson Health Policy Fellows, 312

Role modification, 264

Routing messages, 245–246,
247–248, 249–250

Rural areas: benefits of telehealth
for, 55; children with disabilities
in, serving, 138–144; serving
cancer patients in, 171–176,

330–331; serving the elderly in, 235–242; telerehabilitation in, 268–274; vendor-provider partnership for serving, 284–288

S

St. Alexius Medical Center, North Dakota, 314
St. John's Pleasant Valley Hospital (SJPVH), 194, 197, 198
St. John's Regional Medical Center (SJRMC), 194, 197, 198
Same-day scheduling, 249
SARS outbreak, 343
Satisfaction. *See specific type*
Savings in prison telehealth program, 50, 52–53. *See also* Cost savings
Scheduling: in prison telehealth program, 55, 57; in rural teleconsulting for disabled children, 139–140, 144; and Web-based messaging service, 249
School-based programs, 132, 269, 272
Science Panel on Interactive Communication and Health, 195, 202, 333, 336
Scoring (pricing) of telehealth bills, 316
Scott County Hospital, 146, 147, 148
Security: of on-line communication, 245; sustainable, developing and maintaining, 277–282
Security architecture layers, 278–279
Security audit, 281–282
Security engineering, 281
Security management, 281
Security monitoring and response, 281
Security operations, 281
Security vendor, formalized support from, 280, 281
SEEDS project, 225–230
Selection of technology. *See* Technology selection
SelfhelpMagazine (SHM) Web site, construction and management of, 187–191

Self-monitoring, 92–95, 98
Self-organization, 71–72, 73, 77–78, 96
Self-regulating care, 92–95, 98
Sentara Home Care Services, telehealth disease management program of, 40–44
Service agreement for on-line forums, 191
Service delivery models, different, 31
Shriners Hospitals for Children, telemedicine at, 30–35
*Si*mulated *E*lectronic h*E*alth *D*elivery *S*ystem (SEEDS) project, 225–230
Simulation, distinction between reification and, 213
Simulation-based medical education project, 212–222
Single point of contact (SPOC), developing, 314, 315
Site independence, 290–291, 295
Site management, building capacity for, 343
SoBig computing plague, 278
Social and Family Medicine, University of Crete Medical School, 70
Social aspects, understanding, of medical records information system implementation, 19–27
Social learning theory, concepts from, basing multimedia program on, 195
Social networks, 264
Societal level affecting adoption, 264–265
Software and hardware selection. *See* Technology selection
Software and hardware, using, training for. *See* Technical training
Southern California Chapter of the March of Dimes, 197
Southern Governors' Association (SGA), 312, 313, 314, 315, 318
Specialist-provider interactions, accessibility of, 264
Specialty care, using telehealth for, with elderly veterans, 238–239
Specialty consultations, Internet-based, adoption of, 261–267

Speech teletherapy program, 269, 273–274
Spinal cord-injured patients, telemedicine for, 31–35
Stable revenue streams, 272
Standard operating procedures, uniform, statewide adoption of, 304, 306
Standardized computing platform, 280
Standards, telemedicine, 210
Start-up management team, leadership issues facing, 59–68
Start-up stages, 300, 303–306
State Children's Health Insurance Program (SCHIP), 312, 317
Statewide telemedicine program, policy issues in, addressing, 299–308
Storytelling network, 104, 108–109
Storytelling techniques, use of, 196
Structures, organizational, 74, 82, 83, 84; problems with, 86, 87
Subsidies, 291
Support: caregiver, 116, 175–176, 241; patient, 181–185, 330
Support groups, 116, 181, 182, 184–185
Support, technical, from security vendors, 280, 281
Surrogate primary care physician, 319
Sustainability stage, 300
Symptom management, coordinating, through daily dialogue, 92–95
System life cycle, phases of, virus and vulnerability management within, 280–281
Systems. *See specific type*

T

Target audience: expanding, for Web-based directory service for uninsured, 325; feedback from, importance of, 201; reaching, diagnosing communication infrastructure for, 101–109
Targeted population, clear definition of, requiring, 134

Taskforce on Medical Technology, 312

Teaching model, for telemedicine training program, 204–205

Teams: management, 59–68, 219, 220; virtual, 217, *218*, 219

Technical problems: in bridging the digital divide, 340; in health care information system, 73; in home telecare trial project, 6, 7, 8; with medical records information system, 22–23; in prison telehealth program, 55; in teleconsulting network project, 14, 16; in teledermatology service, 81, 81–82, 84; in telehospice program, 114; with teletherapy, 135

Technical staff, advanced, specific training for, 210

Technical support, from security vendors, 280, 281

Technical track, 206

Technical training: advanced, 210; on automated medication administration system, 156; on clinical information system, 229; on health care information system, 69, 73, 76–77; in home telecare trial project, 5, 8; in home telehealth program, 41–42, 43, 44; lack of, effect of, 203; on medical records information system, 24–25; providing continuing education for, 203–210; in teleconsulting network project, 12, 15, 16; for virtual outreach project, 161–162; for Web-based messaging service, 248, 249

Technological standards, establishing, 34

Technology: deployment of, strategies for, 290–296; fear of, addressing, 272; limitations of, 6, 35, 50, 114, 165, 287; recommendations on, 76; as a trigger for change, 75

Technology design, vendor-provider partnership for, 284–288

Technology partner, locating, 285–286

Technology selection: for bridging the digital divide, 341; for cancer information service, 328; for elder care telehealth services, 237; for ESRD telemedicine program, 119; for home telecare trial project, 4; for home telehealth programs, 40, 41, 42, 286; for interpersonal symptom management, 92, 93; for low-vision telemedicine service, 251, 252, *253*; for medical records information system, 20; for medication administration system, 152–153, 154; for multimedia education for gestational diabetes patients, 194, 196; for rural teleconsulting with disabled children, 139; for statewide telemedicine program, 304; for teleconsulting network project, 12; for teledermatology service, 81, 82, 83, 84; for telehospice program, 112; for telerehabilitation service, 269, 270; for teletherapy treating childhood depression, 130, 132; for transparency, 290–296, 291; for virtual outreach project, 161, 165; for virtual reality distance learning project, 214–216, *217*, 221–222; for Web-based directory service, 326

Tele Doc system, 237

Telecare trial project, problems implementing, 3–9

Telecommunications system, statewide, 303–304

Teleconsultations: patient satisfaction with, 119–120; process of, for disabled children, *141*

Teleconsulting network project, challenges launching, 11–17

Teledermatology service, 81–87

Telediagnosis, issue of, 84–85

Telehealth: benefits of, explaining, 49, *51*; concept of, explaining, 49, *50*; in cyberspace, 212–222; Senate bill on, 313, 314, 316, 317

Telehealth alliance, statewide, benefits of, 55

Telehealth cancer symptom management, 91–99

Telehealth communication in elder care, 235–242

Telehealth encounters, national assessments of, 312, 314

Telehealth Improvement and Modernization Act of 2000, 313

Telehealth listserv, nationwide, 317

Telehospice, role of, in end-of-life care, 111–116

TeleKidcare program, 130, 132

Telemedicine Governance Council, 30, 34

Telemedicine Learning Center (TLC), 204–210

"Telemedicine: Part of the IT Revolution," 203, 211

Telemedicine Research Center, 111, 117

Telemedicine standards, 210

Telemedicine training, 203–210, 304

Tele–mental health services: for childhood depression, determining effectiveness of, 130–136; history of, 130

Tele-oncology practice, financial side of, 171–177

Tele-ophthalmology, process of implementing, for low-vision consultations, 252–260

Teleradiology, 12

Telerehabilitation, approach to, 268–274

Teletherapy for childhood depression, determining effectiveness of, 129–136

Tennessee, crisis telehealth program in, for cost management, 145–149

Test environment, establishment and maintenance of, 280

Texas Infrastructure Fund (TIF) Board, 251, 252

Therapy patients, mental health, serving, 130–136

Therapy-Related Symptom Checklist, 176

Three-group design, reason for, 131

Time, allowing: for attaining satisfaction, 241; for multimedia education program planning, 201

Topeka Veterans Affairs Medical Center (VAMC), 151
Topics of conversation during provider-patient interactions, 120, *121*
TOUCH system, 215–216
Training and education. *See specific type*
Transactional leaders, 63
Transformational leaders, 63
Transmission issues, 291, 292, 293
Transparent technology, program working towards, 289–296
Transportation cost and savings, 53, *54*
Triadic consultations, 81
Trust: implied, in employees, 74; in leaders, issue of, 64, 65, 66
Trust-building, importance of, 67
Tuition for training, 206–207
Turnover, staff, in teleconsulting network project, 15
Two-group design, reason for, 131

U

Ubiquitous evaluation system, 306
Uncertainty levels, effect of: on patient perspectives, 121–122, 181; on provider perspectives, 123, 167
Underserved populations, providing cancer information to, 328–334
Understanding Media: The Extensions of Man (McLuhan), xvii
Uninsured, barriers to access for, addressing, 319–326
Uninsured Connections Network (UCN), 320; Web site of, 321–326
Uninsured Trust Fund Coalition, 320
United Kingdom: home telecare trial in, 3–9; issue of telecare in, 80; teledermatology service in, 81–87; virtual outreach project in, 160–169
U.K. Department of Health, 5
U.K. Department of Health Primary Care Research Consortium, 9
United Nations, 337, 345

United Nations Conference on Trade and Development, *339*, 345
United Nations Development Programme India, 340, *341*, 343, 345
United Nations Population Division, *339*, 345
U.S. Bureau of the Census, 102, 110, 284, 288, 319, 327
U.S. Congress and reimbursement policy, 312–318
U.S. Department of Agriculture, 310
U.S. Department of Commerce, 310, 333
U.S. Department of Health and Human Services, 285, 310, 320, 329, 334, 336
U.S. Government Accounting Office, 236, 243
U.S. health care expenditures, 319
U.S. House Commerce Committee's Subcommittee on Health and the Environment, 315, 317
U.S. House Resolution (HR) 4577, 317
U.S. House Resolution (HR) 5661, 317
U.S. House Ways and Means Health Subcommittee, 315, 317
U.S. Senate bill 2505 (telehealth bill), 313, 314, 316, 317
U.S. Senate Finance Committee, 312, 316, 317
U.S. Senate Health, Education, Labor and Pensions Committee, 312
U.S. White House, 334, 336
United Way, Los Angeles, 102, 110
University at Buffalo Department of Family Medicine, 320
University culture, 306
University Eye Institute (UEI), 251
University Health Center in Sioux Falls, South Dakota, 315
University Medical Center, Tucson, 301
University of Arizona College of Medicine, Department of Pathology, 301
University of California Davis

Health System (UCDHS), 205, 244–250
University of California, Davis (UC Davis), telemedicine training program at, 204–210
University of California, Los Angeles (UCLA), 198
University of California, Los Angeles (UCLA), School of Public Health, 194
University of California, San Francisco, 288
University of Crete Medical School, 70
University of Hawaii (UH), 214, 219
University of Houston College of Optometry (UHCO), 251
University of Iowa, 140
University of Iowa College of Nursing, 237
University of Iowa Hospitals and Clinics, Center for Disabilities and Development (CDD), 139, 140, 141, 143, 144
University of Kansas Medical Center (KUMC): telehospice program involving, 112; teleoncology project at, 171–176; teletherapy at, 129–136
University of Kansas School of Nursing, 225
University of Kentucky, 314
University of Missouri, 312, 313, 314, 315, 316
University of New Mexico (UNM), 46, 47, 214, 217, 219
University of New Mexico (UNM), Center for Telehealth, Health Sciences Center, 219
University of Southern California, 102
University of Tennessee, 314
University of Tennessee Graduate School of Medicine, 147, 150
University of Tennessee Telehealth Network (UTTN), 146, 147, 148
University of Virginia, 316
University of Western Australia, 217
University of Wisconsin, 330
Upgrades, 8, 84, 114, 229, 238

Upper Peninsula Telehealth Network (UPTN), 290–296
Urban areas, serving cancer patients in, 330–331
Usability of equipment, working with vendor for, 286–287
Utilization: of elder care telehealth services, 241; of e-mail, patient-provider, 245; of health care information system, 72, 73; of Internet-based specialty consultations, 263, 266; of Internet-delivered health education system, 331; of multimedia educational program, 201; of statewide telemedicine program, 306; in teleconsulting network project, 14, *15*, 16; of Web-based directory service, 322, *323*, *324*; of Web-based messaging service, 248

V

Value-added service, 263
Values, organizational, assessing, 295
Vendor-provider partnership for home telehealth, 284–288
Vendors, security, technical support from, 280, 281
Venture capital, acquiring, 61
Veterans Affairs Medical Centers (VAMCs), 151, 235–236
Veterans Affairs (VA) system, 235
Veterans, elderly, home telehealth service for, 236–242
Veterans Health Administration (VHA), 92, 93, 94, 98

Veterans Information Systems and Technology Architecture (VistA), 151, 153
Virtual due list (VDL), 154
Virtual health care delivery system, project involving, 225–230
Virtual organizations, 265
Virtual Outreach project, 160–169
Virtual reality, use of, for distance learning, 212–222
Virtual support groups, possibility of, for caregivers, 116
Virtual teams, 217, *218*, 219
Virus and vulnerability management program, developing and maintaining, 277–282
Vision: for national health care system, 98; need for, 34
Vision care, telemedicine service for, 251–260
ViTel Net, 286
Vocational rehabilitation services, 274
Voluntary advisory council, 302
Volunteers, harnessing, for Web site construction and management, 187, 188–189
Vulnerability and virus management program, developing and maintaining, 277–282
Vulnerable populations, providing cancer information to, 328–334

W

Wait times, 35, 82, 84, 85, 86
Web links, 322

Web site construction and management: problems with, 323; successful, 187–191
Web-based directory service, creating, for the uninsured, 320–326
Web-based messaging service, patient-provider, systemwide rollout of, 244–250
WebMD, 181
WebVisit interviews, 246, 247, 250
Welchia computing plague, 278
Wisconsin, underserved populations in, providing cancer information to, 330–331
WNYhelpnet.ORG project, 321–326
Workflow, clinic, and Web-based messaging service, 245–246, 247–248
Workload pressures: in home telecare trial project, 7, 8; in low-vision telemedicine service, 258, 260; in virtual outreach project, 165
World Health Organization Multi-centre Collaboration Network for SARS Diagnosis, 343, 345
World Health Organization (WHO), 71, 77, 79, 337, 338, 339, 343, 344
Written guidelines. *See* Guidelines, developing

Y

Yale University, 332